A Mosaic of America
Volume II, 1865–1940

Second Edition

Lawrence L. Hartzell

Brookdale Community College

KENDALL/HUNT PUBLISHING COMPANY
4050 Westmark Drive   Dubuque, Iowa 52002

Contents

Dedication   vii

Preface   ix

CHAPTER 1 The American South, 1865–1900   **1**

1.1 Jourdon Anderson, "A Letter to My Old Master" (1865)   3

1.2 Address from the Colored Citizens of Norfolk, Va.,
To the People of the United States   6

1.3 Andrew Johnson, "Plan for Reconstruction" (1865)   12

1.4 Carl Schurz, "Report on the Conditions in the South" (1865)   14

1.5 Albion Tourgee, "Letter on Ku Klux Klan Activities" (1870)   23

1.6 Booker T. Washington, "Atlanta Exposition Speech" (1895)   29

1.7 W.E.B. DuBois, "Of Mr. Booker T. Washington and Others"
(1903)   33

CHAPTER 2 Taming the West, 1865–1900   **43**

2.1 Stuart Henry, "Conquering Our Great American Plains"
(1930)   45

2.2 Robert M. Utley, "Wars of the Peace Policy," 1869–1886   49

2.3 T. J. Stiles, "Buffalo Soldiers"   66

2.4 Joseph G. McCoy, "Historical Sketches of the Cattle Trade
of the West and Southwest" (1874)   77

2.5 Robert A. Trennert, "Educating Indian Girls at
Nonreservation Boarding Schools, 1878–1920"   82

2.6 Helen Hunt Jackson, "A Century of Dishonor" (1881)   98

2.7 "Dawes Severalty Act" (1887)   103

CHAPTER 3   **Industrialization and Labor, 1865–1920**   **107**

3.1 William Cronon, "Railroad Time"   109

3.2 Kevin Starr, "Radicalism in Nineteenth-Century
         San Francisco"   118

3.3 John Morrison, "Testimony Before Congress" (1883)   133

3.4 Pullman Strikers, "Statement" (1894)   137

3.5 Knights of Labor, "Constitution" (1878)   139

3.6 Samuel Gompers, "Fundamental Universal Service" (1916)   143

CHAPTER 4   **Politics in the Gilded Age, 1870–1900**   **149**

4.1 William L. Riordan, "Plunkitt of Tammany Hall" (1905)   151

4.2 Jonathan Kandell, "Boss"   165

4.3 Daniel Czitrom, "Big Tim Sullivan and Metropolitan
         Politics in New York, 1889-1913"   172

4.4 "The Ten Commandments of the Grange" (1874)   192

4.5 "Populist Party, Platform" (1892)   194

CHAPTER 5   **Immigration and Popular Culture 1880–1920**   **201**

5.1 Jacob Riis, "The Bohemians Tenement-house
         Cigarmaking" (1890)   203

5.2 John Higham, "Strangers in the Land"   210

5.3 "Restrictions on Chinese Immigration" (1892)   219

5.4 Madison Grant, "Survival of the Unfit" (1918)   221

5.5 Josiah Strong, "Our Country" (1886)   224

5.6 *New York Times*, "Opening Night at Coney Island" (1904) 229

5.7 Steven A. Riess, "The Social Functions of Baseball"   233

CHAPTER 6   The Progressive Era, 1880-1920   245

6.1   Jane Addams, "The Subjective Necessity for Social
Settlements" (1892)   247

6.2   John Dewey, "A Democrat Schoolroom" (1900)   255

6.3   Jane Addams, "Why the Ward Boss Rules" (1898)   258

6.4   *Muller v. Oregon* (1908)   264

6.5   Benjamin B. Lindsey, "The Dangerous Life" (1931)   268

6.6   Maureen A. Flanagan, "Gender and Urban Political
Reform: The City Club and the Woman's City Club
of Chicago in the Progressive Era"   271

CHAPTER 7   Imperialism and World War I, 1880-1920   291

7.1   Alfred Thayer Mahan, "The Influence of Sea Power
upon History" (1890)   293

7.2   Albert J. Beveridge, "The Command of the Pacific "(1902)   298

7.3   Joseph Henry Crooker, "The Menace to America" (1900)   303

7.4   Woodrow Wilson, "War Message to Congress" (1917)   310

7.5   George Norris, "Opposition to U.S. Involvement in
World War I" (1917)   317

7.6   J. William T. Youngs, "The Lafayette Escadrille"   320

7.7   *Schenck v. U.S.* (1919)   345

CHAPTER 8   America in the 1920s   349

8.1   Frederick Lewis Allen, "Prelude: May, 1919" (1930)   351

8.2   Lynn Dumenil, "The Modern Temper"   361

8.3   John D'Emilio and Estelle Friedman, "The Sexual
Revolution of the 1920s"   369

8.4 Jules Tygiel, "Unreconciled Strivings: Baseball in Jim Crow America" 380

8.5 Langston Hughes, "The Negro Artist and the Racial Mountain" (1926) 402

8.6 Poets of the Harlem Renaissance: Claude McKay and Sterling Brown 405

CHAPTER 9 The Great Depression and The New Deal, 1929–1940 **409**

9.1 Magnus Alexander, "A Businessman's Reaction to the Crash" (1929) 411

9.2 Herbert Hoover, "Lincoln's Birthday Radio Address" (1931) 414

9.3 John A. Garraty, "The Big Picture of the Great Depression" 417

9.4 Franklin D. Roosevelt, "First Inaugural Address" (1933) 430

9.5 Carolyn Weaver, "Birth of Entitlement" 435

9.6 Huey Long, "Share Our Wealth" (1935) 443

9.7 Republican Party, "Platform" (1936) 445

Dedication

To the memory of

Jack Hartzell

1938–2001

Preface

It was my intention to compile a reader consisting of primary and secondary sources that my American history students would find insightful and valuable. This collection represents a wide range of approaches to the study of history—political, social, economic, racial, intellectual, gender, ethnic. It covers history from both the "bottom up" and the "top down," giving voice to those historical actors both ignored and celebrated throughout America's past. I hope that these selections bring history to life and fire the imaginations of its readers.

I would like to thank my colleagues—Tom Cioppa, Carl Francese, Fred Fraterrigo, Jess Le Vine, Jack Needle, Jane Scimeca, Karen Sieben, Richard Sorrell, Tony Snyder, and Sherri West—for their continual advice and guidance, and for providing me with a friendly, collaborative working environment. It has also been my pleasure to work with an excellent group of adjunct instructors who have contributed greatly to my professional growth. My appreciation is extended to the staff of the Social Sciences Division for their support and to the Interlibrary Department at the Bankier Library for making my work considerably easier.

Lawrence L. Hartzell
Lincroft, New Jersey
November 2006

CHAPTER 1

The American South
1865–1900

1.1   Jourdon Anderson, "A Letter to My Old Master" (1865)

1.2   Black Residents of Norfolk, "To the American People" (1865)

1.3   Andrew Johnson, "Plan for Reconstruction" (1865)

1.4   Carl Schurz, "Report on the Conditions in the South" (1865)

1.5   Albion Tourgee, "Letter on Ku Klux Klan Activities" (1870)

1.6   Booker T. Washington, "Atlanta Exposition Speech" (1895)

1.7   W.E.B. DuBois, "Of Mr. Booker T. Washington and Others" (1903)

1.1
A Letter to My Old Master (1865)

Jourdon Anderson

This letter from an ex-slave living in Dayton, Ohio, in the summer of 1865 provides an excellent example of the hopes and desires of the freedmen. What does Anderson's letter tell us about how African Americans defined freedom? What kind of things does he value? Compare your answers to those from Document 1.2. Does Anderson want to return to his old plantation? Why or why not?

TO MY OLD MASTER, COLONEL P.H. ANDERSON,
BIG SPRING, TENNESSEE

Sir: I got your letter, and was glad to find that you had not forgotten Jourdon, and that you wanted me to come back and live with you again, promising to do better for me than anybody else can. I have often felt uneasy about you. I thought the Yankees would have hung you long before this, for harboring Rebs they found at your house. I suppose they never heard about your going to Colonel Martin's to kill the Union soldier that was left by his company in their stable. Although you shot at me twice before I left you, I did not want to hear of your being hurt, and am glad you are still living. It would do me good to go back to the dear old home again, and see Miss Mary and Miss Martha and Allen, Esther, Green, and Lee. Give my love to them all, and tell them I hope we will meet in the better world, if not in this. I would have gone back to see you all when I was working in the Nashville Hospital, but one of the neighbors told me that Henry intended to shoot me if he ever got a chance.

I want to know particularly what the good chance is you propose to give me. I am doing tolerably well here. I get twenty-five dollars a month, with victuals and clothing; have a comfortable home for Mandy—the folks

From Lydia Maria Child, *The Freedman's Book* (1865).

call her Mrs. Anderson—and the children—Milly, Jane, and Grundy—go to school and are learning well. The teacher says Grundy has a head for a preacher. They go to Sunday school, and Mandy and me attend church regularly. We are kindly treated. Sometimes we overhear others saying, "Them colored people were slaves" down in Tennessee. The children feel hurt when they hear such remarks; but I tell them it was no disgrace in Tennessee to belong to Colonel Anderson. Many darkeys would have been proud, as I used to be, to call you master. Now if you will write and say what wages you will give me, I will be better able to decide whether it would be to my advantage to move back again.

As to my freedom, which you say I can have, there is nothing to be gained on that score, as I got my free papers in 1864 from the Provost-Marshal General of the Department of Nashville. Mandy says she would be afraid to go back without some proof that you were disposed to treat us justly and kindly; and we have concluded. to test your sincerity by asking you to send us our wages for the time we served you. This will make us forget and forgive old scores, and rely on your justice and friendship in the future. I served you faithfully for thirty-two years, and Mandy twenty years. At twenty-five dollars a month for me, and two dollars a week for Mandy, our earnings would amount to eleven thousand six hundred and eighty dollars. Add to this the interest for the time our wages have been kept back, and deduct what you paid for our clothing, and three doctor's visits to me, and pulling a tooth for Mandy, and the balance will show what we are in justice entitled to. Please send the money by Adam's Express, in care of V. Winters, Esq., Dayton, Ohio. If you fail to pay us for faithful labors in the past, we can have little faith in your promises in the future. We trust the good Maker has opened your eyes to the wrongs which you and your fathers have done to me and my fathers, in making us toil for you for generations without recompense. Here I draw my wages every Saturday night; but in Tennessee there was never any pay-day for the Negroes any more than for the horses and cows. Surely there will be a day of reckoning for those who defraud the laborer of his hire.

In answering this letter, please state if there would be any safety for my Milly and Jane, who are now grown up, and both good-looking girls. You know how it was with poor Matilda and Catherine. I would rather stay here and starve—and die, if it come to that—than have my girls brought to shame by the violence and wickedness of their young masters. You will also please state if there has been any schools opened for the colored children in your neighborhood. The great desire of my life now is to give my children an education, and have them form virtuous habits.

Say howdy to George Carter, and thank him for taking the pistol from you when you were shooting at me.

FROM YOUR OLD SERVANT,
JOURDON ANDERSON

1.2

Address from the Colored Citizens of Norfolk, Va., to the People of the United States (1865)

This petition presents a classic example of the goals black Americans had for freedom at the end of the Civil War. What do these Virginia blacks want out of freedom? How do they propose to reach those goals? How does their definition of freedom compare to that of Jourdon Anderson in Doc. 1.1? Why do you think so many whites opposed the kind of freedom outlined here?

Fellow Citizens:

The undersigned have been appointed a committee, by a public meeting of the colored citizens of Norfolk, held June 5th, 1865, in the Catharine Street Baptist Church, Norfolk, Va., to lay before you a few considerations touching the present position of the colored population of the southern States generally, and with reference to their claim for equal suffrage in particular.

We do not come before the people of the United States asking an impossibility; we simply ask that a Christian and enlightened people shall, at once, concede to us the full enjoyment of those privileges of full citizenship, which, not only, are our undoubted right, but are indispensable to that elevation and prosperity of our people, which must be the desire of every patriot . . .

Address given June 5, 1865.

We believe our present position is by no means so well understood among the loyal masses of the country, otherwise there would be no delay in granting us the express relief which the nature of the case demands. It must not be forgotten that it is the general assumption, in the South, that the effects of the immortal Emancipation Proclamation of President Lincoln go no further than the emancipation of the negroes then in slavery, and that it is only constructively even, that that Proclamation can be said, in any legal sense, to have abolished slavery, and even the late constitutional amendment, if duly ratified, can go no further; neither touch, nor can touch, the slave codes of the various southern States, and the laws respecting free people of color consequent therefrom, which, having been passed before the act of secession, are presumed to have lost none of their vitality, but exists, as a convenient engine for our oppression, until repealed by special acts of the State legislatures. By these laws, in many of the southern States, it is still a crime for colored men to learn or be taught to read, and their children are doomed to ignorance; there is no provision for insuring the legality of our marriages; we have no right to hold real estate; the public streets and the exercise of our ordinary occupations are forbidden us unless we can produce passes from our employers, or licenses from certain officials; in some States the whole free negro population is legally liable to exile from the place of its birth, for no crime but that of color; we have no means of legally making or enforcing contracts of any description; we have no right to testify before the courts in any case in which a white man is one of the parties to the suit—we are taxed without representation, and, in short, so far as legal safeguards of our rights are concerned, we are defenceless before our enemies. While this is our position as regards our legal status, before the State laws, we are still more unfortunately situated as regards our late masters. The people of the North, owing to the greater interest excited by the war, have heard little or nothing, for the past four years, of the blasphemous and horrible theories formerly propounded for the defence and glorification of human slavery, in the press, the pulpit and legislatures of the southern States; but, though they may have forgotten them, let them be assured that these doctrines have by no means faded from the minds of the people of the South; they cling to these delusions still, and only hug them the closer for their recent defeat. Worse than all, they have returned to their homes, with all their old pride and contempt for the negro transformed into bitter hate for the new-made freeman, who aspires to the exercise of his new-found rights, and who has been fighting for the suppression of their rebellion. That this charge is not unfounded, the manner in which it has been recently attempted to enforce the laws above referred to proves. In Richmond, during the three days' sway of the rebel Mayor Mayo, over 800 colored people were arrested, simply for walking the streets without a pass; in the neighboring city of Portsmouth, a Mayor has just been elected, on the avowed platform that this is a white man's government, and our enemies have been heard to boast openly, that soon not a colored man shall be left in the city; in the greater number of counties in this State, county meeting shave been held, at which resolutions have been adopted *deploring*, while accepting, the abolition of slavery, but going on to pledge the planters composing the meeting, to employ no negroes save such as were formerly owned by themselves, without a written recommendation from their late employers, and threatening violence towards those who should do so, thereby keeping us in a state of serfdom, and preventing our free selection of our employers; they have also pledged themselves, in no event, to pay their late adult slaves more than $60 per year for their labor, in the future, out of which, with characteristic generosity, they have decided that we are to find clothes for ourselves and families, and pay our taxes and doctors' bills; in many of the more remote districts individual planters are to be found who still refuse to recognize their negroes as free, forcibly retaining the wives and children of their late escaped slaves; cases have occurred, not far from Richmond itself, in which an attempt to leave the plantation has been punished by shooting to death; and finally, there are numbers of cases, known to ourselves, in the immediate vicinity of this city, in which a faithful performance, by colored men, of the duties or labor contracted for, has been met by a contemptuous and violent refusal of the stipulated compensation. These are facts, and yet the men doing these things are, in many cases, loud in their professions of attachment to the restored Union, while committing these outrages on the most faithful friends that Union can ever have. Even well known Union men have often been found among our oppressors; witness the action of the Tennessee legislature in imposing unheard of disabilities upon us, taking away from us, and giving to the Country Courts, the right of disposing of our children, by apprenticing them to such occupations as the court, not their parents, may see fit to adopt for them; and in this very city, and under the protection of military law, some of our white friends who have nobly distinguished themselves by their efforts in our behalf, have been threatened with arrest by a Union Mayor of this city, for their advocacy of the cause of freedom.

Fellow citizens, the performance of a simple act of justice on your part will reverse all this; we ask for no expensive aid from military forces, stationed throughout the South, overbearing State action, and rendering our government republican only in name; give us the suffrage, and you may rely upon us to secure justice for ourselves, and all Union men, and to keep the State forever in the Union.

While we urge you to this act of simple justice to ourselves, there are many reasons why you should concede us this right in your own interest. It cannot be that you contemplate with satisfaction a prolonged military occupation of the southern States, and yet, without the existence of a larger loyal constituency than, at present, exists in these States, a military occupation will be absolutely necessary, to protect the white Union men of the South, as well as ourselves, and if not absolutely to keep the States in the Union, it will be necessary to prevent treasonable legislation . . .

You have not unreasonable complained of the operation of that clause of the Constitution which has hitherto permitted the slavocracy of the South to wield the political influence which would be represented by a white population equal to three fifths of the whole negro population; but slavery is now abolished, and henceforth the representation will be in proportion to the enumeration of the who population of the South, *including people of color*, and it is worth your consideration if it is desirable or politic that the fomenters of this rebellion against the Union, which has been crushed at the expense of so much blood and treasure, should find themselves, after defeat, more powerful than ever, their political influence enhanced by the additional voting power of the other two fifths of the colored population, by which means four Southern votes will balance in the Congressional and Presidential elections at least seven Northern ones. The honor of your country should be dear to you, as it is, but is that honor advanced, in the eyes of the Christian world, when America alone, of all Christian nations, sustains an unjust distinction against four million and a half of her most loyal people, on the senseless ground of a difference of color? You are anxious that the attention of every man, of every State legislature, and of Congress, should be exclusively directed to redressing the injuries sustained by the country in the late contest; are these objects more likely to be effected amid the political distractions of an embarrassing negro agitation? You are, above all, desirous that no future intestine wars should mar the prosperity and destroy the happiness of the country; will your perfect security from such evils be promoted by the existence of a colored population of four millions and a half, placed, by your enactments, outside the pale of the Constitution, discontented by oppression, with an army of 200,000 colored soldiers, whom you have drilled, disciplined, and armed, but whose attachment to the State you have failed to secure by refusing them citizenship? You are further anxious that your government should be an example to the world of true Republican; but how can you avoid the charge of inconsistency if you leave one eighth of the population of the whole country without any political rights, while bestowing these rights on every immigrant who comes to these shores, perhaps from a despotism, under which he could never exercise the least political right, and had no means of forming any conception of their proper use? . . .

It is hardly necessary here to refute any of the slanders with which our enemies seek to prove our unfitness for the exercise of the right of suffrage. It is true, that many of our people are ignorant, but for *that* these very men are responsible, and decency should prevent *their* use of such an argument. But if our people are ignorant, no people were ever more orderly and obedient to the laws; and no people ever displayed greater earnestness in the acquisition of knowledge. Among no other people could such a revolution have taken place without scenes of license and bloodshed; but in this case, and we say it advisedly, full information of the facts will show that no single disturbance, however, slight, has occurred which has not resulted from the unprovoked aggression of white people, and, if any one doubts how fast the ignorance, which has hitherto cursed our people, is disappearing, 'mid the light of freedom, let him visit the colored schools of this city and neighborhood, in which between two and three thousand pupils are being taught, while, in the evening, in colored schools may be seen, after the labors of the day, hundreds of our adult population from budding manhood to hoary age, toiling, with intensest eagerness, to acquire the invaluable arts of reading and writing, and the rudimentary branches of knowledge. One other objection only will we notice; it is that our people are lazy and idle; and, in support of this allegation, the objectors refer to the crowds of colored people subsisting on Government rations, and flocking into the towns. To the first statement we reply that we are poor, and that thousands of our young and able-bodied men, having been enlisted in the army to fight the battles of their country, it is but reasonable that that country should contribute something to the support of those whose natural protectors that country has taken away. With reference to the crowds collected round the military posts and in the cities, we say that though some may have come there under misapprehensions as to the nature of the freedom they have just received, yet this is not the case with the majority; the colored man knows that freedom means freedom to labor, and to enjoy its fruits, and in that respect evinces at least an equal appreciation of his new position with his late owners; if he is not to be found laboring for these late owners, it is because he cannot trust them and feels safe, in his new-found freedom, nowhere out of the immediate presence of the national forces; if the planters want his labor (and they do,) fair wages and fair treatment will not fail to secure it.

In conclusion, we wish to advise our colored brethren of the State and nation, that the settlement of this question is to a great extent dependent on them, and that supineness on their part will do as much to delay if not defeat the full recognition of their rights as the open opposition of avowed enemies. Then be up and active, and everywhere let associations be formed having for their object the agitation, discussion and enforcement of your claims to equality before the law, and equal rights of suffrage. Your opponents are active; be prepared, and organize to resist their efforts. We would further advise that all political associations of colored men, formed within the limits of the State of Virginia, should communicate the fact of their existence, with the names and post office addresses of their officers, to Joseph T. Wilson, Norfolk, Va., in order that communication and friendly cooperation may be kept up between the different organizations, and facilities afforded for common and united State action, should occasion require it. . . .

In concluding this address, we would now make a last appeal to our fellow-citizens of all classes throughout the nation. Every Christian and humane man must feel that our demands are just; we have shown you that their concession is, for us, necessary, and for you expedient. We are Americans, we know no other country, we love the land of our birth and our fathers, we thank God for the glorious prospect before our country, and we believe that if we do but obey His laws He will yet enthrone her high o'er all the nations of the earth, in glory, wealth and happiness; but this exalted state can never be reached if injustice, ingratitude, and oppression of the helpless, mark the national conduct, treasuring up, as in the past, God's wrath and your misery for a day of reckoning; as the path of justice alone is ever the safe and pleasant way, and the words of Eternal Wisdom have declared that the throne (or nation) shall be established only by righteousness and upholden by mercy. With these reflections we leave our case in the hands of God, and to the consideration of our countrymen.

1.3
Plan for Reconstruction (1865)

Andrew Johnson

Ascending to the presidency after the assassination of Abraham Lincoln, Tennesseean Andrew Johnson began his plan for Reconstruction in May 1865. This document is an example of how Johnson approached the matter, appointing "provisional governors" in every former Confederate state (here, W. W. Holden in North Carolina). Johnson's plan is important in part because of the restrictions he places on suffrage; under his plan, which Southerners can vote?

Whereas the fourth section of the fourth article of the Constitution of the United States declares that the United States shall guarantee to every State in the Union a republican form of government and shall protect each of them against invasion and domestic violence; and

Whereas the President of the United States is by the Constitution made Commander in Chief of the Army and Navy, as well as chief civil executive officer of the United States, and is bound by solemn oath faithfully to execute the office of President of the United States and to take care that the laws be faithfully executed; and

Whereas the rebellion which has been waged by a portion of the people of the United States against the properly constituted authorities of the Government ... and

Whereas it becomes necessary and proper to carry out and enforce the obligations of the United States to the people of North Carolina in securing them in the enjoyment of a republican form of government:

Now, therefore, in obedience to the high and solemn duties imposed upon me by the Constitution of the United States and for the purpose of enabling the loyal people of said State to organize a State government

From James D. Richardson, ed., *Messages and Papers of the Presidents* (Washington D.C.: Government printing office), vol. 6, pp. 312-313.

whereby justice may be established, domestic tranquillity insured, and loyal citizens protected in all their rights of life, liberty, and property, I, Andrew Johnson, President of the United States and Commander in Chief of the Army and Navy of the United States, do hereby appoint William W. Holden provisional governor of the State of North Carolina, whose duty it shall be, at the earliest practicable period, to prescribe such rules and regulations as may be necessary and proper for convening a convention composed of delegates to be chosen by that portion of the people of said State who are loyal to the United States, and no others, for the purpose of altering or amending the constitution thereof, and with authority to exercise within the limits of said State all the powers necessary and proper to enable such loyal people of the State of North Carolina to restore said State to its constitutional relations to the Federal Government and to present such a republican form of State government as will entitle the State to the guaranty of the United States therefor and its people to protection by the United States against invasion, insurrection, and domestic violence: *Provided*, That in any election that may be hereafter held for choosing delegates to any State convention as aforesaid no person shall be qualified as an elector or shall be eligible as a member of such convention unless he shall have previously taken and subscribed the oath of amnesty as set forth in the President's proclamation of May 29, A. D. 1865, and is a voter qualified as prescribed by the constitution and laws of the State of North Carolina in force immediately before the 20th day of May, A. D. 1861, the date of the so-called ordinance of secession; and the said convention, when convened, or the legislature that may be thereafter assembled, will prescribe the qualification of electors and the eligibility of persons to hold office under the constitution and laws of the State—a power the people of the several States composing the Federal Union have rightfully exercised from the origin of the Government to the present time.

And I do hereby direct—

...That the military commander of the department and all officers and persons in the military and naval service aid and assist the said provisional governor in carrying into effect this proclamation; and they are enjoined to abstain from in any way hindering, impeding, or discouraging the loyal people from the organization of a State government as herein authorized....

1.4
Report on the Conditions in the South (1865)

Carl Schurz

Former Union general Carl Schurz was appointed by President Johnson to take a three-month tour of the South and report on the attitudes and behavior of the Southern people on the eve of Reconstruction. Johnson hoped that Schurz's discoveries would provide support for his plan of Reconstruction. What did Schurz find out? What does he think Reconstruction should try to accomplish? Do you think President Johnson would agree?

Sir:…You informed me that your "policy of reconstruction" was merely experimental, and that you would change it if the experiment did not lead to satisfactory results. To aid you in forming your conclusions upon this point I understood to be the object of my mission,…

Condition of Things Immediately after the Close of the War

In the development of the popular spirit in the south since the close of the war two well-marked periods can be distinguished. The first commences with the sudden collapse of the confederacy and the dispersion of its armies, and the second with the first proclamation indicating the "reconstruction policy" of the government.… When the news of Lee's and Johnston's surrenders burst upon the southern country the general consternation was extreme. People held their breath, indulging in the wildest apprehensions as to what was now to come.… Prominent Unionists told me that persons who for four years had scorned to recognize them on the street approached them with smiling faces and both hands extended.

From U.S. Congress, Sentate, 39th Cong., 1st sess., 1865, Ex. Doc. No. 2, pp.1-5, 8, 36-39, 41-44.

Men of standing in the political world expressed serious doubts as to whether the rebel States would ever again occupy their position as States in the Union, or be governed as conquered provinces. The public mind was so despondent that if readmission at some future time under whatever conditions had been promised, it would then have been looked upon as a favor. The most uncompromising rebels prepared for leaving the country. The masses remained in a state of fearful expectancy....

Such was, according to the accounts I received, the character of that first period. The worst apprehensions were gradually relieved as day after day went by without bringing the disasters and inflictions which had been vaguely anticipated, until at last the appearance of the North Carolina proclamation substituted new hopes for them. The development of this second period I was called upon to observe on the spot, and it forms the main subject of this report.

Returning Loyalty

...[T]he white people at large being, under certain conditions, charged with taking the preliminaries of "reconstruction" into their hands, the success of the experiment depends upon the spirit and attitude of those who either attached themselves to the secession cause from the beginning, or, entertaining originally opposite views, at least followed its fortunes from the time that their States had declared their separation from the Union....

I may group the southern people into four classes, each of which exercises an influence upon the development of things in that section:

1. Those who, although having yielded submission to the national government only when obliged to do so, have a clear perception of the irreversible changes produced by the war, and honestly endeavor to accommodate themselves to the new order of things. Many of them are not free from traditional prejudice but open to conviction, and may be expected to act in good faith whatever they do. This class is composed, in its majority, of persons of mature age— planters, merchants, and professional men; some of them are active in the reconstruction movement, but boldness and energy are, with a few individual exceptions, not among their distinguishing qualities.
2. Those whose principal object is to have the States without delay restored to their position and influence in the Union and the people of the States to the absolute control of their home concerns. They are ready, in order to attain that object, to make any ostensible

concession that will not prevent them from arranging things to suit their taste as soon as that object is attained. This class comprises a considerable number, probably a large majority, of the professional politicians who are extremely active in the reconstruction movement. They are loud in their praise of the President's reconstruction policy, and clamorous for the withdrawal of the federal troops and the abolition of the Freedmen's Bureau.

3. The incorrigibles, who still indulge in the swagger which was so customary before and during the war, and still hope for a time when the southern confederacy will achieve its independence. This class consists mostly of young men, and comprises the loiterers of the towns and the idlers of the country. They persecute Union men and negroes whenever they can do so with impunity, insist clamorously upon their "rights," and are extremely impatient of the presence of the federal soldiers. A good many of them have taken the oaths of allegiance and amnesty, and associated themselves with the second class in their political operations. This element is by no means unimportant; it is strong in numbers, deals in brave talk, addresses itself directly and incessantly to the passions and prejudices of the masses, and commands the admiration of the women.

4. The multitude of people who have no definite ideas about the circumstances under which they live and about the course they have to follow; whose intellects are weak, but whose prejudices and impulses are strong, and who are apt to be carried along by those who know how to appeal to the latter....

Feeling towards the Soldiers and the People of the North

...[U]pon the whole, the soldier of the Union is still looked upon as a stranger, an intruder—as the "Yankee," "the enemy."...

It is by no means surprising that prejudices and resentments, which for years were so assiduously cultivated and so violently inflamed, should not have been turned into affection by a defeat; nor are they likely to disappear as long as the southern people continue to brood over their losses and misfortunes. They will gradually subside when those who entertain them cut resolutely loose from the past and embark in a career of new activity on a common field with those whom they have so long considered their enemies.... [A]s long as these feelings exist in their present strength, they will hinder the growth of that reliable kind of loyalty which springs from the heart and clings to the country in good and evil fortune.

Situation of Unionists

...It struck me soon after my arrival in the south that the known Union-ists—I mean those who during the war had been to a certain extent iden-tified with the national cause—were not in communion with the leading social and political circles; and the further my observations extended the clearer it became to me that their existence in the south was of a rather pre-carious nature.... Even Governor [William L.] Sharkey, in the course of a conversation I had with him in the presence of Major General Osterhaus, admitted that, if our troops were then withdrawn, the lives of northern men in Mississippi would not be safe.... [General Osterhaus said]: "There is no doubt whatever that the state of affairs would be intolerable for all Union men, all recent immigrants from the north, and all negroes, the mo-ment the protection of the United States troops were withdrawn."...

Negro Insurrections and Anarchy

...[I do] not deem a negro insurrection probable as long as the freedmen were assured of the direct protection of the national government. When-ever they are in trouble, they raise their eyes up to that power, and al-though they may suffer, yet, as long as that power is visibly present, they continue to hope. But when State authority in the south is fully restored, the federal forces withdrawn, and the Freedmen's Bureau abolished, the colored man will find himself turned over to the mercies of those whom he does not trust. If then an attempt is made to strip him again of those rights which he justly thought he possessed, he will be apt to feel that he can hope for no redress unless he procure it himself. If ever the negro is capable of rising, he will rise then....

There is probably at the present moment no country in the civilized world which contains such an accumulation of anarchical elements as the south. The strife of the antagonistic tendencies here described is aggravat-ed by the passions inflamed and the general impoverishment brought about by a long and exhaustive war, and the south will have to suffer the evils of anarchical disorder until means are found to effect a final settlement of the labor question in accordance with the logic of the great revolution.

The True Problem—Difficulties and Remedies

In seeking remedies for such disorders, we ought to keep in view, above all, the nature of the problem which is to be solved. As to what is commonly termed "reconstruction," it is not only the political machinery of the States and their constitutional relations to the general government, but the whole organism of southern society that must be reconstructed, or rather constructed anew, so as to bring it in harmony with the rest of American society. The difficulties of this task are not to be considered overcome when the people of the south take the oath of allegiance and elect governors and legislatures and members of Congress, and militia captains. That this would be done had become certain as soon as the surrenders of the southern armies had made further resistance impossible, and nothing in the world was left, even to the most uncompromising rebel, but to submit or to emigrate. It was also natural that they should avail themselves of every chance offered them to resume control of their home affairs and to regain their influence in the Union. But this can hardly be called the first step towards the solution of the true problem, and it is a fair question to ask, whether the hasty gratification of their desire to resume such control would not create new embarrassments.

The true nature of the difficulties of the situation is this: The general government of the republic has, by proclaiming the emancipation of the slaves, commenced a great social revolution in the south, but has, as yet, not completed it. Only the negative part of it is accomplished. The slaves are emancipated in point of form, but free labor has not yet been put in the place of slavery in point of fact. And now, in the midst of this critical period of transition, the power which originated the revolution is expected to turn over its whole future development to another power which from the beginning was hostile to it and has never yet entered into its spirit, leaving the class in whose favor it was made completely without power to protect itself and to take an influential part in that development. The history of the world will be searched in vain for a proceeding similar to this which did not lead either to a rapid and violent reaction, or to the most serious trouble and civil disorder. It cannot be said that the conduct of the southern people since the close of the war has exhibited such extraordinary wisdom and self-abnegation as to make them an exception to the rule.

In my dispatches from the south I repeatedly expressed the opinion that the people were not yet in a frame of mind to legislate calmly and understandingly upon the subject of free negro labor. And this I reported to be the opinion of some of our most prominent military commanders and other observing men. It is, indeed, difficult to imagine circumstances more unfavorable for the development of a calm and unprejudiced public opinion than those under which the southern people are at present laboring.

The war has not only defeated their political aspirations, but it has broken up their whole social organization....

In which direction will these people be most apt to turn their eyes? Leaving the prejudice of race out of the question, from early youth they have been acquainted with but one system of labor, and with that one system they have been in the habit of identifying all their interests. They know of no way to help themselves but the one they are accustomed to....

It is certain that every success of free negro labor will augment the number of its friends, and disarm some of the prejudices and assumptions of its opponents. I am convinced one good harvest made by unadulterated free labor in the south would have a far better effect than all the oaths that have been taken, and all the ordinances that have as yet been passed by southern conventions. But how can such a result be attained? The facts enumerated in this report, as well as the news we receive from the south from day to day, must make it evident to every unbiased observer that unadulterated free labor cannot be had at present, unless the national government holds its protective and controlling hand over it.... One reason why the southern people are so slow in accommodating themselves to the new order of things is, that they confidently expect soon to be permitted to regulate matters according to their own notions. Every concession made to them by the government as been taken as an encouragement to persevere in this hope, and, unfortunately for them, this hope is nourished by influences from other parts of the country. Hence their anxiety to have their State governments restored *at once,* to have the troops withdrawn, and the Freedmen's Bureau abolished, although a good many discerning men know well that, in view of the lawless spirit still prevailing, it would be far better for them to have the general order of society firmly maintained by the federal power until things have arrived at a final settlement. Had, from the beginning, the conviction been forced upon them that the adulteration of the new order of things by the admixture of elements belonging to the system. of slavery would under no circumstances be permitted, a much larger number would have launched their energies into the new channel, and, seeing that they could do "no better," faithfully co-operated with the government. It is hope which fixes them in their perverse notions. That hope nourished or fully gratified, they will persevere in the same direction. That hope destroyed, a great many will, by the force of necessity, at once accommodate themselves to the logic of the change. If, therefore, the national government firmly and unequivocally announces its policy not to give up the control of the free-labor reform until it is finally accomplished, the progress of that reform will undoubtedly be far more rapid and far less difficult than it will be if the attitude of the government is such as to permit contrary hopes to be indulged in....

Immigration [and Capital]

[The south would benefit] from immigration of northern people and Europeans.... The south needs capital. But capital is notoriously timid and averse to risk.... Capitalists will be apt to consider—and they are by no means wrong in doing so—that no safe investments can be made in the south as long as southern society is liable to be convulsed by anarchical disorders. No greater encouragement can, therefore, be given to capital to transfer itself to the south than the assurance that the government will continue to control the development of the new social system in the late rebel States until such dangers are averted by a final settlement of things upon a thorough free-labor basis.

How long the national government should continue that control depends upon contingencies. It ought to cease as soon as its objects are attained; and its objects will be attained sooner and with less difficulty if nobody is permitted to indulge in the delusion that it will cease *before* they are attained. This is one of the cases in which a determined policy can accomplish much, while a half-way policy is liable to spoil things already accomplished....

Negro Suffrage

It would seem that the interference of the national authority in the home concerns of the southern States would be rendered less necessary, and the whole problem of political and social reconstruction be much simplified, if, while the masses lately arrayed against the government are permitted to vote, the large majority of those who were always loyal, and are naturally anxious to see the free labor problem successfully solved, were not excluded from all influence upon legislation. In all questions concerning the Union, the national debt, and the future social organization of the south, the feelings of the colored man are naturally in sympathy with the views and aims of the national government. While the southern white fought against the Union, the negro did all he could to aid it; while the southern white sees in the national government his conqueror, the negro sees in it his protector, while the white owes to the national debt his defeat, the negro owes to it his deliverance; while the white considers himself robbed and ruined by the emancipation of the slaves, the negro finds in it the assurance of future prosperity and happiness. In all the important issues the negro would be led by natural impulse to forward the ends of the government, and by making his influence, as part of the voting body, tell upon the legislation of the States, render the interference of the national authority less necessary.

As the most difficult of the pending questions are intimately connected with the status of the negro in southern society, it is obvious that a correct solution can be more easily obtained if he has a voice in the matter. In the right to vote he would find the best permanent protection against oppressive class-legislation, as well as against individual persecution. The relations between the white and black races, even if improved by the gradual wearing off of the present animosities, are likely to remain long under the troubling influence of prejudice. It is a notorious fact that the rights of a man of some political power are far less exposed to violation than those of one who is, in matters of public interest, completely subject to the will of others....

In discussing the matter of negro suffrage I deemed it my duty to confine myself strictly to the practical aspects of the subject. I have, therefore, not touched its moral merits nor discussed the question whether the national government is competent to enlarge the elective franchise in the States lately in rebellion by its own act; I deem it proper, however, to offer a few remarks on the assertion frequently put forth, that the franchise is likely to be extended to the colored man by the voluntary action of the southern whites themselves. My observation leads me to a contrary opinion. Aside from a very few enlightened men, I found but one class of people in favor of the enfranchisement of the blacks: it was the class of Unionists who found themselves politically ostracised and looked upon the enfranchisement of the loyal negroes as the salvation of the whole loyal element. But their numbers and influence are sadly insufficient to secure such a result. The masses are strongly opposed to colored suffrage; anybody that dares to advocate it is stigmatized as a dangerous fanatic; nor do I deem it probable that in the ordinary course of things prejudices will wear off to such an extent as to make it a popular measure....

Deportation of the Freedmen

...[T]he true problem remains, not how to remove the colored man from his present field of labor, but how to make him, where he is, a true freeman and an intelligent and useful citizen. The means are simple: protection by the government until his political and social status enables him to protect himself, offering to his legitimate ambition the stimulant of a perfectly fair chance in life, and granting to him the rights which in every just organization of society are coupled with corresponding duties.

Conclusion

I may sum up all I have said in a few words. If nothing were necessary but to restore the machinery of government in the States lately in rebellion in point of form, the movements made to that end by the people of the south might be considered satisfactory. But if it is required that the southern people should also accommodate themselves to the results of the war in point of spirit, those movements fall far short of what must be insisted upon....

1.5

Letter on Ku Klux Klan Activities (1870)

Albion Tourgee

Albion Tourgee was a carpetbagger—a Northern Republican (Tourgee was born in Ohio) who moved to the South after the Civil War. He quickly became an important political activist in his new home state of North Carolina, working to secure political rights for the former slaves there. In 1868 he was appointed a judge in the state court system, a position he held for six years. This letter recounts the vicious activities of the Ku Klux Klan in North Carolina. What does Tourgee think needs to happen to prevent this kind of violence from continuing?

Greensboro, May 24, 1870
My Dear General [Joseph C. Abbott],

It is my mournful duty to inform you that our friend John W. Stephens, State Senator from Caswell, is dead. He was foully murdered by the Ku-Klux in the Grand Jury room of the Court House on Saturday or Saturday night last. The circumstances attending his murder have not yet fully come to light there. So far as I can learn, I judge these to have been the circumstances: He was one of the Justices of the Peace in that township, and was accustomed to hold court in that room on Saturdays. It is evident that he was set upon by some one while holding this court, or immediately after its close, and disabled by a sudden attack, otherwise there would have been a very sharp resistance, as he was a man, and always went armed to the teeth. He was stabbed five or six times, and then hanged on a hook in the Grand Jury room, where he was found on Sunday morning. Another

Greensboro, May 24, 1870.

brave, honest Republican citizen has met his fate at the hands of these fiends. Warned of his danger, and fully cognizant of the terrible risk which surrounded him, he still manfully refused to quit the field. Against the advice of his friends, against the entreaties of his family, he constantly refused to leave those who had stood by him in the day of his disgrace and peril. He was accustomed to say that 3,000 poor, ignorant, colored Republican voters in that county had stood by him and elected him, at the risk of persecution and starvation, and that he had no idea of abandoning them to the Ku-Klux. He was determined to stay with them, and either put an end to these outrages, or die with the other victims of Rebel hate and national apathy: Nearly six months ago I declared my belief that before the election in August next the Ku-Klux would have killed more men in the State than there would be members to be elected to the Legislature. A good beginning has been made toward the fulfillment of this property.

The following counties have already filled, or nearly so, their respective "quotas:" Jones County, quota full, excess 1; Orange County quota full; excess, 1. Caswell County quota full; excess, 2; Alamance County quota full; excess, 1. Chatham County quota nearly full. Or, to state the matter differently, there have been twelve murders in five counties of the district during the past eighteen months, by bands of disguised villains. In addition to this, from the best information I can derive, I am of the opinion that in this district alone there have been 1,000 outrages of a less serious nature perpetrated by the same masked fiends. Of course this estimate is not made from any absolute record, nor is it possible to ascertain with accuracy the entire number of beatings and other outrages which have been perpetrated. The uselessness, the utter futility of complaint from the lack of ability in the laws to punish is fully known to all. The danger of making such complaint is also well understood. It is therefore not unfrequently by accident that the outrage is found out, and unquestionably it is frequently absolutely concealed. Thus, a respectable, hard working white carpenter was working for a neighbor, when accidentally his shirt was torn, and disclosed his back scarred and beaten. The poor fellow begged for the sake of his wife and children that nothing might be said about it, as the Ku-Klux had threatened to kill him if he disclosed how he had been outraged. Hundreds of cases have come to my notice and that of my solicitor. . . .

Men and women come scarred, mangled, and bruised, and say: "The Ku-Klux came to my house last night and beat me almost to death, and my old woman right smart, and shot into the house, 'bust' the door down, and told me they would kill me if I made complaint; " and the bloody mangled forms attest the truth of their declarations. On being asked if any one knew any of the party it will be ascertained that there was no recognition, or only the most uncertain and doubtful one. In such cases as these nothing can be done by the court. We have not been accustomed to enter them on record. A man of the best standing in Chatham told me that he could count up 200 and upward in that county. In Alamance County, a citizen in conversation one evening enumerated upward of 50 cases which had occurred within his own knowledge, and in one section of the county. He gave it as his opinion that there had been 200 cases in that county. I have no idea that he exceeded the proper estimate. That was six months ago, and I am satisfied that another hundred would not cover the work done in that time.

These crimes have been of every character imaginable. Perhaps the most usual has been the dragging of men and women from their beds, and beating their naked bodies with hickory switches, or as witnesses in an examination the other day said, sticks" between a "switch" and a "club." From 50 to 100 blows is the usual allowance, sometimes 200 and 300 blows are administered. Occasionally an instrument of torture is owned. Thus in one case two women, one 74 years old, were taken out, stripped naked, and beaten with a paddle, with several holes bored through it. The paddle was about 30 inches long, 3 or 4 inches wide, and 1/4 of an inch thick, of Oak. Their bodies were so bruised and beaten that they were sickening to behold. They were white women and of good character until the younger was seduced, and swore her child to its father. Previous to that and so far as others were concerned her character was good.

Again, there is sometimes a fiendish malignity and cunning displayed in the form and character of the outrages. For instance, a colored man was placed astride of a log, and an iron staple driven through his person into the log. In another case, after a band of them had in turn violated a young negro girl, she was forced into bed with a colored man, their bodies were bound together face to face, and the fire from the hearth piled upon them. The K.K.K. rode off and left them, with shouts of laughter. Of course the bed was soon in flames, and somehow they managed to crawl out, though terribly burned and scarred. The house was burned.

I could give other incidents of cruelty, such as hanging up a boy of nine years old until he was nearly dead, to make him tell where his father was hidden, and beating an old negress of 103 years old with garden partings because she would not own that she was afraid of the Ku-Klux. But it is unnecessary to go into further detail. In this district I estimate their offenses as follows, in the past en months: Twelve murders, 9 rapes, 11 rsons,

7 mutilations, ascertained and most of them on record. In some no identification could be made.

Four thousand or 5,000 houses have been broken open, and property or persons taken out. In all cases all arms are taken and destroyed. Seven hundred or 800 persons have been beaten or otherwise maltreated. These of course are partly persons living in the houses which were broken into.

And yet the Government sleeps. The poor disarmed nurses of the Republican party-those men by whose ballots the Republican party holds power-who took their lives in their hands when they cast their ballots for U.S. Grant and other officials-all of us who happen to be beyond the pale of the Governmental regard-must be sacrificed, murdered, scourged, mangled, because some contemptible party scheme might be foiled by doing us justice. I could stand it very well to fight for Uncle Sam, and was never known to refuse an invitation on such an occasion; but his lying down, tied hand and foot with the shackles of the law, to be killed by the very dregs of the rebellion, the scum of the earth, and not allowed either the consolation of fighting or the satisfaction that our "fall" will be noted by the Government, and protection given to others thereby, is somewhat too hard. I am ashamed of the nation that will let its citizens be slain by scores, and scourged by thousands, and offer no remedy or protection. I am ashamed of a State which has not sufficient strength to protect its own officers in the discharge of their duties, nor guarantee the safety of any man's domicile throughout its length and breadth. I am ashamed of a party which, with the reins of power in its hands, has not nerve or decision enough to arm its own adherents, or to protect them from assassinations at the hands of their opponents. A General who in time of war would permit 2,000 or 3,000 of his men to be bushwhacked and destroyed by private treachery even in an enemy's country without any one being punished for it would be worthy of universal execration, and would get it, too. How much more worthy of detestation is a Government which in time of peace will permit such wholesale slaughter of its citizens? It is simple cowardice, inertness, and wholesale demoralization. The wholesale slaughter of the war has dulled our Nation's sense of horror at the shedding of blood, and the habit of regarding the South as simply a laboratory, where every demagogue may carry on his reconstructionary experiments at will, and not as an integral party of the nation itself, has led our our Government to shut its eyes to the atrocities of these times. Unless these evils are speedily remedied, I tell you, General, the Republican party has signed its death warrant. It is a party of cowards or idiots-I don't care which alternative is chosen.

The remedy is in our hands, and we are afraid or too dull to bestir ourselves and use it.

But you will tell me that Congress is ready and wilting to act if it only knew what to do. Like the old Irish woman it wrings its hands and cries, "O Lawk, 0 Lawk; if I only knew which way." And yet this same Congress has the control of the militia and can organize its own force in every county in the United States, and arm more or less of it. This same Congress has the undoubted right to guarantee and provide a republican government, and protect every citizen in "life, liberty, and the pursuit of happiness," as well as the power conferred by the XVth Amendment. And yet we suffer and die in peace and murderers walk abroad with the blood yet fresh upon their garments, unharmed, unquestioned and unchecked. Fifty thousand dollars given to good detectives would secure, if well used, a complete knowledge of all this gigantic organization of murders. In connection with an organized and armed militia, it would result in the apprehension of any number of these Thugs en masque and with blood on their hands. What then is the remedy?

First: Let Congress give to the U.S. Courts, or to Courts of the States under its own laws, cognizance of this class of crimes, as crimes against the nation, and let it prov3ide that this legislation be enforced. Why not, for instance, make going armed and masked or disguised, or masked or disguised in the night time, an act of insurrection or sedition?

Second: Organize militia, National-State militia is a nuisance-and arm as many as may be necessary in each county to enforce its laws.

Third: Put detectives at work to get hold of this whole organization. Its ultimate aim is unquestionably to revolutionize the Government. If we have not pluck enough for this, why then let us just offer our throats to the knife, emasculate ourselves, and be a nation of self-subjugated slaves at once.

And now, Abbott, I have but on thing to say to you. I have very little doubt that I shall be one of the next victims. My steps have been dogged from months, and only a good opportunity has been wanting to secure to me the fate which Stephens has just met, and I speak earnestly upon this matter. I feel that I have a right to do so, and a right to be heard as well, and with this conviction I say to you plainly that any member of Congress who, especially if from the South, does not support, advocate, and urge immediate, active, and thorough measures to put an end to these outrages, and make citizenship a privilege, is a coward, a traitor a fool. The time for action has come, and the man who has now only speeches to make over some Constitutional scarecrow, deserves to be damned.

1.6
Atlanta Exposition Speech (1895)

Booker T. Washington

Given before the Atlanta Cotton States and International Exposition in September 1895, this famous speech by noted African American leader Booker T. Washington gives us insight into his "accommodationist" approach to race relations. What does he mean when he implores whites to "Cast down your bucket where you are"? What does he call on African Americans to do to improve their position in American life?

Mr. President and Gentlemen of the Board of Directors and Citizens.

One-third of the population of the South is of the Negro race. No enterprise seeking the material, civil, or moral welfare of this section can disregard this element of our population and reach the highest success. I but convey to you, Mr. President and Directors, the sentiment of the masses of my race when I say that in no way have the value and manhood of the American Negro been more fittingly and generously recognized than by the managers of this magnificent Exposition at every stage of its progress. It is a recognition that will do more to cement the friendship of the two races than any occurrence since the dawn of our freedom.

Not only this, but the opportunity here afforded will awaken among us a new era of industrial progress. Ignorant and inexperienced, it is not strange that in the first years of our new life we began at the top instead of at the bottom; that a seat in Congress or the state legislature was more sought than real estate or industrial skill; that the political convention or stump speaking had more attractions than starting a dairy farm or truck garden.

A ship lost at sea for many days suddenly sighted a friendly vessel. From the mast of the unfortunate vessel was seen a signal, " Water, water;

From *Up from Slavery* by Booker T. Washington, Doubleday, Page & Co., 1901.

we die of thirst!" The answer from the friendly vessel at once came back, "Cast down your bucket where you are." A second time the signal, "Water, water; send us water!" ran up from the distressed vessel, and was answered, "Cast down your bucket where you are." And a third and fourth signal for water was answered, "Cast down your bucket where you are." The captain of the distressed vessel, at last heeding the injunction, cast down his bucket, and it came up full of fresh, sparkling water from the mouth of the Amazon River. To those of my race who depend on bettering their condition in a foreign land or who underestimate the importance of cultivating friendly relations with the Southern white man, who is their next-door neighbour, I would say: "Cast down your bucket where you are"—cast it down in making friends in every manly way of the people of all races by whom we are surrounded.

Cast it down in agriculture, mechanics, in commerce, in domestic service, and in the professions. And in this connection it is well to bear in mind that whatever other sins the South may be called to bear, when it comes to business, pure and simple, it is in the South that the Negro is given a man's chance in the commercial world, and in nothing is this Exposition more eloquent than in emphasizing this chance. Our greatest danger is that in the great leap from slavery to freedom we may overlook the fact that the masses of us are to live by the productions of our hands, and fail to keep in mind that we shall prosper in proportion as we learn to dignify and glorify common labour and put brains and skill into the common occupations of life; shall prosper in proportion as we learn to draw the line between the superficial and the substantial, the ornamental gewgaws of life and the useful. No race can prosper till it learns that there is as much dignity in tilling a field as in writing a poem. It is at the bottom of life we must begin, and not at the top. Nor should we permit our grievances to overshadow our opportunities.

To those of the white race who look to the incoming of those of foreign birth and strange tongue and habits for the prosperity of the South, were I permitted I would repeat what I say to my own race, "Cast down your bucket where you are." Cast it down among the eight millions of Negroes whose habits you know, whose fidelity and love you have tested in days when to have proved treacherous meant the ruin of your firesides. Cast down your bucket among these people who have, without strikes and labour wars, tilled your fields, cleared your forests, built your railroads and cities, and brought forth treasures from the bowels of the earth, and helped make possible this magnificent representation of the progress of the South. Casting down your bucket among my people, helping and encouraging them as you are doing on these grounds, and to education of head, hand, and heart, you will find that they will buy your surplus land, make blossom the waste places in your fields, and run your factories. While doing this, you can be sure in the future, as in the past, that you and your families will be surrounded by the most patient, faithful, law-abiding, and unresentful people that the world has seen. As we have proved our loyalty to you in the past, in nursing your children, watching by the sick-bed of your mothers and fathers, and often following them with tear-dimmed eyes to their graves, so in the future, in our humble way, we shall stand by you with a devotion that no foreigner can approach, ready to lay down our lives, if need be, in defence of yours, interlacing our industrial, commercial, civil, and religious life with yours in a way that shall make the interests of both races one. In all things that are purely social we can be as separate as the fingers, yet one as the hand in all things essential to mutual progress.

There is no defence or security for any of us except in the highest intelligence and development of all. If anywhere there are efforts tending to curtail the fullest growth of the Negro, let these efforts be turned into stimulating, encouraging, and making him the most useful and intelligent citizen. Effort or means so invested will pay a thousand per cent interest. These efforts will be twice blessed—"blessing him that gives and him that takes."

There is no escape through law of man or God from the inevitable:—

> The laws of changeless justice bind
> Oppressor with oppressed;
> And close as sin and suffering joined
> We march to fate abreast.

Nearly sixteen millions of hands will aid you in pulling the load upward, or they will pull against you the load downward. We shall constitute one-third and more of the ignorance and crime of the South, or one-third its intelligence and progress; we shall contribute one-third to the business and industrial prosperity of the South, or we shall prove a veritable body of death, stagnating, depressing, retarding every effort to advance the body politic.

Gentlemen of the Exposition, as we present to you our humble effort at an exhibition of our progress, you must not expect overmuch. Starting thirty years ago with ownership here and there in a few quilts and pumpkins and chickens (gathered from miscellaneous sources), remember the path that has led from these to the inventions and production of agricultural implements, buggies, steam-engines, newspapers, books, statuary, carving, paintings, the management of drug-stores and banks, has not been trodden without contact with thorns and thistles. While we take pride in what we exhibit as a result of our independent efforts, we do not for a moment forget that our part in this exhibition would fall far short of your expectations but for the constant help that has come to our educational life, not only from the Southern states, but especially from Northern philanthropists, who have made their gifts a constant stream of blessing and encouragement.

The wisest among my race understand that the agitation of questions of social equality is the extremest folly, and that progress in the enjoyment of all the privileges that will come to us must be the result of severe and constant struggle rather than of artificial forcing. No race that has anything to contribute to the markets of the world is long in any degree ostracized. It is important and right that all privileges of the law be ours, but it is vastly more important that we be prepared for the exercises of these privileges. The opportunity to earn a dollar in a factory just now is worth infinitely more than the opportunity to spend a dollar in an opera-house.

In conclusion, may I repeat that nothing in thirty years has given us more hope and encouragement, and drawn us so near to you of the white race, as this opportunity offered by the Exposition; and here bending, as it were, over the altar that represents the results of the struggles of your race and mine, both starting practically empty-handed three decades ago, I pledge that in your effort to work out the great and intricate problem which God has laid at the doors of the South, you shall have at all times the patient, sympathetic help of my race; only let this be constantly in mind, that, while from representations in these buildings of the product of field, of forest, of mine, of factory, letters, and art, much good will come, yet far above and beyond material benefits will be that higher good, that, let us pray God, will come, in a blotting out of sectional differences and racial animosities and suspicions, in a determination to administer absolute justice, in a willing obedience among all classes to the mandates of law. This, this, coupled with our material prosperity, will bring into our beloved South a new heaven and a new earth.

1.7
Of Mr. Booker T. Washington and Others (1903)

W.E.B. DuBois

Taken from his masterly The Souls of Black Folk, *this essay is a classic statement of DuBois's philosophy concerning race relations at the turn of the century. What is DuBois's criticism of Washington? Compare this to Document 1.6; how would you describe the differences between these two powerful leaders?*

Easily the most striking thing in the history of the American Negro since 1876 is the ascendancy of Mr. Booker T. Washington. It began at the time when war memories and ideals were rapidly passing; a day of astonishing commercial development was dawning; a sense of doubt and hesitation overtook the freedmen's sons,—then it was that his leading began. Mr. Washington came, with a single definite programme, at the psychological moment when the nation was a little ashamed of having bestowed so much sentiment on Negroes, and was concentrating its energies on Dollars. His programme of industrial education, conciliation of the South, and submission and silence as to civil and political rights, was not wholly original; the Free Negroes from 1830 up to war-time had striven to build industrial schools, and the American Missionary Association had from the first taught various trades; and Price and others had sought a way of honorable alliance with the best of the Southerners. But Mr. Washington first indissolubly linked these things; he put enthusiasm, unlimited energy, and perfect faith into his programme, and changed it from a by-path into a veritable Way of Life. And the tale of the methods by which he did this is a fascinating study of human life.

It startled the nation to hear a Negro advocating such a programme after many decades of bitter complaint; it startled and won the applause of the South, it interested and won the admiration of the North; and after a confused murmur of protest, it silenced if it did not convert the Negroes themselves.

To gain the sympathy and coöperation of the various elements comprising the white South was Mr. Washington's first task; and this, at the time Tuskegee was founded, seemed, for a black man, well-nigh impossible. And yet ten years later it was done in the word spoken at Atlanta: "In all things purely social we can be as separate as the five fingers, and yet one as the hand in all things essential to mutual progress." This "Atlanta Compromise" is by all odds the most notable thing in Mr. Washington's career. The South interpreted it in different ways: the radicals received it as a complete surrender of the demand for civil and political equality; the conservatives, as a generously conceived working basis for mutual understanding. So both approved it, and to-day its author is certainly the most distinguished Southerner since Jefferson Davis, and the one with the largest personal following.

Next to this achievement comes Mr. Washington's work in gaining place and consideration in the North. Others less shrewd and tactful had formerly essayed to sit on these two stools and had fallen between them; but as Mr. Washington knew the heart of the South from birth and training, so by singular insight he intuitively grasped the spirit of the age which was dominating the North. And so thoroughly did he learn the speech and thought of triumphant commercialism, and the ideals of material prosperity, that the picture of a lone black boy poring over a French grammar amid the weeds and dirt of a neglected home soon seemed to him the acme of absurdities. One wonders what Socrates and St. Francis of Assisi would say to this.

And yet this very singleness of vision and thorough oneness with his age is a mark of the successful man. It is as though Nature must needs make men narrow in order to give them force. So Mr. Washington's cult has gained unquestioning followers, his work has wonderfully prospered, his friends are legion, and his enemies are confounded. To-day he stands as the one recognized spokesman of his ten million fellows, and one of the most notable figures in a nation of seventy millions. One hesitates, therefore, to criticise a life which, beginning with so little, has done so much. And yet the time is come when one may speak in all sincerity and utter courtesy of the mistakes and shortcomings of Mr. Washington's career, as well as of his triumphs, without being thought captious or envious, and without forgetting that it is easier to do ill than well in the world.

The criticism that has hitherto met Mr. Washington has not always been of this broad character. In the South especially has he had to walk warily to avoid the harshest judgments,—and naturally so, for he is dealing with the one subject of deepest sensitiveness to that section. Twice— once when at the Chicago celebration of the Spanish-American War he alluded to the color-prejudice that is "eating away the vitals of the South," and once when he dined with President Roosevelt—has the resulting Southern criticism been violent enough to threaten seriously his popularity. In the North the feeling has several times forced itself into words, that Mr. Washington's counsels of submission overlooked certain elements of true manhood, and that his educational programme was unnecessarily narrow. Usually, however, such criticism has not found open expression, although, too, the spiritual sons of the Abolitionists have not been prepared to acknowledge that the schools founded before Tuskegee, by men of broad ideals and self-sacrificing spirit, were wholly failures or worthy of ridicule. While, then, criticism has not failed to follow Mr. Washington, yet the prevailing public opinion of the land has been but too willing to deliver the solution of a wearisome problem into his hands, and say, "If that is all you and your race ask, take it."

Among his own people, however, Mr. Washington has encountered the strongest and most lasting opposition, amounting at times to bitterness, and even today continuing strong and insistent even though largely silenced in outward expression by the public opinion of the nation. Some of this opposition is, of course, mere envy; the disappointment of displaced demagogues and the spite of narrow minds. But aside from this, there is among educated and thoughtful colored men in all parts of the land a feeling of deep regret, sorrow, and apprehension at the wide currency and ascendancy which some of Mr. Washington's theories have gained. These same men admire his sincerity of purpose, and are willing to forgive much to honest endeavor which is doing something worth the doing. They coöperate with Mr. Washington as far as they conscientiously can; and, indeed, it is no ordinary tribute to this man's tact and power that, steering as he must between so many diverse interests and opinions, he so largely retains the respect of all.

But the hushing of the criticism of honest opponents is a dangerous thing. It leads some of the best of the critics to unfortunate silence and paralysis of effort, and others to burst into speech so passionately and intemperately as to lose listeners. Honest and earnest criticism from those whose interests are most nearly touched,—criticism of writers by readers, of government by those governed, of leaders by those led,—this is the soul of democracy and the safeguard of modern society. If the best of the American Negroes receive by outer pressure a leader whom they had not recognized before, manifestly there is here a certain palpable gain. Yet there is also irreparable loss,—a loss of that peculiarly valuable education which a group receives when by search and criticism it finds and commissions its own leaders. The way in which this is done is at once the most elementary and the nicest problem of social growth. History is but the record of such group-leadership; and yet how infinitely changeful is its type and character! And of all types and kinds, what can be more instructive than the leadership of a group within a group?—that curious double movement where real progress may be negative and actual advance be relative retrogression. All this is the social student's inspiration and despair....

Mr. Washington represents in Negro thought the old attitude of adjustment and submission; but adjustment at such a peculiar time as to make his programme unique. This is an age of unusual economic development, and Mr. Washington's programme naturally takes an economic cast, becoming a gospel of Work and Money to such an extent as apparently almost completely to overshadow the higher aims of life. Moreover, this is an age when the more advanced races are coming in closer contact with the less developed races, and the race-feeling is therefore intensified; and Mr. Washington's programme practically accepts the alleged inferiority of the Negro races. Again, in our own land, the reaction from the sentiment of war time has given impetus to race-prejudice against Negroes, and Mr. Washington withdraws many of the high demands of Negroes as men and American citizens. In other periods of intensified prejudice all the Negro's tendency to self-assertion has been called forth; at this period a policy of submission is advocated. In the history of nearly all other races and peoples the doctrine preached at such crises has been that manly self-respect is worth more than lands and houses, and that a people who voluntarily surrender such respect, or cease striving for it, are not worth civilizing.

In answer to this, it has been claimed that the Negro can survive only through submission. Mr. Washington distinctly asks that black people give up, at least for the present, three things,—

First, political power,
Second, insistence on civil rights
Third, higher education of Negro youth,—

and concentrate all their energies on industrial education, and accumulation of wealth, and the conciliation of the South. This policy has been courageously and insistently advocated for over fifteen years, and has been triumphant for perhaps ten years. As a result of this tender of the palm-branch, what has been the return? In these years there have occurred:

1. The disfranchisement of the Negro.
2. The legal creation of a distinct status of civil inferiority for the Negro.
3. The steady withdrawal of aid from institutions for the higher training of the Negro.

These movements are not, to be sure, direct results of Mr. Washington's teachings; but his propaganda has, without a shadow of doubt, helped their speedier accomplishment. The question then comes: Is it possible, and probable, that nine millions of men can make effective progress in economic lines if they are deprived of political rights, made a servile caste, and allowed only the most meagre chance for developing their exceptional men? If history and reason give any distinct answer to these questions, it is an emphatic *No*. And Mr. Washington thus faces the triple paradox of his career:

1. He is striving nobly to make Negro artisans business men and property-owners; but it is utterly impossible, under modern competitive methods, for workingmen and property-owners to defend their rights and exist without the right of suffrage.
2. He insists on thrift and self-respect, but at the same time counsels a silent submission to civic inferiority such as is bound to sap the manhood of any race in the long run.
3. He advocates common-school and industrial training, and depreciates institutions of higher learning; but neither the Negro common-schools, nor Tuskegee itself, could remain open a day were it not for teachers trained in Negro colleges, or trained by their graduates.

This triple paradox in Mr. Washington's position is the object of criticism by two classes of colored Americans. One class is spiritually descended from Toussaint the Savior, through Gabriel, Vesey, and Turner, and they represent the attitude of revolt and revenge; they hate the white South blindly and distrust the white race generally, and so far as they agree on definite action, think that the Negro only hope lies in emigration beyond the borders of the United States. And yet, by the irony of fate, nothing has more effectually made this programme seem hopeless than the recent course of the United States toward weaker and darker peoples in the West Indies, Hawaii, and the Philippines,—for where in the world may we go and be safe from lying and brute force?

The other class of Negroes who cannot agree with Mr. Washington has hitherto said little aloud. They deprecate the sight of scattered counsels, of internal disagreement; and especially they dislike making their just criticism of a useful and earnest man an excuse for a general discharge of venom from small-minded opponents. Nevertheless, the questions involved are so fundamental and serious that it is difficult to see how men like the Grimkes, Kelly Miller, J. W. E. Bowen, and other representatives of this group, can much longer be silent. Such men feel in conscience bound to ask of this nation three things:

1. The right to vote.
2. Civic equality.
3. The education of youth according to ability.

They acknowledge Mr. Washington's invaluable service in counselling patience and courtesy in such demands; they do not ask that ignorant black men vote when ignorant whites are debarred, or that any reasonable restrictions in the suffrage should not be applied; they know that the low social level of the mass of the race is responsible for much discrimination against it, but they also know, and the nation knows, that relentless color-prejudice is more often a cause than a result of the Negro's degradation; they seek the abatement of this relic of barbarism, and not its systematic encouragement and pampering by all agencies of social power from the Associated Press to the Church of Christ. They advocate, with Mr. Washington, a broad system of Negro common schools supplemented by thorough industrial training; but they are surprised that a man of Mr. Washington's insight cannot see that no such educational system ever has rested or can rest on any other basis than that of the well-equipped college and university, and that insist that there is a demand for a few such institutions throughout the South to train the best of the Negro youth as teachers, professional men, and leaders.

This group of men honor Mr. Washington for his attitude of conciliation toward the white South; they accept the "Atlanta Compromise" in its broadest interpretation; they recognize, with him, many signs of promise, many men of high purpose and fair judgment, in this section; they know that no easy task has been laid upon a region already tottering under heavy burdens. But, nevertheless, they insist that the way to truth and right lies in straightforward honesty, not in indiscriminate flattery; in praising those of the South who do well and criticising uncompromisingly those who do ill; in taking advantage of the opportunities at hand and urging their fellows to do the same, but at the same time in remembering that only a firm adherence to their higher ideals and aspirations will ever keep those ideals within the realm of possibility. They do not expect that the free right to vote to enjoy civic rights, and to be educated, will come in a moment; they do not expect to see the bias and prejudices of years disappear at the blast of a trumpet; but they are absolutely certain that the way for a people to gain their reasonable rights is not by voluntarily throwing them away and insisting that they do not want them; that the way for a people to gain respect is not by continually belittling and ridiculing themselves; that, on the contrary, Negroes must insist continually, in season and out of season, that voting is necessary to modem manhood, that color discrimination is barbarism, and that black boys need education as well as white boys.

In failing thus to state plainly and unequivocally the legitimate demands of their people, even at the cost of opposing an honored leader, the thinking classes of American Negroes would shirk a heavy responsibility,—a responsibility to themselves, a responsibility to the struggling masses, a responsibility to the darker races of men whose future depends so largely on this American experiment, but especially a responsibility to this nation,—this common Fatherland. It is wrong to encourage a man or a people in evil-doing; it is wrong to aid and abet a national crime simply because it is unpopular not to do so. The growing spirit of kindliness and reconciliation between the North and South after the frightful difference of a generation ago ought to be a source of deep congratulation to all, and especially to those whose mistreatment caused the war; but if that reconciliation is to be marked by the industrial slavery and civic death of those same black men, with permanent legislation into a position of inferiority, then those black men, if they are really men, are called upon by every consideration of patriotism and loyalty to oppose such a course by all civilized methods, even though such opposition involves disagreement with Mr. Booker T. Washington. We have no right to sit silently by while the inevitable seeds are sown for a harvest of disaster to our children, black and white....

It would be unjust to Mr. Washington not to acknowledge that in several instances he has opposed movements in the South which were unjust to the Negro; he sent memorials to the Louisiana and Alabama constitutional conventions, he has spoken against lynching, and in other ways has

openly or silently set his influence against sinister schemes and unfortunate happenings. Notwithstanding this, it is equally true to assert that on
the whole the distinct impression left by Mr. Washington's propaganda is,
first, that the South is justified in its present attitude toward the Negro because of the Negro's degradation; secondly, that the prime cause of the
Negro's failure to rise more quickly is his wrong education in the past;
and, thirdly, that his future rise depends primarily on his own efforts. Each
of these propositions is a dangerous half-truth. The supplementary truths
must never be lost sight of: first, slavery and race-prejudice are potent if
not sufficient causes of the Negro's position; second, industrial and common-school training were necessarily slow in planting because they had
to await the black teachers trained by higher institutions,—it being extremely doubtful if any essentially different development was possible,
and certainly a Tuskegee was unthinkable before 1880; and, third, while it
is a great truth to say that the Negro must strive and strive mightily to help
himself, it is equally true that unless his striving be not simply seconded,
but rather aroused and encouraged, by the initiative of the richer and wiser
environing group, he cannot hope for great success.

In his failure to realize and impress this last point, Mr. Washington is
especially to be criticised. His doctrine has tended to make the whites,
North and South, shift the burden of the Negro problem to the Negro's
shoulders and stand aside as critical and rather pessimistic spectators;
when in fact the burden belongs to the nation, and the hands of none of
us are clean if we bend not our energies to righting these great wrongs.

The South ought to be led, by candid and honest criticism, to assert her
better self and do her full duty to the race she has cruelly wronged and is
still wronging. The North—her co-partner in guilt—cannot salve her conscience by plastering it with gold. We cannot settle this problem by diplomacy and suaveness, by "policy" alone. If worse come to worst, can the
moral fibre of this country survive the slow throttling and murder of nine
millions of men?

The black men of America have a duty to perform, a duty stern and
delicate,—a forward movement to oppose a part of the work of their greatest leader. So far as Mr. Washington preaches Thrift, Patience, and Industrial Training for the masses, we must hold up his hands and strive with
him, rejoicing in his honors and glorying in the strength of this Joshua
called of God and of man to lead the headless host. But so far as Mr. Washington apologizes for injustice, North or South, does not rightly value the
privilege and duty of voting, belittles the emasculating effects of caste distinctions, and opposes the higher training and ambition of our brighter

minds,—so far as he, the South, or the Nation, does this,—we must un-
ceasingly and firmly oppose them. By every civilized and peaceful method
we must strive for the rights which the world accords to men, clinging un-
waveringly to those great words which the sons of the Fathers would fain
forget: "We hold these truths to be self-evident: That all men are created
equal; that they are endowed by their Creator with certain unalienable
rights; that among these are life, liberty, and the pursuit of happiness."

CHAPTER 2

Taming the West
1865–1900

2.1 Stuart Henry, "Conquering Our Great American Plains" (1930)

2.2 Robert M. Utley, "Wars of the Peace Policy," 1869–1886

2.3 T. J. Stiles, "Buffalo Soldiers"

2.4 Joseph McCoy, "Historic Sketches of the Cattle Trade of the West and Southwest" (1874)

2.5 Robert A. Trennert, "Educating Indian Girls at Nonreservation Boarding Schools, 1878–1920"

2.6 Helen Hunt Jackson, "A Century of Dishonor" (1881)

2.7 "Dawes Severalty Act" (1887)

2.1
Conquering Our Great American Plains (1930)

Stuart Henry

Taken from his 1930 reminiscence, this document recalls Stuart Henry's experience as the son of a Kansas farmer in 1874, when a plague of grasshoppers devastated the area. What kinds of problems did rural Kansans face in the late nineteenth century besides hordes of insects?

In 1874 came a gigantic calamity in the form of a raid of grasshoppers, which ate up every bit of green vegetation from the Rocky Mountains to and beyond the Missouri River. I recall that when coming home late one afternoon for supper I stepped back surprised to see what became known as Rocky Mountain locusts covering the side of the house. Already inside, they feasted on the curtains. Clouds of them promptly settled down on the whole country—everywhere, unavoidable. People set about killing them to save gardens, but this soon proved ridiculous. Specially contrived machines, pushed by horses, scooped up the hoppers in grain fields by the barrelful to burn them. This, too, was then nonsensical. Vast hordes, myriad. In a week grain fields, gardens, shrubs, vines, had been eaten down to the ground or to the bark. Nothing could be done. You sat by and saw everything go.

When autumn came with the country devastated, the population despaired again when seeing the insects remaining for the winter with the apparent plan of being on hand for the next season. It seemed that they could be counted on as a curse for all time, since the Rocky Mountain locusts, as the name indicates, appeared new to science, to the civilized world. No one, accordingly, knew of their habits. And their ingenuity confounded close observers. As if intending to stay permanently on the plains, they bored holes only in hard ground, in roads and other firm places, for their winter occupancy. Intelligently did they avoid soft ground, since tenancy there would be more easily, more apt to be, disturbed.

To add to the terror of the locust invasion was the general accompaniment of weather tending always to be dry. Kansans—"people of the south wind." This poetic Indian meaning might bear a still more distinctive signification if it ran "people of the hot southwest wind." For continental western Kansas, lying in the exact center of the United States, turned out to be subject in summer to burning south or southwest winds untempered by cooling salt breezes creeping up from the Gulf of Mexico or cooling zephyrs descending from Canada. The middle area often missed the relief that either the southern or northern areas might experience. And a steady hot current of air, though mild in velocity, brought the dreaded dry times.

How one hated to see the heavens seal their cisterns and the plains to be sear! A few showers would dash upon the ground and run to cover in the creek and river beds, not stopping to penetrate to roots. Matters seemed, indeed, to be made worse by these spurts of moisture, the blazing sun promptly coming out afterward, baking the earth harder.

Almost hilarious, many of the old-timers during such months! They underwent the stark privations in very fair style, having been shown to be prophets with honor in their own land.

"Hee-hee! Didn't I tell you so? This ain't no farmin' country. Too droughty. Lucky fer cattle if lucky fer anything. An' these 'ere Easterners ruinin' the buffalo grass by plowin' it up! Spilin' everything. Yaps that want to farm better stay back East where there ain't anything better to do. They have driv' out the Texas cattle trade. What have they got left? Mighty little, by cracky!"

People still often considered the plains fit at best for very light spring crops. If these shrank up just before harvest, there would be left after June nothing to fall back upon during the rest of the year. The small corn areas along the streams then resembled patches of sticks. The local livestock in 1874 had to be disposed of, fodder lacking. Pitiful little vegetable gardens shriveled. The few flower plots planted by housewives were at first bravely watered. Like tiny, ghastly totem poles did the scarred stalks afterward look.

In a hot droughty summer most of the wells and springs gave out early. Water in creeks trickled so shallowly that dogs lay panting in them while hardly able to immerse more than their paws. Then the burning spell! The southwest wind blew at frequent intervals out of its Sahara ovens, sweeping the land with a flinty dust. You thought of it as a finely textured burial shroud. People told the old joke: "We'd have had to soak our pigs overnight so that they could hold swill." The nights proved as debilitating as the days, since humanity couldn't sleep for the heat. This was the worst of it—they couldn't sleep. No part of each twenty-four hours furnished forgetfulness of the nightmare of failure.

In that country of poor farming and upon a population heedless about laying by supplies for a scarce period, the disaster of 1874 doubled its effect. One conceded: Of what use to work? Farmers, of course, stood out of a job. They loafed in town from midsummer on. For many said they could hardly have plowed or broken prairie. The lumps of sod needed to be knocked up by axes. Seven months before there would be a thing to do. Locusts and scanty rainfall together!

One watched the office men in towns lounging day after day at their doors or hanging out of their windows, with nothing on hand. Business collapsed. It looked like an idiotic insult to ask anyone for what he owed. Tillers of soil could not be counted on to pay anyhow till after harvest, once a year, and now, in 1874, no harvest. The merchants, townsmen in general, were expected to cash up from month to month. They stared blankly at the streets, trying to figure how they could get through the winter with their money and credit mostly gone up the spout. The sight of farmers dawdling in stores and saloons added to the dismalness. What if *next* year brought a blank? Too awful to contemplate! Meanwhile—it looked like sheer unavoidable starvation.

Moral stamina? One knew how the women slouched around red-hot cookstoves three times a day for the regular if skimpy meals. Some strength *must* be kept up, some flesh *must* be kept on bones. Even wives who had had a little pardonable vanity left quit trying to save their complexions. They let their tresses go dry and stick out any way. Hair got crinkly, few bothering much about brushes and combs. Hollow-eyed, fagged out, the fair sex came to care little how they looked, what they wore. The story was told of seeing on a street a woman in a garment she had sewed together from the halves of different flour sacks without taking the pains to remove their brands, the result being shocking. Men swore and played poker no more. Fathers dreaded to face their children, who grew raggeder. As for their dirtiness, who, you might almost ask, hardly dared spare water to wash them? Husbands hated to go home to meals, for they must meet the appeals of their wives to climb on wagons and strike out for back home.

"Sell for what you can get, John—give it away—leave it—only let's get out. I don't have to ride on a railroad. A schooner headed east looks awful good to me."

Prayer meetings being held, a few of the men who had not gone to church dropped in and sat before pulpits, heads bowed, humbled in respect. They wondered now if there might be some virtue in supplication. At least they risked no money nor chances by attending meeting. Anything, even prayer, to see mud puddles drowning out the hoppers! But the believers in the great god luck—the majority—stood, in the main, by their guns. They didn't think petitions by four-hundred-dollar-a-year ministers had enough breeze behind them to be shot clear up to Heaven so that the yelpings could be heard there. Wouldn't luck bring a favorable year next time, since this one could be called a ripper? Herein lay the dependable thing about luck: It always changes....

What with federal and other public aid and a steady immigration with money in larger sums, the population lived through the great grasshopper year mainly from necessity as well as pluck. It was a close call. But the locusts or a drought or both the next year would practically wipe out this early folk. A mighty and unsuspected blessing, however, intervened. Since low and moister regions than the Rocky Mountains cause its grasshopper progeny to die before maturity, one raid will not continue elsewhere its severest damage into the following years. This is what took place on the plains in the spring of 1875, though it could not have been foreseen by the disheartened people. In that year and the year or two afterward this insect did not cause the harm suffered in 1874.

Also the seed grain supplied by Eastern charity made good, and the fortunate season in 1875 brought ample crops to meet good prices. Buoyant faith at once reestablished itself....The god luck had again veered. The plains now reigned in prosperity and was freely wagered on in terms of a wet, though glowing, future.

2.2
Wars of the Peace Policy, 1869–1886

Robert M. Utley

In this essay, historian Robert Utley describes the armed conflicts between the U.S. Army and Native Americans in the wake of the 1868 treaty. According to Utley, what led to these "wars," and what consequences did they bring to Indians on the Plains?

However representative of the Indian Wars were the nearly unnoticed adventures of Lieutenant [Walter S.] Schuyler and [Kiowa Indian leader] Pago-to-goodle, it was the big headline-grabbing uprisings that captured public attention and often decreed changes in the Indians' fortunes. One after another, such conflicts marked the years of the Peace Policy and dashed its bright hopes. In one sense, it is an irony that so many wars broke out under the mantle of the Peace Policy, but in another sense it is readily understandable. The Peace Policy aimed at placing all Indians on reservations, where they could be kept away from the settlements and travel routes and where ultimately they could be civilized. The Indians often had other ideas—if not at first, then after they had sampled the reality of life on the reservation. Virtually every major war of the two decades after Appomattox was fought to force Indians on to newly created reservations or to make them go back to reservations from which they had fled. From such perspective, it is not surprising that warfare characterized the Peace Policy.

As the years passed, moreover, the Peace Policy ceased to command the wide support it had at first. The army, in particular, grew more openly critical. Except for an occasional Lieutenant Drew or Colonel Grierson, officers scoffed at the notion of conquest by kindness, and they had little use for the idealistic yet often corrupt people and purposes of the Indian Bureau. As General Sheridan remarked simplistically in 1869, "If a white man commits murder or robs, we hang him or send him to the penitentiary; if an Indian does the same, we have been in the habit of giving him more blankets." And as Lieutenant Schuyler observed at the Camp Verde Reservation, the Indians "can be governed for the present only with a hand of iron, which is a manner of governing totally unknown to the agents of the Indian Bureau, most of whom are afraid of the Indians and are willing to do anything to conciliate them." Western sentiment, always militant, encouraged the army in its view of the Peace Policy. "Let sniveling quakers give place to bluff soldiers," ran a typical editorial comment.

Who is friendly and who is not? military officers not unreasonably asked the civilian authorities. Those on the reservation were friendly and the exclusive responsibility of the Indian Bureau, came the answer; those off the reservation were hostile and the responsibility of the army. Superficially, it seemed a logical solution to a chronic dilemma. It drew a line that no one, including the Indians, could mistake. But as the record of the Fort Sill "city of refuge" demonstrated, a reservation could harbor a great many Indians of unfriendly disposition. Unfortunately, except for the rare Satanta who bragged of his exploits, their individual identities remained unknown or unprovable. Aggravating the army's frustration, garrisons on or near reservations had to watch helplessly while civilian corruption and mismanagement—or so it seemed to them—prodded Indians toward an armed hostility that would have to be suppressed at the risk of army lives. As General Sherman complained to a congressional committee in 1874: "The Indian Bureau keeps feeding and clothing the Indians, till they get fat and saucy, and then we are only notified that the Indians are troublesome, and are going to war, after it is too late to provide a remedy."

Except by government decree, moreover, Indians off the reservation were not necessarily belligerent. They might be out hunting, or headed for a visit with friends in another tribe, or simply wandering about seeing the country. Even a whole band off the reservation did not automatically mean hostility. Indeed, few such could be clearly labeled friendly or hostile; ambiguity more accurately described their temper. Was Black Kettle's village on the Washita friendly or hostile? No chief and no band more diligently pursued peace. Yet it was the trail of a party of Black Kettle's young men, their hands stained with the blood of Kansas settlers, that led Custer's cavalry to the luckless chief's winter lodges. The army never learned to discriminate between the guilty and the innocent simply because rarely was a group of Indians unmistakably one or the other.

The army did not pursue its Indian-fighting mission very creatively. Occasionally a General Crook recognized his foes as superb guerrilla fighters who called for techniques quite different than had Robert E. Lee's gray legions. Crook fought Indians like Indians and usually, in fact, with Indians. But the army as an institution never evolved a doctrine of Indian warfare, never taught its aspiring officers at West Point the difference between conventional and unconventional war, and never issued official guidance for troops in the field.

Lacking a formal doctrine of unconventional war, the army waged conventional war. Heavy columns of infantry and cavalry, locked to slow moving supply trains, crawled about the vast western distances in search of Indians who could scatter and vanish almost instantly. The conventional tactics of the Scott, Casey, and Upton manuals sometimes worked, by routing an adversary that had foolishly decided to stand and fight on the white soldiers' terms, by smashing a village whose inhabitants had grown careless, or by wearing down a quarry through persistent campaigning that made surrender preferable to constant fatigue and insecurity. But most such offensives merely broke down the grain-fed cavalry horses and ended with the troops devoting as much effort to keeping themselves supplied as to chasing Indians.

But when they worked, these offensives worked with a vengeance. They were a forerunner of "total war" against entire populations, as pioneered by Sherman and Sheridan against the Confederacy. Under the guidance and inspiration of these two leaders—the one now General in Chief of the army, the other heading the strategic Division of the Missouri, embracing all the Great Plains—the army set forth to find the enemy in their winter camps, to kill or drive them from their lodges, to destroy their ponies, food, and shelter, and to hound them mercilessly across a frigid landscape until they gave up. If women and children got hurt or killed, it was lamentable, but justified because it resolved the issue quickly and decisively, and thus more humanely. Although prosecuted along conventional lines and often an exercise in logistical futility, this approach yielded an occasional victory, such as the Washita, that saved it from serious challenge.

No better than the army did the Indians adapt to new conditions. The westward surge of the white people after the Civil War confronted them with a crisis of apocalyptic implications, yet they met it, like the army, in the same old ways. Despite the common danger, tribal particularism and intertribal animosities remained as strong as ever. Sometimes tribes came together in alliance against an especially visible threat from the whites, but rarely did such an alliance hang together for very long. Even unity within a tribe proved elusive. Factions differed on how to deal with the white encroachment; some resisted, some accommodated, and some wavered and even oscillated between the two extremes. The highly individual character of tribal society inhibited the rise of leaders who could bring together diverse opinions, and, to make matters worse, the proliferation of "government chiefs" demoralized the traditional political organization. As one astute observer remarked, army officers, Indian superintendents and commissioners, and even agents had created so many chiefs that "Indian chiefs, like brevets in the army, are become so common they are not properly respected."

Nor did fighting methods change. Indian culture still developed a superb fighting man. Warriors still practiced guerrilla tactics masterfully and made uncanny use of terrain, vegetation, and other natural conditions, all to the anguish of their military antagonists. But Indian culture also continued to emphasize the individual and withhold from any man the power of command, except through personal influence. Thus team discipline tended to collapse when opportunities for personal distinction or differing opinions on strategy or tactics arose. Man for man, the warrior far surpassed his blue clad adversary in virtually every test of military proficiency; but unit for unit—however great the numbers—the Indians could not come close to matching the discipline and organization of the army. When Indians made the mistake of standing and fighting on the army's terms, they usually lost.

In the end, however, the relative fighting qualities of the opponents made little difference. Despite all the wars of the Peace Policy, the Indians did not succumb to military conquest, The army contributed to the final collapse, of course, with "war houses" scattered all through the Indian country and with campaigns that hastened an outcome ordained by more significant forces. More than the army, railroads, settlements, and all the numbers, technology, and other trappings of an aggressive and highly organized society brought defeat to the Indians. Every white advance came at the expense of resources, especially wild game, essential to the Indian way of life. As the open land and its natural bounty shrank, the reservation offered the only alternative to extinction. For the Indians, General Sherman's jest held deadly portent: "I think it would be wise," he said of the Sioux insistence on hunting on the Republican River, "to invite all the sportsmen of England & America there this fall for a Grand Buffalo hunt, and make one grand sweep of them all."

Yet the Indians' armed resistance to the westward movement, and the army's armed response, form dramatic and significant chapters in the history of both peoples and of the frontiers across which they faced each other. In the Trans-Mississippi West, the final and most intense phase coincided with the final phase of the westward migration and settlement of the whites and was a direct consequence of the Peace Policy's imperative to confine all Indians to reservations.

Kintpuash had tried the reservation and did not like it. An able, ambitious young man, he and other Modoc leaders had signed a treaty in 1864 ceding their homeland among the lake-dotted, lava-scored plateaus of southern Oregon and northern California and had agreed to live on a reservation with Klamaths and Snakes. Homesick, bullied by the more numerous Klamaths, some sixty to seventy families followed Kintpuash back to their old homes on Lost River, just south of the Oregon-California boundary. As more and more whites took up homesteads on the ceded lands, tensions rose. Officials of the Indian Bureau pressed Kintpuash— with other whites, they knew him as Captain Jack—to go back to the reservation. Persuasion failing, they asked the army to use force. That move provoked the Modoc War of 1872–73.

At dawn on November 29, 1872, cavalry attacked the village of Kintpuash. After an exchange of fire, the Indians fled, later crossing Tule Lake in boats. Another party of Modocs, under a leader the whites called Hooker Jim, rode around the east side of the lake, killing settlers along the way. On the lake's southern shore they united in a wild expanse of black lava that nature had piled into a gigantic fortress. They knew its every fissure, cavern, and passageway. Patches of grass subsisted their cattle. Sagebrush and greasewood yielded fuel. Water came from Tule Lake. As the big army that quickly assembled discovered, it could not be penetrated by assault, reduced by artillery bombardment, or taken by siege. It swiftly drew national attention as "Captain Jack's Stronghold."

Kintpuash conducted the defense with great skill. For four months, with only about sixty fighting men, he held off an army whose numbers ultimately approached a thousand. Again the government decided to try diplomacy. A peace commission arrived and erected a lone tent on the plain outside the lava beds. Negotiations commenced. So did Kintpuash's troubles. Factionalism accomplished what an army could not. Hooker Jim and others challenged Kintpuash's course and taunted him for refusing to kill the peace commissioners in a bold stroke aimed at winning a reservation on Lost River. Ridiculed and humiliated, he finally agreed. On Good Friday, April 11, 1873, the Modoc leaders suddenly interrupted the peace talks, drew hidden weapons, and fell on the white negotiators. One escaped, but three were left on the ground shot, stabbed, and stripped. (Miraculously, one later recovered.)

The deed sealed the fate of the Modocs, for the head of the commission was none other than the commander of the military department, Edward R. S. Canby, who thus gained dubious distinction as the only regular army general slain by Indians in the entire history of the Indian Wars. (Others called general, such as Custer, held the rank by brevet or volunteer, not regular, commissions.) Foolishly the Modocs had called down upon themselves the wrath of an outraged nation. The army responded with more troops and better leadership at the same time that quarrels among the Modoc leadership intensified. Finally the Indians scattered from the lava beds and were run down, group by small group, by pursuing columns of soldiers. On June 1 a detachment found Kintpuash and his family hiding in a cave. His "legs had given out," he explained.

Against people who had treacherously murdered a popular war hero, the precepts of the Peace Policy could not be expected to govern. Kintpuash and three others involved in Canby's death died on the gallows; their heads were cut off and shipped to the Army Medical Museum in Washington. A furious General Sherman demanded that Kintpuash's followers, who had compiled such an extraordinary record of skill and courage in holding the lava beds, be scattered among other tribes "so that the name of Modoc should cease." In October 1873, 155 in number, they were resettled fifteen hundred miles to the east, in Indian Territory. The name did not cease, but their demand to live in their homeland ceased to be heard.

The Modoc War—more accurately, the slaying of General Canby—badly crippled the Peace Policy. Newspapers everywhere saw it as dramatic evidence that Indians could not be trusted or reasoned with. Whether favoring extermination or civilization, editors judged Canby's death a grievous blow to the Peace Policy. As always, however, events on the Great Plains more profoundly influenced public opinion and shaped policy than those elsewhere in the West. Throughout the 1870s, warfare with Plains Indians rose to a thunderous finale on the Little Bighorn in 1876 that was almost universally regarded as marking the demise of the Peace Policy. Like the Modoc War, the Plains wars centered chiefly on the issue of whether or not tribes were to live on reservations as demanded by the Peace Policy.

On the southern Plains, the big nomadic tribes had agreed to reservations in the Medicine Lodge treaties. They actually lived there—Kiowas and Comanches at Fort Sill, Cheyennes and Arapahos at Darlington—because General Sheridan's winter operations of 1868–69, especially Custer's persistent and wide-ranging marches, had made fugitive life tiring and insecure. But reservation life proved confining; clothing and ration issues scant, of poor quality, and badly selected for Indian wants; and the encroachments of white cattlemen, whiskey peddlers, horse thieves, and other opportunists unnerving, if not demoralizing. Particularly ominous to the Indians, white hunters slaughtered the buffalo for their hides alone, leaving carcasses by the hundreds of thousands to rot on the prairies. Kiowas and Comanches regularly raided in Texas and Mexico, as they always had, while Cheyennes and Arapahos raided less often in Kansas. Discontent and mutual aggression finally boiled over in the Red River War of 1874–75.

For a time, while Satanta and Big Tree languished in the Texas penitentiary and the government held 124 women and children seized in an attack on a fugitive Comanche village, reservation-based raiders had restrained themselves. But the release of these captives, in exchange for promises of good behavior, had removed the restraint. The spring and summer of 1874 found Indians raiding in Texas and Kansas with new ferocity. In particular, Comanches and Cheyennes attacked a camp of white hide hunters at Adobe Walls in the Texas Panhandle, where Kit Carson had fought the Kiowas in 1864, and Kiowas under Lone Wolf ambushed a detachment of Texas Rangers near the site of the Salt Creek Massacre of 1871. These aggressions provoked the government to lift the ban against military operations on Indian reservations. Suddenly army officers at the Fort Sill and Darlington agencies were compiling lists of "friendly" Indians. Everyone else, sure to be classed as "hostiles," headed west, beyond the reservation boundaries. Some eighteen hundred Cheyennes, two thousand Comanches, and one thousand Kiowas moved in large encampments among the breaks surrounding the headwaters of the Washita River and the various forks of the Red, in the Texas Panhandle—hence the designation "Red River War."

Suddenly this country, hitherto so remote and secure, swarmed with soldiers. From north, east, south, and west, five columns converged. One routed the Indians at the base of the caprock near the mouth of Palo Duro Canyon. Another fell on a Comanche village nestled deep in the canyon itself. August sun parched the land and dried the water holes. September brought days of rain, bank-full streams, prairies of mud, and an ordeal the Indians remembered as "the wrinkled-hand chase." Winter loosed blizzards and numbing cold. Through it all, the soldiers kept after the Indians. There were few clashes and little bloodshed, but gradually the exhaustion of the chase, the discomforts of weather and hunger, and, above all, the constant gnawing fear of soldiers storming into their camps at dawn wore them down. As early as October, some had tired and drifted back to the reservation. By the spring of 1875, all had returned.

At the agencies the Indians discovered white officials behaving with a sternness uncharacteristic of the Peace Policy. Throughout the winter, as parties straggled in from the west, army officers confined leaders who were somewhat capriciously judged guilty of particular "crimes" or simply of functioning as "ringleaders." Satanta found no disposition toward leniency; back he went to the Texas Penitentiary, where three years later, in despair, he threw himself from an upper window to his death. As spring came to Fort Sill, soldiers herded seventy-four Indians, shackled and chained, aboard eight wagons. Among them were such noted chiefs as Gray Beard, Minimic, and Medicine Water of the Cheyennes; Lone Wolf, Woman's Heart, and White Horse of the Kiowas; and Black Horse of the Comanches. With women wailing their grief, the caravan moved out and headed for the railroad. After days of travel the Indians, so recently at large on the Staked Plains, found themselves enclosed by the thick walls and bastions of an ancient Spanish fortress on the Florida coast.

The army had gained a clear victory, not only over the Indians but over the more extreme proponents of the Peace Policy. From his Chicago headquarters General Sheridan had directed the strategy of convergence. Generals John Pope and Christopher C. Augur had overseen its execution. At least two field officers, Colonels Nelson A. Miles and Ranald S. Mackenzie, had won great distinction in carrying it out. Both had gained battlefield victories, Miles in the caprock fight, and Mackenzie in the celebrated charge into Palo Duro Canyon. But in the end it was not combat success but convergence, unremittingly prosecuted, that had won the war. Confinement of the "ringleaders" far from their homes and families helped ensure that another war would not occur. Never again did Kiowas, Comanches, Cheyennes, or Arapahos revolt against their reservation overlords. Never again did Texas and Kansas settlers suffer aggression from these tribes. Nor did Generals Sherman and Sheridan forget the lessons of the Red River War as they turned their attention to the northern Plains.

Here, Sioux, Northern Cheyenne, and Northern Arapaho had yet to be finally brought within the reservation system. Oglalas and Brules drew rations at the Red Cloud and Spotted Tail agencies in northwestern Nebraska, where these two chiefs maneuvered tortuously between the opposing forces of white officialdom and their own people. Other Sioux formed tenuous connections with agencies along the Missouri River, the eastern border of the Great Sioux Reservation—Hunkpapas and Blackfeet at Grand River, Miniconjous and Sans Arc at Cheyenne River, and still others at

Crow Creek and Lower Brule. Cheyennes and Arapahos mingled with Sioux at Red Cloud. In all, these agencies counted perhaps twenty-five thousand adherents.

But the strength of the adherence wavered with the seasons and the competing influence of rival chiefs, for off to the west roamed a hard core of kinsmen who had no intention of abandoning the free life of the chase for the dubious attractions of the reservation. They looked for leadership to a chief of surpassing influence. Of compelling countenance and commanding demeanor, quick of thought and emphatic of judgment, Sitting Bull held power not only as war and political chief but also as religious functionary. "He had a big brain and a good one," recalled an old warrior, "a strong heart and a generous one." At the agency Indians he hurled a taunt: "You are fools to make yourselves slaves to a piece of fat bacon, some hard-tack, and a little sugar and coffee." And in fact, many did not. Nothing prevented them from sampling the old hunting life in the summer and the hardtack and coffee in winter. Back and forth they shuttled between the agencies and the camps of Sitting Bull and other "nontreaty" chiefs.

These "northern Indians" stirred up constant trouble. While on the reservation, they kept the agencies in turmoil, for they were ungovernable, a danger to white officials, and a bad influence on the agency Indians. While off the reservation, they did not always keep to the unceded hunting grounds guaranteed by the Treaty of 1868, but sometimes raided along the Platte and among the Montana settlements at the head of the Missouri and Yellowstone rivers.

That the whites called them hostiles and accused them of breaking the treaty while also enjoying its bounty did not bother these hunting bands. They could point to some treaty violations by the other side as well. For one thing, in 1873 surveyors laid out a route for the Northern Pacific Railroad along the northern margins of the unceded territory. For another, and most infuriating, in 1874 "Long Hair" Custer led his soldiers into the Black Hills, part of the Great Sioux Reservation itself, and there found gold. Miners swarmed into the Indian country, and the government, making only a token effort to keep them out, hesitantly broached the subject of buying the part of the reservation that contained the Black Hills. Then late in 1875, runners arrived in the winter camps of the hunting bands with a stern message from the Great Father: Come to the agencies at once or be considered hostiles against whom the army would make war.

They ignored the summons, and as spring turned to summer in 1876 they discovered blue columns converging on their hunting grounds. In

March, one attacked an Oglala camp on Powder River but bungled the fol-
low-up and retreated under assaults of bitter cold and deep snow. As the
snow melted, the fugitive camps swelled. Worsening conditions at the
agencies, the Black Hills issue, and the attempt to take away the freedom
to roam the unceded territory set off an unusually large spring migration
of agency Indians to the camps of the hunting bands. June found them
coming together in a village that steadily expanded as it moved slowly
westward across the streams flowing northward into the Yellowstone.
These Indians were not looking for a fight, but, as never before, they were
proud, confident, and at the height of their power. Chiefs of ability forti-
fied the leadership of Sitting Bull—Black Moon, Gall, Hump, Lame Deer,
Dirty Moccasins, Lame White Man, and the incomparable Crazy Horse.
Since his triumph as head of the party that decoyed Captain Fetterman
out of Fort Phil Kearny ten years earlier, Crazy Horse had emerged as a
splendid war leader and uncompromising foe of reservations.

By mid-June the Indians camped on a creek that ran into a river they
knew as the Greasy Grass. Earlier, on the Rosebud, they had staged their
annual Sun Dance. Sitting Bull had experienced a vision, in which he saw
many dead soldiers "falling right into our camp." The people had thrilled
to the image and the promise. Now scouts brought word of soldiers
marching down the Rosebud. Crazy Horse led a large force to do battle.
For six hours they fought, and after the Indians called off the fight the soldiers retreated.

But this was not the triumph foretold by Sitting Bull. Soldiers had not
fallen into their camp. Down to the Greasy Grass the village moved, and
here the largest number yet of agency Indians joined the alliance. Six separate tribal circles—Hunkpapa, Oglala, Miniconjou, Sang Arc, Blackfoot,
Northern Cheyenne—extended for three miles along the banks of the
Greasy Grass. The village probably counted twelve hundred lodges and
mustered almost two thousand fighting men.

True to Sitting Bull's prophecy, many soldiers were in fact about to fall
into this village. As in the Red River War, General Sheridan had plotted a
strategy of convergence. Advancing from the south, General Crook had
struck the camp on Powder River on March 17 but had been driven back
by winter. In May he sallied forth again, only to be stopped and turned back
at the Battle of the Rosebud on June 17. Meantime, General Alfred H. Terry
approached from the east, and Colonel John Gibbon from the west. They
joined on the Yellowstone at the mouth of the Rosebud. From here Terry
launched a striking force of some six hundred cavalry, under the same Long
Hair Custer who had invaded the Black Hills two years earlier. Custer

followed the Indian trail up the Rosebud, across the Wolf Mountains, and down to the Greasy Grass, which his map labeled the Little Bighorn. The village there, because of the recent arrivals of agency Indians, contained about three times as many warriors as he had expected. On the scorching Sunday of June 25, 1876, his soldiers fell into it.

George Armstrong Custer presided over one of the most complete disasters in American military annals. A century later it still commanded public fascination and fueled heated controversy. More immediately, the Sioux and Cheyennes discovered what the Modocs had so painfully learned: the slaying of a big white chief could spell the doom of a people. Custer's Last Stand shocked and outraged Americans, shook the Peace Policy to the verge of collapse, brought a flood of soldiers to the Indian country, and afforded rationalization for forcing the agency chiefs, hitherto held back by the militant opposition of the northern Indians, to sell the Black Hills. An "agreement"—it resembled a treaty in all but name—legitimized the sale. For the Sioux and Cheyennes, final defeat lurked unseen in their soaring victory amid the brown hills overlooking the Greasy Grass.

Once again, winter combined with soldiers who could brave its blasts destroyed Indian resistance. Until the first snows the Sioux and Cheyennes, now fragmented in bands, easily eluded the big armies that ponderously gave chase. But winter, as usual, made them vulnerable. In the frigid, misty dawn of November 25, 1876, eleven hundred cavalrymen under Colonel Ranald S. Mackenzie burst into the Cheyenne village of Dull Knife and Little Wolf in a canyon of the Bighorn Mountains. Forty Cheyennes died, and the rest watched helplessly from the bluffs as the soldiers burned their tipis, clothing, and winter food supply. That night the temperature plunged to thirty below zero. Eleven babies froze to death at their mothers' breasts.

The suffering Cheyennes took refuge with Crazy Horse, but the soldiers tracked down these people too. In January 1877, on Tongue River, Sioux and Cheyenne warriors clashed with "walk-a-heap" bluecoats in a fight that petered out in a blinding blizzard. These soldiers had built a rude fort at the mouth of the Tongue, and they kept to the field all winter. Tired and discouraged, the Indians opened talks with the soldier chief at this fort. He wore a huge overcoat, and they called him "Bear's Coat."

He was the same Colonel Nelson A. Miles who had so resolutely pursued the southern Plains tribes in the Red River War.

Bear's Coat's combination of fight and talk, together with peace feelers put out from Red Cloud Agency through the agency chiefs, gradually strengthened the peace elements in the hostile camps. Spring saw the surrender of almost all the fugitives. On May 6, 1877, Crazy Horse led his Oglalas into Red Cloud Agency and threw his weapons on the ground in token of surrender. Four months later, amid circumstances that are still confusing, he died in a guardhouse scuffle, stabbed by either a soldier's bayonet or another Indian's knife. "It is good," said a fellow chief sadly, "he has looked for death and it has come."

The previous October, in a tense meeting between the lines, Sitting Bull told Bear's Coat that the Great Spirit had made him an Indian, and not an agency Indian. Rather than go to the reservation, he had led his people northward to the land of the "Great Mother." He got along well with her redcoats, but he and his people could not find enough food. Bear's Coat watched the boundary line like a hawk and prevented them from riding into Montana to hunt buffalo. Year after year, as they grew hungrier and hungrier, families and groups slipped away to surrender and go to the reservation. At last, in July 1881, Sitting Bull and about fifty families presented themselves at Fort Buford, Montana, the last vestige of the mighty alliance that had overwhelmed Long Hair Custer five years earlier. Sitting Bull handed his rifle to his eight-year-old son and told him to give it to the soldier chief. "I wish it to be remembered," he said, "that I was the last man of my tribe to surrender my rifle, and this day have given it to you."…

By 1881, when the surrender of Sitting Bull marked the close of the Plains wars, all tribes of the American West save one had been compelled by military force to go to, or return to, their reservations. Of them all, only the Apaches had not yet been made to face the truth that the reservation represented their only possible destiny. At one place or another in the Southwest, Apache warfare had been virtually continuous since Spanish colonial times. In the early 1870s General Crook had seemed to be on the verge of ending it permanently. His masterful Tonto Basin campaign of 1872–73 had brought about the collapse of the most troublesome Apache groups and their confinement on the reservations set up earlier by Vincent Colyer and General Howard. But Crook went north to do less than brilliantly against the Sioux, and the iron military regime relaxed. At the same time the Indian Bureau decided to do away with the multiplicity of small reservations and to concentrate all Apaches west of the Rio Grande on a single reservation. A hot, barren, malarial flat along Arizona's Gila River, San Carlos was a terrible place to live. The final phases of Indian warfare in the United States grew out of the refusal of two powerful Apache leaders and their followers to settle permanently on the San Carlos Reservation.

These leaders were Victorio and Geronimo. Victorio of the Mimbres had learned his skills from the great Mangas Coloradas, whom he equaled in courage, stamina, cunning, and leadership. He wanted peace with the whites, and for a time, with Loco, he had pursued it. But soon he saw that few whites were as trustworthy as the good Lieutenant Drew, and the command to settle at San Carlos banished all such notions. Geronimo, of the Chiricahuas, emerged as a leader shortly after the death of Cochise in 1874. Short, thick, scowling, and ill-tempered, he exhibited few appealing traits, even to his own people. But of all Apache leaders, his cousin later remembered, "Geronimo seemed to be the most intelligent and resourceful as well as the most vigorous and farsighted. In times of danger he was a man to be relied upon." No less than Victorio did Geronimo find the order to move to San Carlos in 1876 offensive.

For two years, 1877–79, Victorio tried to find a solution to the dilemma that the government's concentration program had thrust upon him. He even attempted to live at San Carlos. "That horrible summer!" recalled one of his followers. "There was nothing but cactus, rattlesnakes, heat, rocks, and insects. No game; no edible plants. Many, many of our people died of starvation." Victorio also tried to live on his old reservation at Ojo Caliente, but the government had decided to close that place down. He tried to settle with the Mescaleros on the Fort Stanton Reservation, east of the Rio Grande, but that did not work. In fact, nothing worked, and on September 4, 1879, he and sixty warriors attacked a contingent of black cavalrymen near Ojo Caliente in the opening clash of the Victorio War.

In Texas, New Mexico, and Chihuahua, Victorio exacted a terrible price for the government's attempt to put him at San Carlos. With fresh numbers from the Mescalero Reservation, he counted between 125 and 150 warriors. Here and there they darted with lightning speed, cutting down isolated sheepherders and waylaying hapless travelers. Time and again they eluded the soldiers, both American and Mexican, who combed the mountains and deserts in an exhausting and mostly vain effort to destroy the marauders. In July 1880, in the hot, barren wastes of western Texas, Victorio found himself, for a change, thwarted by hard-riding units of black troopers who expertly kept him from the few waterholes and ultimately forced him into Mexico. Hungry, destitute, and low on ammunition, the raiders began to tire. Eastward they drifted, into the parched deserts of Chihuahua, seemingly without plan or purpose. By October 1880 they camped amid three low peaks rising sharply from the vast desert plain. Tres Castillos, the Mexicans called them.

At dawn on October 15 the Apaches awoke to the crash of gunfire and the shouts of Mexican soldiers and Tarahumara Indian allies. Their horse herd lost, the Indians scrambled up the boulder-strewn slope of one of the hills, and there they fought back. All day and into the night the two sides exchanged fire. In the dark the Indians tried to slip away, but failed. Singing the death chant, they turned to throwing up rock fortifications for a fight to the last. At daybreak they watched as the Mexicans began filtering upward among the boulders. The struggle was desperate and bloody and, in its final stages, hand-to-hand. When the smoke and dust cleared, seventy-eight Apaches lay dead among the rocks and another sixty-eight herded together as captives. Among the dead was Victorio.

At the time of Victorio's death, Geronimo was living, none too contentedly, at San Carlos. Besides its repugnant natural conditions, the reservation festered with intrigue, intertribal rivalries, incompetent and corrupt agents, and conflict between civil and military officials. White settlers pressed in on the reservation boundaries. Almost any spark could touch off an explosion. It came in August 1881. A medicine man had been preaching a new religion that whites regarded as incendiary. In an attempt to arrest him, the army got into a fight with his followers, shot and killed the prophet, and had to quell a mutiny among the Apache scouts. Frightened by the resulting military activity, Geronimo and other leaders, with seventy-four people, broke out and headed for Mexico.

An especially daring raid in the following spring drew attention to the deteriorating state of affairs in Arizona. Geronimo and others swooped down on San Carlos, killed the police chief, and forced old Loco and several hundred people to return to Mexico with them. That event prodded the government to decisive action. Early in September 1882 a familiar figure reappeared in Arizona—the "Gray Fox," General Crook. At once he clamped military rule on San Carlos. To keep the peace here and later to go after the "renegades" in Mexico, he recruited five companies of Apache scouts—"the wildest I could get"—and placed them under his brightest, most energetic young officers. Skilled packers organized efficient and sturdy mule trains. No cumbersome wagons would limit mobility.

The Sierra Madre of Mexico had always afforded Apaches an impregnable fortress. Its steep ridges, piled one on another toward towering peaks and perpetually shadowing plunging gorges and canyons walled in vertical rock, sheltered and protected these Indians and provided secure bases for raiding in all directions, on both sides of the international border. One Chiricahua group, the Nednhis, had made this wilderness their home for generations. Their chief, Juh, surpassed all others in power.

Geronimo, Nachez (son of Cochise), Chato, Chihuahua, Loco, Bonito, battle-scarred old Nana (who had ridden with Victorio but had escaped Tres Castillos), and others deferred to Juh. But one day Juh fell from a cliffside trail to his death, and increasingly the captains of the Apaches in the Sierra Madre looked to Geronimo for guidance. From their mountain lairs they continued to raid. In a foray of special ferocity, in March 1883 Chato and twenty-five warriors slashed across Arizona and New Mexico, and then faded back into Mexico. In response, Crook marched.

A surprise attack by Apache scouts on Chato's camp high in the Sierra Madre gave notice to all the fugitives that their fortress had been breached. Where Mexican troops had never ventured, Americans had penetrated, and at the head of other Apaches. It came as enough of a shock that one by one the band leaders drifted in to talk with the Gray Fox. Geronimo, who had been raiding in Chihuahua, came last. Squatting around smoky campfires, the Indians listened to the harsh words of this general who so uncharacteristically wore a canvas suit and rode a mule. Surrender, he told them in a threat that he and all his listeners knew he could not carry out, or he would kill them all. At night, in long arguments among themselves, the chiefs debated what to do. Crook's success in reaching them in previously inaccessible refuges, combined with his ability to enlist their own people against them, tipped the balance. "We give ourselves up," Geronimo at last announced, "do with us as you please."

The surrender turned out to be only temporary. Back at San Carlos, tensions began building almost at once. A people accustomed to freedom found military rule irksome; the men especially bridled at the ban on beating their wives and on brewing the volatile intoxicant *tiswin*. In May 1885 off they went again, some 134 people, including Geronimo, Nachez, Chihuahua, and Nana. Once again they hid themselves deep in the Sierra Madre. Once again they discovered white officers leading their own people against them. And once again they quickly tired of keeping always on the run, always apprehensive of a sudden surprise attack. They sent word to the officer in charge of one of the scout units, Captain Emmet Crawford, that they wanted to talk. But before a meeting could be arranged, Mexican militia attacked the scouts, and the captain fell with a bullet in his brain. Later Geronimo and others met with Crawford's lieutenant, Marion P. Maus, and told him they wanted to talk with General Crook.

The meeting took place at Canyon de los Embudos, twelve miles south of the border, on March 25, 1886. Seated on the sides of a pleasantly shaded ravine, the general and the Apaches parleyed. As he had done two years earlier, Crook spoke sternly. Now the terms were harsher. The men with their families must go to a place of confinement in the East for two years, and only then could they return to San Carlos. Otherwise, Crook vowed, "I'll keep after you and kill the last one, if it takes fifty years." After two days of argument among themselves, the Apache chiefs accepted Crook's terms. While the general hastened north to telegraph the good news to his superiors, the Indians moved slowly toward the border. Along the way they found a whiskey peddler. In the midst of a drinking bout Geronimo and Nachez had second thoughts. With twenty men and thirteen women, they stampeded back to the Sierra Madre.

This development profoundly discouraged General Crook. Worse, it brought him into conflict with General Sheridan, who had succeeded Sherman as head of the army. Sheridan had never trusted the Apache scouts, and he thought Crook should use regulars instead. Now he issued orders that not only implicitly criticized Crook's methods but required him to break his word to the Indians who had not fled with Geronimo and Nachez. Rather than carry out such orders, Crook asked to be relieved. Sheridan lost no time in dispatching a replacement, Nelson A. Miles, now a brigadier general. It was a hard blow to the Gray Fox, for he and Miles had long been bitter rivals, personally as well as professionally. Bear's Coat welcomed the chance to succeed where Crook had failed.

Astutely, Miles made a great show of employing regular soldiers against the Apaches, but in the end he quietly adopted Crook's methods. Apache scouts combed the Sierra Madre, keeping the quarry on the run. As a special peace emissary, Miles sent Lieutenant Charles B. Gatewood, whom the Indians knew as a friend, to see if he could find and persuade them to give up. Ironically, Gatewood was a Crook protégé.

As in the past, the little band of fugitives soon tired of running. On August 24, 1886, they admitted Gatewood and two Indian companions to their camp. At considerable peril to his life, Gatewood stated the new terms: The Apaches must go to Florida and wait for the President to decide their ultimate fate. Geronimo said he and Nachez would give up, but only if they could return to San Carlos. Then Gatewood played his high card. At San Carlos Geronimo would find none of his kinsmen, only rival tribes. All the Chiricahuas, even those who had loyally served Crook as scouts, had been herded aboard railway cars and deported to Florida. Stunned, the Indians debated for a long time, but at last they told Gatewood that they would give up to General Miles personally. In Skeleton Canyon, just north of the border, Geronimo faced Miles and handed over his rifle.

A trainload of Apaches rattling across the Arizona desert toward far-off Florida signaled the end of armed resistance to the reservation system.

Every important Indian war since 1870 had been essentially a war not of concentration but of rebellion—of Indians rebelling against reservations they had already accepted in theory if not in fact. Geronimo and his tiny band of followers were the last holdouts, and they only because the wilds of Mexico offered them a haven denied to most other tribes. Thus the wars of the Peace Policy, and indeed the Indian Wars of the United States, came to a close in Skeleton Canyon, Arizona, on September 4, 1886.

2.3
Buffalo Soldiers

T. J. Stiles

Stiles's article tells the story of the famous African American cavalrymen in the post-Civil War West, often referred to as the "Buffalo Soldiers." What role did these black troops play in the military activities against Native Americans in the West, and why do you think that role was long forgotten or ignored?

On September 24, 1868, MAJ. GEORGE A. FORSYTH MUST have wondered if he would live to see the next morning. He lay stretched out beside the rotting carcass of his dead horse, in the willow brush and tall grass that covered a small island in the dry bed of the Arikaree River, on the vast plains of eastern Colorado Territory. All around him lay dead and wounded men—his men. And beyond the empty riverbanks, just out of rifle shot, circled the 700 Cheyenne and Oglala warriors who had kept the major's detachment trapped on this island since the 17th.

Full-scale war with the tribes of the Great Plains had just erupted; Forsyth had taken his 50 handpicked scouts out of Fort Hays in Kansas on a march to find the enemy. But the Native Americans had found Forsyth first.

On the 17th, the Cheyenne war chief the soldiers called Roman Nose had led hundreds of fighters on a dawn charge against Forsyth's camp. Their storm of bullets and arrows laid waste to his horse herd and left many of his men dead or wounded. The major himself collapsed as a slug tore into each leg and another creased his scalp. By the 24th, repeated charges and stealthy sniping had turned half his scouts into casualties; a horrific stench now rose from the dead men and animals. The survivors, who at first had used their fallen mounts as protection, now resorted to eating the horses' decaying flesh.

From *Smithsonian*, December 1998 by T.J. Stiles. Reprinted by permission of the author.

Unknown to Forsyth, a company of cavalry was searching for him. Two of his scouts had slipped through the besieging Indians and made their way to Fort Wallace in Kansas, where they had alerted Capt. Louis H. Carpenter, an old Civil War comrade of the major's.

The next day, the beleaguered scouts on that maldorous little island noticed that the Indians had drawn off. Then they saw why: in the distance they discovered movement, which gradually took the form of mounted men…cavalrymen…black cavalrymen. They were Captain Carpenter's troopers, pounding across the dry grass. This unit went by the name of Company H, 10th Cavalry—but Forsyth's men may indeed have known them by the name that the African-American troops earned from their Indian foes: they were the buffalo soldiers.

Forsyth's fight entered Western legend as the Battle of Beecher's Island, but few remember that he was rescued so dramatically by black troops. Despite a recent wave of interest in the professional African-American soldiers of the 19th century, many writers have treated them as a footnote to the history of the frontier. In fact, black regulars took center stage in the Army's great Western drama, shouldering combat responsibilities far out of proportion to their numbers (which averaged 10 percent of the military's total strength). Over the course of three decades on the frontier, the buffalo soldiers emerged as the most professional experienced and effective troops in the service.

When Carpenter led his company into Forsyth's grim camp, only three years had passed since the end of the Civil War. Some 180,000 African-Americans had carried arms for the Union, filling out regiments, divisions, even an entire corps (the 25th, part of which occupied Richmond in the war's closing days). These were all-volunteer units, however, established for the duration of the war. Not one company in the standing Regular Army was open to African-American recruits. But on July 28, 1866, Congress provided for four Regular Army infantry regiments(the 38th, 39th, 40th and 41st) and two of Cavalry 9th and 10th), to be composed exclusively of black enlisted men. The Army would *have* to accept African-Americans.

Almost immediately, the new black regulars found themselves in combat on the frontier. Lt. Col. George Armstrong Custer's wife, Elizabeth, described an incident in June 1867 (based on an account in one of her husband's letters), when 300 Cheyennes swept down on Fort Wallace, where Custer was in command. A squad of black infantrymen from the 38th had arrived to pick up supplies when the white garrison spilled out to form a firing line.

Suddenly, a wagon pulled by four mules tore out to the line of battle, Elizabeth wrote. "It was filled with Negroes, standing up, all firing in the direction of the Indians. The driver lashed the mules with his blacksnake, and roared at them as they ran. When the skirmish line was reached, the colored men leaped out and began firing again. No one had ordered them to leave their picket-station, but they were determined that no soldiering should be carried on in which their valor was not proved."

Despite the brave showing, the 38th Infantry was not to last. On March 3, 1869, a new law ordained a general reduction in the Army: the 38th and 41st regiments were consolidated into the new 24th Infantry, and the 39th and 40th merged to create the 25th Infantry. Occasionally, companies from the 24th and 25th infantries served with their mounted counterparts, some times engaging in heavy combat. The lion's share of adventure fell to the special corps of black Seminole scouts—Indians of largely African descent (SMITHSONIAN, August 1991)—who served with the 24th Infantry under Lt. John Bullis. On the whole, however, the African-American infantry regiments missed out on much of the glory won by the black cavalry.

Throughout the frontier era, black soldiers endured nearly unbearable conditions. Indeed, they complained of receiving the worst of everything, including surplus equipment and cast-off horses; many white officers openly bemoaned their assignments and some abused their troops. Maybe worst of all was local prejudice—and the Army did little if anything to help. In Texas, for example, when a sheriff killed a black medal of Honor recipient, shooting him in the back, nothing was done. A Nebraskan who killed three black soldiers, including another Medal of Honor winner, also went unpunished. And it was nearly impossible for African-American soldiers to get commissions. One man from the 9th Cavalry said of the regiments at Fort Robinson, late in the century, "not a single colored soldier has been promoted from the ranks to the grade of an officer…the army is decidedly against it."

The demands of frontier warfare, however, led to wide dispersion of most regiments, which placed tremendous importance on the leadership qualities of noncommissioned officers. That was certainly true of the 9th Cavalry, scattered across the rough Texas landscape in tiny, undermanned posts. Yet the 9th's sergeants and corporals were precisely the men whom the Army thought most unsuited to soldiering and command: in the early years they were mostly former slaves, drawn primarily from the plantation country of Louisiana and Mississippi. Often illiterate in the beginning, these officers—and their troopers—displayed a voracious appetite for education, and they ultimately set the standard for professionalism. Desertion rates for many regiments surpassed 25 percent a year; not so among the buffalo soldier. As the service newspaper reported, "The Ninth Cavalry astonished the Army by reporting not a single desertion for twelve months."

Before 1867 came to a close, the 9th Cavalry's raw recruits won the respect of every armed opponent anywhere close to Texas. Christmas day found Capt. William Frohock and Company K on a patrol at the Pecos River, 75 miles east of Fort Stockton. The troopers settle for the night in empty Fort Lancaster, a long-abandoned post. Three men, privates Anderson Trimble, Edward Bowers and William Sharpe, stood guard over the horse herd as the troops stretched out to sleep.

The next day, Trimble, Bowers and Sharpe found themselves surrounded by armed men on horseback. They were lassoed and dragged to their deaths behind their assailant's horses. Meanwhile, the strangers turned to the company holed up in Fort Lancaster.

Captain Frohock had trouble making out just who was firing on his detachment (the attackers were most likely Lipans, Kickapoos and Mexican outlaws). In the flurry of shouting men, ricocheting bullets, swirling dust and pounding hooves, he estimated that at least 900 opponents encircled his men. If his guess was correct, it meant that Company K—fewer than 70 troopers—faced more men than served in the entire 9th Cavalry.

The inexperienced buffalo soldiers threw down a curtain of fire from their seven-shot Spencer carbines. For hours they fought, pumping bullets out of their carbines so fast the barrels grew blisteringly hot. Finally the enemy drew off, carrying away 20 dead and scores of wounded. The buffalo soldiers had triumphed; never again would the Lipans and Kickapoos dare to attack them so directly.

For eight years, the 9th Cavalry fought numerous pitched battles against Lipans, Kickapoos, Kiowas, Comanches—and the people destined to be their most determined foes, the Apaches. Then in late 1875, Col. Edward Hatch took the regiment into the Apache homeland, the New Mexico Territory. There he assumed the role of department commander, and his men devoted themselves to battling various Apache war parties that frequently struck out on raids off the reservations.

These warriors had long since mastered mountain guerrilla warfare. Unlike the Sioux, Cheyennes, Kiowas or Comanches, who fought primarily to keep ranchers and hunters off their homelands, the Apaches had lived for centuries among Hispanic settlements, alternately raiding and trading with neighboring villages. They knew how to lay expert ambushes in the steep cliffs lining the valleys of the Southwest, how to throw off pursuers by leaving behind elaborate dummy camps, how to camouflage cuts in telegraph lines by splicing them with leather thongs.

The 9th was in the field constantly. Pvt. Henry Bush remembered being "continuously on scouting service which subjected us to great exposure, such as sleeping in rains and snows in the mountains unprotected from the elements, sometimes no sleep for two days, sometimes subsisting on the most meager diet, sometimes marches of ninety miles…in hot scorching sun." And when they did make contact, the fighting was ferocious.

In January 1877, Capt. Charles D. Beyer learned that a party of Apaches had broken out of the San Carlos reservation in Arizona and had crossed into new Mexico. He issued orders to Lt. Henry Wright to mount six troopers and three Navajo scouts and find their trail. On a cold, clear, winter day, the detachment of buffalo soldiers clambered up through the rocky Florida Mountains, riding right up to the edge of a camp of more than 40 Apaches.

The troops immediately saw how precarious their situation was: ten men, deep in the mountains and far from help, surrounded by nearly five times their number. Even worse, they no longer carried the rapid-firing Spencer carbines, which carried seven rounds in a tubular magazine; they now used single-shot Springfields, while many Apaches wielded new multi-shot Winchesters.

Lieutenant Wright decided to brazen it out. He trotted his horse straight into the heart of the camp, followed by his tiny squad, and shouted for the Apache chiefs to meet him in council. The troopers slid off their saddles as Wright spoke to the Indians through a Navajo scout. He and his men, he said, would be happy to accept their surrender. The chiefs apparently did not laugh; as the negotiations continued, the soldiers noticed that the women and children were silently slipping away while the warriors encircled the detachment.

Suddenly Wright shouted for his men to break through the ring. At the first step forward, the Apaches shouldered their rifles. In an instant, 26-year-old Cpl. Clinton Greaves swiveled his carbine toward the closest warrior and squeezed off a single round. Leaping toward the line of warriors, he seized the barrel of his weapon and arced its wooden shoulder stock through the air, slamming it into the body of one of his foes.

As this powerful trooper—"a big fine looking soldier," another trooper recalled—swung left and right, the rest of the detachment fired and reloaded madly. Lieutenant Wright shot down a nearby Apache; privates Dick Mackadoo and Richard Epps shot three more warriors as lead snapped through the air in every direction. The troopers frantically mounted and galloped through the opening Corporal Greaves had created. After a few seconds more of intense fighting, the Apaches themselves scattered to the mountain peaks for cover, intending to challenge the soldiers from afar. The troopers not only managed to get away unscathed, but left with 11 Apache horses.

Wright and his men earned nearly legendary status within the regiment for their brave stand in the Florida Mountains. But the highest recognition of all went to Corporal Greaves: on June 26, 1879, he became the second trooper in the 9th Cavalry to earn the Medal of Honor.

Soon the regiment came to grips with the leader who would prove to be its deadliest enemy of all: Victorio, chief of the Warm Springs band of Apaches. Tension had been building as the Bureau of Indian Affairs tried to shift his people to the San Carlos reservation in Arizona. After two escapes from San Carlos, Victorio and his band were permitted to remain at the reservation in their native New Mexico. Just when a measure of peace seemed to be in hand, lawmen arrive to arrest the chief for murder. In August 1879, he fled the reservation with 60 followers, soon to multiply to more than 300. The Victorio War had begun.

The men of the 9th Cavalry quickly learned how Victorio had won his reputation as a great war chief. He selected as one of his first targets the horse herd of Company E; on September 4, the Indians killed five troopers, wounded three more and rode off with 46 animals. Shortly afterward, Victorio unleashed a well-planned ambush in the canyon of the Los Animas River, leaving as many as eight buffalo soldiers dead or wounded.

After these setbacks, Col. Hatch assigned Maj. Albert B. Morrow to lead the pursuit. Morrow's hard-riding troopers repeatedly made contact with Victorio's forces, engaging in bitter but indecisive fighting. The skillful Apache would slip away over the border into Mexico, where the 9th Cavalry's scouts could not follow.

On May 13, 1880, Sgt. George Jordan of Company K learned precisely where the Apaches were. This native of Tennessee had just made camp with 25 men at a stage station, having spent a long day escorting a train of supply wagons. As the detachment prepared for a well-earned night of rest, a courier rode in with a desperate message: Victorio was headed for the settlement of Fort Tularosa.

The sergeant called his men together. "They all said they would go on as far as they could," Jordan reported. At 8 o'clock in the evening, they began a hard march for the endangered village. At about 6 the next morning, the tired troopers rode into the silent town, its women and children peering out apprehensively through shuttered windows. "When they recognized us as troops," he recalled, "they came out of their houses waving towels and handkerchiefs for joy."

Sergeant Jordan boasted more than ten years of experience in the 9th Cavalry; he knew what it meant to command a detachment, and he knew how to fight the Apaches. After a brief rest, he set his men to work building a stockade. By the end of the afternoon, they were done; the men had not slept for at least 24 hours, but they could now lead the residents inside a hastily built fort.

As the sun dipped down to the west, Sergeant Jordan stood outside the stockade talking to a civilian when a shot cracked the quiet evening. Instantly dozens of bullets spattered the ground as Jordan and his companion sprinted for the fort. Jordan reported, "but we repulsed them each time, and when they finally saw that we were masters of the situation they turned their attention to the stock and tried to run it off." Head-on attacks against an entrenched foe were not the Apache way; Victorio soon pulled away. "The whole action was short but exciting while it lasted, and after it was all over the townspeople congratulated us for having repulsed a band of more than 100." Congress congratulated Jordan with the Medal of Honor.

Nine days later, a unit of Indian scouts severely shot up Victorio's camp, sending the chief flying into Mexico with Morrow's command snapping at his heels. The move set the stage for the final, decisive phase of the campaign—and shifted the burden to the rest of the buffalo soldiers;: the men of the 10th Calvary, led by Col. Benjamin Grierson, and those of the 24th and 25th infantries.

Grierson believed Victorio would reenter the United States in western Texas; to stop him, he decided to case a net to ensnare the chief no matter which direction her turned. The key was water: only a handful of springs dotted the dry mountains southeast of El Paso. By guarding the most important water holes, and by posting a network of scouts along the Rio Grande, he could block any attempt to penetrate West Texas.

The night of July 29 found Grierson at Tenaja de los Palmos, a strategic water hole between Fort Quitman (to the west on the Rio Grande) and Eagle Springs (15 miles to the east). He had with him a half-dozen buffalo soldiers, one white officer and his 20-year-old son, Robert. Earlier that day, Grierson and his men had been met by three African-American troopers bearing a critical dispatch from the Rio Grande: the Apaches had been seen crossing the river into Texas.

It was no ordinary buffalo soldier who led the couriers; it was Lt.

Henry O. Flipper, the first black graduate of West Point and an office of the 10th Cavalry. "I rode 98 miles in 22 hours mostly at night, through a country the Indians were expected to traverse," he wrote. " I had no bad effects from the hard ride till I reached [Grierson's] tent. When I attempted to dismount, I found I was stiff and sore and fell from my horse to the ground"…

After resting, Flipper left with orders that all available troops should make haste for Grierson's position. Meanwhile the colonel and his men spent the night throwing up two stone breastworks atop the rocky ridge overlooking the water hole. Despite the desperate odds, Grierson had decided to make a stand. If he could deny Victorio access to the water in that canyon, he was certain that the Apaches would have to turn back to Mexico. The next morning, at about 4 o'clock, Lt. Leighton Finley rode in with reinforcements: a mere ten cavalrymen.

Young Robert Grierson would later scrawl in his journal a vivid account of the events that followed. Sometime after 8, as the little party finished breakfast, the scouts south of camp sent up the cry "Here come the Indians!" Then he saw them: dozens of long-haired warriors, rifles held at the ready as they nudged their horses through the canyon southeast of their position on the ridge.

As a dense cluster of Apaches rode slowly across the rough trail, the Indians heard the sound of galloping horses. Down Finley's buffalo soldiers came, snapping off shots as they thundered into the valley. "Several Indians hid in a hollow till Lt. F. passed, & then fired on his party," Robert wrote. "He had them on both sides of him & poured it into them thick & vice versa. The rifles sounded splendidly and you could hear the balls singing. Just as Lt. Finley was about to dislodge the Indians from behind a ledge, Capt. Viele's and Lt. Colladay's companies came & in the smoke and dust took F. for Indians and fired on him."

Capt. Charles Viele, Lieutenant Flipper and the troopers of Company C had just arrived from Fort Quitman. Now they fired on Finley by mistake; fortunately, both Viele and Finley pulled their men back to Grierson's breastworks. "All got back about the same time," wrote Robert, except one black trooper whose horse had been shot; after him galloped the resurgent warriors, convinced now that the battle had turned in their favor. "He got along as be he could—the Indians were nearly on him—he turned & fired his revolver & this checked them some."

Grierson ordered his men to fire. "We then let fly from our fortifications at the Indians about 300 yards off & golly!! You ought to've seen 'em turn tail & strike for the hills." In four hours of desperate fighting, the

Apaches lost seven men; the 10 th Cavalry, one trooper. The battle left Victorio short on food and water, and saddled with dead and wounded; he had no choice but to retreat to Mexico.

In early August, he returned and slipped past Grierson's men on his way to another strategic water hole, Rattlesnake Springs. Determined to get there first, Grierson and his men covered 65 miles in 21 hours. The buffalo soldiers outpaced their fast-moving Indian foes as Grierson led them on a parallel path, keeping to the far side of a mountain range to mask their presence from the enemy.

The 10th Cavalry won the race, arriving in the early hours of August 6. "We go there and at once took position for a fight," Flipper recalled. Grierson laid out an elaborate ambush, sending Captain Viele with companies C and G to occupy the walls of the valley above the springs. "No lights or fires were allowed and we had to eat cold suppers without coffee," Flipper continued. "If [the Apaches] once got in as far as the spring, we would have them surrounded and every vantage point occupied.

At 2 in the afternoon, the long, ragged band of Apaches rode into sight, ambling slowly through the bunchgrass and rocks and cactus on their tired horses. The Indians in the lead sensed that something was wrong and stopped their advance. When Viele saw them grow cautious, he gave orders to commence firing. The first of eight volleys of rifle fire erupted from valley walls; Victorio's men scrambled for cover.

The master of the ambush had been ambushed himself—but the trap had been sprung too soon, and the long-range fire did little damage to the Indians. The Apaches, however, were desperate for water. Victorio rallied his men for an attack. Warriors on horseback surged across the valley floor, screaming their defiance and losing shots at the dug-in buffalo soldiers. Just as the Apaches neared the springs, Capt. Louis H. Carpenter and Lt. Thaddeus Winfield Jones led companies H and B on a charge from one flak, crashing into the Apaches with carbines blazing. Victorio's men withdrew once again.

Over the next two hours, the firing died away to silence; Grierson knew better than to stage a pointless assault on Apaches holed up in the rocks. Then, as so often happened in battle, the unexpected occurred. At 4 o'clock a line of wagons rounded a mountain eight miles southeast of the water hole. A party of warriors emerged from the rocks and scampered onto their ponies, undoubtedly relieved to find an easy target beyond the reach of Grierson's men (and probably hoping to get some water as well).

Suddenly the Apaches pulled up short—for out of the wagons poured the buffalo soldiers of the 24th Infantry, the escort for this supply train for the 10th Cavalry. These foot soldiers unleashed a devastating fire across the valley floor. The Indians turned and fled; and within few days they fell back to Mexico.

On October 14, 1880, Mexican troops trapped Victorio's badly reduced forces, killing the great chief in the final assault. But the victory had already been won. The Victorio War was perhaps the most difficult campaign ever waged against the Apaches. It was also one of the few Apache wars fought largely by regular troops, not Apache scouts enlisted by the Army—and those troops were largely buffalo soldiers. They out-marched, out-fought and out-generaled a foe often considered to be the hardest marching, hardest fighting, most skillful enemy in frontier history.

Over the remaining years of the frontier era, the buffalo soldiers stayed at the center of events. The 10th Cavalry, for example, played a significant role in the last major act of Indian warfare in the Southwest: the Geronimo Campaign of 1885-86. The 9th Cavalry and the 25th Infantry also joined operations against the Sioux in 1890-91.

Lieutenant Flipper, however, endured a sad sequel to the Victorio War. As the only African-American line officer in the 10th, he remained the object of special hatred by many of his fellow officers. As quartermaster at Fort Davis, Texas, in July 1881 he discovered commissary money was missing from his trunk. On December 8, 1881, a court-martial found Flipper innocent of embezzling the funds—but guilty of "conduct unbecoming an officer. (Historians believe the court-martial occurred as a result of Flipper's friendship, albeit platonic, with a white woman.) Expelled from the military, he worked as a civil engineer, and as a translator, but he failed in his increasing efforts to clear his name. Finally, on December 13, 1976, after long campaigning by Flipper's descendants and defenders, the Army's board of corrections exonerated him, issuing an honorable discharge 36 years after his death.

As the buffalo soldiers watched the promising age of Reconstruction—the nation's first civil rights era—come crashing down into the rubble of segregation, they saw themselves as the last bastion of public service for African-Americans. "They are possessed of the notion," wrote one chaplain. "That the colored people of the whole country are more or less affected by their conduct in the Army."

In the Spanish-American War and in the Philippine insurrections, these regiments added pages to their thick record of accomplishments. Ironically, these units were largely kept out of combat in the two world wars, although African-American volunteers and draftees fought courageously in France, Italy and Germany. Yet even those who saw combat suffered severe prejudice; only a handful received awards for valor. On January 13, 1997, President Bill Clinton took a small step to rectify this injustice by awarding the Medal of Honor to seven African-Americans who had served in World War II.

In recent years, interest in the buffalo soldiers has flourished. They have been commemorated with a postage stamp, historical-reenactment groups and a 1997 cable television movie. Much of the new recognition stems from the efforts of one black officer who strongly identifies with his 19th-century predecessors. In 1982 he arrived at Fort Leavenworth, Kansas (birthplace of the 10th Cavalry), and was dismayed to find not one memorial to the buffalo soldiers' "incredible contribution to the American West." That officer was Colin Powell. In 1992, he returned to Fort Leavenworth—this time as chairman of the Joint Chiefs of Staff—to dedicate a monument by sculptor Eddie Dixon. It was a fitting tribute from a military that hesitated to accept African-Americans, learned to depend on them, and finally—under the leadership of a modern black soldier—has come to honor their memory.

2.4
Historical Sketches of the Cattle Trade of the West and Southwest

Joseph G. McCoy

This excerpt from McCoy's memoir of life as a cowboy details two fascinating aspects of driving cattle from Texas to Kansas: exactly how cowboys interact with their cattle to accomplish a drive successfully, and how drivers deal with the business end of their work once they have gotten their cattle to market. McCoy's discussion of the dual nature of cowboy life reminds us that the romantic image of this "American hero" was considerably more complex than we realize.

We left the herd fairly started upon the trail for the northern market. Of these trails there are several, on leading to Baxter Springs and Chetopa, another called the "old Shawnee trail" leaving Red river and running eastward, crossing the Arkansas not far above Fort Gibson, thence bending westward up the Arkansas river; but the principal trail now traveled is more direct and is known as "Chisholm trail," so named from a semi-civilized Indian who is said to have traveled it first. It is more direct, has more prairie, less timber, more small streams and less large ones, and altogether better grass and fewer flies—no civilized Indian tax or wild Indian disturbances—than any other route yet driven over, and is also much shorter in distance because direct from Red river to Kansas. Twenty-five to thirty-five days is the usual time required to bring a drove from Red River to the Southern line of Kansas, a distance of between 250 and 300 miles, and an excellent country to drive over. So many cattle have been driven over the trail in the last few years that a broad highway is tread out

---

From *Cattle Trade of the West and Southwest* by Joseph G. McCoy.

looking much like a national highway; so plain, a fool could not fail to keep in it.

One remarkable feature is observable as being worthy of note, and that is how completely the herd becomes broken to follow the trail. Certain cattle will take the lead, and others will select certain places in the line, and certain ones bring up the rear, and the same cattle can be seen at their post, marching along like a column of soldiers, every day during the entire journey, unless they become lame, when they will fall back to the rear. A herd of one thousand cattle will stretch out from one to two miles whilst traveling on the trail, and is a very beautiful sight, inspiring the drover with enthusiasm akin to that enkindled in the breast of the military by the sight of marching columns of men. Certain cow-boys are appointed to ride beside the leaders and so control the herd, whilst others ride beside and behind. keeping everything in its place and moving on, the camp wagon and "cavvie-yard" bringing up the rear. When an ordinary creek or small river is reached the leaders are usually easily induced to go in , and although it may be swimming, yet they scarce hesitate, but plunge through to the northern shore and continue the journey, the balance of the herd following as fast as they arrive. Often, however, at large rivers, when swollen by floods, difficulty is experienced in getting over, especially is this the case when the herd gets massed together. Then they become unwieldy and are hard to induce to take the water. Sometimes days are spent, and much damage to the condition of the herd done, in getting across a single stream. But if the herd is well broken and properly managed, this difficulty is not often experienced.

As soon as the leaders can be induced to take to the water, and strike out for the opposite shore, the balance will follow with but little trouble. Often the drover can induce the leaders to follow him into and across the river, by riding ahead of them into the water and, if need be, swimming his horse in the lead to the opposite shore, whilst the entire herd follow much in the same order that it travels on the trail. It sometimes occurs that the herd will become unmanageable and frightened after entering the water and refuse to strike out to either shore, but gather around their leaders and swim in a circle round and round very similar to milling on the ground when frightened. The aspect is that of a mass of heads and horns, the bodies being out of sight in the water, and it is not uncommon to loose numbers by drowning. When the herd gets to milling in the water—to break this mill and induce the leaders to launch out for the shore the drover swims his cow pony into the center of the mill and, if possible, frightens the mass of struggling whirling cattle, into separation. Not un-frequently the drover is unhorsed and compelled to swim for his life; often taking a swimming steer by the tail, and thus be safely and speedily towed to the shore.

Swimming herds of cattle across swollen rivers is not listed as one of the pleasurable events in the drover's trip to the northern market. It is the scarcity of large rivers that constitutes one of the most powerful arguments in favor of the Chisholm trail. Nevertheless it is not entirely free from this objection, especially during rainy seasons. When the herd is over the stream he next job is to get the camp wagon over. This is done by draw-ing it near the water's edge and, after detaching the oxen and swimming them over, a number of picket ropes are tied together, sufficient to reach across the river, and attached to the wagon which is then pushed into the water and drawn to the opposite shore, whereupon the team is attached and the wagon drawn on to solid ground.

Few occupations are more cheerful, lively and pleasant than that of the cow-boy on a fine day or night; but when the storm comes, then is his manhood and often his skill and bravery put to test. When the night is inky dark and the lurid lightning flashes its zig-zag course athwart the heavens, and the coarse thunder jars the earth, the winds moan fresh and lively over the prairie, the electric balls dance from tip to tip of the cattle's horns then the position of the cow-boy on duty is trying far more than romantic.

When the storm breaks over his head, the least occurrence unusual, such as the breaking of a dry week or stick, or a sudden and near flash of lightning, will start the herd, as if by magic, all at an instant, upon a wild rush. And woe to the horse, or man, or camp that may be in their path The only possible show for safety is to mount and ride with them until you can get outside the stampeding column. It is customary to train cattle to listen to the noise of the herder. Who sings in a voice more sonorous than musi-cal a lullaby consisting of a few short monosyllables. A stranger to the busi-ness of stock driving will scarce credit the statement that the wildest herd will not run so long as they can hear distinctly the voice of the herder above the din of the storm. But if by any mishap the herd gets off on a real stampede. It is by bold, dashing, reckless riding in the darkest of nights, and by adroit, skillful management that it is checked and brought under control. The moment the herd is off, the cow-boy turns his horse at full speed down the retreating column, and seeks to get up beside the leaders, which he does not attempt to stop suddenly, for such an effort would be futile, but turns them to the left or right hand, and gradually curves them into a circle, the circumference of which is narrowed down as fast as possible, until the whole herd is rushing wildly round and round on as small a piece of ground as possible for them to occupy. Then the cow-boy begins his lullaby note in a loud voice, which has a great effect in quieting the herd. When all is still, and the herd will over its scare, they are returned to their bed-ground, or held where stopped until daylight.

After a drive of twenty-five to one hundred days, the herd arrives in Western Kansas, whither in advance, its owner has come, and decided what point at which he will make his headquarters. Straightway a good herding place is sought out and the herd, upon its arrival, placed thereon, to remain until the buyer is found, who is diligently sought after: but if not found as soon as the cattle are fat, they are shipped to market. But the drover has a decided preference for selling on firm principle, for there he feels at home and self possessed: but when he goes on the cars he is out of his element and doing something he don't understand much about, and don't wish to learn, especially at the price it has cost many cattle shippers.

We have in a former paper said that Texan drovers, as a class, were clanish and easily gulled by promises of high prices for their stock. As an illustration of these statements, we cite a certain secret meeting of the drovers held at one of the camps in '67, whereat they all, after talking the matter over, pledged themselves to hold their cattle for three cents per pound, gross, and to sell none for less. One of the principal arguments used was that their cattle must be worth that price, or those Illinoisans would not be expending so much money and labor in preparing facilities for shipping them. To this resolution they adhered persistently, refusing $2.75 per 100 lbs, for fully 10,000 head, and afterwards failing to get their three cents on the prairie for their cattle, shipped them to Chicago on their own account and sold them there at $2.25 to $2.50 per 100 lbs, and out of that paid a freight of $150 per car, realizing from ten to fifteen dollars per head less than they had haughtily refused upon the prairie. Some of them refused to accept these prices, and packed their cattle upon their own account. Their disappointment and chagrin at their failure to force a buyer to pay three cents per pound for cattle, was great and bitter, but their refusal to accept the offer of 2-3/4 cents per pound was great good fortune to the would-be buyers, for at that price $100,000 would have been lost on ten thousand head of cattle. An attempt was made the following year to form a combination to put up prices; but a burnt child dreads the fire and the attempted combination failed, and every drover looked out sharply for himself.

Now one instance touching their susceptibility to being gulled by fine promises. In the fall of 1867, when Texan cattle were selling at from $24 to $28 per head in Chicago, a well dressed, smooth-tongued individual put in an appearance at Abilene and claimed to be the representative of a certain(bogus) packing company of Chicago, and was desirous of purchasing several thousand head of cattle. He would pay Chicago prices at Abilene, or rather than be particular, five or ten dollars per head more than the same cattle would sell for in Chicago. It was astonishing to see how eagerly certain drovers fell into his trap and bargained their cattle off to him at $35 per head at Abilene, fully $15 more than they would pay out. But mark you, the buyer so "child-like and bland," could only pay the little sum of twenty-five dollars down on 400 to 800 head, but would pay the balance when he got to Leavenworth with the cattle, he being afraid to bring his wealth up in that wild country. In the meantime they would load the cattle on the cars, bill them in the name of the buyer, and of course everything would be all right. Strange as it may appear, several of the hitherto most suspicious drovers of 1867, fell in with this swindlers' scheme, and were actually about to let him ship their herds off, on a mere verbal promise, when the parties in charge of the Yards, seeing that the drovers were about to be defrauded out of their stock, posted them to have the cattle billed in their own name, and then if the pay was not forthcoming they would have possession of their own stock without troublesome litigation, as every man of sense anticipated the would have. When the swindler after various excuses for his failures to pay at Leavenworth, Quincy and Chicago, all the while trying to get the cattle into his own hands, found that he must come down with the cash, he very plainly told the Texan to go to hades with his cattle. Instead of obeying this warm parting injunction of his new found, high-priced buyer, he turned his cattle over to a regular commission and received about $26 per head at Chicago less freight charges, or almost $18 per head at Abilene instead of the $35 per head.

2.5
Educating Indian Girls at Nonreservation Boarding Schools, 1878–1920

Robert A. Trennert

Arizona State University historian Robert A. Trennert addresses the federal government's policy of sending young Indian girls to schools to be "Americanized." What were the specific goals of the Bureau of Indian Affairs education policy? According to Trennert, were those goals met? How did the schools "encourage" Native American girls to assimilate?

During the latter part of the nineteenth century the Bureau of Indian Affairs made an intensive effort to assimilate the Indian into American society. One important aspect of the government's acculturation program was Indian education. By means of reservation day schools, reservation boarding schools, and off-reservation industrial schools, the federal government attempted to obliterate the cultural heritage of Indian youths and replace it with the values of Anglo-American society. One of the more notable aspects of this program was the removal of young Indian women from their tribal homes to government schools in an effort to transform them into a government version of the ideal American woman. This program of assimilationist education, despite some accomplishments, generally failed to attain its goals. This study is a review of the education of Indian women at the institutions that best typified the government program—the off-reservation industrial training schools. An understanding of this educational system provides some insight into the impact of the acculturation effort on the native population. Simultaneously, it illustrates some of the prevalent national images regarding both Indians and women.

The concept of educating native women first gained momentum among eighteenth-century New England missionaries who recommended that Indian girls might benefit from formal training in housekeeping. This idea matured to the point that, by the 1840s, the federal government had committed itself to educating Indian girls in the hope that women trained as good housewives would help their mates assimilate. A basic premise of this educational effort rested on the necessary elimination of Indian culture. Although recent scholarship has suggested that the division of labor between the sexes within Indian societies was rather equitable, mid-nineteenth-century Americans accepted a vision of Native American women as slaves toiling endlessly for their selfish, slovenly husbands and fathers in an atmosphere of immorality, degradation, and lust. Any cursory glance at contemporary literature provides striking evidence of this belief. Joel D. Steele, for example, in his 1876 history of the American nation described Indian society in the following terms: "The Indian was a barbarian.... Labor he considered degrading, and fit only for women. His squaw, therefore, built his wigwam, cut his wood, and carried his burdens when he journeyed. While he hunted or fished, she cleared the land...and dressed skins."

Government officials and humanitarian reformers shared Steele's opinion. Secretary of the Interior Carl Schurz, a noted reformer, stated in 1881 that "the Indian woman has so far been only a beast of burden. The girl, when arrived at maturity, was disposed of like an article of trade. The Indian wife was treated by her husband alternately with animal fondness and with the cruel brutality of the slave driver." Neither Steele nor Schurz was unique in his day; both expressed the general opinion of American society. From this perspective, if women were to be incorporated into American society, their sexual role and social standing stood in need of change.

The movement to educate Indian girls reflected new trends in women's education. Radical changes in the economic and social life of late nineteenth-century America set up a movement away from the traditional academy education of young women. Economic opportunity created by the industrial revolution combined with the decline of the family as a significant economic unit produced a demand for vocational preparation for women. The new school discipline of "domestic science," a modern, home-making technique, developed as a means to bring stability and scientific management to the American family and provide skills to the increasing number of women entering the work force. In the years following the Civil

War, increased emphasis was placed on domestic and vocational education as schools incorporated the new discipline into their curriculum. Similar emphasis appeared in government planning for the education of Indian women as a means of their forced acculturation. However, educators skirted the question of whether native women should be trained for industry or homemaking.

During the 1870s, with the tribes being confined to reservations, the government intensified its efforts to provide education for Indian youth of both sexes. The establishment of the industrial training schools at the end of the decade accelerated the commitment to educate Indian women. These schools got their start in 1878 when Captain Richard Henry Pratt, in charge of a group of Indian prisoners at Fort Marion, Florida, persuaded the government to educate eighteen of the younger male inmates at Hampton Normal Institute, an all-black school in Virginia, run by General Samuel C. Armstrong. Within six months Pratt and Armstrong were pleased enough with the results of their experiment to request more students. Both men strongly believed that girls should be added to the program, and Armstrong even went so far as to stipulate that Hampton would take more Indian students only on condition that half be women. At first Indian Commissioner Ezra A. Hayt rejected the proposal, primarily because he questioned the morality of allowing Indian women to mix with black men, but Armstrong's argument that "without educated women there is no civilization" finally prevailed. Thus, when Pratt journeyed west in the fall of 1878 to recruit more students, he fully expected half to be women.

Pratt was permitted to enlist fifty Indian students on his trip up the Missouri River. Mrs. Pratt went along to aid with the enlistment of girls. Although they found very little problem in recruiting a group of boys, they had numerous difficulties locating girls. At Fort Berthold, for instance, the Indians objected to having their young women taken away from home. Pratt interpreted this objection in terms of his own ethnocentric beliefs, maintaining that Indian tribes made their "squaws" do all the work. "They are too valuable in the capacity of drudge during the years they should be at school to be spared to go,"' he reported. Ultimately it required the help of local missionaries to secure four female students. Even then there were unexpected problems. As Pratt noted, "One of the girls [age ten] was especially bright and there was a general desire to save her from the degradation of her Indian surroundings. The mother [age twenty-six] said that education and civilization would make her child look upon her as a savage, and that unless she could go with her child and learn too, the child could not come." Pratt included both mother and daughter. Not all the missionaries and government agents, however, shared Pratt's enthusiasm. At Cheyenne River and other agencies a number of officials echoed the sentiments of Commissioner Hayt regarding the morality of admitting girls to a black school, and they succeeded in blocking recruitment. As a result, only nine girls were sent to Hampton.

Although the educational experiences of the first Indian girls to attend Hampton have not been well documented, a few things are evident. The girls were kept under strict supervision and were separated from the boys except during times of classroom instruction. In addition, the girls were kept apart from black pupils. Most of the academic work was focused on learning the English language, and the girls also received instruction in household skills. The small number of girls, of course, made it difficult to implement a general educational plan. Moreover, considerable opposition remained to educating Indian women at Hampton. Many prominent reformers expected confrontations, or even worse, love affairs, between black and red. Others expressed concern that Indian students in an all-black setting would not receive sufficient incentive and demanded they have the benefit of direct contact with white citizens.

Captain Pratt himself wanted to separate the Indians and blacks, and despite the fact that no racial trouble surfaced at Hampton, he pressured the government to create a school solely for Indians. Indian contact with blacks did not fit in with his plans for native education, and he reminded Secretary Schurz that Indians could become useful citizens only "through living among our people." The government consented, and in the summer of 1879 Pratt was authorized to open a school at Carlisle Barracks, Pennsylvania, "provided both boys and girls are educated in said school." Thus, while Hampton continued to develop its own Indian program, it was soon accompanied by Carlisle and other all-Indian schools.

Under the guidance of General Armstrong at Hampton and Captain Pratt at Carlisle, a program for Indian women developed over a period of several years. Although these men differed on the question of racial mixing, they agreed on what Indian girls should be learning. By 1880, with fifty-seven Indian girls at Carlisle and about twenty at Hampton, the outlines of the program began to emerge. As rapidly as possible the girls were placed in a system that put maximum emphasis on domestic chores. Academic learning clearly played a subordinate role. The girls spent no more than half a day in the classroom and devoted the rest of their time to domestic work. At Carlisle the first arrivals were instructed in "the manufacture and mending of garments, the use of the sewing machine, laundry work, cooking, and the routine of household duties pertaining to their sex."

Discipline went hand in hand with work experience. Both Pratt and Armstrong possessed military backgrounds and insisted that girls be taught strict obedience. General Armstrong believed that obedience was completely foreign to the native mind and that discipline was a corollary to civilization. Girls, he thought, were more unmanageable than boys because of their "inherited spirit of independence." To instill the necessary discipline, the entire school routine was organized in martial fashion, and every facet of student life followed a strict timetable. Students who violated the rules were punished, sometimes by corporal means, but more commonly by ridicule. Although this discipline was perhaps no more severe than that in many non-Indian schools of the day, it contrasted dramatically with tribal educational patterns that often mixed learning with play. Thus, when Armstrong offered assurances that children accepted "the penalty gratefully as part of [her] education in the good road," it might be viewed with a bit of skepticism.

Another integral part of the program centered on the idea of placing girls among white families to learn by association. The "outing" system, as it was soon called, began almost as quickly as the schools received students. Through this system Pratt expected to take Indian girls directly from their traditional homes and in three years make them acceptable for placement in public schools and private homes. By 1881 both Carlisle and Hampton were placing girls in white homes, most of which were located in rural Pennsylvania or New England. Here the girls were expected to become independent, secure a working knowledge of the English language, and acquire useful domestic skills. Students were usually sent to a family on an individual, basis, although in a few cases several young women were placed in the same home. Emily Bowen, an outing program sponsor in Woodstock, Connecticut, reveals something of white motives for participation in the service. Miss Bowen, a former teacher, heard of Pratt's school in 1880 and became convinced that God had called upon her to "lift up the lowly." Hesitating to endure the dangers of the frontier, she volunteered instead to take eight Indian girls into her home to "educate them to return and be a blessing to their people." Bowen proposed to teach the girls "practical things, such as housework, sewing, and all that is necessary to make home comfortable and pleasant." In this manner, she hoped, the girls under her charge would take the "true missionary spirit" with them on their return to their people.

Having set the women's education program in motion, Pratt and his colleagues took time to reflect on just what result they anticipated from the training. In his 1881 report to Commissioner Hiram Price, Pratt charted out his expectations. Essentially he viewed the education of native girls as a supportive factor in the more important work of training boys. To enter American society, the Indian male needed a mate who would encourage his success and prevent any backsliding. "Of what avail is it," Pratt asked, "that the man be hard-working and industrious, providing by his labor food and clothing for his household, if the wife, unskilled in cookery, unused to the needle, with no habits of order or neatness, makes what might be a cheerful, happy hone only a wretched abode of filth and squalor?" Pratt charged Indian women with clinging to "heathen rites and superstitions" and passing them on to their children. They were, in effect, unfit as mothers and wives. Thus, a woman's education was supremely important, not so much for her oven benefit as for that of her husband. Pratt did acknowledge that girls were required to learn more than boys. An Indian male needed only to learn a single trade; the woman, on the other hand, "must learn to sew and to cook, to wash and iron, she must learn lessons of neatness, order, and economy, for without a practical knowledge of all these she cannot make a home."

The size of the girls' program increased dramatically during the 1880s. The government was so taken with the apparent success of Carlisle and Hampton that it began to open similar schools in the West. As the industrial schools expanded, however, the women's program became institutionalized, causing a substantial deviation from the original concept. One reason for this change involved economic factors. The Indian schools, which for decades received $167 a year per student, suffered a chronic lack of funds; thus, to remain self-sufficient, they found themselves relying upon student labor whenever possible. Because they already believed in the educational value of manual labor, it was not a large step for school officials to begin relying upon student labor to keep the schools operating. By the mid-1880s, with hundreds of women attending the industrial schools, student labor had assumed a significant role in school operations. Thus, girls, originally expected to receive a useful education, found themselves becoming move important as an economic factor in the survival of the schools.

The girls' work program that developed at Hampton is typical of the increasing reliance on Indian labor. By 1883 the women's training section was divided into such departments as sewing, housekeeping, and laundry, each in the charge of a white matron or a black graduate. The forty-one girls assigned to the sewing department made the school's bedding, wardrobe, and curtains. At Winona Lodge, the dormitory for Indian girls that also supported the housework division, the matron described the work routine as follows: "All of the Indian girls, from eight to twenty-four years old, make their own clothes, wash and iron them, care for their rooms, and a great many of them take care of the teachers' rooms. Besides this they have extra work, such as sweeping, dusting, and scrubbing the corridors, stairs, hall, sewing-room, chapel, and cleaning other parts of the building." In addition, a large group of Indian girls worked in the school laundry doing the institution's wash.

Conditions were even more rigorous at western schools where a lack of labor put additional demands on female students. At Genoa, Nebraska, the superintendent reported that the few girls enrolled in that school were kept busy doing housework. With the exception of the laundry, which was detailed to the boys, girls were responsible for the sewing and repair of garments, including their own clothes, the small boys' wear, underwear for the large boys, and table linen. The kitchen, dining room, and dormitories were also maintained by women students. Similar circumstances prevailed at Albuquerque, where Superintendent P. F. Burke complained of having to use boys for domestic chores. He was much relieved when enough girls enrolled to allow "the making of the beds, sweeping, and cleaning both the boys' and girls' sleeping apartments." Because of inadequate facilities there were no girls enrolled when the Phoenix school opened in 1891; but as soon as a permanent building was constructed, Superintendent Wellington Rich requested twenty girls "to take the places now filled by boys in the several domestic departments of the school." Such uses of student labor were justified as a method of preparing girls for the duties of home life.

Some employees of the Indian Service recognized that assembly line chores alone were not guaranteed to accomplish the goals of the program. Josephine Mayo, the girls' matron at Genoa, reported in 1886 that the work program was too "wholesale" to produce effective housewives. "Making a dozen beds and clearing a dormitory does not teach them to make a room attractive and homelike," she remarked. Nor did cooking large quantities of a single item "supply a family with a pleasant and healthy variety of food, nicely cooked." The matron believed that Indian girls needed to be taught in circumstances similar to those they were expected to occupy. She therefore stated that small cottages be utilized in which girls could be instructed in the care of younger students and perform all the duties of a housewife. Although Mayo expressed a perceptive concern for the inherent problems of the system, her remarks had little impact on federal school officials. In the meantime, schools were expected to run effectively, and women continued to perform much of the required labor.

Not all the girls' programs, of course, were as routine or chore orient-ed as the ones cited above. Several of the larger institutions made sincere efforts to train young Indian women as efficient householders. Girls were taught to care for children, to set tables, prepare meals, and make domes-tic repairs. After 1896 Haskell Institute in Kansas provided women with basic commercial skills in stenography, typing, and bookkeeping. Nurs-ing, too, received attention at some schools. A number of teachers, though conventional in their views of Indian women's role, succeeded in relaxing the rigid school atmosphere. Teachers at Hampton, for instance, regular-ly invited small groups of girls to their rooms for informal discussions. Here girls, freed from the restraints of the classroom, could express their feelings and receive some personal encouragement. Many institutions per-mitted their girls to have a dress "with at least some imitation of prevail-ing style" and urged them to take pride in their appearance.

The industrial schools reached their peak between 1890 and 1910. Dur-ing this period as many as twenty-five nonreservation schools were in op-eration. The number of Indian women enrolled may have reached three thousand per annum during this period and females composed between 40 and 50 percent of the student body of most schools. The large number of young women can be attributed to several factors: girls were easier to recruit, they presented fewer disciplinary problems and could be more readily placed in the "outing system," and after 1892 they could be sent to school without parental consent.

Women's education also became more efficient and standardized dur-ing the 1890s. This was due in large part to the activities of Thomas J. Mor-gan, who served as Indian commissioner from 1889 to 1893. Morgan advocated the education of Indian women as an important part of the ac-culturation process, believing that properly run schools could remove girls from the "degradation" of camp life and place them on a level with "their more favored white sisters." The commissioner hoped to accomplish this feat by completely systematizing the government's educational program. "So far as possible," he urged, "there should be a uniform course of study, similar methods of instruction, the same textbooks, and a carefully organ-ized and well understood system of industrial training." His suggestions received considerable support, and by 1890, when he issued his "Rules for Indian Schools," the standardization of the Indian schools had begun. Mor-gan, like Pratt before him, fully expected his concert of education to rapid-ly produce American citizens. The results were not what the commissioner expected. While standardization proved more efficient, it also exacerbated some of the problems of the women's educational program.

Under the direction of Morgan and his successors, the Indian schools of the era became monuments to regimentation from which there was no escape. This development is obvious in the increasing emphasis on military organization. By the mid-nineties most girls were fully incorporated into the soldierly routine. As one superintendent noted, all students were organized into companies on the first day of school. Like the boys, the girls wore uniforms and were led by student officers who followed army drill regulations. Every aspect of student life was regulated. Anna Moore, a Pima girl attending the Phoenix Indian School, remembered life in the girls' battalion as one of marching "to a military tune" and having to drill at five in the morning. Most school officials were united in their praise of military organization. Regimentation served to develop a work ethic; it broke the students' sense of "Indian time" and ordered their life. The merits of military organization, drill, and routine in connection with discipline were explained by one official who stated that "it teaches patriotism, obedience, courage, courtesy, promptness, and constancy."

Domestic science continued to dominate the women's program. Academic preparation for women never received much emphasis by industrial school administrators despite Morgan's promise that "literary" training would occupy half the students' time. By 1900 the commissioner's office was reminding school officials that "higher education in the sense ordinarily used has no place in the curriculum of Indian schools." With so little emphasis on academics, it is not surprising that few pupils ever completed the eight-year course required for graduation. Most students spent their time learning to read and write English, make simple calculations, and perhaps pick up a bit of history. One reason for the lack of emphasis on academics was that by 1900 many school administrators had come to feel that Indians were incapable of learning more. One school superintendent did not consider his "literary" graduates capable of accomplishing much in white society, while another educator described the natives as a "child race." Little wonder, then, that the schools continued to emphasize domestic work as the most useful kind of training for women.

In 1901 the Bureau of Indian Affairs published a *Course of Study for the Indian Schools.* This document makes obvious the heavy reliance placed on domestic science and the extent to which the work program had become institutionalized. There are several notable features of the course of study. It makes clear that the Indian Bureau had lowered its expectations for Indian women. It also illustrates the scientific emphasis that had been added to domestic training over the years. Considerable attention was given to protection from disease and unsanitary conditions, nutrition, and an orderly approach to household duties. The section on housekeeping, for example, emphasized the necessity of learning by doing. Indian girls were to be assured that because their grandmothers did things in a certain way was no reason for them to do the same. Sound management of financial affairs was also stressed. Notably absent, however, was any commitment to book learning. In its place were slogans like "Learn the dignity of serving, rather than being served."

The extent to which every feature of the girls' program was directed toward the making of proper middle-class housewives can be seen in the numerous directives handed down by the government. By the early twentieth century every detail of school life was regulated. In 1904 Superintendent of Indian Schools Estelle Reed issued a three-page circular on the proper method of making a bed. Much of this training bore little relationship to the reservation environment to which students would return. A few programs were entirely divorced from reality. The cooking course at Sherman Institute in California, for instance, taught girls to prepare formal meals including the serving of raw oysters, shrimp cocktails, and croquettes. In another instance, Hampton teachers devoted some of their energies to discussing attractive flower arrangements and the proper selection of decorative pictures.

Another popular program was the "industrial" cottage. These originated in 1883 at Hampton when the school enrolled several married Indian couples to serve as examples for the students. The couples were quartered in small frame houses while learning to maintain attractive and happy homes. Although the married students did not long remain at Hampton, school officials began to use the cottages as model homes where squads of Indian girls might practice living in white-style homes. By 1900 similar cottages were in use at western schools. The industrial cottage at Phoenix, for example, operated a "well-regulated household" run by nine girls under a matron's supervision. The "family" (with no males present) cleaned and decorated the cottage, did the regular routine of cooking, washing, and sewing, and tended to the poultry and livestock in an effort "to train them to the practical and social enjoyment of the higher life of a real home."

The outing system also continued to be an integral part of the girls' program. As time went on, however, and the system was adopted at western locations, the original purposes of the outings faded. Initially designed as a vehicle for acculturation, the program at many locations became a means of providing servants to white householders. At Phoenix, for example, female pupils formed a pool of cheap labor available to perform domestic services for local families. From the opening of the school in 1891, demands for student labor always exceeded the pool's capacity. One superintendent estimated that he could easily put two hundred girls to work. Moreover, not all employers were interested in the welfare of the student. As the Phoenix superintendent stated in 1894, "The hiring of Indian youth is not looked upon by the people of this valley from a philanthropic standpoint. It is simply a matter of business." In theory, school authorities could return pupils to school at any time it appeared they were not receiving educational benefits; but as one newspaper reported, "What a howl would go up from residents of this valley if the superintendent would exercise this authority."

Even social and religious activities served an educational purpose. When Mrs. Merial Dorchester, wife of the superintendent of Indian schools, made a tour of western school facilities in the early 1890s, she recommended that school girls organize chapters of the King's Daughters, a Christian service organization. Several institutions implemented the program. At these locations girls were organized by age into "circles" to spend spare time producing handcrafted goods for charity. School officials supported such activity because the necessity of raising their own funds to pay dues instilled in the girls a spirit of Christian industry. The manufacture of goods for charity also enhanced their sense of service to others. Said one school superintendent, the organization is "effective in furnishing a spur to individual effort and makes the school routine more bearable by breaking the monotony of it." Although maintaining a nonsectarian stance, the schools encouraged all types of religious activity as an effective method of teaching Christian values and removing the girls from the home influence.

An important factor in understanding the women's program at the industrial schools is the reaction of the girls themselves. This presents some problems, however, since most school girls left no record of their experiences. Moreover, many of the observations that have survived were published in closely controlled school magazines that omitted any unfavorable remarks. Only a few reliable reminiscences have been produced, and even these are not very informative. Despite such limitations, however, several points are evident. The reaction of Indian girls to their education varied greatly. Some came willingly and with the approval of their parents. Once enrolled in school, many of these individuals took a keen interest in their education, accepted discipline as good for them, and worked hard to learn the ways of white society. An undetermined number may have come to school to escape intolerable conditions at home. Some evidence suggests that schools offered safe havens from overbearing parents who threatened to harm their children. For other girls the decision to attend a nonreservation school was made at considerable emotional expense, requiring a break with conservative parents, relatives, and tribesmen. In a few cases young women even lost their opportunity to marry men of their own tribe as they became dedicated to outside lifestyle.

Many girls disliked school and longed to return home. The reasons are not hard to find. The hard work, discipline, and punishment were often oppressive. One Hopi girl recalled having to get down on her knees each Saturday and scrub the floor of the huge dining hall. "A patch of floor was scrubbed, then rinsed and wiped, and another section was attacked. The work was slow and hard on the knees," she remembered. Pima school girl Moore experienced similar conditions working in the dining hall at Phoenix: "My little helpers and I hadn't even reached our teen-aged years yet, and this work seemed so hard! If we were not finished when the 8:00 a.m. whistle sounded, the dining room matron would go around strapping us while we were still on our hands and knees.... We just dreaded the sore bottoms." In a number of instances, teachers and matrons added to the trauma by their dictatorial and unsympathetic attitudes. A few girls ran away from school. Those who were caught received humiliating punishment. Runaway girls might be put to work in the school yard cutting grass with scissors or doing some other meaningless drudgery. In a few cases recalcitrant young ladies had their hair cut off. Such experiences left many girls bitter and anxious to return to the old of way of life.

The experiences of Indian girls when they returned home after years of schooling illustrate some of the problems in evaluating the success of the government program. For many years school officials reported great success for returned students. Accounts in articles and official documents maintained that numbers of girls had returned home, married, and established good homes. The Indian Bureau itself made occasional surveys purporting to show that returned students were doing well, keeping neat homes and speaking English. These accounts contained a certain amount of truth. Some graduates adapted their education to the reservation environment and succeeded quite well. Many of these success stories were well publicized. There is considerable evidence to suggest, however, that the reports were overly optimistic and that most returning girls encountered problems.

A disturbingly large number of girls returned to traditional life upon returning home. The reasons are rather obvious. As early as 1882, the principal of Hampton's Indian Division reported that "there is absolutely no position of dignity to which an Indian girl after three years' training can look forward to with any reasonable confidence." Although conditions improved somewhat as time went on, work opportunities remained minimal. Girls were usually trained in only one specialty. As the superintendent of the Albuquerque school reported, girls usually returned home with no relevant skills. Some spent their entire school stay working in a laundry or sewing room, and though they became expert in one field, they had nothing to help them on the reservation. As the Meriam report later noted, some Indian girls spent so much time in school laundries that the institutions were in violation of state child labor laws. In another instance, one teacher noted how girls were taught to cook on gas ranges, while back on the reservation they had only campfires.

Moreover, the girls' educational achievements were not always appreciated at home. Elizabeth White tells the story of returning to her Hopi home an accomplished cook only to find that her family shunned the cakes and pies she made in place of traditional food, called her "as foolish as a white woman," and treated her as an outcast. As she later lamented, her school-taught domestic skills were inappropriate for the Hopis. Girls who refused to wear traditional dress at home were treated in like manner. Under these circumstances, many chose to cast off their learning, to marry, and return to traditional living. Those young women who dedicated themselves to living in the white man's style often found that reservations were intolerable, and unable to live in the manner to which they had become accustomed, they preferred to return to the cities. Once there the former students tended to become maids, although an undetermined number ended up as prostitutes and dance hall girls.

Employment opportunities for educated Indian woman also pointed up some of the difficulties with the industrial schools. In fairness, it must be admitted that trained women probably had more opportunities than their male counterparts. Most of those who chose to work could do so; however, all positions were at the most menial level. If a girl elected to live within the white community, her employment choices were severely limited. About the only job available was that of domestic service, a carryover from the outing system. In this regard, the Indian schools did operate as employment agencies, finding jobs for their former students with local families. Despite the fact that some Indian women may have later come to feel that their work, despite its demeaning nature; provided some benefits for use in later life, many of their jobs proved unbearably hard. After being verbally abused, one former student wrote that "I never had any Lady say things like that to me." Another reported on her job, "I had been working so hard ever since

I came here cleaning house and lots of ironing. I just got through ironing now I'm very tired my feet get so tired standing all morning." Unfortunately, few respectable jobs beyond domestic labor were available. Occasionally girls were trained as nurses or secretaries only to discover that they could find no work in Anglo society.

The largest employer of Indian girls proved to be the Indian Bureau. Many former students were able to secure positions at Indian agencies and schools; in fact, had it not been for the employment of former students by the paternalistic Indian service, few would have found any use for their training. The nature of the government positions available to Indian girls is revealing. Almost all jobs were menial in nature; only a few Indian girls were able to become teachers, and none worked as administrators. They were, rather, hired as laundresses, cooks, seamstresses, nurses' helpers, and assistant matrons. Often these employees received little more than room, board, and government rations, and even those who managed to be hired as teachers and nurses received less pay than their white counterparts. Summing up the situation in 1905, Indian Commissioner Francis E. Leupp noted that whites clearly outnumbered Indian workers in such areas as supervisors, clerks, teachers, matrons, and housekeepers, but the gap narrowed with seamstresses and laundresses. Indian girls could find work, but only in the artificial environment of Indian agencies and schools located at remote western points and protected by a paternalistic government. Here they continued to perform tasks of domestic nature without promise of advancement. Nor were they assimilated into the dominant society as had been the original intent of their education.

School administrators were reluctant to admit the failings of the system. As early as the 1880s some criticism began to surface, but for the most part it was lost in the enthusiasm for training in a nonreservation environment. After 1900, however, critics became more vocal and persistent, arguing that the Indian community did not approve of this type of education, that most students gained little, and that employment opportunities were limited at best. More important, this type of education contributed little to the acculturation effort. As one opponent wrote, "To educate the Indian out of his [or her] home surroundings is to fill him with false ideas and to endow him with habits which are destructive to his peace of mind and usefulness to his community when the educational work is completed." Commissioner Leupp (1905–1909) was even more vocal. He generally accepted the increasingly prevalent theory that Indians were childlike in nature and incapable of assimilating into white society on an equal basis. Leupp suggested that the system failed to produce self-reliant Indians and, instead of giving Indian children a useful education, protected them in an artificial environment. Other school officials echoed the same sentiments. In this particular respect it was suggested that boarding school students were provided with all the comforts of civilization at no cost and thus failed to develop the proper attitude toward work. Upon returning to the reservations, therefore, they did not exert themselves and lapsed into traditionalism.

Despite increasing criticism, the women's educational program at the nonreservation schools operated without much change until after 1920. Girls were still taught skills of doubtful value, were hired out as maids through the outing system, did most of the domestic labor at the schools, and returned to the reservation either to assume traditional life or accept some menial government job. By the late twenties, however, the movement to reform Indian education began to have some impact. Relying upon such studies as the 1928 Meriam Report, reformers began to demand a complete change in the Indian educational system. Among their suggestions were that industrial boarding schools be phased out and the emphasis on work training be reduced. Critics like John Collier argued that the policy of removing girls from their homes to educate them for a life among whites had failed. Instead, girls were discouraged from returning to the reservation and had received little to prepare them for a home life. Collier's arguments eventually won out, especially after he became Indian commissioner in 1933. Thus ended this particular attempt to convert Native American women into middle-class American housewives.

The education program for Indian women at the industrial schools from 1878 to 1920 failed to attain its goals. Although there were a few individual success stories, on the whole Indian girls did not assimilate into American society as the result of their education. School authorities, unfortunately, made little attempt to accommodate the native society and tried instead to force Indian girls into the mold of an alien society. As a result, the federal schools did not train Indian women for the conditions they faced upon returning home. Instead, women were trained for an imaginary situation that administrators of Indian education believed must exist under the American system. Taking native girls from their home environment, where learning was informally conducted by parents and relatives, and placing them in a foreign, structured atmosphere accomplished more confusion and hostility than acculturation.

Racial beliefs also hindered success. Despite the attempts of school officials and kindhearted citizens to convince Indian girls of their equality, their program conveyed an entirely different impression, due in part to the fact that some school officials believed that Indians were indeed inferior. Students were treated as substandard and as outcasts. Promises made to students that once educated and trained they would obtain employment and status in American society proved patently misleading. Few rewarding jobs were available in white society, and status was an impossibility.

2.6
A Century of Dishonor (1881)

Helen Hunt Jackson

*Born in Massachusetts, Helen Hunt Jackson moved to Colorado in
1875. She quickly became an advocate for the rights of Native
Americans, publishing her classic* A Century of Dishonor *in 1881.
In this entry, the conclusion of that book, she criticizes the federal
government's dealings with the Indians. According to Jackson, how
have the Indians of the West suffered at the government's hands, and
what is the solution to their plight?*

There are within the limits of the United States between two hundred
and fifty and three hundred thousand Indians, exclusive of those in
Alaska. The names of the different tribes and bands, as entered in the statistical tables of the Indian Office Reports, number nearly three hundred.
One of the most careful estimates which have been made of their numbers and localities gives them as follows: "In Minnesota and States east of
the Mississippi, about 32,500; in Nebraska, Kansas, and the Indian Territory, 70,650; in the Territories of Dakota, Montana, Wyoming, and Idaho,
65,000; in Nevada and the Territories of Colorado, New Mexico, Utah, and
Arizona; 84,000; and on the Pacific slope, 48,000."

Of these, 130,000 are self-supporting on their own reservations, "receiving nothing from the Government except interest on their own mon-
eys, or annuities granted them in consideration of the cession of their
lands to the United States."

This fact alone would seem sufficient to dispose forever of the accusation, so persistently brought against the Indian, that he will not work.

Of the remainder, 84,000 are partially supported by the Government—
the interest money due them and their annuities, as provided by treaty,
being inadequate to their subsistence on the reservations where they are
confined. In many cases, however, these Indians furnish a large part of
their support—the White River Utes, for instance, who are reported by

the Indian Bureau as getting sixty-six per cent of their living by "root-dig-ging, hunting, and fishing;" the Squaxin band, in Washington Territory, as earning seventy-five per cent, and the Chippewas of Lake Superior as earning fifty per cent in the same way. These facts also would seem to dis-pose of the accusation that the Indian will not work.

There are about 55,000 who never visit an agency, over whom the Gov-ernment does not pretend to have either control or care. These 55,000 "sub-sist by hunting, fishing, on roots, nuts, berries, etc., and by begging and stealing;" and this also seems to dispose of the accusation that the Indian will not "work for a living." There remains a small portion, about 31,000, that are entirely subsisted by the Government.

There is not among these three hundred bands of Indians one which has not suffered cruelly at the hands either of the Government or of white settlers. The poorer, the more insignificant, the more helpless the band, the more certain the cruelty and outrage to which they have been subjected. This is especially true of the bands on the Pacific slope. These Indians found themselves of a sudden surrounded by and caught up in the great influx of gold-seeking settlers, as helpless creatures on a shore are caught up in a tidal wave. There was not time for the Government to make treaties; not even time for communities to make laws. The tale of the wrongs, the oppressions, the murders of the Pacific-slope Indians in the last thirty years would be a volume by itself, and is too monstrous to be believed.

It makes little difference, however, where one opens the record of the history of the Indians; every page and every year has its dark stain. The story of one tribe is the story of all, varied only by differences of time and place; but neither time nor place makes any difference in the main facts. Colorado is as greedy and unjust in 1880 as was Georgia in 1830, and Ohio in 1795; and the United States Government breaks promises now as deft-ly as then, and with an added ingenuity from long practice.

One of its strongest supports in so doing is the wide-spread sentiment among the people of dislike to the Indian, of impatience with his presence as a "barrier to civilization," and distrust of it as a possible danger. The old tales of the frontier life, with its horrors of Indian warfare, have grad-ually, by two or three generations' telling, produced in the average mind something like an hereditary instinct of unquestioning and unreasoning aversion which it is almost impossible to dislodge or soften.

There are hundreds of pages of unimpeachable testimony on the side of the Indian; but it goes for nothing, is set down as sentimentalism or partisanship, tossed aside and forgotten.

President after president has appointed commission after commission to inquire into and report upon Indian affairs, and to make suggestions as to the best methods of managing them. The reports are filled with eloquent statements of wrongs done to the Indians, of perfidies on the part of the Government; they counsel, as earnestly as words can, a trial of the simple and unperplexing expedients of telling truth, keeping promises, making fair bargains, dealing justly in all ways and all things. These reports are bound up with the Government's Annual Reports, and that is the end of them. It would probably be no exaggeration to say that not one American citizen out of ten thousand ever sees them or knows that they exist, and yet any one of them, circulated throughout the country, read by the right-thinking, right-feeling men and women of this land, would be of itself a "campaign document" that would initiate a revolution which would not subside until the Indians' wrongs were, so far as is now left possible, righted.

In 1869 President Grant appointed a commission of nine men, representing the influence and philanthropy of six leading States, to visit the different Indian reservations, and to "examine all matters appertaining to Indian affairs."

In the report of this commission are such paragraphs as the following: "To assert that 'the Indian will not work' is as true as it would be to say that the white man will not work.

"Why should the Indian be expected to plant corn, fence lands, build houses, or do anything but get food from day to day, when experience has taught him that the product of his labor will be seized by the white man to-morrow? The most industrious white man would become a drone under similar circumstances. Nevertheless, many of the Indians" (the commissioners might more forcibly have said 130,000 of the Indians) "are already at work, and furnish ample refutation of the assertion that 'the Indian will not work.' There is no escape from the inexorable logic of facts.

"The history of the Government connections with the Indians is a shameful record of broken treaties and unfulfilled promises. The history of the border white man's connection with the Indians is a sickening record of murder, outrage, robbery, and wrongs committed by the former, as the rule, and occasional savage outbreaks and unspeakably barbarous deeds of retaliation by the latter, as the exception.

"Taught by the Government that they had rights entitled to respect, when those rights have been assailed by the rapacity of the white man, the arm which should have been raised to protect them has ever been ready to sustain the aggressor.

"The testimony of some of the highest military officers of the United States is on record to the effect that, in our Indian wars, almost without exception, the first aggressions have been made by the white man; and the assertion is supported by every civilian of reputation who has studied the subject. In addition to the class of robbers and outlaws who find impunity in their nefarious pursuits on the frontiers, there is a large class of professedly reputable men who use every means in their power to bring on Indian wars for the sake of the profit to be realized from the presence of troops and the expenditure of Government funds in their midst. They proclaim death to the Indians at all times in words and publications, making no distinction between the innocent and the guilty. They rate the lowest class of men to the perpetration of the darkest deeds against their victims, and as judges and jurymen shield them from the justice due to their crimes. Every crime committed by a white man against an Indian is concealed or paliated. Every offence committed by an Indian against a white man is borne on the wings of the post or the telegraph to the remotest corner of the land, clothed with all the horrors which the reality or imagination can throw around it. Against such influences as these the people of the United States need to be warned."

To assume that it would be easy, or by any one sudden stroke of legislative policy possible, to undo the mischief and hurt of the long past, set the Indian policy of the country right for the future, and make the Indians at once safe and happy, is the blunder of a hasty and uninformed judgment. The notion which seems to be growing more prevalent, that simply to make all Indians at once citizens of the United States would be a sovereign and instantaneous panacea for all their ills and all the Government's perplexities, is a very inconsiderate one. To administer complete citizenship of a sudden, all round, to all Indians, barbarous and civilized alike, would be as grotesque a blunder as to dose them all round with any one medicine, irrespective of the symptoms and needs of their diseases. It would kill more than it would cure. Nevertheless, it is true, as was well stated by one of the superintendents of Indian Affairs in 1857, that, "so long as they are not citizens of the United States, their rights of property must remain insecure against invasion. The doors of the federal tribunals being barred against them while wards and dependents, they can only partially exercise the rights of free government, or give to those who make, execute, and construe the few laws they are allowed to enact, dignity sufficient to make them respectable. While they continue individually to gather the crumbs that fall from the table of the United States, idleness, improvidence, and indebtedness will be the rule, and industry, thrift, and freedom from debt the exception. The utter absence of individual title to particular lands deprives every one among them of the chief incentive to labor and exertion—the very mainspring on which the prosperity of a people depends."

All judicious plans and measures for their safety and salvation must embody provisions for their becoming citizens as fast as they are fit, and must protect them till then in every right and particular in which our laws protect other "persons" who are not citizens.

There is a disposition in a certain class of minds to be impatient with any protestation against wrong which is unaccompanied or unprepared with a quick and exact scheme of remedy. This is illogical. When pioneers in a new country find a tract of poisonous and swampy wilderness to be reclaimed, they do not withhold their hands from fire and axe till they see clearly which way roads should run, where good water will spring, and what crops will best grow on the redeemed land. They first clear the swamp. So with this poisonous and baffling part of the domain of our national affairs—let us first "clear the swamp."

However great perplexity and difficulty there may be in the details of any and every plan possible for doing at this late day anything like justice to the Indian, however hard it may be for good statesmen and good men to agree upon the things that ought to be done, there certainly is, or ought to be, no perplexity whatever, no difficulty whatever, in agreeing upon certain things that ought not to be done, and which must cease to be done before the first steps can be taken toward righting the wrongs, curing the ills, and wiping out the disgrace to us of the present condition of our Indians.

Cheating, robbing, breaking promises—these three are clearly things which must cease to be done. One more thing, also, and that is the refusal of the protection of the law to the Indian's rights of property, " of life, liberty, and the pursuit of happiness."

When these four things have ceased to be done, time, statesmanship, philanthropy, and Christianity can slowly and surely do the rest. Till these four things have ceased to be done, statesmanship and philanthropy alike must work in vain, and even Christianity can reap but small harvest.

2.7
Dawes Severalty Act (1887)

The Dawes Severalty Act was the final major nineteenth-century treaty between the government and the Plains Indians. Compare it to Documents 2.2 and 2.3. What are its goals? Allotments of land to Indians were a controversial part of this bill; why?

Be it enacted by the Senate and House of Representatives of the United States of America in Congress assembled, That in all cases where any tribe or band of Indians has been, or shall hereafter be, located upon any reservation created for their use, either by treaty stipulation or by virtue of an act of Congress or executive order setting apart the same for their use, the President of the United States be, and he hereby is, authorized, whenever in his opinion any reservation or any part thereof of such Indians is advantageous for agricultural and grazing purposes, to cause said reservation, or any part thereof, to be surveyed, or resurveyed if necessary, and to allot the lands in said reservation in severalty to any Indian located thereon in quantities as follows:

To each head of a family, one-quarter of a section;
To each single person over eighteen years of age, one-eighth of a section;
To each orphan child under eighteen years of age, one-eighth of a section; and
To each other single person under eighteen years now living, or who may be born prior to the date of the order of the President directing an allotment of the lands embraced in any reservation, one-sixteenth of a section:

Provided, That in case there is not sufficient land in any of said reservations to allot lands to each individual of the classes above named in quantities as above provided, the lands embraced in such reservation or reservations shall be allotted to each individual of each of said classes pro rata in accordance with the provisions of this act: And provided further, That where the treaty or act of Congress setting apart such reservation provides the allotment of lands in severalty in quantities in excess of those herein provided, the President, in making allotments upon such reservation, shall allot the lands to each individual Indian belonging thereon in quantity as specified in such treaty or act: And provided further, That when the lands allotted are only valuable for grazing purposes, an additional allotment of such grazing lands, in quantities as above provided, shall be made to each individual.

SEC. 2. That all allotments set apart under the provisions of this act shall be selected by the Indians, heads of families selecting for their minor children, and the agents shall select for each orphan child, and in such manner as to embrace the improvements of the Indians making the selection. Where the improvements of two or more Indians have been made on the same legal subdivision of land, unless they shall otherwise agree, a provisional line may be run dividing said lands between them, and the amount to which each is entitled shall be equalized in the assignment of the remainder of the land to which they are entitled under his act: Provided, That if any one entitled to an allotment shall fail to make a selection within four years after the President shall direct that allotments may be made on a particular reservation, the Secretary of the Interior may direct the agent of such tribe or band, if such there be, and if there be no agent, then a special agent appointed for that purpose, to make a selection for such Indian, which selection shall be allotted as in cases where selections are made by the Indians, and patents shall issue in like manner....

SEC. 5. That upon the approval of the allotments provided for in this act by the Secretary of the Interior, he shall cause patents to issue therefor in the name of the allottees, which patents shall be of the legal effect, and declare that the United States does and will hold the land thus allotted, for the period of twenty-five years, in trust for the sole use and benefit of the Indian to whom such allotment shall have been made, or, in case of his decease, of his heirs according to the laws of the State or Territory where such land is located, and that at the expiration of said period the United States will convey the same by patent to said Indian, or his heirs as aforesaid, in fee, discharged of said trust and free of all charge or incumbrance whatsoever: Provided, That the President of the United States may in any case in his discretion extend the period. And if any conveyance shall be made of the lands set apart and allotted as herein provided, or any contract made touching the same, before the expiration of the time above mentioned, such conveyance or contract shall be absolutely null and void: Provided, That the law of descent and partition in force in the State or Territory where such lands are situate shall apply thereto after patents therefor have been executed and delivered, except as herein otherwise provided; and the laws of the State of Kansas regulating the descent and partition of real estate shall, so far as practicable, apply to all lands in the Indian Territory which may be allotted in severalty under the provisions of this act: And provided further, That at any time after lands have been allotted to all the Indians of any tribe as herein provided, or sooner if in the opinion of the President it shall be for the best interests of said tribe, it shall be lawful for the Secretary of the Interior to negotiate with such Indian tribe for the purchase and release by said tribe, in conformity with the treaty or statute under which such reservation is held, of such portions of its reservation not allotted as such tribe shall, from time to time, consent to sell, on such terms and conditions as shall be considered just and equitable between the United States and said tribe of Indians, which purchase shall not be complete until ratified by Congress, and the form and manner of executing such release prescribed by Congress: Provided however, That all lands adapted to agriculture, with or without irrigation so sold or released to the United States by any Indian tribe shall be held by the United States for the sale purpose of securing homes to actual settlers and shall be disposed of by the United States to actual and bona fide settlers only tracts not exceding one hundred and sixty acres to any one person, on such terms as Congress shall prescribe, subject to grants which Congress may make in aid of education: And provided further, That no patents shall issue therefor except to the person so taking the same as and homestead, or his heirs, and after the expiration of five years occupancy therof as such homestead; and any conveyance of said lands taken as a homestead, or any contract touching the same, or lieu thereon, created prior to the date of such patent, shall be null and void. And the sums agreed to be paid by the United States as purchase money for any portion of any such reservation shall be held in the Treasury of the United States for the sole use of the tribe or tribes Indians; to whom such reservations belonged; and the same, with interest thereon at three per cent per annum, shall be at all times subject to appropriation by Congress for the education and civilization of such tribe or tribes of Indians or the members thereof. The patents aforesaid shall be recorded in the General Land Office, and afterward delivered, free of charge, to the allottee entitled thereto. And if any religious society or other organization is now occupying any of the public lands to which this act is applicable, for religious or educationl work among the Indians, the Secretary of the Interior is hereby authorized to confirm such occupation to such society or organization, in quantity not exceeding one hundred and sixty acres in any one tract, so long as the same shall be so occupied, on such terms as he shall deem just; but nothing herein contained shall change or alter any claim of such society for religious or educational purposes heretofore granted by law. And hereafter in the employment of Indian police, or any other employes in the public service among any of the Indian tribes or bands affected by this act, and where Indians can perform the duties required, those Indians who have availed themselves of the provisions of this act and become citizens of the United States shall be preferred.

SEC. 6. That upon the completion of said allotments and the patenting of the lands to said allottees, each and every member of the respective bands or tribes of Indians to whom allotments have been made shall have the benefit of and be subject to the laws, both civil and criminal, of the State or Territory in which they may reside; and no Territory shall pass or enforce any law denying any such Indian within its jurisdiction the equal protection of the law. And every Indian born within the territorial limits of the United States to whom allotments shall have been made under the provisions of this act, or under any law or treaty, and every Indian born within the territorial limits of the United States who has voluntarily taken up, within said limits, his residence separate and apart from any tribe of Indians therein, and has adopted the habits of civilized life, is hereby declared to be a citizen of the United States, and is entitled to all the rights, privileges, and immunities of such citizens, whether said Indian has been or not, by birth or otherwise, a member of any tribe of Indians within the territorial limits of the United States without in any manner affecting the right of any such Indian to tribal or other property.

CHAPTER 3

Industrialization and Labor, 1865–1920

3.1   William Cronon, "Railroad Time"

3.2   Kevin Starr, "Radicalism in Nineteenth Century San Francisco"

3.3   John Morrison, "Testimony Before Congress" (1883)

3.4   Pullman Strikers, "Statement" (1894)

3.5   Knights of Labor, "Constitution" (1878)

3.6   Samuel Gompers, "Fundamental Universal Service" (1916)

3.1
Railroad Time

William Cronon

Excerpted from Cronon's book **Nature's Metropolis: Chicago and the Great West,** *this entry argues that "to understand Chicago . . . , one must first understand the railroad." Cronon discusses how railroads changed our understanding of time and space, and thereby changing our understanding of ourselves. How would you describe Cronon's argument here? Is it persuasive?*

As Chicagoans and other Americans groped for language to convey their excitement at the railroad, they found themselves drawn to two metaphors that would recur endlessly in booster rhetoric. On the one hand, they assimilated the railroad to the doctrine of natural advantages... The railroad's presence was no less inevitable, no less "natural," than the lakes and rivers with which it competed. Wealth would come to Chicago because its "system of railroads branching in every possible direction throughout the length and breadth of the producing district" made it "the natural outlet and market" for its region. A writer for the Lakeside Monthly went so far as to argue that Chicago could expect a speedy recovery from its disastrous 1871 fire because the railroads constituted a natural force compelling it back to economic health. "The routes of traffic passing through this city," he wrote, are as truly "natural" routes as though the great lakes were a mountain-chain, and the Mississippi, instead of flowing to the tropics, swept around the southern base of that impassable range, and emptied its volume, swollen by a score of great tributaries into the waters of New York, Delaware, or Chesapeake Bay. The routes thus established, not merely by capital, but by nature and necessity, are as true fixed facts as are the Mississippi and the Lakes; and they are far more commanding....

From *Uncommon Ground,* edited by William Cronon. Copyright© 1995 by William Cronon. Used by permission of W. W. Norton & Company, Inc.

People who wrote of the railroad in this way never paused to explain how so "natural" a route could be constructed from rails, ties, and locomotives. Instead, they seemed to see it less as an artificial invention than as a force of nature, a geographical power so irresistible that people must shape their lives according to its dictates.

Wherever the rails went, they brought sudden sweeping change to the landscapes and communities through which they passed, suggesting the second metaphor that occurs repeatedly in nineteenth-century prose about them. Railroads were more than just natural; their power to transform landscapes partook of the supernatural; drawing upon a mysterious creative energy that was beyond human influence or knowledge. The steam engine on the prairie evoked genies and wands and the magic that could make dreams come true merely by wishing them so. "Railroads," wrote one Chicagoan, "are talismanic wands. They have a charming power. They do wonders—they work miracles. They are better than laws; they are essentially, politically and religiously—the pioneer, and vanguard of civilization." Because the flat glaciated landscape was peculiarly suited to railroads, "adapted as it is by nature for their advantageous construction," the arrival of these "powerful iron agencies" meant that the land would "spring at once into teeming life and animation."

When the locomotive appeared on the horizon, it soon called forth "the wave of population ...rolling a mighty tide of subjugation over the prairies," with "hamlets, towns and cities ...springing up like magic and realizing in a day the old time history of an age." One editor compared such villages to the quail that "whirls up before the whistle of the engines."

Nobody probably intended such metaphors literally, so we can if we choose read them as mere rhetorical excess. There seems little question, though, that many nineteenth-century Americans did feel genuine awe in the face of the new technology. The locomotive was an inanimate object that had somehow sprung to life, the mechanical herald of a new age. People who described it by appealing to nature and magic—often in the same breath—were seeking some analogue that would help them make sense of a phenomenon unlike any they had encountered before. Our own faith in technology has been so chastened by our knowledge of Faust's bargain—also magical, but finally hollow and self-destructive—that we may find it hard to take seriously the rhetoric of wonder as applied to so profane an object as a railroad locomotive. We recognize such rhetoric as an exercise in mystification. Those who shrouded the railroad in the language of deep mystery, making it seem the expression of a universal life-force beyond human ken, obscured the social and economic processes that lay behind it. Despite the metaphors it evoked, the railroad was neither a direct product of nature nor the creation of a sorcerer's magic. It was a human invention at the heart of an equally human economic system. "Nature," wrote one booster who came closer than most to this perspective, "built Chicago through her artificer, Man."

Still, writers who waxed poetic about the railroad were surely right to regard it as much more than just a machine. It touched all facets of American life in the second half of the nineteenth century, insinuating itself into virtually every aspect of the national landscape. As Caroline Kirkland remarked in 1858 in describing the sunset over an Illinois prairie community, "Fancy the rail gone, and we have neither telegraph, nor schoolhouse, nor anything of all this but the sunset,—and even that we could not be there to see in spring-time," because of the mud that would prevent us from reaching the place. The railroad left almost nothing unchanged: that was its magic. To those whose lives it touched, it seemed at once so ordinary and so extraordinary—so second nature—that the landscape became unimaginable without it. The railroad would replace the waterways of first nature with the myriad complexities of its own geography, thereby becoming the unnatural instrument of a supposedly "natural" destiny. It would rapidly emerge as the chief link connecting Chicago with the towns and rural lands around it, so the city came finally to seem like an artificial spider suspended at the center of a great steel web. To understand Chicago and its emerging relationship to the Great West, one must first understand the railroad.

Railroad Time

Compared with earlier transport systems—lakes, river, and canals, on the one hand, and rural roads, on the other—railroads exhibited several key innovations. For one, they broke much more radically with geography. Railroad engineers certainly had to consider any environmental factors that might affect a line's operating costs—the relative steepness of topographic gradients, the bearing load of subsoil structures, the bridgeability of watercourses, and so no. Still, their chief task was to draw the straightest possible line between market centers that might contribute traffic to the road. The same principle applied to nonrail transport systems as well, but the railroads came closer to realizing it than any of their water-based competitors.

As a result, the boosters' geographical determinism affected railroads only indirectly, as a kind of cost-benefit analysis that engineers performed in selecting from among a nearly infinite set of possible routes. Railroads did follow existing rivers and valleys to reach existing harbors and towns—but not because of mysterious environmental forces. Such places usually offered the largest concentrations of prospective customers for freight and passenger traffic. Railroad engineers sought above all to route their lines through country that promises high market demand and low operating cost. Nineteenth-century rhetoric might present the railroad network as "natural," but it was actually the most artificial transportation system yet constructed on land.

The railroads' liberation from geography took many subtle forms. Aside from being able to go virtually anyplace where potential demand was great enough, they could also operate quite independently of the climatic factors that had bedeviled earlier forms of transportation. Farmers who used a railroad like the Galena and Chicago Union probably regarded its invulnerability to mud as its single greatest attraction. No longer did trade and travel have to stop during set seasons of the year.

The railroads also alleviated many of the worst effects of winter. The period from November to April had always been the dullest season of the business year, when trade ground to a virtual halt for farmers and merchants alike. With the railroad, rural farmers could travel to urban markets whenever they had the need and funds to do so, even in the deep cold of February. Chicagoans no longer had to wait for months on end to view the latest fashions from New York. As one railroad promoter wryly remarked, "It is against the policy of Americans to remain locked up by ice on half of the year." The railroads could not break the wheel of the seasons entirely: the fall harvest, for instance, remained a particularly active time for travel, straining all forms of transportation. But they did reduce the seasonal economic cycles that followed the rising and falling curves of temperature and precipitation.

Just as the railroad changed the ways people experienced the seasons of the year, so too did it begin to change their relationship to the hours of the day. No earlier invention had so fundamentally altered people's expectations of how long it took to travel between two distant points on the continent, for no earlier form of transportation had ever moved people so quickly. In prerailroad days, before the Michigan Southern made its triumphal entrance into Chicago on February 20, 1852, the trip from new York took well over two weeks; shortly thereafter, it took less than two days. Even more striking was the accelerated flow of information after the arrival of the telegraph in 1848: messages that had once taken weeks to travel between Chicago and the East Coast now took minutes and seconds. Railroad and telegraph systems would expand in tandem, often following the same routes, and together they shrank the whole perceptual universe of North America. Because people experience distance more in hours than in miles, New York, Chicago, and the Great West quite literally grew closer as the lines of wire and rail proliferated among them.

Conversely, time accelerated and became more valuable the greater the distance one could travel in any given period. Once farmers had access to a railroad, most no longer thought it worth their while to spend a week or more driving a team of horses over bad roads to sell their crops in Chicago. More than twice as much wheat came to Chicago in 1852 via the Galena and Chicago Union than came in farmers' wagons, the latter having fallen by half in just the previous year. In 1860, Chicago received almost a hundred times more wheat by rail than by wagon; ten years later, no one even bothered to keep statistics on the latter. Beneath these seemingly straightforward commodity movements lay a much subtler cultural change: farmers now valued their time too much to contemplate making extended wagon journeys of the sort they had taken for granted just ten or twenty years earlier. As one Chicagoan later remembered, the railroad relieved "the farmers at every stopping place from their long and tedious journeys by team, enabling them to utilize their own labor, and the services of their teams , in improving their farms, and adding every season to the amount of grain sown," thereby increasing the pace of agricultural improvement throughout the hinterland landscape.

As railroads decreased the cost of distance and increase the value of time, they also raised peoples' expectations about the regularity and reliability of transportation services. Earlier forms of western transport had involved single vehicles carrying small loads. The individuals or firms that ran them operated on a limited scale and had little ability to predict other hazards. As a result, canal boats, steamships, and road vehicles had trouble keeping regular schedules. As one frustrated eastern traveler reported of his western journey in 1851, "For a boat to lie at her wharf hours after the time set for starting, and by innumerable stops to prolong her trip a day or two beyond the promised time, is an event of common occurrence." Because people had no choice but to tolerate such delays, they had to plan very loose schedules for when they might be able to conduct business, receive shipments, or complete a trip. With so erratic a transformation system, one could no place a very high value on one's own time. "Indeed," the same traveler reported, "time does not yet seem to enter as an element into Western thought. It answers about as well to do a thing next week as this; to wait a day or two for a boat, as to meet it at the hour appointed; and so on through all the details of life."

Because railroads ran more quickly and reliably, and could carry more people and goods over greater distances, they changed this irregular sense of time. Trains too could be delayed. But whereas earlier western stage and steamship operators had measured their service by how many trips they made in the course of a week, railroads measured the same service in terms of the scheduled trips they made in a day. On this scale, a train delayed by several hours was very late indeed, a fact that suggests how railroads changed people's ability to schedule and predict their use of time. The long-term consequence was to move timekeeping into the realm of the mechanical clock, away from the various natural cycles which had formerly marked the flow of time.

Distinctions that had once been crucial in dividing the days and months of the year—separating night from day, wet times from dry, hot times from cold, good weather from bad—gradually became less important to travel even if they did not disappear altogether. No longer did one have to stop traveling and find lodging for the night when the sun went down; no longer did one have to delay a journey until ice disappeared from rivers or lakes; no longer did one have to fear snowstorms as a lief-threatening hazard on the open road. When one boarded a train, one entered a world separated from the outside by its own peculiar environment and sense of time. Train passengers had less and less need to interact physically with the landscapes through which they were passing. They became spectators who could enjoy watching the world go by instead of working their way across it on foot or horseback. Unless an accident occurred—and railroad accidents, like those of steamboats, entailed horrors of a sort never before seen—the train promised what its passengers increasingly came to expect: the safety and clockwork regularity of an artificial universe.

The most dramatic proof that this new universe had extended its influence to the outside worked came in 1883, when the major railroad companies imposed on North America new, "standard" times to replace the hundreds of "local" times which had previously been used to set clocks throughout the country. Before the invention of standard time, clocks were set according to the rules of astronomy: noon was the moment when the sun stood highest in the midday sky. By this strict astronomical definition every locale had a different noon, depending on the line of longitude it occupied. When clocks read noon in Chicago, it was 11:50 A.M. in St. Louis, 11:38 A.M. in St. Paul, 11:27 A.M. in Omaha, and 12:18 P.M. in Detroit, with every possible variation in between. For companies trying to operate trains between these various points, the different local times were a scheduling nightmare. Railroads around the country set their clocks by no fewer than fifty-three different standards—and thereby created a deadly risk for everyone who rode them. Two trains running on the same tracks at the same moment but with clocks showing different times could well find themselves unexpectedly occupying the same space, with disastrous consequences.

And so, on November 18, 1883, the railroad companies carved up the continent into four time zones, in each of which all clocks would be set to exactly the same time. At noon, Chicago jewelers moved their clocks back by nine minutes and thirty-three seconds in order to match the local time of the ninetieth meridian. The Chicago Tribune likened the event to Joshua's having made the sun stand still, and announced, "The railroads of this country demonstrated yesterday that the hand of time can be moved backward about as easily as Columbus demonstrated that an egg can be made to stand on end." Although the U.S. government would not officially acknowledge the change until 1918, everyone else quickly abandoned local sun time and set clocks by railroad time instead. Railroad schedules thus redefined the hours of the day: sunrise over Chicago would henceforth come ten minutes sooner and the noonday sun would hang a little lower in the sky.

The railroads broke with the sun in one other respect as well. All previous forms of land transport had relied on biological sources to power their movement, in the form of food calories consumed by people, horses, or oxen to move vehicles and goods through space. All such energy ultimately derived from the sun, and its use was strictly constrained by the physiological ability of animal metabolisms to convert food into work. Speed of movement had well-defined biological limits, as did the total quantity of work that people or animals could perform in a day; a good-sized man might deliver two to three horsepower-hours in the course of a hard ten-hour day, while a horse might deliver eight to ten horsepower-hours during the same period. The railroad broke this age-old restrictive relationship between biological energy and movement, much as the steamboat had done for water transport several decades earlier. Although early locomotives burned wood, they gradually shifted toward coal, and so ended their reliance on biological energy sources by replacing them with fossil fuel. Locomotives were not more efficient than horses, but they could consume vastly greater quantities of fuel much more quickly, and thus had much higher limits for work, speed, and endurance. Typical locomotives of the 1850s could deliver well over three hundred horsepower. By the Civil War, they could pull enormous loads at better than twenty miles per hour for hours on end—far longer than horses or people could move a tiny fraction of that load at less then half that speed. No longer would solar energy and animal physiology set limits to human movement across the landscape.

The greater speed, distance, volume, and power of railroads enabled them to break free from the economic and environmental constraints of earlier transport systems. Compared with its predecessors, railroad geography rested on differences in degree that people experienced as differences in kind, shifting the human sense of scale in a way that itself became second nature in subtle ways. With the possible exception of great armies, no human organization had ever posed such extensive and elaborate management problems before. The railroads moved immense volumes of goods and people at high speeds on closely time schedules over great distances, creating a far-flung network in which responsibility for the entire system fell to a small group of managers. Operating such a system required concentrations of private capital greater than ever before. By 1860, total American investment in canals, which had been the largest comparable corporate enterprises, was still less than $200 million after forty years of operation, while railroad investment, more than tripling in the preceding single decade, had already passed $1.1 *billion*. Unlike their predecessors, the corporations that ran railroads generally owned the entire operation: lands, rails, locomotives, cars, and stations, not to mention the labor and fuel that kept everything moving. The companies that operated stagecoaches, ships, and canal boats generally paid only their vehicles' operating costs, not the expense of maintaining the right of way, while canal companies and toll roads maintained the right of way without owning or running vehicles themselves. Railroads did both and simultaneously incurred large fuel, labor, and equipment costs. Although such extensive ownership rights conferred great power, with them came truly daunting levels of risk and responsibility as well. Running a railroad meant trying to achieve unprecedented levels of coordination among engineering technologies, management structures, labor practices, freight rates, resource flows, and—not least—natural environments, all spread over thousands of square miles of land.

Control of this sort required techniques for gathering and interpreting information at a level much more detailed than had previously been typical of most business enterprises. The railroads faced as much of a challenge in processing data as in moving people or freight. For every station, managers had to set rates, maintain schedules, and keep records of what the firm was hauling at how much cost during which period to time, so that in the end the corporate account books would all balance. Managing this accounting problem generated vast new quantities of statistics which themselves helped revolutionize the American economy by making possible increasingly intricate analyses of trade and production. Responsibility for using the new statistics fell into the hands of a new class of managers, engineers, and accountants whose emerging professional skills became essential to the system as a whole. Out of their work would come an increasingly hierarchical power structure which gradually proliferated through the entire economy.

At the most abstract level, the railroads' hierarchies of corporate wealth and managerial power represented a vast new concentration of capital. Whether one understands that word to mean the accumulated surplus value extracted from rail workers, the aggregate financial investments represented by company stock, or the real resources and equipment required to operate trains, it carries one basic implication. As perceived by those who ran it, a railroad was a pool of capital designed to make more capital. Railroads spent money moving goods and passengers in order to earn a profit out of the difference between their receipts and their operating expenses. Actual practice did not always turn out so happily, but this at least was the theory of the enterprise: invested capital would grow or at least earn back costs so that the system as a whole could expand. Because investments and costs were enormous, everything that moved by railroad— and every place through which the railroad ran—became linked to the imperatives of corporate capital. The railroad thus became the chief device for introducing a new capitalist logic to the geography of the Great West.

3.2
Radicalism in Nineteenth-Century San Francisco

Kevin Starr

The best known historian of California, Kevin Starr here describes the origins of radical union activity in San Francisco. According to Starr, why did radicalism rise and fall in its influence on laborers and on the political system in California? What was its long-term impact on society? What does the life of Denis Kearney tell us about the problems facing radical leaders in the late nineteenth century?

In order to understand the intensity of labor strife in California during the Depression of the 1930s, one must grasp a simple but elusive dynamic in the labor culture of the state, which was centered in and controlled by San Francisco. Radicalism—as a program, a style, a mode of fiery rhetoric and symbolic gesture—had deep, very deep, roots on the West Coast. It also stood in a fixed relationship to organized labor. Time and again, radical leaders, appearing from nowhere, galvanized the labor movement in San Francisco with fiery, violent language, then disappeared or were pushed aside by more centrist successors. Perhaps this tension arose from the extremes of poverty and wealth so evident in the city by the 1870s; perhaps it possessed even deeper roots in the uncertainties of the Gold Rush, when men were transformed by wealth or went to ruin side by side in sight of one another. Whatever the nexus of causes, San Francisco functioned as the left edge of America in more than its geography. By the mid-1930s many feared that radicalism had asserted not its dialectic with mainstream labor, but its dominance. But this is to anticipate history. It is better to begin with the Gold Rush.

During the first years of the Gold Rush, labor had the advantage. The Gold Rush created an instant need for workers of every sort to build cities and towns and to service the mining economy. A washerwoman could charge $20 for laundering a dozen items of clothing. A carpenter could make a minimum of $14 a day in late 1849, and daily wages approaching

From *Endanger Dreams: The Great Depression in California* by Kevin Starr, pages 3-15. Reprinted by permission of Oxford University Press, Inc.

118

$20 were not uncommon. An unskilled laborer could make $8 or more per day in San Francisco. Of equal importance to these high wages, the Gold Rush restored the dignity of labor; for every miner, no matter what his education or occupation in the Eastern states, was by definition a manual laborer. In the mines and in the cities as well, social distinctions blurred as men of various backgrounds rolled up their sleeves and performed physical work. In later years, the memory of this physical labor survived as a cherished tradition, a badge of Forty-Niner status in men who had remade themselves in the Gold Rush. A society which began as an epic of labor in the mines and prized labor so highly when instant cities had to be constructed, a society in which many of the bourgeoisie had begun their careers in shirt sleeves, however temporarily, created a subliminal affinity for labor that remained part of the local culture. For a few short years everyone had been a worker, and by and through physical work California itself had been established.

On a day-to-day basis, less subliminal realities asserted themselves. Sensing the power created by their scarcity, skilled and semi-skilled workers in frontier San Francisco organized themselves so as to control jobs and job sites. In-groups, nearly always white, excluded out-groups, frequently Hispanic or foreigners, which also meant Australians. Such exclusion, enforced by violence, did not constitute trade unionism, but neither was it mere thuggery despite its basis in force; for workers were showing the rudiments of social organization, however crudely expressed. In November 1849 the carpenters and joiners of San Francisco organized a strike demanding $16 a day. They received $13 a day for half a month, $14 a day for the second two weeks. Their strike represented a quantum leap in social organization over the job-protection groups formed earlier that year. By 1859 there were two formal unions in San Francisco, the Typographical Society, the first trade union on the Pacific Coast, and the Teamsters Union, and these organizations were to turn followed by associations (unions would be too strong a term) of longshoremen, shipwrights, plasterers, bricklayers, hodcarriers, and others. Such protective organizations were becoming increasingly necessary, for the golden age of Gold Rush labor was passing. The more San Francisco grew in population, the more workers became available. By 1853 carpenters who had been making $14 a day in 1849 were working for $8; this was still a very high wage for the United States at this period, but already the suggestion was emerging that California's protected labor market would not last forever.

The Civil War postponed the inevitable. Cut off from the East by the conflict, the San Francisco Bay Area developed its own manufacturing capacity, as in the case of the Union Iron and Brass Works of San Francisco founded in 1849. By 1864 some 250 ironworkers were employed there at the peak of the season, manufacturing, repairing, or refitting the intricate iron and brass fittings necessary for the mining and ship-repair industries and constructing the boilers (one hundred a year) which were the main source of industrial energy in that era. Not surprisingly, the ironmoulders and boilermakers of San Francisco organized. In April 1864 they struck, successfully, for $4 for a ten-hour day. The previous year, the San Francisco Trade Union Council, the first citywide labor organization, was formed. The Council represented fifteen labor organizations and as many as three thousand workers.

Employers were organizing as well, beginning with a restaurant owners' association formed in 1861, which defeated a citywide waiters' strike in 1863. Thus encouraged, manufacturers formed an Employers Association in 1864 whose primary target was the militant and successful Machinists and Boilermakers Union. In an effort to break the strike of April 1864, the Association recruited skilled ironworkers from the East. The union sent representatives down to Panama to meet the newcomers before they took ship to San Francisco. By the time the strikebreakers reached the city, they had joined the union. Beaten in the strike, the Association began to target union leaders for discharge. By the last 1860s the Machinists and Boilermakers Union had been shorn of its leadership, and rollbacks and takeaways had begun.

The single most contested point of struggle in the 1860s was the eight-hour day. The radical nature of this demand is difficult to grasp in our era. The bakers of San Francisco, as an example, were working seven days a week, fourteen to fifteen hours a day, in October 1863, when they struck unsuccessfully for a twelve-hour day and no Sunday work. In June 1867 Chinese workers struck the Central Pacific for a twelve-hour day and $40 a month. (They were receiving $30.) In a world where such inhumanly long hours were acceptable, the demand for an eight-hour day posed a radical threat to the established order. The fact that the eight-hour day constituted a serious demand in San Francisco in the 1860s asserted the underlying radical tradition that was already forming. Caulkers won this concession in December 1865, followed by the shipwrights and joiners in January 1866. The printer unionist Alexander M. Kenaday and carpenter unionist A. M. Winn forged the eight-hour-day movement in the mid- and late 1860s into a well-organized crusade that helped send Irish-born Eugene Casserly, a Democrat, to the United States Senate in 1860.

Starting life as a carpenter, A. M. Winn had prospered in San Francisco as a building contractor and real estate speculator. With the outbreak of the Civil War, Winn won appointment as brigadier general in the state militia. Having thus crossed class barriers so dramatically, Winn kept his working-class connections in a distinctive blend of pro-labor activism and *haute bourgeois* prosperity that said something very important about San Francisco: a carpenter had become a contractor and a militia general while remaining a union activist. On 3 June 1867 General Winn led two thousand workers on parade in San Francisco in support of the eight-hour-a-day platform. By 1868 a league of fifty eight-hour-a-day organizations had been formed throughout the state. The league succeeded in getting an eight-hour expectation passed through the legislature. Without enforcement provisions, however, and with the labor pool expanding, this law remained by a prophetic gesture on the books: a tribute to the strength of labor in San Francisco.

With the transcontinental railroad approaching completion in 1869, employers predicted the influx of thousands of skilled, semi-skilled, and unskilled workers into California, putting an end to San Francisco's protected labor market. In 1869 employers established a California Labor and Employment Exchange to encourage migration. The fact that thousands of Chinese and Irish, laid off from construction crews now that the railroad work was winding down, were pouring into San Francisco exacerbated the situation. In the late 1870s San Francisco erupted into class conflict that through mass meetings and incendiary rhetoric raised the specter—and very nearly the substance—of revolution.

San Francisco novelist Gertrude Atherton described the 1870s as terrible, and for once she was not exaggerating. When the banking house of Jay Cooke failed on 18 September 1873, the New York Stock Exchange closed for ten days, and the United States was plunged into the worst depression the country had ever experienced. A year later, the Panic reached California, putting an abrupt end to the boom ushered in by silver from the Comstock Lode. In late August 1875 the Bank of California, the premier financial institution of the Far West, closed its doors after a run on its deposits; and its secretary and presiding genius, William Chapman Ralston, who had been secretly making unauthorized loans to his many enterprises from Bank funds, swam out into the chilly waters off North Beach and died from either stroke, heart attack, or suicide. The Bank of California took a number of other San Francisco banks down with it, either permanently or for a period of time. Money dried up, and capital-scarce ventures, including Ralston's Palace Hotel, the largest hostelry in the Northern Hemisphere, went into remission.

Worse: some 154,300 immigrants had poured into California between 1873 and 1875, more than the total immigration of the 1856-1867 period.

About a quarter of these newcomers were factory workers dislocated by the Panic in the East, and most of them soon found themselves milling about San Francisco looking for work, their presence ominously added to the Irish and the Chinese left unemployed by the completion of the transcontinental railroad. The eight-hour day had long since become a thing of the past as thousands of unemployed men idled around fires blazing in the empty sandlots of San Francisco, passing a bottle if one were available, muttering desperately to each other about the lack of jobs. Elsewhere in the city —in waterfront sheds, in squatters' tents in the outlying districts—an increasing number of homeless women and their ragged offspring kept shabby house as their men tramped the streets in search of work. In one short decade, a workers' paradise had become a wasteland of unemployment.

In late July 1877 the central committee of the San Francisco chapter of the Workingmen's Party of the United States called for a rally of the unemployed on the evening of the 23rd on the sandlots in front of City Hall. Eight thousand men showed up. A rally of such size in such dire times terrified the establishment. In and of itself, the Workingmen's Party—an American offshoot of the International Workingmen's Association, more commonly known as the First International, founded in London in 1864 under the leadership of Karl Marx—raised the specter of revolution through its stated goals and its identification with the uprising of the Paris Commune in 1871. That incident—the seizing of the city by radicals, the shooting of prominent citizens, including the Archbishop of Paris, the re-seizure of the city by the army, followed by the mass execution of seventeen thousand *communards*, including women and children—functioned as an overture, a chillingly prophetic paradigm, to a century of revolutions that was to follow.

If this suggestion of Paris were not disconcerting enough to the oligarchy of San Francisco, the Workingmen's Party of the United States was in sympathy with the railroad strike that had broken out in the East six days before the scheduled San Francisco rally, and many of its members had participated actively in the struggle. Never before had the nation witnessed such an effective walkout, bringing the railroad system in the East and parts of the Midwest to a halt, followed by the use of federal troops to suppress the strikers. The sight of blue-coated regulars marching against civilian strikers in Martinsburg, West Virginia; Cumberland, Maryland; Baltimore, Reading, and Pittsburgh, where most of the violence occurred, including a number of deaths, offered the nation a chilling reenactment of the suppression of the Paris Commune. In St. Louis, the strikers actually seized the city, governing it in *de facto* rebellion for two weeks before federal troops gained control.

All this was occurring even as the first San Francisco Workingmen's Party rally was in the planning stages. Rumors swept the city: the workers planned to set fire to the Pacific Mail Steamship Company docks, where Chinese immigrants landed, then burn down Chinatown. On the day of the rally, a group of workers was arrested for parading the streets with a banner advertising the time and place of the meeting. The San Francisco police and the state militia went on alert.

In its early stages at least, the rally itself threatened to prove anti-climactic. Sensitive to the fears gripping the oligarchy who controlled the city government, the Workingmen's Party officials on the platform confined their remarks to expressions of support for the striking railroad workers in the East and to generic condemnations of the capitalist system. But then some young thugs on the outskirts of the crowd—hoodlums they were called, a local term which soon entered the American language—began to beat up a hapless Chinese man who chanced to be passing by. A policeman arrested one particularly violent hoodlum, but his confreres seized him back. "On to Chinatown!'" they screamed, and many followed. Never in its quarter century of American existence had San Francisco witnessed such rioting as the sacking of Chinatown which followed. Although the toll was relatively minor—the destruction of twenty Chinese laundries, some damage to the Chinese Methodist Mission—the specter of similar sackings elsewhere in the city drove the already edgy oligarchy into full alert. The day following the riot, businessman William T. Coleman, leader of the Vigilance Committees of 1851 and 1856, was asked to head up a hastily organized Committee of Public Safety. Four thousand volunteers were rapidly organized into public safety brigades, each man armed with a hickory pickaxe handle attached to his wrist by a leather thong.

The next evening, 24 July 1877, a thousand men gathered for a rally before the United States mint on Mission Street. Only the presence of armed state militia prevented them from sacking the nearby Mission Woolen Mills, an important employer of Chinese workers. On the next evening, a crowd gathered in front of the Pacific Mail docks, where Chinese workers arrived from the Far East. Blocked from the docks and depot by the police and by the Committee of Public Safety patrols, the men set fire to a nearby lumberyard, then retreated to an adjacent hill from which they harassed firefighters with stones. The police and their pickaxe-handle auxiliaries charged the hill. Gunfire broke out. When it was over, four rioters lay dead, and San Francisco had its miniaturist replay of Paris six years earlier and a parallel to the strike-struck cities of the East.

Twelve hundred militiamen, 252 policemen, and four thousand pickaxe-handle vigilantes patrolled the city. The Army in the nearby Presidio was put on alert, and three Navy gunboats took up positions offshore. Not since the Civil War itself had so much governmental and para-governmental firepower been lined up, both in San Francisco and the East, against civilians in a state of *de facto* or threatened insurrection. More rioting followed on the evening of the 26th, but by then a well-advertised instruction disseminated to the militia and the police to shoot to kill anyone destroying property or interfering with firefighters took the momentum out of the rioters, who remained quiet and disbanded on the 27th. On 28 July, Governor William Irwin felt confident enough to telegraph the Secretary of the Navy and thank him for the gunboats, now no longer necessary. Within the next few weeks, the militia went home and the Committee of Public Safety disbanded its pickaxe-handle brigade.

The events of the week 22 to 28 July 1877 blended reality and gesture. The riots were real (four deaths, property loss); but the reaction from government and the oligarchy—the police, the soldiers, the vigilantes, the offshore gunboats—while responding to a real threat, was also excessive, energized as it was by fears coming from the railroad strike in the east with its attendant suggestion of revolution. Throughout the week, San Francisco was acting out a symbolic scenario of insurrection and repression. The strikes and repressions in the East were for real: real grievances, a very real work stoppage, a real commune in St. Louis, purposeful strikers, troops advancing with rifles and bayonets. In far-off San Francisco, by terms of organizational sophistication, violence, deaths, property loss, or effect on the nation (no railroads ceased to run, no vital traffic halted in the harbor) should have been relegated to the status of a sideshow: except for the fact that the sideshow touched even deeper fears of revolt. Had American gunboats ever before been placed in position against an American city—other than in the Civil War? Had the rioting in San Francisco grown worse, would the Secretary of the Navy, with the governor's approval, have ordered the shelling of San Francisco? Something deeper was at work here: something about the role San Francisco was destined to play in the national encounter with the rhetoric of European-style revolution and the reaction such rhetoric provoked from the right.

In terms of the protestors, the acting out had been fumbling and inept: three disorganized riots, perpetrated by apolitical hoodlums bent on some anarchistic burning of laundries and bashing of Chinese. But now, in the aftermath of the week of 22 July 1877, the radicals would escalate their symbolic response to the police, the militia, the pickaxe-handle brigade, the offshore gunboats: first on the level of fiery revolutionary rhetoric, then later as an organized political party that, for a brief moment, assumed control of California itself

Among the pickaxe-handle men patrolling that late July 1877 was one Denis Kearney, age thirty, a native of County Cork who had settled in San Francisco in 1872 after a fourteen-year career at sea. Having risen from cabin boy to first mate on American vessels and more important, having saved his money, Kearney sank his savings into a drayage business, which he managed meticulously. A sailor since the age of eleven, Kearney struggled manfully to make up for lost time. He spent the years 1872 to 1877 building his business and pursuing a course of self-improvement. At the public library he read Darwin and Spencer and newspapers from the great world and dreamed of a political career. On Sundays he attended discussions at the Lyceum for Self Culture, a reading and debate forum for working people bent upon self-improvement.

A small man, highly strung, with fierce blue eyes and a drooping mustache, Denis Kearney took himself very seriously, even when others considered him more than a bit of a fool. Kearney wanted desperately to lead, to play a role in the world, and he groped toward that goal with the ursine clumsiness of a sporadic autodidact, speaking over-loud in a thick brogue he never lost. At meetings of the Lyceum for Self Culture or of the Draymen and Teamsters Union, Kearney was wont to take the floor and deliver himself of harangues on innumerable subjects, rambling and pompous, which elicited catcalls and groans from the audience. His favorite topic, ironically, was the shiftlessness of working people. They smoked; they drank; they had irregular domestic arrangements; they lacked ambition. He, by contrast—and Kearney frequently referred to his own situation—neither smoked nor drank and had a respectable wife (the former Miss Mary Ann Leary), four well-cared-for children, a drayage business. Workingmen idled in saloons or at amusement parks in their off-hours. He read books at the public library. They were priest-ridden. He had seen through the sham of organized religion. No wonder employers preferred the Chinese, so orderly and diligent, so productive and self-disciplined! When the call came from the Committee of Public Safety for volunteers, Denis Kearney went on patrol with a pickaxe handle, protecting businesses which employed Chinese labor from irate white workers.

Two months later, on the evening of 16 September 1877, Denis Kearney was addressing a torchlight gathering of these selfsame workers in an empty San Francisco sandlot, telling them that the Chinese were taking their jobs. Five days later he was telling another gathering of the unemployed that they, all twenty thousand of them, should be armed and drilling so as to defy the police, the militia, the Committee of Safety. Within sixty days, the bumbling autodidact on the right had become a Jack Cade embodiment of revolution. Patrolling with his pickaxe handle in late July, Denis Kearney sensed not only the power of the oligarchy but the force of the irate workers as well. Wanting so desperately to lead, he saw in the unemployed a power which could be his as well, provided he could take proper hold. The very reason he feared and criticized the workers—because he, too, was one of them: vulnerable, clumsy, and Irish despite his sailing master's certificate, his drayage business, his teetotalism, the long hours spent deciphering closely printed books whose language he could barely comprehend—this very point of identification now became an axis on which Kearney could rotate 180 degrees and head off in the opposite direction. The Yankee capitalist Coleman might tie a pickaxe handle to his wrist with a leather thong, but Kearney would never sit down to dinner in Coleman's dining room. As far as Coleman and his class were concerned, Denis Kearney, drayman, student of Darwin and Spencer, was just another disposable Irishman. As workers, cooks, and housemen, the oligarchy preferred the Chinese.

In August 1877 Denis Kearney applied for membership in the Workingmen's Party of the United States. Flabbergasted that such a known baiter of the working class should be seeking admission to its ranks, the Party rejected his application. Kearney determined to found his own party, which he did, the short-lived Workingmen's Trade and Labor Union of San Francisco. It dissolved after two meetings. On the 21st of September Kearney made his first appearance as a sandlot orator before a crowd of two hundred. Seven hundred came to hear him two nights later. Time, place, the press of events, and inordinate ambition had transformed the fool with his rambling, bromidic monologues into the charismatic demagogue voicing the seething resentments of the unemployed with their angry cries of "The Chinese must go!"

Kearney's second attempt at forming a party met with more success. The platform adopted on 5 October 1877 by the newly organized Workingmen's Party of California seethed with high, if angry, moral purpose. The United States, it argued, must become a workers' republic—by means of the ballot box. The imperatives of religion, humanity, and patriotism demanded nothing less. The Chinese, unfortunately, had no claim on this moral commonwealth. For Kearney and his followers, "John," as the Chinese laborers was called, was strictly a dehumanized tool of the capitalist class, working longer hours for less money and making minimal demands on his employers. Brought in to do the servile work of Gold Rush California (there were fifty-four Chinese in California in 1848, more than twenty-five thousand in 1852), the Chinese were banned from the mines, frequently through violence. The construction of the transcontinental railroad, in which the Chinese achieved an epic of engineering and labor, kept them employed—and socially—through the 1860s; but when the Chinese began to migrate into San Francisco in the depressed 1870s seeking industrial employment, trouble began. They were permitted to fish and to open laundries, for white workers had no desire to become fishermen until the Italians arrived in the 1880s; nor did whites want to go into the laundry business, with the exception fo the deluxe specialty operations conducted by the French. But when the Chinese sought industrial, draying, or longshoring jobs, when they edged toward the periphery of the construction trades, their willingness to work for low wages and their high productivity threatened white workers, employed and unemployed alike. The first union labels in the United States appeared on cigar boxes in San Francisco in the 1870s: white bands to differentiate work done by members of the Cigarmakers Union from cigars made in Chinese shops. Union kilns stamped their bricks with a small cross to distinguish their product from bricks baked by "the heathen Chinese."

And now the anti-Chinese violence of July , followed by the incendiary speeches of Denis Kearney and the 16 October manifesto issued by the Workingmen's Party which announced: "We have made no secret of our intentions. We make none. Before you and the world, we declare that the Chinamen must leave our shores. We declare that white men, and women, and boys, and girls, cannot live as the people of the great republic should and compete with the Single Chinese coolies in the labor market. We declare that we cannot hope to drive the Chinaman away by working cheaper than he does. None but an enemy would expect it of us; none but an idiot could hope for success; none but a degraded coward and slave would make the effort. To an American, death is preferable to life on a par with the Chinese."

At this point, the plot thickens—and in such a way as to reassert and reinforce the expressive, mimetic aspects of far-Left/far-Right conflict in San Francisco. First of all, Denis Kearney, firebrand revolutionist, became an ongoing media event. In an effort to sell newspapers through sensationalism, the San Francisco *Chronicle* covered Kearney's speeches at great length. The more incendiary the speech, the more extensive the coverage. There was even a suspicion, later denied by Kearney, that *Chronicle* reporter Chester Hull helped the ill-educated drayman prepare his more incendiary harangues, which always managed to appear *verbatim* and at great length in the next morning's *Chronicle* as if they had been previously transmitted to Mr. Hull in written copy or prepared by him in the first place. Or perhaps Hull merely rewrote Kearney's incoherent harangues, polishing their language, heightening their ferocity, after they were delivered?

Whatever the sequence, the language is certainly not a *verbatim* transcript. Whether Hull wrote Kearney's speeches before or after they were delivered, the fiery demagogue drew much of his power not so much from his speeches as they were delivered, but as they were reported in the next morning's *Chronicle*. Like a modern celebrity, Kearney assumed an existence halfway between event and heightened, even fabricated reportage. Denis Kearney drew his strength not merely from the realities of his massive, incoherent resentments and his semi-literate preachments, but from the celebrity's ability to be real and unreal simultaneously: to become, that is, a symbolic presence removed from ordinary reality and allowed an extraordinary latitude of behavior and statement, like a figure in a dream— or a nightmare. How else could Denis Kearney say what he said, all those violent, reckless things, unless there existed a tacit agreement in his audience, including those he baited, that Kearney was not real in the same way that other labor leaders were real? He was, rather, a collective creation of a deeply divided community, allowed to say the unsayable so that language might suffice for action and true revolution be avoided.

Take, for example, Kearney's ferocious speech of 29 October 1877. Railroad magnate Charles Crocker, the construction genius of the Big Four, was in the process of consolidating his hold on an entire city block atop Nob Hill bounded by California, Sacramento, Taylor and Jones Streets, today the site of Grace Cathedral. One householder, however, refused to be bought out, so Crocker had the home of his obstinate neighbor surrounded on three sides by a high wooden fence that blocked out the sunlight. What a perfect place, Kearney and his colleagues decided, for a sandlot rally—atop Nob Hill within shouting distance of the Crocker, Stanford, Huntington, Hopkins, and Flood mansion sites. Several thousand men crossed a sandlot on the evening of 29 October to hear Kearney, his fierce eyes and mustache Hitlerian in the torchlight, give vent, according to the next day's *Chronicle*, to the most incendiary utterances thus far record-ed on the Pacific Coast.

"The Central pacific railroad men are thieves, and will soon feel the power of the working men," the *Chronicle* reports Kearney as saying. "When I have thoroughly organized my party, we will march through the city and compel and compel the thieves to give up their plunder. I will lead you to the City Hall, clean out the police force, hang the Prosecuting Attorney, burn every book that has a particle of law in it, and then enact new laws for the working men. I will give the Central Stanford and his crowd will have to take the consequences. I will give Crocker until November 29th to take down the fence around Jung's house, and if he doesn't do it, I will lead the workingmen up there and tear it down, and give Crocker the worst beating with the sticks that a man ever got."

If Kearney actually said all this a mere three months after San Francisco stood under *de facto* martial law, then how were such threats received by his audience? As realistic possibilities? Or as stylized rhetoric in a conflict that had already been removed to a symbolic level once the perceived threat of an actual revolution had been faced and put down the previous July? Kearney's threats evoked actions more horrible than anything attempted in the July riots. This was a call for revolution. Why, then, were not the pickaxe handles immediately issued to the bourgeois vigilantes, or the gunboats summoned once again to anchor offshore?

Recklessly, Kearney plunged ahead. "If I give an order to hang Crock-er," he was reported to have told a rally at the corner of Stockton and Green a few nights later, "it will be done." Kearney's colleague, mean-while, the marginally competent physician C. C. O'Donnell, was giving Kearney a run for his money. "When thoroughly organized," O'Donnell told a rally on 15 October, "we could plant our flag on Telegraph Hill, and our cannons, too, and blow the Mail steamers and their Chinese freight out of the waters"—a threat he repeated on the 25th. "They have got to stop this importation of Chinese," ranted the doctor on 2 November, "or you will see Jackson Street run knee deep in blood."

By the evening of 3 November, after two weeks of such language, the oligarchy had had enough. The latitude tacitly granted Kearney and his followers in the matter of language collapsed. Kearney had pushed it too far. The verbal mimesis of revolution as a way of offering subliminal release had begun to sound too much like revolution itself. The militia was called out, and Kearney was arrested even as he was speaking to a mass meeting in front of Dr. O'Donnell's office. The next night three other Work-ingmen leaders were taken into custody. A fifth was arrested when he visited the other four in jail, where they remained under heavy bail. The militia continued to patrol.

If one considers American society inherently stable, these events hover on the edge of the comic: an *opéra bouffe* of revolution in a provincial American city. But things suddenly did not seem so stable to San Franciscans in November 1877. The leadership of the Chinese Six companies, among others, was now taking Kearney's language as an actual threat. The Six Companies politely informed the city that should the Chinese quarter be once again invaded, the residents—despite the fact that "our countrymen are better acquainted with peaceful vocations than the scenes of strife"—were prepared to defend themselves and their property to the death.

Even Kearney and his colleagues realized that they had pushed street theater beyond permissible limits. Impressed by the austerities of the city jail, they wrote to the mayor claiming they had been misreported by the press and promising, somewhat contradictorily, to hold no more outdoor meetings nor use any more incendiary language. Despite two tries, the district attorney could not gain a conviction in Superior Court, and by Thanksgiving the San Francisco Six (there had been another arrest) went free, charges dismissed. The even-handedness of the court, dismissing two separate sets of charges on constitutional grounds, suggested that however frighteningly Kearney and his colleagues had bespoken themselves, fears of actual revolution had begun to subside in the community. As many as ten thousand workers paraded with Kearney and his colleagues on Thanksgiving Day, and in the evening they voted to nominate delegates to attend the State Constitutional Convention scheduled to meet in Sacramento in April 1879.

Thus the Workingmen transformed themselves into a *bona fide* party, committed not to revolution, but to the reform of California through an adjustment of its constitution. The rank and file of the movement had seen the dead end of revolution as Kearney and O'Donnell had luridly summoned it forth from the platform, and the leadership of the Workingmen's Party realized that it now had a chance to play politics instead of talking violence. Slowly, the leadership began to squeeze Kearney out of the picture. Kearney was owned lock, stock, and barrel by the *Chronicle*, went one rumor. He had promised the oligarchy to fade from the scene, went another report, in exchange for $5,000.

In an effort to regain his position, Kearney reverted to that which had taken him from obscurity in the first place, violent language. "When the Chinese question is settled," he said in December, "we can discuss whether it would be better to hand, shoot, or cut the capitalist to pieces." In January

1878 Kearney was reported to have said, month other things: "Are you courageous? How many of you have got muskets? Up hands, who have got muskets? How many of you have got about ten feet of rope in your pocket? Well, you must be ready and arm yourselves. This thing has got too hot. There is a white heat in this thing now, and you must be ready when I issue a call for 10,000 men."

This last remark brought the Committee of Safety back into session, although patrols were not sent out. Kearney and five others were arrested and jailed. Several companies of militia were mustered, and the gunboat *Lackawanna* took up its accustomed position off the Pacific Mail docks. For Denis Kearney, the magic had worked. It was like old times. Once again, he was the imprisoned martyr, his name on everyone's lips.

Only now, he had pushed it twice too often and twice too far. The San Francisco Board of Supervisors and the California State legislature each passed severe anti-incitement ordinances. Signed by the Governor on 19 January 1878, the state law authorized two years in prison and a $5,000 fine for use of incendiary language or any other form of incitement. The legislature also appropriated funds to expand the San Francisco police force and gave the governor a $20,0000 contingency fund to deal with public disturbances.

More than ever, the growing anti-Kearney faction in the leadership of the Workingmen's Party was realizing that it could not talk revolution and run candidates for office simultaneously. Although Kearney was acquitted for the third time on 22 January 1878, he went into rapid decline. In May he was deposed from the presidency of the Party. At the Constitutional Convention which met in Sacramento from 28 September 1878 to 3 March 1879, the fifty delegates from the Workingmen's Party (out of a total of 149) allied themselves with Granger delegates from the agricultural counties and helped fashion a document which won voter approval by a mere ten thousand votes, thanks mainly to Granger support. While placing restrictions on corporate power, the railroad especially, the new constitution was not a radical document. The delegates rejected such extreme proposals as a unicameral legislature and the banishment of the Chinese from most forms of employment and trade. With eleven state senators, seventeen assemblymen, and one member of the railroad commission in its ranks, the Workingmen's Party had made the transition to respectability.

Anti-Chinese agitation flared up again in San Francisco in February 1880, with the familiar ritual of nighttime sandlot rallies by torchlight and, by day, harassment of industries employing the loathed Mongolian. Cowed employers discharged nearly a thousand Chinese workers in San

Francisco and Oakland. Once again, the oligarchy formed a Committee of Safety, and there was talk of a direct appeal to President Rutherford B. Hayes to send in federal troops to quell the disturbances. Kearney leapt into the fray with an incendiary speech that earned him six months in the county jail and a $1,000 fine. He served a few months before being released on appeal. Kearney made one last sandlot speech—a cautious one—to the crowd of supporters who escorted him out of prison; but already, as the Workingmen's Party was being invaded and colonized by the Greenback Labor Party headquartered in Chicago and the renascent Democratic Party of California, Kearney's brand of politics as rhetorically violent street that was becoming increasingly passe. Sensing this, Kearney allied himself with the Greenback labor movement and was elected to the national executive committee in Chicago. Cut off from the sandlots, disciplined by the protocols of an earnest organization of Midwestern Protestant agrarians, Denis Kearney lost his role as rhetorical firebrand. He also lost his interest in politics.

A decade earlier, Kearney had entered public life comically, as a bumbling lyceum orator, and now he exited it in the same style, as a proprietor of a coffee and donut stand in a squatters' village, Mooneysville, at Ocean Beach. Largely organized by Kearney and Con Mooney, after whom the enterprise was named, the Mooneysville squatters attempted to occupy disputed beachfront property at the base of Sutro Heights by setting up concession stands there and claiming ownership. The fact that a subsidiary of the Southern Pacific, the Park and Ocean Railroad Company, claimed the property added to the *opéra bouffe* of it all. Once again, Denis Kearney, this time behind the counter in an apron, dispensing coffee and donuts at ten cents a round, was taking on the capitalist establishment. "The news is painful in the extreme," gloated the Town Crier column in the *California Advertiser* for 29 December 1883, "for when we look back on his glorious career from the time that he sold his horse and dray for a mess of agitation pottage up to the date he made trips to the East and posed as an Irish orator, utterly ignorant of the English grammar, we have always figured on Denis as either the next Vice-President of the United States or Poundkeeper of San Francisco." On the morning of 31 January 1884, Golden Gate Park employees assisted by the San Francisco police dismantled Mooneysville. "Let the Romans do it!" Kearney exclaimed as the park workers tore down his coffee and donut stand. He was standing on sand as he made his last public speech.

3.3
Testimony Before Congress (1883)

John Morrison

A New York City machinist, Morrison testified before a Senate committee investigating union activity in 1883. How does Morrison compare his contemporary work experiences with those of earlier years? Why might the Senate be interested in Morrison's opinion and those of workers like him?

Q. Is there any difference between the conditions under which machinery is made now and those which existed ten years ago?—A. A great deal of difference.

Q. State the differences as well as you can.—A. Well, the trade has been subdivided and those subdivisions have been again subdivided, so that a man never learns the machinist's trade now. Ten years ago he learned, not the whole of the trade, but a fair portion of it. Also, there is more machinery used in the business, which again makes machinery. In the case of making the sewing-machine, for instance, you find that the trade is so subdivided that a man is not considered a machinist at all. Hence it is merely laborers' work and it is laborers that work at that branch of our trade. The different branches of the trade are divided and subdivided so that one man may make just a particular part of a machine and may not know anything whatever about another part of the same machine. In that way machinery is produced a great deal cheaper than it used to be formerly, and in fact, through this system of work, 100 men are able to do now what it took 300 or 400 men to do fifteen years ago. By the use of machinery and the subdivision of the trade they so simplify the work that it is made a great deal easier and put together a great deal faster. There is no system of apprenticeship, I may say, in the business. You simply go in and

From Report of the Committee of the Senate upon the Relations between Labor and Capital, *48th Congress (1885)*, pp. 755–759.

learn whatever branch you are put at, and you stay at that unless you are changed to another.

Q. Does a man learn his branch very rapidly?—A. Yes, sir, he can learn his portion of the business very rapidly. Of course he becomes very expert at it, doing that all the time and nothing else, and therefore he is able to do a great deal more work in that particular branch than if he were a general hand and expected to do everything in the business as it came along.…

Q. Do you know from reading the papers or from your general knowledge of the business whether there are other places in other cities or other parts of the country that those men could have gone and got work?—A. I know from general reports of the condition of our trade that the same condition existed throughout the country generally.

Q. Then those men could not have bettered themselves by going to any other place, you think?—A. Not in a body.

Q. I am requested to ask you this question: Dividing the public, as is commonly done, into the upper, middle, and lower classes, to which class would you assign the average workingman of your trade at the time when you entered it, and to which class you would assign him now?—A. I now assign them to the lower class. At the time I entered the trade I should assign them as merely hanging on to the middle class; ready to drop out at any time.

Q. What is the character of the social intercourse of those workingmen? Answer first with reference to their intercourse with other people outside of their own trade—merchants, employers, and others.—A. Are you asking what sort of social intercourse exists between the machinists and the merchants? If you are, there is none whatever, or very little if any.

Q. What sort of social intercourse exists among the machinists themselves and their families, as to visiting, entertaining one another, and having little parties and other forms of sociability, those little things that go to make up the social pleasures of life?—A. In fact with the married folks that has died out—such things as birthday parties, picnics, and so on. The machinists to-day are on such small pay, and the cost of living is so high, that they have very little, if anything, to spend for recreation, and the machinist has to content himself with enjoying himself at home, either fighting with his wife or licking his children.

Q. I hope that is not a common amusement in the trade. Was it so ten years ago?—A. It was not; from the fact that they then sought enjoyment in other places, and had a little more money to spend. But since they have had no organization worth speaking of, of course their pay has gone down. At that time they had a form of organization in some way or other which seemed to keep up the wages, and there was more life left in the machinist then; he had more ambition, he felt more like seeking enjoyment outside, and in reading and such things, but now it is changed to the opposite; the machinist has no such desires.

Q. What is the social air about the ordinary machinist's house? Are there evidences of happiness, and joy, and hilarity, or is the general atmosphere solemn, and somber, and gloomy?—A. To explain that fully, I would state first of all, that machinists have got to work ten hours a day in New York, and that they are compelled to work very hard. In fact the machinists of America are compelled to do about one-third more work than the machinists do in England in a day. Therefore, when they come home they are naturally played out from shoving the file, or using the hammer or the chisel, or whatever it may be, such long hours. They are pretty well played out when they come home, and the first thing they think of is having something to eat and sitting down, and resting, and then of striking a bed. Of course when a man is dragged out in that way he is naturally cranky, and he makes all around him cranky; so, instead of a pleasant house it is every day expecting to lose his job by competition from his fellow-workman, there being so many out of employment, and no places for them, and his wages being pulled down through their competition, looking at all times to be thrown out of work in that way, and staring starvation in the face makes him feel sad, and the head of the house being sad, of course the whole family are the same, so the house looks like a dull prison instead of a home.

Q. Do you mean to say that that is the general condition of the machinists in New York and in this vicinity?—A. That is their general condition, with, of course, a good many exceptions. That is the general condition to the best of my knowledge.

Q. Where do you work?—A. I would rather not have it in print. Perhaps I would have to go Monday morning if I did. We are so situated in the machinist's trade that we daren't let them know much about us. If they know that we open our mouths on the labor question, and try to form organizations, we are quietly told that "business is slack," and we have got to go.

Q. Do you know of anybody being discharged for making speeches on the labor question?—A. Yes; I do know of several. A little less than a year ago several members of the organization that I belong to were discharged because it was discovered that they were members of the organization.

Q. Do you say those men were members of the same organization that you belong to?—A. Yes, sir, but not working in the same place where I work. And in fact many of my trade have been on the "black list," and have had to leave town to find work.

Q. Are the machinists here generally contented, or are they in a state of discontent and unrest?—A. There is mostly a general feeling of discontent, and you will find among the machinists the most radical workingmen, with the most revolutionary ideas. You will find that they don't so much give their thoughts simply to trades unions and other efforts of that kind, but they go far beyond that, they only look for relief through the ballot or through a revolution, a forcible revolution....

Q. You say they look for relief through a forcible revolution. In the alternative of a forcible revolution have they considered what form of government they would establish?—A. Yes; some of them have and some of them have not.

Q. What kind of government would they establish?—A. Yes. They want to form a government such as this was intended to be, a government "of the people, for the people, and by the people"—different entirely from the present form of government.

3.4
Statement (1894)

Pullman Strikers

*Industrialist George Pullman reacted to the Panic of 1893 by firing
some workers and cutting wages for others who lived in the "company
town" of Pullman, Illinois, where they rented homes, went to church,
and shopped in stores owned by Pullman. Although not unionized, the
Pullman workers walked off the job, and subsequent sympathy strikes
by other workers shut down railroad traffic in nearby Chicago. In this
statement, how do the striking employees characterize Pullman's
behavior? What are their grievances?*

Mr. President and Brothers of the American Railway Union: We struck
at Pullman because we were without hope. We joined the American
Railway Union because it gave us a glimmer of hope. Twenty thousand
souls, men, women, and little ones, have their eyes turned toward this convention today, straining eagerly through dark despondency for a glimmer
of the heavensent message you alone can give us on this earth.

In stating to this body our grievances it is hard to tell where to begin.
You all must know that the proximate cause of our strike was the discharge
of two members of our grievance committee the day after George M. Pullman, himself, and Thomas H. Wickes, his second vice-president, had guaranteed them absolute immunity. The more remote causes are still
imminent. Five reductions in wages, in work, and in conditions of employment swept through the shops at Pullman between May and December, 1893. The last was the most severe, amounting to nearly thirty per cent,
and our rents had not fallen. We owed Pullman $70,000 when we struck
May 11. We owe him twice as much today. He does not evict us for two
reasons: One, the force of popular sentiment and public opinion; the other

---

From *U.S. Congress, House, U.S. Strike Commission,* Report on the Chicago Strike
of June-July, 1894 *(U.S. Government Printing Office, 1895).*

because he hopes to starve us out, to break through in the back of the American Railway Union, and to deduct from our miserable wages when we are forced to return to him the last dollar we owe him for the occupancy of his houses.

Rents all over the city in every quarter of its vast extent have fallen, in some cases to one-half. Residences, compared with which ours are hovels, can be had a few miles away at the price we have been contributing to make a millionaire a billionaire. What we pay $15 for in Pullman is leased for $8 in Roseland; and remember that just as no man or woman of our 4,000 toilers has ever felt the friendly pressure of George M. Pullman's hand, so no man or woman of us all has ever owned or can ever hope to own one inch of George M. Pullman's land. Why, even the very streets are his. His ground has never been platted of record, and today he may debar any man who has acquiring rights as his tenant from walking in his highways. And those streets; do you know what he has named them? He says after the four great inventors in methods of transportation. And do you know what their names are? Why, Fulton, Stephenson, Watt, and Pullman.

Water which Pullman buys from the city at 8 cents a thousand gallons he retails to us at 500 per cent advance and claims he is losing $400 a month on it. Gas which sells at 75 cents per thousand feet in Hyde Park, just north of us, he sells for $2.25. When we went to tell him our grievances he said we were all his "children."

Pullman, both the man and the town, is an ulcer on the body politic. He owns the houses, the schoolhouses, and churches of God in the town he gave his once humble name. The revenue he derives from these, the wages he pays out with one hand—the Pullman Palace Car Company, he takes back with the other—the Pullman Land Association. He is able by this to bid under any contract car shop in this country. His competitors in business, to meet this, must reduce the wages of their men. This gives him the excuse to reduce ours to conform to the market. His business rivals must in turn scale down; so must he. And thus the merry war—the dance of skeletons bathed in human tears—goes on, and it will go on, brothers, forever, unless you, the American Railway Union, stop it; end it; crush it out.

3.5
Constitution (1878)

Knights of Labor

*Terrence Powderly became the president of the Knights of Labor in
1879. The Knights was the largest national labor union of its day,
reaching a peak of membership and influence in 1886. Here, in this
excerpt from his autobiography, Powderly presents the constitution of
the organization as it existed when he took office. What is the Knights'
unique perspective on the relationship of workers to the Industrial
Revolution? What kinds of values and behaviors does it advocate?*

The first committee on constitution of the order of the Knights of Labor,
appointed by Mr. Stephens, consisted of representatives Robert
Schilling. Chairman; Ralph Beaumont, Thomas King, T. V. Powderly, and
George S. Boyle. Two members of this committee, Messrs. Schilling and
Powderly, were members of the Industrial Brotherhood; and though neither one knew that the other would be present, both brought with them a
sufficient supply of constitutions of the I. B. to supply the body. The adoption of the preamble was left to these two, and a glance at it will show
what changes were made in the declaration of principles whose history
has been traced down from year to year since it was first adopted by the
National Labor Union of 1866.

The committee on constitution adopted the constitution of the Industrial Brotherhood so far as practicable. The constitution, when printed, bore
the same legend on the title page as was adopted at the Rochester meeting
in 1874. The following is the preamble adopted at Reading, January 3, 1878:

> "When bad men combine, the good must associate, else they will
> fall, one by one, an unpitied sacrifice in a contemptible struggle."

From *Terrence v. Powderly*, Thirty Years of Labor (1889).

Preamble

The recent alarming development and aggression of aggregated wealth, which, unless checked, will invariably lead to the pauperization and hopeless degradation of the toiling masses, render it imperative, if we desire to enjoy the blessings of life, that a check should be placed upon its power and upon unjust accumulation, and a system adopted which will secure to the laborer the fruits of his toil; and as this much-desired object can only be accomplished by the thorough unification of labor, and the united efforts of those who obey the divine injunction that "In the sweat of thy brow shalt thou eat bread," we have formed the * * * * * * with a view of securing the organization and direction, by cooperative effort, of the power of the industrial classes; and we submit to the world the objects sought to be accomplished by our organization, calling upon all who believe in securing "the greatest good to the greatest number" to aid and assist us:—

I. To bring within the folds of organization every department of productive industry, making knowledge a stand-point for action, and industrial and moral worth, not wealth, the true standard of individual and national greatness.

II. To secure to the toilers a proper share of the wealth that they create: more of the leisure that rightfully belongs to them; more societary advantages; more of the benefits, privileges, and emoluments of the world: in a word, all those rights and privileges necessary to make them capable of enjoying, appreciating, defending and perpetuating the blessings of good government.

III. To arrive at the true condition of the producing masses in their educational, moral, and financial condition, by demanding from the various governments the establishment of bureaus of Labor Statistics.

IV. The establishment of co-operative institutions, productive and distributive.

V. The reserving of the public lands—the heritage of the people—or the actual settler;—not another acre for railroads or speculators.

VI. The abrogation of all laws that do not bear equally upon capital and labor, the removal of unjust technicalities, delays, and discriminations in the administration of justice, and the adopting of measures providing for the health and safety of those engaged in mining, manufacturing, or building pursuits.

VII. The enactment. of laws to compel chartered corporations to pay their employes weekly, in full, for labor performed during the preceding week, in the lawful money of the country.

VIII. The enactment of laws giving mechanics and laborers a first lien on their work for their full wages.

IX. The abolishment of the contract system on national, State, and municipal work.

X. The substitution of arbitration for strikes, whenever and wherever employers and employees are willing to meet on equitable grounds.

XI. The prohibition of the employment of children in workshops, mines and factories before attaining their fourteenth year.

XII. To abolish the system of letting out by contract the labor of convicts in our prisons and reformatory institutions.

XIII. To secure for both sexes equal pay for equal work.

XIV. The reduction of the hours of labor to eight per day, so that the laborers may have more time for social, enjoyment and intellectual improvement, and be enabled to reap the advantages conferred by the laborsaving machinery which their brains have created.

XV. To prevail upon governments to establish a purely national circulating medium, based upon the faith and resources of the nation, and issued directly to the people, without the intervention of any system of banking corporations, which money shall be a legal tender in payment of all debts, public or private....

In accepting the preamble of the Industrial Brotherhood, the convention fully realized that for the most part the reforms which were asked for in that preamble must one day come through political agitation and action. The chief aim of those who presented the document to the convention was to place something on the front page of the constitution which, it was hoped, every workingman would in time read and ponder over. It was their hope that by keeping those measures, so fraught with interest to the people, constantly before the eye of the worker, he would become educated in the science of politics to that extent that he would know that those things that were wrong in our political system were wrong simply because he did not attend to his political duties in a proper manner; that the righting of such things as were wrong would not be done by those who had the management of political affairs up to that time, but by himself....

...The belief was prevalent until a short time ago among working men, that only the man who was engaged in manual toil could be called a workingman. The man who labored at the bench or anvil; the man who held the throttle of the engine, or delved in the everlasting gloom of the coal mine, did not believe that the man who made the drawings from which he forged, turned, or dug could be classed as a worker. The draughtsman, the time-keeper, the clerk, the school teacher, the civil engineer, the editor, the reporter, or the worst paid, most abused and illy appreciated of all toilers—woman—could not be called a worker. It was essential that the mechanics of America should know who were workers. A more wide-spread knowledge of the true definition of the word labor must be arrived at, and the true relations existing between all men who labor must be more clearly defined. Narrow prejudice, born of the injustice and oppressions of the past, must be overcome, and all who interest themselves in producing for the world's good must be made to understand that their interests are identical. All the way down the centuries of time in which the man who worked was held in bondage or servitude, either wholly or partially, he was brought directly in contact with the overseer, the superintendent, or the boss. From these he seldom received a word of kindness; indeed it was the recognized rule to treat all men who toiled as if they were of inferior clay.

It was necessary to teach the laborer that it was not essential for him to grovel in the dust at the feet of a master in order to win his title deed to everlasting bliss in the hereafter, and it can not be wondered at that many who strove to better the condition of the toiler lost all respect for religion when they saw that those who affected to be the most devout worshipers at the foot of the heavenly throne, were the most tyrannical of task masters when dealing with the poor and lowly, whose unfortunate lot was cast within the shadow of their heartless supervision....

...Knowledge for the workingman meant that he should be able to detect the difference between the real and the sham. Whenever a learned man said that which did not appear to be just to labor, he was to be questioned, publicly questioned, as to his base of actual facts. All through the centuries toilers have erected the brass and granite monuments of the world's greatness and have thrown up on hillside and plain the material for other homes than their own. The weary feet of toil have trodden the earth, and strong hands have formed the pillars of the bondage of old. All along the blood-stained march of the years that have flown, the struggling ones have given to earth more of richness in the sweat which fell to earth from their throbbing foreheads; the grain which lifted its head for long ages of time under the care of the toiler, has been enriched by the sweat, the blood, and the flesh of the poor, plodding men of toil. While the sun kissed to warmth and life the wheat and corn which their hands nurtured and cared for, they received the husks and stalks as their recompense for labor done. Their masters took the grain for themselves, but lifted no hand in its production....

3.6
Fundamental Universal Service (1916)

Samuel Gompers

Gompers was the first president of the American Federation of Labor (AFL), taking office in 1886 and holding it for all but one of the next thirty-eight years. The AFL was a trade union, organizing skilled workers by craft rather than by industry. Gompers and the AFL worked for "bread and butter unionism," focusing almost exclusively on workplace issues like wages, working conditions, and benefits. In this document, Gompers discusses the "eternal problem" of labor and the Industrial Revolution. How do his views compare with those of the Knights in Document 3.5? Which approach seems more effective to you?

In the world's development and progress there has been an agency that has brought opportunity into the lives of millions—universally misunderstood, inspired by highest idealism, untutored and often clumsy is its efforts to accomplish results—the labor movement.

1. Eternal Problem of Labor is Control of Property

The eternal problem with which the labor movement has to cope is control of property—to bring property into such relations to human life that it will serve and not injure. The struggle has been long and hard but the day is past when the labor movement has to justify its right to be classified as a necessary agency with a function to perform in achieving grater freedom and justice. Its claim to acceptance as an instrumentality for achieving human progress is based upon the nature and the value of the service it renders. It was born out of efforts of workers to think out modern phases of that world-old universal problem—property.

From *American Federationist*, November 1916, pp. 1037ff.

Trade unions regard property and the laws of property as human institutions, tended for service in the development of individuality, giving each a feeling of security and assurance and independence, which mean freedom to direct and control his life.

2. The Struggle for Equal Opportunity

The progress of history has been toward establishing equal opportunity for all, for the development and expression of individuality. As the problems of rights have been thought out they have had also to be fought out— for back of ideals there must be aggressive assertiveness that grows out of conviction. New ideals are revolutionizing forces. Sometimes changes have been brought about by appeals to reason and ultimately to self-interest, and we call the process evolution. Sometimes the wronged classes have had to establish new ideals of human rights by sacrificing life and blood, and we call the process revolution. Sometimes the oppressed classes have had to maintain their rights and compel recognition of responsibility by interposing their economic power, and we call it a strike. But whatever the process, whether evolution, revolution, or strike, surely though often slowly, the customs and institution of one period have given way to wider ideals and greater opportunity for greater numbers.

In our own country the Declaration of Independence of the American Colonies not only created a new nation but set forth a new concept of human rights, the right to life, liberty, and the pursuit of happiness. The Civil War which resulted in the liberation of four million human slaves from chattel bondage gave, aye, even a broader meaning to the principle of human liberty.

One king's head cleared the way for a reasonable attitude indispensable for evolutionary progress. The French revolution with Louis XVI at the guillotine tore the roots of feudalism loose from their grip on Europe. Progress whether evolutionary or revolutionary up to the Nineteenth Century put agencies of control into ever widening groups of property owners, until there remained disinherited politically as well as economically only those who held no property but who worked for others. With the decline of feudalism, which did impose a degree of responsibility upon the overlord for the well-being of his serfs and villeins and assured them permanence of relations, there developed the modern industrial system, under which relations between those who worked and those who hired became purely industrial, impersonal, regarded by employers as a part of their mechanism for profits.

3. The Industrial Order and a Propertyless Working Class

Under this industrial order employes lost standing as individuals. As wage-earners only and as factors in great industrial systems they no longer owned the tools of production, they lost even a qualified ownership of land or property, they became part of the machinery of production and distribution, without permanence of employment or assurance of securing the necessities of livelihood. Under such conditions there could be no dignity of life or service, no opportunity for individuality, no freedom—but the crushing irresponsible power of employers threatened to grind the creative energy out of one generation only to seize upon the next generation weakened by inherited tendencies due to economic oppression until the masses of the nations sank to sweatshop standards. Undernourished weaklings who work long hours and are denied the right to direct their own lives do not normally have strong, resourceful, masterful children.

Out of their needs, out of their oppression, out of their weakness, wage-earners evolved an agency for their protection. They reasoned that if they were denied the right to a voice in determining the terms under which they worked, they would fold their arms and refuse to work. Human labor power is necessary to coordinate the machinery and the process of production. By striking, by withholding labor power, wage-earners can bring employers to an appreciation of the value of the human element in production. That service, so customary that employers have taken it for granted, is part of a human life. When all reason fails, strikes can put better understanding into the minds of the employers and induce them to a proper regard for employes. Thus by the trade unions those who participate in the processes of industry have fought and won opportunity to a voice in management in industry. Those who use the tools have a right to say how long, for what returns and under what conditions they will use the tools.

Trade unions are a very potent agency in the terrific struggle for industrial freedom which must precede real freedom, freedom for self-direction and self-control.

Men and women can not live during working hours under autocratic conditions, and instantly become sons and daughters of freedom as they step outside the shop gates.

The experiences of the habits of the shop are indelibly ground into the souls and minds of the workers.

Democracy must come in the factory and the shop before it can be realized in the life of the nation. So long as the factory boss has irresponsible power to hire and fire, to dole out the lowest wages for which men and women or children an work, his employes have no rights that must be respected, no sense of self-respect or dignity, no real freedom.

Long hours of work, low wages, insanitary conditions of work and waste of human power affect not only the workers but their home life, their children and their children's children.

It is somewhat startling to find cynical disregard for the human element in production coexistent with a growing appreciation of the value of human life and more sensitive consciences. But these conditions are bound up with concepts of property and property rights. Unchallenged control over large holdings and capital gives employers power—indeterminate, irresponsible, all-pervading power—over the lives of those who work for wages. Only by interposing a force which gives a power similar to that of property can wage-earners secure recognition of their rights—that force is economic organization. Through trade unions they match economic power with economic power and their power is the more fundamental. It is control over creative activity....

6. The Trade Union Stands for Humanity

The trade union seeks to exalt human life—to demand justice and opportunity for all those who furnish native service to the world. It protects the weak and oppressed and destroys the power of the arrogant: It is the great human democratizing force.

This is its service to humanity—a universal service that brings a message of hope to all. Misery, distress, present injustice are bearable if there is a way out to better things—exclude the hope and life is plunged into blackness. Trade unionism is that in which wage-earners put their faith. The achievements of trade unionism justify their faith. There is no universal service in any field of activity which does not uplift all humanity. Service to humanity does in a sense further self-interests but only when these are not subversive to the welfare of fellow beings and workers. The opportunities for better life and greater freedom won by the workers are shared with all other members of society. The agency devised by wage-earners—the principle of economic organization—is universal in its application and benignant service to all who work. The universality of the principle is recently being made more apparent by the cleavage separating workers from those who live by the toil of others and recognizing the community of interests among all producers—both those who work with their minds and hands or with their minds only. The cleavage is the basis for the new championship of trade unionism by teachers, actors, authors, government employes, etc. It demonstrates that economic organization can perform a service for all workers.

In the early development of the trade union its function is chiefly protective and militant, as it becomes an established social agency its functions become constructive. It is based upon elemental power, stronger, more vital than political power. It is an organism next to primitive life forces.

It is a world-old movement that has led the workers out of slavery into serfdom, out of serfdom into legal, physical freedom, and has given that freedom a real meaning in political and economic relations of society.

It is a service that is as wide as the universe and as lasting. It seeks to make workers entirely free of legal mortgage which property owners have held over their opportunities and their lives. The achievements of the trade union movement will go down through the ages with the glory of impersonal immortality that has secured opportunity for all of all generations.

CHAPTER 4

Politics in the Gilded Age, 1870–1900

4.1   William L. Riordan, "Plunkitt of Tammany Hall" (1905)

4.2   Jonathan Kandell, "Boss"

4.3   Daniel Czitrom, "Big Tim Sullivan and Metropolitan Politics in New York, 1880-1913"

4.4   "The Ten Commandments of the Grange" (1874)

4.5   "Populist Party, Platform" (1892)

4.1
Plunkitt of Tammany Hall (1905)

William L. Riordan

George Washington Plunkitt was a ward boss in the Tammany Hall political machine that ran New York City politics for much of the nineteenth and early twentieth centuries. In this transcription of interviews he gave to New York Evening Post *reporter William Riordan, Plunkitt explains the basis for urban machine politics at the turn of the century. What does Plunkitt mean by "I seen my opportunities and I took 'em"? What is civil service, and why is it so bad? According to Plunkitt, how should politicians behave? What characteristics should they have?*

Honest Graft and Dishonest Graft

Everybody is talkin' these days about Tammany men growin' rich on graft, but nobody thinks of drawin' the distinction between honest graft and dishonest graft. There's all the difference in the world between the two. Yes, many of our men have grown rich in politics. I have myself. I've made a big fortune out of the game, and I'm gettin' richer every day, but I've not gone in for dishonest graft—blackmailin' gamblers, saloonkeepers, disorderly people, etc.—and neither has any of the men who have made big fortunes in politics.

There's an honest graft, and I'm an example of how it works. I might sum up the whole thing by sayin': "I seen my opportunities and I took 'em."

Just let me explain by examples. My party's in power in the city, and it's goin' to undertake a lot of public improvements. Well, I'm tipped off, say, that they're going to lay out a new park at a certain place.

I see my opportunity and I take it. I go to that place and I buy up all the land I can in the neighborhood. Then the board of this or that makes its plan public, and there is a rush to get my land, which nobody cared particular for before.

Ain't it perfectly honest to charge a good price and make a profit on my investment and foresight? Of course, it is. Well, that's honest graft.

Or supposin' it's a new bridge they're goin' to build. I get tipped off and I buy as much property as I can that has to be taken for approaches. I sell at my own price later on and drop some more money in the bank.

Wouldn't you? It's just like lookin' ahead in Wall Street or in the coffee or cotton market. It's honest graft, and I'm lookin' for it every day in the year. I will tell you frankly that I've got a good lot of it, too.

I'll tell you of one case. They were goin' to fix up a big park, no matter where. I got on to it, and went lookin' about for land in that neighborhood.

I could get nothin' at' a bargain but a big piece of swamp, but I took it fast enough and held on to it. What turned out was just what I counted on. They couldn't make the park complete without Plunkitt's swamp, and they had to pay a good price for it. Anything dishonest in that?

Up in the watershed I made some money, too. I bought up several bits of land there some years ago and made a pretty good guess that they would be bought up for water purposes later by the city.

Somehow, I always guessed about right, and shouldn't I enjoy the profit of my foresight? It was rather amusin' when the condemnation commissioners came along and found piece after piece of the land in the name of George Plunkitt of the Fifteenth Assembly District, New York City. They wondered how I knew just what to buy. The answer is—I seen my opportunity and I took it. I haven't confined myself to land; anything that pays is in my line.

For instance, the city is repavin' a street and has several hundred thousand old granite blocks to sell. I am on hand to buy, and I know just what they are worth.

How? Never mind that. I had a sort of monopoly of this business for a while, but once a newspaper tried to do me. It got some outside men to come over from Brooklyn and New Jersey to bid against me.

Was I done? Not much. I went to each of the men and said: "How many of these 250,000 stones do you want?" One said 20,000, and another wanted 15,000, and other wanted 10,000. I said: "All right, let me bid for the lot, and I'll give each of you all you want for nothin'."

They agreed, of course. Then the auctioneer yelled: "How much am I bid for these 250,000 fine pavin' stones?"

"Two dollars and fifty cents," says I.

"Two dollars and fifty cents!" screamed the auctioneer. "Oh, that's a joke! Give me a real bid."

He found the bid was real enough My rivals stood silent. I got the lot for $2.50 and gave them their share. That's how the attempt to do Plunkitt ended, and that's how all such attempts end.

I've told you how I got rich by honest graft. Now, let me tell you that most politicians who are accused of robbin' the city get rich the same way.

They didn't steal a dollar from the city treasury. They just seen their opportunities and took them. That is why, when a reform administration comes in and spends a half million dollars in tryin' to find the public robberies they talked about in the campaign, they don't find them.

The books are always all right. The money in the city treasury is all right. Everything is all right. All they can show is that the Tammany heads of departments looked after their friends, within the law, and gave them what opportunities they could to make honest graft. Now, let me tell you that's never goin' to hurt Tammany with the people. Every good man looks after his friends, and any man who doesn't isn't likely to be popular. If I have a good thing to hand out in private life, I give it to a friend. Why shouldn't I do the same in public life?

Another kind of honest graft. Tammany has raised a good many salaries. There was an awful howl by the reformers, but don't you know that Tammany gains ten votes for every one it lost by salary raisin?

The Wall Street banker thinks it shameful to raise a department clerk's salary from $1500 to $1800 a year, but every man who draws a salary himself says: "That's all right. I wish it was me." And he feels very much like votin' the Tammany ticket on election day, just out of sympathy.

Tammany was beat in 1901 because the people were deceived into believin' that it worked dishonest graft. They didn't draw a distinction between dishonest and honest graft, but they saw that some Tammany men grew rich, and supposed they had been robbin' the city treasury or levyin' blackmail on disorderly houses, or workin' in with the gamblers and lawbreakers.

As a matter of policy, if nothing else, why should the Tammany leaders go into such dirty business, when there is so much honest graft lyin' around when they are in power? Did you ever consider that?

Now, in conclusion, I want to say that I don't own a dishonest dollar. If my worst enemy was given the job of writin' my epitaph when I'm gone, he couldn't do more than write:

"George W. Plunkitt. He Seen His Opportunities, and He Took 'Em."

How to Become a Statesman

There's thousands of young men in this city who will go to the polls for the first time next November. Among them will be many who have watched the careers of successful men in politics, and who are longin' to make names and fortunes for themselves at the same game. It is to these youths that I want to give advice. First, let me say that I am in a position to give what the courts call expert testimony on the subject. I don't think you can easily find a better example than I am of success in politics. After forty years' experience at the game I am—well, I'm George Washington Plunkitt. Everybody knows what figure I cut in the greatest organization on earth, and if you hear people say that I've laid away a million or so since I was a butcher's boy in Washington Market, don't come to me for an indignant denial. I'm pretty comfortable, thank you.

Now, havin' qualified as an expert, as the lawyers say, I am goin' to give advice free to the young men who are goin' to cast their first votes, and who are lookin' forward to political glory and lots of cash. Some young men think they can learn how to be successful in politics from books, and they cram their heads with all sorts of college rot. They couldn't make a bigger mistake. Now, understand me, I ain't sayin' nothin' against colleges. I guess they'll have to exist as long as there's bookworms, and I suppose they do some good in a certain way, but they don't count in politics. In fact, a young man who has gone through the college course is handicapped at the outset. He may succeed in politics, but the chances are 100 to 1 against him.

Another mistake: some young men think that the best way to prepare for the political game is to practice speakin' and becomin' orators. That's all wrong. We've got some orators in Tammany Hall, but they're chiefly ornamental. You never heard of Charlie Murphy delivering a speech, did you? Or Richard Croker, or John Kelly, or any other man who has been a real power in the organization? Look at the thirty-six district leaders of Tammany Hall today. How many of them travel on their tongues? Maybe one or two, and they don't count when business is doin' at Tammany Hall. The men who rule have practiced keepin' their tongues still, not exercisin' them: So you want to drop the orator idea unless you mean to go into politics just to perform the skyrocket act.

Now, I've told you what not to do; I guess I can explain best what to do to succeed in politics by tellin' you what I did. After goin" through the apprenticeship of the business while I was a boy by workin' around the district headquarters and hustlin' about the polls on election day, I set out when I cast my first vote to win fame and money in New York City politics. Did I offer my services to the district leader as a stump-speaker? Not much. The woods are always full of speakers. Did I get up a book on municipal government and show it to the leader? I wasn't such a fool. What I did was to get some marketable goods before goin' to the leaders. What do I mean by marketable goods? Let me tell you: I had a cousin, a young man who didn't take any particular interest in politics. I went to him and said: "Tommy, I'm goin' to be a politician, and I want to get a followin'; can I count on you?" He said: "Sure, George." That's how I started in business. I got a marketable commodity—one vote. Then I went to the district leader and told him I could command two votes on election day, Tommy's and any own. He smiled on me and told me to go ahead. If I had offered him a speech or a bookful of learnin', he would have said, "Oh, forget it!"

That was beginnin' business in a small way, wasn't it? But that is the only way to become a real lastin' statesman. I soon branched out. Two young men in the flat next to mine were school friends. I went to them, just as I went to Tommy, and they agreed to stand by me. Then I had a followin' of three voters and I began to get a bit chesty. Whenever I dropped into district headquarters, everybody shook hands with me, and the leader one day honored me by lightin' a match for my cigar. And so it went on like a snowball rollin' down a hill. I worked the flat-house that I lived in from the basement to the top floor, and I got about a dozen. young men to follow me. Then I tackled the next house and so on down the block and around the comer. Before long I had sixty men back of me, and formed the George Washington Plunkitt Association.

What did the district leader say then when I called at headquarters? I didn't have to call at headquarters. He came after me and said: "George, what do you want? If you don't see what you want, ask for it. Wouldn't you like to have a job or two in the departments for your friends?" I said: "I'll think it over; I haven't yet decided what the George Washington Plunkitt Association will do in the next campaign." You ought to have seen how I was courted and petted then by the leaders of the rival organizations. I had marketable goods and there was bids for them from all sides, and I was a risin' man in politics. As time went on, and my association grew, I thought I would like to go to the Assembly. I just had to hint at what I wanted, and three different organizations offered me the nomination. Afterwards, I went to the Board of Aldermen, then to the State Senate, then became leader of the district, and so on up and up till I became a statesman.

That is the way and the only way to make a lastin' success in politics. If you are goin' to cast your first vote next November and want to go into politics, do as I did. Get a following', if it's only one man, and then go to the district leader and say: "I want to join the organization. I've got one man who'll follow me through thick and thin." The leader won't laugh at your one-man followin'. He'll shake your hand warmly, offer to propose you for membership in his club, take you down to the corner for a drink and ask you to call again. But go to him and say: "I took first prize at college in Aristotle; I can recite all Shakespeare forwards and backwards; there ain't-nothin' in science that ain't as familiar to me as blockades on the elevated roads and I'm the real thing in the way of silver-tongued orators." What will he answer? He'll probably say: "I guess you are not to blame for your misfortunes, but we have no use for you here."

The Curse of Civil Service Reform

This civil service law is the biggest fraud of the age. It is the curse of the nation. There can't be no real patriotism while it lasts. How are you goin' to interest our young men in their country if you have no offices to give them when they work for their party? Just look at things in this city today. There are ten thousand good offices, but we can't get at more than a few hundred of them. How are we goin' to provide for the thousands of men who worked for the Tammany ticket? It can't be done. These men were full of patriotism a short time ago. They expected to be servin' their city, but when we tell them that we can't place them, do you think their patriotism is goin' to last? Not much. They say: "What's the use of workin' for your country anyhow? There's nothin' in the game." And what can they do? I don't know, but I'll tell you what I do know. I know more than one young man in past years who worked for the ticket and was just overflowin' with patriotism, but when he was knocked out by the civil service humbug he got to hate his country and became an Anarchist.

This ain't no exaggeration. I have good reason for sayin' that most of the Anarchists in this city today are men who ran up against civil service examinations. Isn't it enough to make a man sour on his country when he wants to serve it and won't be allowed unless he answers a lot of fool questions about the number of cubic inches of water in the Atlantic and the quality of sand in the Sahara desert? There was once a bright young man in my district who tackled one of these examinations. The next I heard of him he had settled down in Herr Most's saloon smokin' and drinkin' beer and talkin' socialism all day. Before that time he had never drank anything but whisky. I knew what was comin' when a young Irishman drops whisky and takes to beer and long pipes in a German saloon. That young man is today one of the wildest Anarchists in town. And just to think! He might be a patriot but for that cussed civil service.

Say, did you hear about that Civil Service Reform Association kickin' because the tax commissioners want to put their fifty-five deputies on the exempt list, and fire the outfit left to them by Low? That's civil service for you. Just think! Fifty-five Republicans and mug-wumps holdin' $3000 and $4000 and $5000 jobs in the tax department when 1555 good Tammany men are ready and willin' to take their places! It's an outrage! What did the people mean when they voted for Tammany? What is representative government, anyhow? Is it all a fake that this is a government of the people, by the people and for the people? If it isn't a fake, then why isn't the people's voice obeyed and Tammany men put in all the offices?

When the people elected Tammany, they knew just what they were doin'. We didn't put up any false pretenses. We didn't go in for humbug civil service and all that rot. We stood as we have always stood, for rewardin' the men that won the victory. They call that the spoils system. All right; Tammany is for the spoils system, and when we go in we fire every anti-Tammany man from office that can be fired under the law. It's an elastic sort of law and you can bet it will be stretched to the limit. Of course the Republican State Civil Service Board will stand in the way of our local Civil Service Commission all it can; but say!—suppose we carry the State sometime, won't we fire the upstate Board all right? Or we'll make it work in harmony with the local board, and that means that Tammany will get everything in sight. I know that the civil service humbug is stuck into the constitution, too, but, as Tim Campbell said: "What's the constitution among friends?"

Say, the people's voice is smothered by the cursed civil service law; it is the root of all evil in our government. You hear of this thing or that thing goin' wrong in the nation, the State or the city. Look down beneath the surface and you can trace everything wrong to civil service. I have studied the subject and I know. The civil service humbug is underminin' our institutions and if a halt ain't called soon this great republic will tumble down like a Park Avenue house when they were buildin' the subway, and on its ruins will rise another Russian government.

This is an awful serious proposition. Free silver and the tariff and imperialism and the Panama Canal are triflin' issues when compared to it. We could worry along without any of these things, but civil service is sappin' the foundation of the whole shootin' match. Let me argue it out for you. I ain't up on sillygisms, but I can give you some arguments that nobody can answer.

First, this great and glorious country was built up by political parties; second, parties can't hold together if their workers don't get the offices when they win; third, if the parties go to pieces, the government they built up must go to pieces, too; fourth, then there'll be h– – – to pay.

Could anything be clearer than that? Say, honest now; can you answer that argument? Of course you won't deny that the government was built up by the great parties. That's history, and you can't go back of the returns. As to my second proposition, you can't deny that either. When parties can't get offices, they'll bust. They ain't far from the bustin' point now, with all this civil service business keepin' most of the good things from them. How are you goin' to keep up patriotism if this thing goes on? You can't do it. Let me tell you that patriotism has been dying out fast for the last twenty years. Before then when a party won, its workers got every-thing in sight. That was somethin' to make a man patriotic. Now, when a party wins and its men come forward and ask for their rewards, the reply is, "Nothin' doin', unless you can answer a list of questions about Egypt-ian mummies and how many years it will take for a bird to wear out a mass of iron as big as the earth by steppin' on it once in a century?"

I have studied politics and men for forty-five years, and I see how things are driftin'. Sad indeed is the change that has come over the young men, even in my district, where I try to keep up the fire of patriotism by gettin' a lot of jobs for my constituents, whether Tammany is in or out. The boys and men don't get excited any more when they see a United States flag or hear "The Star-Spangled Banner." They don't care no more for fire-crackers on the Fourth of July. And why should they? What is there in it for them? They know that no matter how hard they work for their country in a campaign, the jobs will go to fellows who can tell about the mummies and the bird steppin' on the iron. Are you surprised then that the young men of the country are beginnin' to look coldly on the flag and don't care to put up a nickel for firecrackers?

Say, let me tell of one case. After the battle of San Juan Hill, the Amer-icans found a dead man with a light complexion, red hair and blue eyes. They could see he wasn't a Spaniard, although he had on a Spanish uni-form. Several officers looked him over, and then a private of the Seventy-first Regiment saw him and yelled, "Good Lord, that's Flaherty." That man grew up in my district, and he was once the most patriotic American boy on the West Side. He couldn't see a flag without yellin' himself hoarse.

Now, how did he come to be lying dead with a Spanish uniform on? I found out all about it, and I'll vouch for the story. Well, in the municipal campaign of 1897, that young man, chockful of patriotism, worked day and night for the Tammany ticket. Tammany won, and the young man determined to devote his life to the service of the city. He picked out a place that would suit him, and sent in his application to the head of the department. He got a reply that he must take a civil service examination to get the place. He didn't know what these examinations were, so he went, all light-hearted, to the Civil Service Board. He read the questions about the mummies, the bird on the iron, and all the other fool questions—and he left that office an enemy of the country that he had loved so well. The mummies and the bird blasted his patriotism. He went to Cuba, enlisted in the Spanish army at the breakin' out of the war, and died fightin' his country.

That is but one victim of the infamous civil service. If that young man had not run up against the civil examination, but had been allowed to serve his country as he wished, he would be in a good office today, drawin' a good salary. Ah, how many young men have had their patriotism blasted in the same way!

Now, what is goin' to happen when civil service crushes out patriotism? Only one thing can happen: the republic will go to pieces. Then a czar or a sultan will turn up, which brings me to the fourthly of my argument—that is, there will be h– – – to pay. And that ain't no lie.

Tammany Leaders Not Bookworms

You hear a lot of talk about the Tammany district leaders bein' illiterate men. If illiterate means havin' common sense, we plead guilty. But if they mean that the Tammany leaders ain't got no education and ain't gents they don't know what they're talkin' about. Of course, we ain't all bookworms and college professors. If we were, Tammany might win an election once in four thousand years. Most of the leaders are plain American citizens, of the people; and near to the people, and they have all the education they need to whip the dudes who part their name in the middle and to run the City Government. We've got bookworms, too, in the organization. But we don't make them district leaders. We keep them for ornaments on parade days.

Tammany Hall is a great big machine, with every part adjusted delicate to do its own particular work. It runs so smooth that you wouldn't think it was a complicated affair, but it is. Every district leader is fitted to the district he runs and he wouldn't exactly fit any other district. That's the reason Tammany never makes the mistake the Fusion outfit always makes of sendin' men into the districts who don' know the people, and have no sympathy with their peculiarities. We don't put a silk stockin' on the Bowery, nor do we make a man who is handy with his fists leader of the Twenty-ninth. The Fusionists make about the same sort of a mistake that a repeater made at an election in Albany several years ago. He was hired to go to the polls early in a half-dozen election districts and vote on other men's names before these men reached the polls. At one place, when he was asked his name by the poll clerk, he had the nerve to answer "William Croswell Doane."

"Come off. You ain't Bishop Doane, " said the poll clerk.

"The hell I ain't, you – – – –!" yelled the repeater.

Now, that is the sort of bad judgment the Fusionists are guilty of. They don't pick men to suit the work they have to do.

Take me, for instance. My district, the Fifteenth, is made up of all sorts of people and a cosmopolitan is needed to run it successful. I'm a cosmopolitan. When I get into the silk-stockin' part of the district, I can talk grammar and all that with the best of them. I went to school three winters when I was a boy, and I learned a lot of fancy stuff that I keep for occasions. There ain't a silk stockin' in the district who ain't proud to be seen talkin' with George Washington Plunkitt, and maybe they learn a thing or two from their talks with me. There's one man in the district, a big banker, who said to me one day: "George, you can sling the most vigorous English I ever heard. You remind me of Senator Hoar of Massachusetts." Of course, that was puttin' it on too thick; but say, honest, I like Senator Hoar's speeches. He once quoted in the United States Senate some of my remarks on the curse of civil service, and, though he didn't agree with me all together, I noticed that our ideas are alike in some things, and we both have the knack of puttin ' things strong, only he put on more frills to suit his audience.

As for the common people of the district, I am at home with them at all times. When I go among them, I don't try to show off my grammar, or talk about the Constitution, or how many volts there is in electricity or make it appear in any way that I am better educated than they are. They wouldn't stand for that sort of thing. No; I drop all monkeyshines. So you see, I've got to be several sorts of a man in a single day, a lightnin' change artist, so to speak. But I am one sort of man always in one respect: I stick to my friends high and low, do them a good turn whenever I get a chance, and hunt up all the jobs going for my constituents. There ain't a man in New York who's got such a scent for political jobs as I have. When I get up in the mornin' I can almost tell every time whether a job has become vacant over night, and what department it's in and I'm the first man on the ground to get it. Only last week I turned up at the office of Water Register Savage at 9 a.m. and told him I wanted a vacant place in his office for one of my constituents. "How did you know that O'Brien had got out?" he asked me. "I smelled it in the air when I got up this mornin'," I answered. Now, that was the fact. I didn't know there was a man in the department named O'Brien, much less that he had got out, but my scent led me to the Water Register's office, and it don't often lead me wrong.

A cosmopolitan ain't needed in all the other districts, but our men are just the kind to rule. There's Dan Finn, in the Battery district, bluff, jolly Dan, who is now on the bench. Maybe you'd think that a court justice is not the man to hold a district like that, but you're mistaken. Most of the voters of the district are the janitors of the big office buildings on lower Broadway and their helpers. These janitors are the most dignified and haughtiest of men. Even I would have trouble in holding them. Nothin' less than a judge on the bench is good enough for them. Dan does the dignity act with the janitors, and when he is with the boys he hangs up the ermine in the closet and becomes a jolly good fellow.

Big Tom Foley, leader of the Second District, fits in exactly, too. Tom sells whisky, and good whisky, and he is able to take care of himself against a half dozen thugs if he runs up against them on Cherry Hill or in Chatham Square. Pat Ryder and Johnnie Ahearn of the Third and Fourth Districts are just the men for the places. Ahearn's constituents are about half Irishmen and half Jews. He is as popular with one race as with the other. He eats corned beef and kosher meat with equal nonchalance, and it's all the same to him whether he takes off his hat in the church or pulls it down over his ears in the synagogue.

The other downtown leaders, Barney Martin of the Fifth, Tim Sullivan of the Sixth, Pat Keahon of the Seventh, Florrie Sullivan of the Eighth, Frank Goodwin of the Ninth, Julius Harburger of the Tenth, Pete Dooling of the Eleventh, Joe Scully of the Twelfth, Johnnie Oakley of the Fourteenth, and Pat Keenan of the Sixteenth are just built to suit the people they have to deal with. They don't go in for literary business much downtown, but these men are all real gents, and that's what the people want—even the poorest tenement dwellers. As you go farther uptown you find a rather different kind of district leader. There's Victor Dowling who was until lately the leader of the Twenty-fourth. He's a lulu. He knows the Latin grammar backward. What's strange, he's a sensible young fellow, too. About once in a century we come across a fellow like that in Tammany politics. James J. Martin, leader of the Twenty-seventh, is also something of a high-toner and publishes a law paper, while Thomas E. Rush, of the Twenty-ninth, is a lawyer, and Isaac Hopper, of the Thirty-first, is a big contractor.

The downtown leaders wouldn't do uptown, and vice versa. So, you see, these fool critics don't know what they're talkin' about when they criticize Tammany Hall, the most perfect political machine on earth.

On the Use of Money in Politics

The civil service gang is always howlin' about candidates and officehold-ers puttin' up money for campaigns and about corporations chippin' in. They might as well howl about givin' contributions to churches. A politi-cal organization has to have money for its business as well as a church, and who has more right to put up than the men who get the good things that are goin'? Take, for instance, a great political concern like Tammany Hall. It does missionary work like a church, it's got big expenses and it's got to be supported by the faithful. If a corporation sends in a check to help the good work of the Tammany Society, why shouldn't we take it like other missionary societies? Of course, the day may come when we'll reject the money of the rich as tainted, but it hadn't come when I left Tammany Hall at 11:25 A.M. today.

Not long ago some newspapers had fits because the Assemblyman from my district said he had put up $500 when he was nominated for the Assembly last year. Every politician in town laughed at these papers. I don't think there was even a Citizens' Union man who didn't know that candidates of both parties have to chip in for campaign expenses. The sums they pay are accordin' to their salaries and the length of their terms of office, if elected. Even candidates for the Supreme Court have to fall in line. A Supreme Court Judge in New York County gets $17,500 a year, and he's expected, when nominated, to help along the good cause with a year's salary. Why not? He has fourteen years on the bench ahead of him, and ten thousand other lawyers would be willin' to put up twice as much to be in his shoes. Now, I ain't sayin' that we sell nominations. That's a dif-ferent thing altogether. There's no auction and no regular biddin'. The man is picked out and somehow he gets to understand what's expected of him in the way of a contribution, and he ponies up—all from gratitude to the organization that honored him, see?

Let me tell you an instance that shows the difference between sellin' nominations and arrangin' them in the way I described. A few years ago a Republican district leader controlled the nomination for Congress in his Congressional district. Four men wanted it. At first the leader asked for bids privately, but decided at last that the best thing to do was to get the four men together in the back room of a certain saloon and have an open auction. When he had his men lined up, he got on a chair, told about the value of the goods for sale, and asked for bids in regular auctioneer style. The highest bidder got the nomination for $5000. Now, that wasn't right at all. These things ought to be always fixed up nice and quiet.

As to officeholders, they would be ingrates if they didn't contribute to the organization that put them in office. They needn't be assessed. That would be against the law. But they know what's expected of them, and if they happen to forget they can be reminded polite and courteous. Dan Donegan, who used to be the Wiskinkie of the Tammany Society, and received contributions from grateful officeholders, had a pleasant way of remindin'. If a man forgot his duty to the organization that made him, Dan would call on the man, smile as sweet as you please and say: "You haven't been round at the Hall lately, have you?" If the man tried to slide around the question, Dan would say: "It's gettin' awful cold." Then he would have a fit of shiverin' and walk away. What could be more polite and, at the same time, more to the point? No force, no threats—only a little shiverin' which any man is liable to even in summer.

Just here, I want to charge one more crime to the infamous civil service law. It has made men turn ungrateful. A dozen years ago, when there wasn't much civil service business in the city government, and when the administration could turn out almost any man holdin' office, Dan's shiver took effect every time and there was no ingratitude in the city departments. But when the civil service law came in and all the clerks got lead-pipe cinches on their jobs, ingratitude spread right away. Dan shivered and shook till his bones rattled, but many of the city employees only laughed at him. One day, I remember, he tackled a clerk in the Public Works Department, who used to give up pretty regular, and, after the usual question, began to shiver. The clerk smiled. Dan shook till his hat fell off. The clerk took ten cents out of his pocket, handed it to Dan and said: "Poor man! Go and get a drink to warm yourself up." Wasn't that shameful? And yet, if it hadn't been for the civil service law, that clerk would be contributin' right along to this day.

The civil service law don't cover everything, however. There's lots of good jobs outside its clutch, and the men that get them are grateful every time. I'm not speakin' of Tammany Hall alone, remember! It's the same with the Republican Federal and State officeholders, and every organization that has or has had jobs to give out—except, of course, the Citizens' Union. The Cits held office only a couple of years and, knowin' that they would never be in again, each Cit officeholder held on for dear life to every dollar that came his way.

Some people say they can't understand what becomes of all the money that's collected for campaigns. They would understand fast enough if they were district leaders. There's never been half enough money to go around. Besides the expenses for meetin's, bands and all that, there's the bigger bill for the district workers who get men to the polls. These workers are mostly men who want to serve their country but can't get jobs in the city departments on account of the civil service law. They do the next best thing by keepin' track of the voters and seein' that they come to the polls and vote the right way. Some of these deservin' citizens have to make enough on registration and election days to keep them the rest of the year. Isn't it right that they should get a share of the campaign money?

Just remember that there's thirty-five Assembly districts in New York County, and thirty-six district leaders reachin' out for the Tammany dough-bag for somethin' to keep up the patriotism of ten thousand workers, and you wouldn't wonder that the cry for more, more, is goin' up from every district organization now and forevermore. Amen.

4.2
Boss

Jonathan Kandell

If Plunkitt focuses on urban politics from the bottom up, this article looks at it from the opposite perspective. Kandell's article centers on William Marcy "Boss" Tweed, the kingpin of Tammany Hall in the 1860s. He describes Tweed's rise to power and eventual fall, concentrating on explaining the techniques Tweed employed.

When the official ceremony capping the restoration of New York City's historic Tweed Courthouse was held last December, the wily rascal who built it was back in the place he loved best—the spotlight. Although he never actually became mayor of New York, William Marcy "Boss" Tweed ruled and plundered the city so shamelessly in the years right after the Civil War that his name became synonymous with corruption and chicanery. But by now Tweed, too, has undergone something of a redo.

"He played an indispensable role because the city was growing exponentially in every direction and needed a politician with a strong hand and a broad vision at the helm," says Kenneth Jackson, president of the New-York Historical Society. Jackson, who is also a professor of history at Columbia University, even compares Tweed to former mayor Rudolph Giuliani. "The city was in such chaos back then that it needed someone—like Giuliani in September—who appeared to be in control."

According to Leo Hershkowitz, the historian who has been Tweed's most emphatic champion, "he was intensely loyal, warmhearted, outgoing, and given to aiding the underdog and underprivileged." Other Tweed authorities wonder whether anybody but a powerful crook could have pulled New York City together in that frenzied time. "Could honest men act as effectively as thieves?" asks urban historian Seymour Mandelbaum.

Decidedly not, Tweed himself asserted. "New York politics were always dishonest," he once told a committee investigating him. "This population is too hopelessly split up into races and factions to govern it...except by the bribery of patronage and corruption."

Tweed knew what he was talking about. Born in 1823, he grew up on the Lower East Side, which would soon be teeming with immigrants. His father, Richard, of Scottish descent, was an industrious chair maker who provided his wife and four children with a middle-class livelihood. But by mid-century it was impossible to escape the sights, sounds and smells of poverty. Life spilled out from the tenements and shops into the crowded streets. Sewage pipes burst during heavy rains. Pushcarts and horsedrawn wagons paralyzed traffic.

A youthful brawler and school dropout, at age 21 Tweed settled down and married Mary Jane Skaden, the daughter of a brush factory owner, with whom he had ten children. He joined his father-in-law's business and became the leader of the local volunteer fire company. A beefy six-footer, he enjoyed the rowdy bonhomie of the firehouse. He once surprised a colleague with a raucous bachelor party, leading a 25-piece band that awakened the man's entire neighborhood. Tweed "was young and good looking then, with fine dark brown hair and clear, gritty eyes," according to an acquaintance. "He was a tip-top dancer and never [lacked] a partner." But what excited Tweed most was beating rival fire companies to the scene of a fire. Running beside his mates as they pulled their fire wagon, he would blow a trumpet and shout: Jump her, boys! Jump her lively!"

In those years, fire fighting could be a pathway into politics, a career, Tweed admitted, that was "the only thing 1 get crazy on." With the backing of Tammany Hall, the notorious machine that had wielded power in Manhattan's Democratic Party for years, he became an alderman. Elected to Congress, he quickly grew bored in Washington and decided his future looked brighter back home. "As to spending my time hearing a lot of snoozers discuss the tariff and...the mails from Paducah to Schoharie, I don't think I'm [up to] doing that," he told a friend.

The New York City he returned to in 1855 had 630,000 inhabitants, more than half foreign-born, including 175,000 recent arrivals from Ireland and another 95,000 or so from Germany. Native-born New Yorkers recoiled from the mass of destitute newcomers, but Tweed viewed them as his natural constituency. After he was elected to the Board of Supervisors, which oversaw the financing of public projects throughout the city, he was able to court immigrants with jobs, welfare and street repairs. All he asked in return was their votes.

Meanwhile, Tweed was beginning to demonstrate the potent blend of gall and guile that would eventually boost him to Tammany's top tier. Presiding over a meeting to choose the Democratic nominee for a minor civil post, he realized that his own candidate would lose in an open vote. "Said I to the secretary: 'Have a motion made to dispense with the calling of the roll,'" Tweed later recalled. He then asked all in favor of his candidate to shout aye. "Carried! The meeting is adjourned!" yelled Tweed. Pandemonium broke out, and a pistol-waving delegate threatened to blow Tweed's head off. "I was scared, but I didn't say so," said Tweed, who managed to keep the gunman at bay just long enough to get away.

The Civil War widened the breach between the city's haves and havenots. The well-to-do could pay others to take their place in the army ranks, but the poor were saddled with conscription by lottery, and they rebelled. In July 1863, draft rioters battled police, looted and burned shops and homes, and lynched blacks. It took days to quell the uprising, which left hundreds dead and dozens of buildings destroyed.

The Board of Supervisors, urged on by Tweed, came up with an acceptable alternative to conscription, promising to pay some 30,000 "volunteers" $777 each for military service, a sum equivalent to about two years of an average worker's salary. The clever plan was financed not by raising taxes but by loans from banks and the state.

The end of the Civil War brought a dramatic upturn in New York's fortunes, but huge sums of money had to be spent for new railroads, streets, docks, warehouses and offices. Tweed placed several cronies—the so-called Tweed Ring—in key city posts. They included the former District Attorney, A. Oakey Hall, a silver-tongued playwright and actor who became Tweed's handpicked mayor. But just as important were the people he had placed on the Board of Supervisors. "Pretty nearly every person who had business or furnished supplies for [city] works had a friend in the Board of Supervisors...," Tweed later acknowledged.

In 1867 Tweed got himself elected state senator. By his own account, it cost him about $600,000 in bribes to convince the Senate to pass a charter granting a degree of home rule to the city, which gave New York more control over its budget and its ability to raise money.

It also vastly expanded Tweed's power, and much of it he wielded compassionately. He poured huge amounts of public funds into Catholic schools and charities. He improved water supplies, sewage disposal and streets. And because Central Park was far removed from most immigrant neighborhoods, Tweed built smaller parks nearer the poor. "He provided food and coal at Christmas, took women and children on summer boat rides, intervened on behalf of those who got in trouble with the law, and found jobs for people," says Mike Wallace, a historian at John Jay College of Criminal Justice in New York and coauthor of *Gotham: A History of New York City to 1898*. "But he was using the immigrants to consolidate his power base."

Tweed also reached out to the affluent. "He helped the elite with their cultural institutions," says Thomas Bender, an urban historian at New York University. "We wouldn't have the Metropolitan Museum of Art or the American Museum of Natural History had he not manipulated the state legislature to pass their charters."

Tweed managed this without raising taxes. Instead, the city issued bonds. New York's debt nearly tripled in four years. Most of it was held by banks and trust companies, and as old bonds fell due, new ones were issued to pay for them.

There was a huge hidden cost built into New York's development: the "commissions" charged by the Tweed Ring. Contractors doing jobs for the city were asked to hand in vastly inflated invoices for their work and then allowed to collect 35 percent of the total. Tweed, who had by then been chosen Grand Sachem, or leader, of Tammany, himself kept 25 percent, and the remaining 40 percent was doled out to associates. The Boss insisted that the bulk of his take went to pay off bureaucrats, politicians and judges as part of the cost of getting things done. "It was a time when there was no professional civil service or control over budgets," says Kenneth Jackson. "Tweed sort of ran the city like I run my house: Money comes in and out—and who knows where it's going?"

Tweed had other sources of enrichment, not the least of which were the political favors he did for such notorious robber barons as the financier Jay Gould and railway magnate Cornelius Vanderbilt. Gould, in return, rewarded Tweed with a seat on the board of his Erie railway.

But Tweed took special satisfaction from the times when the city's most upstanding businessmen had to swallow their pride and plead for his help. As Tweed later related, in 1868 construction of the Brooklyn Bridge was held up because Manhattan's $1.5 million share had not been approved by the Board of Aldermen. The head of the bridge company, Henry Cruse Murphy, was desperate. Tweed agreed to meet him. It would take $55,000 or $65,000 in bribes, Tweed told Murphy, to get the aldermen to pass the bridge appropriation. Murphy agreed and soon, or so the story goes, a bag with cash was sent to Tweed's office. Construction did not proceed, however, until the Boss himself had received 560 shares of Brooklyn Bridge stock worth $56,000, plus a seat on the board.

Tweed enjoyed flaunting his wealth. A story is told that one Christmas Tweed gave $50,000 to a Lower East Side immigrant district. He had initially announced a $5,000 donation but upped the ante when a judge shouted: "Oh Boss, add another naught to it." Tweed bellowed with laughter. "Well, here goes," he said, writing in the new amount.

He was an extravagant, exuberant host. His brawny good looks vanished as his body bloated to nearly 300 pounds. But at a Tammany Hall celebration, he was still agile enough to lead the party regulars in a mock tomahawk procession into the banquet room. He is said to have had his daughter's wedding done by Delmonico's, the legendary restaurant, for $13,000—almost twice his official yearly salary as a public servant. He kept large country house in Greenwich, Connecticut, and entertained intimates with lavishly catered cruises on two steam-powered yachts.

The collapse of the Tweed Ring came with unexpected swiftness in 1871. The cause was a spectacular boondoggle—the building at 52 Chambers Street in Manhattan that would soon be dubbed the Tweed Courthouse. Nearly a decade after work on it had begun in 1862, the courthouse still was not complete. Tweed, who as commissioner of public works was in charge of the project, declined to release budgetary details. Then, an obscure politician, James O'Brien, embittered because Tweed had failed to give him a satisfactory share of city graft, turned over the secret books to the *New York Times.*

The *Times* published a series of scathing stories on huge cost overruns. Among the revelations: the marble for the courthouse came from a quarry partly owned by Tweed. He and his cronies apparently felt so secure about bilking the city that they occasionally indulged in bits of sly humor. For example, a $33,283 check made out to one Fillipo Donnarumma was endorsed by "Phillip F. Dummy." Another check was paid to the order of "T. C. Cash."

And yet, in its design and materials, the courthouse was first-class all the way. "When you look at the quality of the stone and cast iron and stained glass and the attention to detail," says John Waite, the architect in charge of the building's recent restoration, "you have to conclude that even though Tweed may have taken a lot of money out of the construction, he still left behind one of New York's great landmarks."

Be that as it may, the courthouse scandal confirmed rumors that New York was borrowing excessively and that only a fraction of the money was making its way into tangible improvements. Banks refused to endorse new securities, and the city's credit rating plummeted. Even politicians who were deeply beholden to Tweed realized they had little choice but to turn their backs on him.

By then the press had transformed Tweed into a pariah. At the head of the pack was Thomas Nast, the *Harper's Weekly* cartoonist, who depicted the Boss as a leering, ham-fisted, obese giant swathed in garish three-piece suits. A rabid anti-Catholic, Nast was especially biased against the Irish, invariably portraying them as drunks with unshaven, apelike faces. Tweed feared Nast's acerbic cartoons more than he did the *Times'* stinging tirades. "I don't care a straw for your newspaper articles—my constituents don't know how to read," the Boss reportedly was driven to complain. "But they can't help seeing them damned pictures."

On October 26, 1871, Tweed was arrested on multiple charges. Not long after that, he was ousted from Tammany after landslide losses by the machine's candidates. As it turned out, it took two trials but prosecutors were able to convict Tweed for failing to audit claims against the city. That and a civil action to recover the city's money were enough to keep him in jail for many of his remaining years. Suffering from diabetes and a heart condition, he died at age 55 on April 12, 1878, in the Ludlow Street jail, a relatively comfortable facility he had helped finance a decade earlier.

On the day of Tweed's funeral, thousands gathered to pay their respects in front of his daughter's house on East 77th Street, where the coffin awaited transfer for burial. At the Tweed family plot in the Green-Wood cemetery in Brooklyn, newspaper reporters noted that most of the nearly 1,500 mourners present at the interment were poor New Yorkers who had somehow arranged round-trip transportation to that rural cemetery. No elected official of importance showed up.

Notwithstanding efforts by some historians to give Tweed his due, his ill repute lives on. Indeed, only a Republican mayor—Rudolph Giuliani, in 1999—could have approved the restoration of the courthouse, says John Dyson, Giuliani's adviser on the project. "The Democrats were too scared to take on something like this because it was linked to Tweed."

The building was used as a courthouse until 1926, after which it housed municipal offices. Located just behind City Hall, within a half mile of the site of the World Trade Center, it was pressed into service after September 11 as a rest and command center for firefighters and other rescue workers. Though covered with dust when the twin towers collapsed, it suffered no structural damage. Scraping away more than a century of grime and paint has revealed the sumptuous Tweed-era marble and multicolored brickwork on the walls and 28-foot-high ceilings. A spectacular laylight with flowers, birds, frogs and squirrels painted on amber-, ruby- and emerald-tinted glass has been replicated based on fragments of the original window found throughout the building. On the exterior, master stoneworkers, some of them born in China and trained in traditional masonry schools there, have extensively repaired the Neo-Renaissance pilasters and column capitals, whose cracked stone acanthus leaves were hanging precariously three stories above the street.

If Tweed has been watching the courthouse goings-on from some precinct clubhouse in the sky, it surely has not escaped his attention that the cost of the restoration—some $85 million—has turned out to be more than double the initial estimate. City officials say the building was in far worse shape than they thought.

The refurbished courthouse will not be used as such. Instead, sometime in the next two years, the Museum of the City of New York will relocate there from its current premises on upper Fifth Avenue. According to city officials, the museum, famed for its collections of historical photographs, costumes, furniture and decorative objects, will have to spend some $40 million more—before overruns—to turn the courthouse into a suitable venue for exhibitions. And with that, Tweed's monument to graft will become the main showcase for New York's proud history.

4.3

Underworlds and Underdogs: Big Tim Sullivan and Metropolitan Politics in New York, 1889-1913

Daniel Czitrom

In this essay, historian Daniel Czitrom tells the story of the rise to political power of "Big Tim" Sullivan at the turn of the twentieth century. Czitrom argues that Sullivan's acquisition of political status derives from Sullivan's creation of a new "public persona." What are the elements of that persona as described by Czitrom, and how does it explain Sullivan's political career?

I believe in liberality. I am a thorough New Yorker and have no narrow prejudices. I never ask a hungry man about his past; I feed him, not because he is good, but because he needs food. Help your neighbor but keep your nose out of his affairs…I never sued a man in my life and no man was ever arrested on my complaint. I am square with my friends, and all I ask is a square deal in return. But even if I don't get that, I am still with my friends.

–Timothy D. ("Big Tim") Sullivan, 1907

On April 17, 1889, members of the New York State Assembly crowded around an obscure young colleague as he angrily and tearfully defended himself against charges that he was the boon companion of thieves, burglars, and murderers. Timothy D. Sullivan had first been elected to represent the Five Points slum district of New York City in 1886, at the age of twenty-three. His accuser was the formidable Thomas F. Byrnes, chief inspector of the New York police department, hero of a popular series of mystery novels, and the most famous detective in the nation. Sullivan had angered the inspector by opposing a bill that would have given city po-

lice the power to jail on sight any person who had ever been arrested. After learning that his two saloons had been suddenly "pulled" for excise law violations and after reading Byrnes's denunciations of him in the New York press, Sullivan disregarded the advice of friends, rose on the assembly floor, and made what everyone agreed was an extraordinary response. "The speech," reported the *New York Herald*," was given in the peculiar tone and language of a genuine Fourth Warder, and while it was interesting in that respect to the countrymen, its tone was so manly that Tim gained much sympathy. If the Inspector's bill had come up today it would have been beaten out of sight."

Sullivan's defense consisted of an autobiographical sketch stressing his impoverished and fatherless childhood, the saintly influence of his mother, the necessity that he go to work at age seven, and his steady progress from bootblack and newsboy to wholesale news dealer. He had known some thieves in school and on the street, as there were a good many in his district. But Sullivan, in rejecting Byrnes's guilt-by-association charge, proudly detailed his own commitment to honest work "and outlined such a busy, struggling life that, when, at the conclusion, he asked if he had any time or money to spend with thieves, there was a 'No' on nearly every member's lips."

This story already contained the key elements of the "honest Bowery boy" narrative at the core of Tim Sullivan's enormous personal popularity and political power in New York. For the next twenty-five years, Sullivan effectively cultivated a public persona, the character of Big Tim, on the way to creating a new metropolitan political style. That style was rooted in a deep knowledge of city street life, particularly as experienced by the city's immigrant and tenement populations. It ingeniously fused traditional machine politics, the techniques (and profits) of commercialized entertainment, and influence within New York's underworld. Sullivan and his circle used it to accumulate enormous political and cultural power. Significantly, Sullivan consistently celebrated the strong guiding hand of women in his own personal development. That celebration translated into a social feminism combining support for woman suffrage and protective welfare legislation with the promotion of a heterosocial popular culture.

Hotly contested by politicos, journalists, business partners, and constituents, the public character of Big Tim had many sides. Sullivan himself left no private papers or diaries and only a few brief letters. Historians attempting to reconstruct the life and thought of the private man are utterly dependent on journalistic accounts, what others said about him, and attention to Sullivan's own construction of a persona. The battles over Big

Tim's true meaning and significance illuminate the complex connections among machine politics, the urban underworld, commercial entertainment, and the emerging welfare state. As a Tammany boss, Sullivan ruled the political districts below Fourteenth Street when that area had the highest population density and percentage of immigrants in the city. As an entrepreneur of vaudeville, amusement parks, and motions pictures, Sullivan amassed a personal fortune by consciously pleasing his public in entertainment as well as in politics. As a political protector of certain figures in the city's flourishing vice economy, he left himself open to charges from middle-class reformers that he was "King of the Underworld."

Over the years Sullivan countered those charges with an ethnic- and class-inflected rhetoric and restatements of his own personal honesty and probity. At the same time, he effectively socialized portions of the vice economy, particularly gambling and the alcohol trade, to support welfare activities in his district. Sullivan understood that the term *underworld*, popularized in the 1890s, was ambiguous, evincing contradictory meanings in the cosmopolis. The underworld was simultaneously a zone of pleasure for visiting businessmen, tourists, and slummers; raw material for journalists and guidebook writers; a potent political weapon for upstate politicians; an economic and organizational resource for Tammany Hall and the police department; and a space associated with the commercial amusements of the city. Sullivan understood, too, that enormous political and economic power could be created by exploiting the structural fact of transience so central to metropolitan life.

Sullivan was born on July 23, 1863, at 125 Greenwich Street, in a neighborhood and city still smoldering from the most violent and destructive civil rebellion in the nations' history. The racial, class, and political hatreds that had exploded in the draft riots only a week before, between Irish immigrants and blacks, tenement house dwellers and the uptown elite, and working poor and the Metropolitan police, would haunt the city's collective memory for decades to come. Sullivan's parents, Daniel O. and Catherine Connelly Sullivan, had been part of the great Irish migration into the city during the 1840s. Like many New York families of their class and background, the Sullivans moved frequently from tenement to tenement within the neighborhood near the lower Hudson River docks. For them, as for the vast majority of the half-million people packed into the roughly two-square-mile area south of Fourteenth Street, housing and health conditions were abominable.

Daniel Sullivan died around 1867, leaving his twenty-six-year-old widow Catherine, with four small children. She remarried soon after and moved, with her new husband, Lawrence Mulligan, an Irish immigrant laborer three years younger than herself, to the Five Points district in lower Manhattan. As the geographical center of the city's burgeoning Irish community, the Points had been notorious for decades as the worst slum in the nation. It was very likely the most thoroughly chronicled neighborhood in the United States, a favorite subject for city journalists, foreign visitors like Charles Dickens, and popular novelists. The 1870 manuscript census shows the Mulligan/Sullivan household of ten, including five children and three boarders, living in a packed wooden tenement at 25 Baxter Street. Dysentery, consumption, and heart disease had killed 3 of the building's 51 residents in the previous year alone. In the surrounding election district, 99 people had died out of a total population of 3,680, for an annual death rate of about 1 in 37.

If the less empathic sanitary inspectors of the day routinely labeled portions of the downtown population as ignorant and depraved, some also tried to distinguish the "poor, yet respectable, hard-working persons," or " the laboring classes,' from the "vicious, intemperate, and degraded." Such distinctions must have been especially important within a family not only struggling to get a living but also warring against itself. Tim Sullivan's stepfather, Lawrence Mulligan, was s violent alcoholic who beat his wife and children. His behavior led to Tim's early decision never to drink alcohol. In reminiscences about his life, Sullivan carefully excluded any mention of Mulligan's role or presence, an act of willful amnesia. The public construction of his childhood, so important to his political identity, would always emphasize the powerful presence of his mother, who took in neighborhood laundry to make ends meet, and his older sister, who went to work in a garment sweatshop when she was fourteen.

At age seven Sullivan started working on Manhattan's Newspaper Row, bundling papers for delivery at $1.50 per week. He also worked as a bootblack in the Fourth Precinct police station house on Oak Street. He completed his course at the Elm Street grammar school at age eleven and was eligible to attend the free high school on Twenty-third Street, but as he later recalled, "as free as it was, it was not free enough for me to go there." Sullivan gained his real education as he progressed to wholesale news dealer. He won a local reputation as a leader and patron of poor newsboys. "He not only furnished my working capital," recalled the Bowery writer Owen Kildare, "but also taught me a few tricks of the trade and advised me to invest my five pennies in just one, the best selling paper of the period." By age eighteen he was working for five different papers, establishing connections with news dealers all over the city, and serving as manager for a large circulation agency. His job took him as far north as Fifty-ninth Street and gave him an intimate knowledge of the city's geography in a time when most Fourth Warders might spend their entire lives without ever venturing above Fourteenth Street.

Sullivan, grown to over six feet tall and weighing two hundred pounds, with a round handsome face, bright smile, and piercing blue eyes, had an imposing physical presence that was an important asset in a day when local political careers frequently began as extensions of masculine prowess or athletic skill. The widely repeated story of how he won the Second District Democratic nomination for the state assembly in 1886, at age twenty-three, may well be apocryphal, but its persistent retelling reinforces this point. Sullivan, so the tale went, encountered a local prizefighter beating up a woman in front of the Tombs, the city prison on Centre Street. He intervened, conquered the rough in a fair fight, and thereby won great reputation among the male youth of the district.

Sullivan's 1889 fight with Inspector Byrnes attracted publicity from the city press and the attention of the Tammany leadership. It gave him a double-edged celebrity that would define the basic tension in his political persona; in future campaigns he would proudly recall how Byrnes's attacks "made a man of me." The *New York Times,* for example, supported Byrnes and attacked Sullivan for "attracting attention to himself and the criminal resorts which he keeps." A reporter assigned to visit Sullivan's small saloon on Doyers Street, right off the Bowery, cast himself as an explorer in a dangerous foreign land: "It is safe to say that there are not a hundred people in this city who live above Canal street who know where Doyers street is, and if they did they would shun it as a the plague....It is narrow and dirty, and in the day time is repulsive enough to keep anybody from trying to penetrate its mysteries, but at night, in addition to its ugliness, it looks dangerous."

Such newspaper attacks served only to increase Sullivan's standing with downtown voters and Richard Croker, the shrewd, taciturn, and menacing leader of Tammany Hall. After the electoral triumph of 1892, in which Tammany swept city offices and helped return Grover Cleveland to the White House, Croker made Sullivan the leader for the new Third Assembly District, a populous, polyglot area bisected by the Bowery, and not previously a Tammany stronghold. Sullivan sold off his saloons, won election to the state senate in 1893, and concentrated on creating the powerful fiefdom that would dominate the political life of lower Manhattan. A tightly knit group of literal and figurative kin ran this machine within the machine: first cousin Timothy P. ("Little Tim") Sullivan, a canny lawyer and political power in his own right; half brother Lawrence ("Larry") Mulligan; and three other Sullivan "cousins," the brothers Florence, Christopher, and Dennis Sullivan. By 1895, the *Tammany Times* hailed Big Tim as "the political ruler of down-town New York" and "the most popular man on the East Side." Tammany's enemies grudgingly acknowledged his district to be "the most perfectly organized and the strongest in New York."

Big Tim's election to the state senate in 1893 solidified the Sullivan machine's control of the Bowery district. This was a sprawling, multiethnic area of some three hundred thousand people, crowded into the tenement-lined streets surrounding Manhattan's busiest boulevard. The mile-long Bowery was the shopping and commercial center for a vast, largely foreign-born, and poor population. Workers with irregular hours (railroad men, streetcar drivers, printers, and restaurant employees), as well as transients and the unemployed, found shelter in Bowery lodging houses. These were jammed alongside theaters, concert saloons, lager beer gardens, dime museums, restaurants, oyster bars, pawnshops, clothing stores, and jewelry shops. At night the Bowery was "probably the most brilliantly lighted thoroughfare on this planet," a magnet for tourists, sailors, slummers, and others in search of a good time or a cheap place to spend the night. Late nineteenth-century observers had long noted the distinctly German flavor of Bowery life, but other languages, increasingly heard in the theaters, tenements, and shops, reflected the new immigration to Manhattan's Lower East Side: Yiddish, Italian, Chinese, Greek. Tammany Hall as an institution remained, of course, distinctly Irish, as reflected in the overwhelming number of Irish district leaders and patronage appointees. How to organize new immigrant voters and to make them regular Democrats in the face of strong Republican and Socialist appeals was the central political task facing the Sullivan machine.

Operating out of his modest three-story clubhouse, Sullivan hitched electoral politics to the commercial flash of the Bowery. Huge, carnivalesque summer chowders gave tenement dwellers a much appreciated escape to the country. Although these summer excursions were by no means invented by Sullivan, he developed them into a new sort of extravaganza, remembered by Al Smith and others as always the biggest Tammany affairs of the year. As many as ten thousand five-dollar tickets might be sold; but the great majority of those who came did not pay, obtaining their tickets from saloonkeepers, businessmen, and others who brought them in large bunches as campaign contributions.

The chowder began with Tim himself leading a street parade to an East

River dock where steamboats ferried the eager picnickers up to Harlem River Park or out to College Point, Long Island. The all-day celebration typically included a clam fritter breakfast, amateur track and field competition, fish and chicken dinner, beer, band music and dancing, and a late night return with torchlight parade and fireworks. Sideshow entertainments ran the gamut from impromptu prize fights to pickup baseball games to pie-eating contests to the awarding of a barrel of flour to the couple with the largest family. Gambling was ubiquitous, with stakes ranging from pennies to thousands of dollars. The assortment of games reflected the ethnic mixture of the crowds who eagerly played Italian *saginetto*, Jewish *stuss*, and Chinese *fan-tan*, alongside the less exotic poker, craps, and monte. Speechmaking was held to a minimum, but scores of politicians from all over the city paid their respects and mingled.

Sullivan's friendship with two older, Tammany-connected New York theatrical producers helps explain the enormous success of his chowders. Henry C. Miner, prosperous owner of five vaudeville theaters, preceded Sullivan as district leader in the Third and donated the clubhouse at 207 Bowery, next door to his thriving People's Theatre. After relinquishing the post to devote more time to his business and to run for Congress, Miner took the much younger Sullivan under his wing, introducing him to theatrical society in New York and Saratoga. An even closer ally was George J. Kraus, proprietor of two Bowery and Tenderloin concert saloons. Kraus's experience as a musician, caterer, bookkeeper, law clerk, and theater manager made him the perfect producer for these events. Sullivan and Kraus formed a partnership in 1896 that eventually managed several burlesque houses and music halls.

With his own origins in the crowded, life-threatening tenements of the Five Points, Sullivan understood the deep significance of democratizing public and commercial recreational space in the city. Tenement dwellers especially appreciated greater opportunities to get out of the house and enjoy themselves. As a state senator in the 1890s, Sullivan first grasped the possibilities for using state power to improve the living conditions of his constituents through his intimate involvement with the creation, sale, and regulation of commercial leisure. Sullivan championed a liberal policy of state licensing for leisure activities associated with the bachelor male subculture of the city, such as boxing and horse racing. In Albany, he led the movement to legalize and regulate professional boxing, and he had a commercial interest in several city athletic clubs that sponsored matches. After the turn of the century, he became more identified with protecting (and investing in) heterosocial popular amusements such as vaudeville, motion pictures, and Coney Island's Dreamland.

In the depression winter of 1894, Sullivan also started the tradition of feeding thousands of poor people a free Christmas dinner. Under the direction of Kraus, the suppers were served in relays to all comers by election district captains and other local politicians at Sullivan's Bowery headquarters, which could seat about 250 at a time. Enough turkey, ham, stuffing, potatoes, bread, beer, pie, and coffee were provided for as many as 5,000 hungry diners, most of them single men from the neighborhood lodging houses. Local vaudeville singers and musicians entertained at these feasts, once described by the senator as "the best Christmas meal every gotten up with the object of making people forget they are poor."

In 1903 Sullivan began giving away shoes and wool socks every February to as many as six thousand people who lined up for blocks around the Bowery clubhouse. The inspiration for this practice was a kindly female schoolteacher who had arranged to get the impoverished young Tim a free pair of shoes during one of the brutal winters of his childhood. Sullivan's charity was not, of course, the only brand available on the Bowery. But it was famous for its total lack of conditions—no distinctions made between the deserving and the undeserving, no hoe investigations, no questions asked. "Help your neighbor, but keep your nose out of his affairs," Sullivan said in 1907, explaining his creed. "I stand with the poet of my people, John Boyle O'Reilly, against the charity that only helps when you surrender the pride of self-respect: 'Organized charity, scrimped and iced,/In the name of a cautious, statistical Christ.'" The innovative food and clothing giveaways and the popular summer chowders were widely covered in the press. They became simultaneously the most tangible and the most symbolic expressions of the Sullivan base of support among lower Manhattan's tenement and floating population—those New Yorkers most vulnerable to the worst economic and social insecurities of metropolitan life.

The Sullivan machine was not all bread and circuses. It carefully organized the Bowery neighborhood using scores of loyal election district captains, each of whom might be responsible for an area containing several thousand people. A large number of the captains were Germans, Jews, and Italians; many were attorneys, liquor dealers, merchants, or the community influentials. Big Tim himself often led groups of workers in early morning treks to uptown public works, making sure the men got the employment he had promised them. He also regularly visited the city prison and local police courts, offering bail money, the promise of a job, or simple encouragement to petty thieves, vagrants, and other down on their luck.

In an era when the New York State vote frequently determined the outcome of presidential elections, Sullivan's controversial efforts to mobilize the Bowery's large, semitransient population had national implications. He employed street-level, physical intimidation at the ballot box both to control and to expand the suffrage. It was the latter that most troubled Sullivan's critics, as in 1893 when, during his state senate campaign, the *New York Herald* routinely stigmatized Sullivan's supporters as "bullet headed, short haired, small eyed, smooth shaven, and crafty looking, with heavy, vicious features, which speak of dissipation and brutality, ready to fight at a moment's notice." The *New York Tribune* appeared most disturbed by Sullivan's success with the lodging house men, as an editorial noted uneasily that district registration exceeded that for 1892, a presidential election year. During an 1984 state senate investigation into police corruption and election fraud, Big Tim. and Florence Sullivan were among those prominently accused of interfering with patrolmen assigned to maintain order at polling places and of physically beating Republican poll watchers who challenged voters' credentials. But none of the Sullivans were called to testify, perhaps because the Republican-dominated committee recognized that both parties were deeply implicated in the practices of machine politics.

Court records show that Big Tim himself personally bailed out men arrested on election law violations, putting up thousands of dollars in cash or pledging his own property as security. He also arranged for legal counsel from the pool of politically ambitious lawyers at the machine's disposal. The defendants were mostly Italians and Jews, often ex-cons, petty criminals, or aggressive district captains, eager to please their leaders by stretching the ambiguous registration and naturalization laws as far as possible. The Sullivan machine occasionally employed rival gangs for strong-arm support at election time, especially during the rare but bruising intra-Tammany primary fights. The largest and most notorious of these were the Jewish Monk Eastman gang and the Italian Paul Kelly Association, whose bitter feuding sometimes exploded into gunfire on Lower East Side streets.

The Sullivan machine's self-conception of its strength rested on a political version of the American work ethic and a notion of service that ironically inverted the ideals of genteel reformers. The Sullivans were nothing if not dedicated businessmen, political entrepreneurs as fiercely proud of their enterprise and as eager to chalk up success to individual initiative as any captain of industry. "All this talk about psychological power and personal magnetism over man is fine business for pretty writing," Big Tim observed in 1909,"but when you get down to brass tacks it's the work that does the business...It's just plenty of work, keep your temper or throw it away, be on the level, and don't put on any airs, because God and the people hate a chesty man." The Tammany leader was successful precisely because he was working at his business on the Fourth of July and Christmas, tending all year round to the personal obligations that translated into votes on election day.

Charges that the "King of the Bowery" was in reality "King of the Underworld" rang loudest at the turn of the century when Tim Sullivan emerged as the preeminent symbol of Tammany's connections with the carnal pleasure of gambling, drinking, prostitution, and commercial entertainments. With the creation of Greater New York, a vast metropolis of three hundred square miles and over three million people, the political stakes had never been higher. Charges that the city ran "wide open" became a regular, election-time rallying cry for Tammany's opponents. A crucial tactic for Sullivan's enemies was the elision of any differences between his interest in burlesque houses and his alleged profits from prostitution and "white slavery," or between his support for Sunday drinking and Sunday vaudevillian his supposed roles as head of a secret "vice commission" that controlled all of New Yorks' gambling.

For example, Sullivan and his partner George Kraus remodeled the Volks Garden Music Hall on East Fourteenth Street, previously a church, and reopened it in September 1898 as the fourteen hundred-seat Dewey Theatre, named for the hero of Manila. Sullivan's political clout ensured lenient treatment from municipal department responsible for fire safety and building permits and the continuation of a concert saloon license. The Dewey, with a novel policy of changing its program every week and presenting matinee and evening performances each day, quickly became one of the most popular theaters in the Union Square district. A typical program might include turns by singers, dialect comedians, performing monkeys, Irish clog dancers, chorus girls, acrobats, and pantomimists. Shows usually concluded with one-act musical burlesques with titles such as "King of the Hobo Ring," "A Wild Night in Washington," and "The Divorce Court." The black minstrel team of Bert Williams and George Walker appeared there regularly. Profits from the Dewey alone netted Sullivan around $25,000 a year, enabling him to purchase title to the property that first year for a reported $167,000 mortgage.

Sullivan's new burlesque and vaudeville house became an issue in the very close 1898 gubernatorial campaign in which Theodore Roosevelt narrowly defeated Tammany's Augustus Van Wyck, brother of Robert Van Wyck, mayor of New York City. To Frank Moss, prominent Republican attorney, counsel for the Society for the Prevention of Crime, and former city police commissioner, Sullivan's theatrical venture epitomized the wide open city. "What shall we say today," he asked a Cooper Union election rally, "about the Dewey Theatre, openly run with a city license, under police surveillance, patronized by men, women, and children, upon whose stage have been given those shows which have kindled unquenchable flames of passion in the breasts of hundreds of its patrons—a theatre boasting the Tammany cause, displaying the Tammany emblems, right opposite Tammany Hall." It was like all those "horrible concert halls and gardens besprinkling the Bowery and other streets in the city, running under license, which, while being by law under constant police observation, are patronized by men, women, and children, who see dances so immoral that the imported oriental dance of 'Little Egypt' would be a Sunday school lesson to their participants."

In fact, the accusations that echoed throughout the city press had all been aired the previous year in the course of the state assembly's Mazet committee investigation into city corruption under Tammany rule. Moss had served as the chief counsel for that strictly partisan, highly selective inquiry, an effort by the state Republican machine to embarrass Tammany. But the Mazet hearings resulted in no indictments or resignations and produced no political earthquake. The notion of a secret, highly centralized, perfectly controlled "Gambling Commission," attractive as it was to Tammany's opponents and the newspapers, was nonetheless impossible to prove. It was all untrue, claimed Sullivan. "It was here during the whole session of the Mazet committee. Why didn't they subpoena me? They know they have nothing against me. They make a lot of talk, but they haven't a particle of proof."

The most explosive and potentially damaging charge against Sullivan alleged that he directly profited from the growing prostitution trade on the Lower East Side. In the fall of 1900, an Episcopal bishop, Henry C. Potter, began to speak out publicly on the issue in response to complaints of open soliciting by prostitutes, pimps, and their runners on the streets and in the tenements. This was a sensitive point, too, for members of the expanding Jewish community, disturbed to see so many of their daughters and sisters forced by poverty into at least casual prostitution. An angry Richard Croker warned that any Tammany leader accepting vice tribute must resign, and he heatedly denied any personal involvement, declaring to his district chiefs, "Some people think that you leaders walk down to me every little while with handfuls of money collected from these people. I am not talking for political effect." Sullivan and his close ally, East Side district leader Martin Engel, had difficult private meetings with Croker, who announced creation of Tammany's own antivice committee for the purpos of investigating the moral conditions of the city. Skeptical reporters wondered out loud "how Martin Engel and Tim Sullivan make a living."

Sullivan became a special target of the fusion campaign that ousted Tammany in the vitriolic elections of 1901. William Travers Jerome styled his candidacy for district attorney "a movement against the protection of vice and crime," a strategy that helped sway many East Side Jewish voters from the Democrats. Jerome repeatedly attacked Sullivan, reviving and embellishing the old charges made by Inspector Byrnes in 1889. On his home turf, at Miner's Bowery Theatre, Sullivan dismissed Jerome as "a liar, a four carat lawyer, a collegiate." He ridiculed Jerome's threat to invade the East Side with outside poll watchers: "If Jerome brings down a lot of football playing, hair-mattressed college athletes to run the polls by force, I will say now that there won't be enough ambulances in New York to carry them away."

Did Sullivan and Engel, in fact, control and grow rich from the mushrooming East Side underworld, its prostitution, gambling, and related criminal activity? That is a difficult question to answer. Engel, one of the first Jews to achieve power within Tammany, no doubt had enormous authority within the increasingly Jewish redlight district centered on Allen Street. His brother Max owned 102 Allen, one of the most notorious fifty-cent houses in the neighborhood. But he manifested his real influence as a bail bondsman and fixer in the crowded halls of the nearby Essex Market Courthouse, the local police court. After making a fortune in the wholesale poultry business, Engel had begun to make himself useful to Tammany by regularly putting up various properties, worth around two hundred thousand dollars, as surety for accused criminals. By the mid-1890s Engel had come to dominate the day-to-day business of the Essex Market court, which, as the place where accused criminals directly confronted the police power of the state, was a critical site of political pull on the Lower East Side.

Some of Sullivan's loyal lieutenants on the Lower East Side undoubetedly had a direct involvement with prostitution, and they enjoyed some political and legal protection in exchange for financial contributions. For his part, Tim Sullivan always vehemently denied any personal connection to the prostitution flourishing below Fourteenth Street. "Nobody who knows me well," he declared in 1901, "will believe that I would take a penny from any woman, much less from the poor creatures who are more to be pitied than any other human beings on earth. I'd be afraid to take a cent from a poor woman of the streets for fear my old mother would see it. I'd a good deal rather break into a bank and rob the safe. That would be more a manly and decent way of getting money." No solid evidence ever emerged linking him to prostitution or white slavery. Nonetheless, shortly after the 1901 election, partly in response to all the unfavorable publicity, both Sullivan and Engel resigned their district leaderships. Their replacements were Little Tim Sullivan and Florence Sullivan. The latter quickly acted to deflect the vice charges against the Sullivan clan by personally leading invasions of East Side brothels, throwing furniture out on the street and roughing up neighborhood pimps.

Sullivan's main connection with the city's vice economy was gambling, not prostitution. He was himself a chronic, flamboyant, and, by all accounts, poor gambler, losing heavily at horse racing and cards all his life. He always tried to turn his habit to economic and political advantage by investing in gambling enterprises and insisting on a democractic approach to betting. Sullivan helped organize the Metropolitan Jockey Club and became a principal investor in its Jamaica racetrack. He offered protection to the scores of small pool rooms, policy joints, and stuss houses that dotted the East Side in exchange for using them as all-purpose hiring halls. Gamblers were expected to make five-dollar-per-day payments known as "CODs" to big Tim's friends and supporters, usually for doing nothing. Private social clubs throughout the East Side brought professional gamblers and professional politicans together across ethnic lines. The Hesper Club on Second Avenue, founded around 1900 and dominated by the Sullivan clan, was the most prestigious of these, a place where Irish and Jewish Democrats came together for fund raisers, poker parties, annual balls, and outings.

The 1901 election of Seth Low as mayor and the overall fusion sweep portended drastic changes for both Sullivan and Tammany as a whole. In 1902, after sixteen years as Tammany's leader, Croker, now a multi-millionaire largely through real estate investments, finally retired to breed racehorses at his English estate. Sullivan himself could have replaced Croker, but he preferred to maintain his semi-independent power base and, instead, threw his considerable influence behind Charles F. Murphy, who ruled Tammany until his death in 1924. With Murphy's ascendancy, Sullivan began to withdraw from direct involvement in city politics, preferring to stay in the backgound and concentrate on expanding his business interests.

He was elected to Congress in 1902 and 1904, but the House, dominated by Republicans, bored him. He missed the Bowery and declared that in Washington "they don't think any more of a congressman than they would of a wooden Indian in front of a cigar store. Why, they hitch horses to Congressmen whenever they want to use them." His stay in Washington, however brief, made him less of a provincial Tammany figure and opened his eyes to the commercial potential of national theatrical circuits. In 1904 he put up $5,000 to help John W. Considine, an ambitious theater manager in Seattle, purchase four small-time vaudeville houses in the Pacific Northwest. Considine had begun his career in the dance halls and honky-tonks of the Alaska gold rush, and with further financial assistance from Sullivan, he began mining the more lucrative Klondike of nationally organized vaudeville.

By 1907 the Sullivan-Considine firm controlled or owned about forty midsized theaters, mostly west of Chicago, as well as a very profitable booking agency. Some of the biggest names in early twentieth-century show business, including Charlie Chaplin and Will Rogers, got their start touring the circuit's popularly priced "ten-twent-thirt" houses, run by Considine with industrial precision. Sullivan's half interest in the company brought him as much as $20,000 a month, or around $200,000 each year. When the company sold its assets in 1914 to Loew Theatrical Enterprise (which added feature motion pictures to the live acts), the Sullivan estate's share of the stock was estimated to be worth at least $750,000.

Sullivan's involvement with the early New York movie industry brought a steady stream of income from another popular yet somewhat disreputable form of leisure. By 1908 Manhattan alone had some two hundred vaudeville houses, storefront nickelodeons, and penny arcades projecting motion pictures to audiences. Nearly one-third of these were concentrated on the Lower East Side, and although no official records of Sullivan's interest in this trade survive, both he and cousin Little Tim evidently received several thousand dollars each month from direct nickelodeon investments and the granting of informal licenses to operate in their territory.

As movies became a booming feature of the commercial amusement scene, the Sullivans made a political and business alliance with William Fox, the archetypal Jewish immigrant movie mogul. Fox pioneered the so-called small-time vaudeville that combined the cheap admission and movie program of the nickelodeon with live performances and a more "high-class" environment. In 1908 Fox paid $100,000 for a one-year lease on two Sullivan vaudeville theaters in prime locations, the Dewey on Fourteenth Street and the Gotham on One Hundred and Twenty-fifth Street. The trade press soon called the Dewey "the best run and most profitable" movie house in New York. Fox's relatively clean, comfortable theaters mixed seven or eight vaudeville acts with movies, attracted a more middle-class patronage, and anticipated the gaudy movie palaces of the teens.

Fox became a leader, too, in organizing New York City motion picture exhibitors in response to continual wrangling over city licenses and suits brought for violations of the Sunday blue laws. The key spokesman for Fox's interests and ultimately the Moving Picture Exhibitors Association was Gustavus A. Rogers, a Jewish attorney from the Lower East Side and longtime lieutenant for Florence Sullivan. Simultaneously, as Tammany leader on the Board of Alderman, Little Tim Sullivan led the fight for city ordinances allowing Sunday vaudeville and movies. Big Tim claimed in 1907 that "the best way to ruin a large cosmopolitan city like ours, which virtually lives off our visiting strangers, is to enforce or keep on the statute books such blue laws which don't belong to our age."

Sullivan had become a wealthy man and generosity with money was an important part of the mystique. His geniality about it perhaps reflected a keen personal satisfaction at having traveled so far from the desperate insecurity of his childhood. But the political charity may have also substituted for the home life Sullivan lacked as an adult. He married Nellie Fitzgerald in 1886, but they became estranged and had no children. An illegitimate daughter, born in 1896, surfaced publicly only after his death, during the fight over his estate. He had no real home, dividing his time between an apartment in the Bowery's Occidental Hotel, a house on East Fourth Street, Albany hotels, and long vacations to Europe and Hot Springs, Arkansas. Sullivan could have retired comfortably, but in 1908 he decided to return to the New York State Senate. Sullivan refocused his political attention on legislative work in Albany as he withdrew from city politics and the internal affairs of Tammany Hall.

In the final stage of his life Sullivan embodied and contributed to an important shift in Tammany and the Democratic Party—an expansion from a personal, service-based politics to one more centered on legislative achievements in social welfare. In the 1890s, as Robert F. Wesser has argued, Democrats stood basically for "personal liberty, negative government, and local autonomy." By the end of Word War I, they had become identified with an economic and social liberalism stressing "labor and social reform as well as a broad advocacy and defense of the interests and values of immigrant groups and ethnic minorities." Sullivan's last years in Albany both exemplified and furthered this change.

Sullivan had always publicly identified himself with the city's working class. Over the years he had quietly and effectively intervened in labor disputes and had persuaded large caterers and music hall proprietors to employ unionized waiters, bartenders, and musicians exclusively. While running for Congress in 1902 he had told supporters, "I never sat a day in the Senate without being glad as I wasn't on the front end of a motor car or on the rear, as a conductor." But in his final years in Albany he began translating his longtime rhetorical identification with working-class voters into important legislative achievements. A key collaborator in this last phase of his life was the young Frances Perkins.

In 1911, in response to massive, socialist-led organizing drives in new York City's garment district and in the aftermath of the disastrous Triangle Shirtwaist fire, Democrats in Albany set up the Factory Investigating Commission (FIC) to survey working conditions throughout the state. For nearly four years, under the leadership of Senator Robert F. Wagner and Assembly man Al Smith, the FIC conducted an unprecedented series of public hearings and on-site inspections that ultimately produced laws that dramatically improved state industrial conditions. Both Wagner and Smith were deeply affected by what they saw in the canneries, textile shops, and candy factories they visited. They were also changed by their collaboration with social Progressives such as Frances Perkins. Eventually appointed the first secretary of labor under Franklin D. Roosevelt, at the time Perkins was a lobbyist for the National Consumers' League and already an expert on comparative wage and hour rates around the state. Her first real political triumph, and the fight that brought her to public attention, was the passage in the final moments of the 1912 legislative session of the fifty-four-hour law limiting the hours of labor for about four hundred thousand women in New York factories.

In both published and private versions of that battle, Perkins portrayed Tim Sullivan as her first political mentor. Unlike Wagner, Smith, Charles F. Murphy, or the haughty young state senator Franklin Roosevelt, Sullivan impressed her as the only politician who accepted the principle of the bill and was willing to guide it through the rough shoals of the legislature. As Perkins recalled in interviews with an oral historian: "'Well,' he said, 'me sister was a poor girl and she went out to work when she was young. I feel kinda sorry for them poor girls that work the way you say they work. I'd like to do them a good turn. I'd like to do you a good turn. You don't know much about this parliamentary stuff, do you?'" With Sullivan's aid in the senate, she outwitted opposition to the measure by accepting an amended assembly version that exempted about ten thousand cannery workers—a compromise that neither manufacturers nor reluctant De-mocrats believed she would accept.

After a tumultuous, last-minute vote in which two wavers switched and voted no, the bill's supporters called for a reconsideration. Perkins frantically telephoned the boat dock where Big Tim and his cousin, Sen. Christy Sullivan, were just about to leave Albany for New York City, be-lieving the bill had safely passed. They rushed back to the capitol, running up the steep hill, "one red-faced and puffing, one white-faced and gasp-ing," and dramatically burst into the senate chamber. Their hands were upraised, and they were yelling to be recorded in the affirmative. The bill passed, and as Perkins recalled the scene, "The Senate and galleries broke into roars of applause....The Sullivans were heroes. I got some of it."

Sullivan tied his views on labor to an outspoken support for woman suffrage. "Years ago," he noted in a 1910 campaign speech, "if you stood on a corner most anywhere down here early in the morning you would see twenty men to one woman going to work. But it's different now. Now, there's about as many women going past the corner to work every morn-ing as there are men. They break about even. If women are going to be the toilers I'm going to give them all the protection I can." As one of the first prominent Tammany men to support the vote for women, Sullivan became a close ally of Harriot Stanton Blatch, leader of the Equality League of Self-Supporting Women. The two shared a basic understanding of the connec-tions between women's economic status and their political rights. Blatch, daughter of Elizabeth Cady Stanton, was part of a new generation of women leaders making a labor-based appeal for suffrage. "It is with woman as a worker that the suffrage has to do," she argued. "It is because she is the worker the state should have the value of her thought." Blatch combined militant street demonstrations with backroom political lobby-ing. She and Sullivan struck up a friendship during her regular trips to Albany to testify before legislative committees and press for suffrage bills. He told her that workingmen who came to Albany were listened to far more respectfully than working women. "And," Blatch wrote in 1912, "he has declared again and again that he wants to give women the same ad-vantage as men enjoy in dealing with the legislators who incline a listen-ing ear to the voters of their district." Sullivan made his argument repeatedly before the senate and also became a popular speaker before women's groups around the state.

Sullivan's views dovetailed with his defense of the broadest possible franchise, a politics of inclusion when it came to voting. Always sensitive about defending the voting rights of recent immigrants, casual laborers, the very poor, and transients in his district, he made an explicit analogy between women and blacks. Independent of the question of women's economic status, he told the senate in 1911, they deserved the suffrage. "Just recollect that less than fifty years ago you would not let a man vote on account of his color; because his color was not right he could not vote....It's going to come and you can't stop it." But opposition and fence straddling by Tammany powers like Murphy and Smith continued to help defeat woman suffrage measures in New York until 1917 when, four years after Sullivan's death, the urban immigrant vote provided the margin of victory in a statewide referendum.

Big Tim's political career came full circle with passage of the so-called Sullivan Law. The politician whose public identity had for years been routinely associated with the city's underworld authored the state's first gun control legislation, making it a felony to carry a concealed weapon and requiring the licensing and registration of small firearms. Sullivan introduced the measure partly in response to a marked increase in highly publicized violent street crime below Fourteenth Street. "The gun toter and the tough man—I don't want his vote," he insisted in his 1910 election campaign. "There are a lot of good, law-abiding people in the lower east side. They do not like to have the red badge of shame waved over that part of the city. They have no sympathy with the tough men, the men who tote guns and use them far too frequently."

Yet Sullivan remained a favorite target for sensational and nativist exposés. Writing in *McClure's* in 1909, George Kibbe Turner dredged up the twenty-year-old charges of Inspector Byrnes, portrayed Sullivan as a white slaver, and held him responsible for positioning Tammany to control the city primarily through its alliance with professional criminals. In an emotional campaign speech, made to a packed house at Miner's Bower Theatre, Sullivan responded by denying any involvement with prostitution and noting that he had made money from his theatrical interests. He paid special tribute to his mother and then moved the crowds with their melodramatic story of how a kindly female schoolteacher had arranged for him to get a free pair of shoes during a hard winter, thus inspiring his own grand of charity.

Sullivan's end was both bizarre and pathetic. He had decided to return to Congress in 1912, anticipating a national Democratic victory that could give him the influence in Washington previously denied him under Republican rule. He never took his seat. In July 1912 he began to suffer from severe mental disorders that included bouts of manic depression, delusions of food poisoning, violent hallucinations, and threats of suicide.

In September 1912, after the funeral of his wife, from whom he had been separated for many years, Sullivan had a complete nervous breakdown. Desperate family members had him committed to a private sanitarium in Yonkers. In January 1913, a sheriff's jury declared him "a lunatic and incapable of managing himself or his affairs" and implied that his illness was caused by tertiary syphilis—although this point did not make it into most press accounts. One doctor described Sullivan as "absolutely dominated by delusions of terrifying apprehension, fear, conspiracy, plot, attempts of poisoning, and efforts to do him bodily harm in every conceivable direction....He had an expression which was consistent with his mental trait. It was one of terror and depression, and it was impossible to divert his attention or to engage him in conversation in any subject whatever apart from the terrifying delusions and hallucinations." A court-appointed committee of family and close friends took charge of his business and personal affairs and shuttled Sullivan between sanitariums, trips to mineral baths in Germany, and private home care.

He lived out his last few months in the seclusion of his brother Patrick's country house in Eastchester, in the Bronx. He had virtually no contact with the press or his friends; the few who saw him found a haggard, thin, and melancholy man who occasionally brightened when talk turned to old Bowery days. Publicly, the family held out hope for recovery. He ran away a few times to the city by catching rides on freight trains, but he would inevitably call to be picked up. On August 31, 1913, during an all-night card game that had put his male nurses to sleep, Tim disappeared for the last time. For two weeks the city's press was filled with conflicting rumors and stories about his whereabouts. Old cronies swore to reports that they had seen and talked with him on the Bowery, or Fourteenth Street, or Fifth Avenue. Others feared suicide. Finally, on September 13, a patrolman assigned to the Bellevue Morgue recognized an unmarked, mangled body as that of Big Tim, just before it was to be shipped off for a pauper's burial in Potter's Field. Sullivan, it turned out, had been run over by a train on the night he slipped away, perhaps as he tried to hop a freight. The body of one of New York's best-known citizens had lain unidentified in the Fordham and Bellevue morgues for thirteen days before being sent downtown for final disposal.

As many as seventy-five thousand people lined the Bowery for a funeral procession described as one of the largest in New York history and remarkable for its class and ethnic diversity. "There were statesmen and prizefighters," the New York Sun reported, "judges, actors, men of affairs, police officials, women splendidly gowned and scrubwomen, panhandlers and philanthropists—never was there more strangely heterogeneous gathering." Even his oldest enemies now recognized that he could not be dismissed as merely the chum of criminals. As the *New York World* put it, "he welcomed the title of 'King of the Underworld' in the sense that he had won his kingship through his friendship for the underdog."

His career and fortune were rooted in the merger of politics and show business. Sullivan thus helped shape a key feature of modern American life. His power had rested upon an uncanny and shrewd melding of job patronage and legal services, charity and poor relief, urban carnival, protection of gambling and the saloon trade, and tolerance for a broad range of commercial entertainments. He supported the vote for women and their full inclusion in the newly emerging world of mass culture. Sullivan's sensitivity to women's issues no doubt reflected his own female-centered upbringing. But in a deeper sense, the evolution of Sullivan's metropolitan style suggests that an explicit ideology of gender informed the political and legislative agenda of the emerging welfare state. Above all, as a pure product of life among the city's poorest tenement Irish, Big Tim saw as no one else before him the political and cultural power latent in an urban underclass too easily dismissed as inherently criminal, depraved and vicious.

4.4

The Ten Commandments of the Grange (1874)

The National Grange of the Patrons of Husbandry, or simply the Grange, as it was known, was created in 1867 and became the most important farm organization of its day. Strongest in the Midwest, the Grange tried to help break down the isolation of rural life by giving farmers a communal outlet for social and educational activities. It eventually became a political force in several Midwestern states for a brief time in the 1870s. This document provides insight into the philosophy of the Grange. According to this entry, what problems do farmers face? What solutions to those problems are proposed here?

1. Thou shalt love the Grange with all thy heart and with all thy soul and thou shalt love thy brother granger as thyself.

2. Thou shalt not suffer the name of the Grange to be evil spoken of, but shall severely chastise the wretch who speaks of it with contempt.

3. Remember that Saturday is Grange day. On it thou shalt set aside thy hoe and rake, and sewing machine, and wash thy-self, and appear before the Master in the Grange with smiles and songs, and hearty cheer. On the fourth week thou shalt not appear empty handed, but shalt thereby bring a pair of ducks, a turkey roasted by fire, a cake baked in the oven, and pies and fruits in abundance for the Harvest Feast. So shalt thou eat and be merry, and "frights and fears" shall be remembered no more.

From "The Ten Commandments of the Grange," *Oshkosh Weekly Times,* 16 December 1874. Reprinted in D. Sven Nordin, *Rich Harvest: A History of the Grange, 1876–1900* (Jackson: University Press of Mississippi, 1974).

4. Honor thy Master, and all who sit in authority over thee, that the days of the Granges may be long in the land which Uncle Sam hath given thee.

5. Thou shalt not go to law.

6. Thou shalt do no business on tick. Pay as thou goest, as much as in thee lieth.

7. Thou shalt not leave thy straw but shalt surely stack it for thy cattle in the winter.

8. Thou shalt support the Granger's store for thus it becometh thee to fulfill the laws of business.

9. Thou shalt by all means have thy life insured in the Grange Life Insurance Company, that thy wife and little ones may have friends when thou art cremated and gathered unto thy fathers.

10. Thou shalt have no Jewish middlemen between thy farm and Liverpool to fatten on thy honest toil, but shalt surely charter thine own ships, and sell thine own produce, and use thine own brains. This is the last and best commandment. On this hang all the law, and profits, and if there be any others they are these.

    Choke monopolies, break up rings, vote for honest men, fear God and make money. So shalt thou prosper and sorrow and hard times shall flee away.

4.5
Platform (1892)

Populist Party

The People's, or Populist, Party was formed in 1892 as a major third-party challenge to Republicans and Democrats. It comes directly out of the Farmers' Alliance movement of the 1870s and 1880s, but the Populists also claim the Grange as one of its ancestors. This platform indicates that the Populists have much in common with Grangers. How do the Populists describe the state of affairs in 1890s America, and how does that description compare with that in Document 4.3? What solutions do the Populists offer as a way out of the degraded condition in which farmers find themselves? Why does the federal government play such a prominent role in those solutions?

Assembled upon the 116th anniversary of the Declaration of Independence, People's Party of America, in their first national convention, invoking upon their action the blessing of Almighty God, puts forth, in the name and on behalf of the people of this country, the following preamble and declaration of principles:—

PREAMBLE:

The conditions which surround us best justify our cooperation: we meet in the midst of a nation brought to the verge of moral, political, and material ruin. Corruption dominates the ballot-box, the legislatures, the Congress, and touches even the ermine of the bench. The people are demoralized; most of the States have been compelled to isolate the voters at the polling-places to prevent universal intimidation or bribery. The newspapers are largely subsidized or muzzled; public opinion silenced; business prostrated; our homes covered with mortgages; labor impoverished; and the land concentrating in the hands of the capitalists. The urban workmen are denied the right of organization for self-protection; imported pauperized labor beats down their wages; a hireling standing army, unrecognized by our laws, is established to shoot them down, and they are rapidly degenerating into European conditions. The fruits of the toil of millions are boldly stolen to build up colossal fortunes for a few, unprecedented in the history of mankind; and the possessors of these, in turn, despise the republic and endanger liberty. From the same prolific womb of governmental injustice we breed the two great classes tramps and millionaires.

The national power to create money is appropriated to enrich bondholders; a vast public debt, payable in legal tender currency, has been funded into gold-beating bonds, thereby adding millions to the burdens of the people.

Silver, which has been accepted as coin since the dawn of history, has been demonetized to add to the purchasing power of gold by decreasing the value of all forms of property as well as human labor; and the supply of currency is purposely abridged to fatten usurers, bankrupt enterprise, and enslave industry. A vast conspiracy against mankind has been organized on two continents, and it is rapidly taking possession of the world. If not met and overthrown at once, it forebodes terrible social convulsions, the destruction of civilization, or the establishment of an absolute despotism.

We have witnessed for more than a quarter of a century the struggles of the two great political parties for power and plunder, while grievous wrongs have been inflicted upon the suffering people. We charge that the controlling influences dominating both these parties have permitted the existing dreadful conditions to develop without serious effort to prevent or restrain them. Neither do they now promise us any substantial reform. They have agreed together to ignore in the coming campaign every issue but one. They propose to drown the outcries of a plundered people with the uproar of a sham battle over the tariff, so that capitalists, corporations, national banks, rings, trusts, watered stock, the demonetization of silver, and the oppressions of the usurers may all be lost sight of. They propose to sacrifice our homes, lives and children on the altar of mammon; to destroy the multitude in order to secure corruption funds from the millionaires.

Assembled on the anniversary of the birthday of the nation, and filled with the spirit of the grand general and chieftain who established our independence, we seek to restore the government of the Republic to the hands of "the plain people," with whose class it originated. We assert our purposes to be identical with the purposes of the National Constitution, "to form a more perfect union and establish justice, insure domestic tranquillity, provide for the common defence, promote the general welfare, and secure the blessings of liberty for ourselves and our posterity." We declare that this republic can only endure as a free government while built upon the love of the whole people for each other and for the nation; that it cannot be pinned together by bayonets; that the civil war is over, and that every passion and resentment which grew out of it must die with it; and that we must be in fact, as we are in name, one united brotherhood of freemen.

Our country finds itself confronted by conditions for which there is no precedent in the history of the world; our annual agricultural productions amount to billions of dollars in value, which must, within a few weeks or months, be exchanged for billions of dollars of commodities consumed in their production; the existing currency supply is wholly inadequate to make this exchange; the results are falling prices, the formation of combines and rings, the impoverishment of the producing class. We pledge ourselves, if given power, we will labor to correct these evils by wise and reasonable legislation, in accordance with the terms of our platform. We believe that the powers of government—in other words, of the people—should be expanded (as in the case of the postal service) as rapidly and as far as the good sense of an intelligent people and the teachings of experience shall justify, to the end that oppression, injustice, and poverty shall eventually cease in the land.

While our sympathies as a party of reform are naturally upon the side of every proposition which will tend to make men intelligent, virtuous, and temperate, we nevertheless regard these questions—important as they are—as secondary to the great issues now pressing for solution, and upon which not only our individual prosperity but the very existence of free institutions depends; and we ask all men to first help us to determine whether we are to have a republic to administer before we differ as to the conditions upon which it is to be administered; believing that the forces of reform this day organized will never cease to move forward until every wrong is remedied, and equal rights and equal privileges securely established for all the men and women of this country.

We declare, therefore,—

First. That the union of the labor forces of the United States this day consummated shall be permanent and perpetual; may its spirit enter all hearts for the salvation of the republic and the uplifting of mankind!

Second. Wealth belongs to him who creates it, and every dollar taken from industry without an equivalent is robbery. "If any will not work, neither shall he eat." The interests of rural and civic labor are the same; their enemies are identical.

Third. We believe that the time has come when the railroad corporations will either own the people or the people must own the railroads; and, should the government enter upon the work of owning and managing all railroads, we should favor an amendment to the Constitution by which all persons engaged in the government service shall be placed under a civil service regulation of the most rigid character, so as to prevent the increase of the power of the national administration by the use of such additional government employees.

First, *Money.* We demand a national currency, safe, sound, and flexible, issued by the general government only, a full legal tender for all debts, public and private, and that, without the use of banking corporations, a just, equitable, and efficient means of distribution direct to the people, at a tax not to exceed two per cent per annum, to be provided as set forth in the subtreasury plan of the Farmers' Alliance, or a better system; also, by payments in discharge of its obligations for public improvements.

- We demand free and unlimited coinage of silver and gold at the present legal ratio of sixteen to one.
- We demand that the amount of circulating medium be speedily increased to not less than fifty dollars per capita.
- We demand a graduated income tax.
- We believe that the money of the country should be kept as much as possible in the hands of the people, and hence we demand that I all state and national revenues shall be limited to the necessary expenses of the government economically and honestly administered.
- We demand that postal savings banks be established by the government for the safe deposit of the earnings of the people and to facilitate exchange.

Second, *Transportation.* Transportation being a means of exchange and a public necessity, the government should own and operate the railroads in the interest of the people.

- The telegraph and telephone, like the post-office system, being a necessity for the transmission of news, should be owned and operated by the government in the interest of the people.

Third, *Land.* The land, including all the natural sources of wealth, is the heritage of the people, and should not be monopolized for speculative purposes, and alien ownership of land should be prohibited. All land now held by railroads and other corporations in excess of their actual needs, and all lands now owned by aliens, should be reclaimed by the government and held for actual settlers only.

RESOLUTIONS

Whereas, Other questions have been presented for our consideration, we hereby submit the following, not as a part of the platform of the People's party, but as resolutions expressive of the sentiment of this convention.

- *Resolved,* That we demand a free ballot and a fair count in all elections, and pledge ourselves to secure it to every legal voter without federal intervention, through the adoption by the States of the unperverted Australian or secret ballot system.
- *Resolved,* That the revenue derived from a graduated income tax should be applied to the reduction of the burden of taxation now resting upon the domestic industries of this country.
- *Resolved,* That we pledge *our* support to fair and liberal pensions to ex-Union soldiers and sailors.
- *Resolved,* That we condemn the fallacy of protecting American labor under the present system, which opens our ports to the pauper and criminal classes of the world, and crowds out our wage-earners; and we denounce the present ineffective laws against contract labor, and demand the further restriction of undesirable immigration.
- *Resolved,* That we cordially sympathize with the efforts of organized workingmen to shorten the hours of labor, and demand a rigid enforcement of the existing eight-hour law on government work, and ask that a penalty clause be added to the said law.

- *Resolved,* That we regard the maintenance of a large standing army of mercenaries, known as the Pinkerton system, as a menace to our liberties, and we demand its abolition; and we condemn *the recent invasion of the Territory of Wyoming* by the hired assassins of plutocracy, assisted by federal officials.
- *Resolved,* That we commend to the favorable consideration of the people and the reform press the legislative system known as the initiative and referendum.
- *Resolved,* That we favor a constitutional provision limiting the office of President and Vice-President to one term, and providing for the election of senators of the United States by a direct vote of the people.
- *Resolved,* That we oppose any subsidy or national aid to any private corporation for any purpose.
- *Resolved,* That this convention sympathizes with the Knights of Labor and their righteous contest with the tyrannical combine of clothing manufacturers of Rochester, and declares it to be the duty of all who hate tyranny and oppression to refuse to purchase the goods made by said manufacturers, or to patronize any merchants who sell such goods.

CHAPTER 5

Immigration and Popular Culture, 1880–1920

5.1   Jacob Riis, "The Bohemians and Tenement-House Cigarmaking" (1890)

5.2   John Higham, "Strangers in the Land"

5.3   "Restrictions on Chinese Immigration" (1892)

5.4   Madison Grant, "Survival of the Unfit" (1918)

5.5   Josiah Strong, "Our Country" (1886)

5.6   *New York Times*, "Opening Night at Coney Island" (1904)

5.7   Steven A. Riess, "The Social Functions of Baseball"

5.1

The Bohemians — Tenement-house Cigarmaking (1890)

Jacob Riis

This chapter from Riis's famous book, How the Other Half Lives, *describes the living and working conditions of immigrants from Bohemia on the Lower East Side of New York City. What picture of immigrant life does Riis create here? How does he account for the conditions he depicts, and what solution does he foresee to the problems the Bohemians face?*

Evil as the part is which the tenement plays in Jewtown as the pretext for circumventing the law that was made to benefit and relieve the tenant, we have not far to go to find it in even a worse role. If the tenement is here continually dragged into the eye of public condemnation and scorn, it is because in one way or another it is found directly responsible for, or intimately associated with, three-fourths of the miseries of the poor. In the Bohemian quarter it is made the vehicle for enforcing upon a proud race a slavery as real as any that ever disgraced the South. Not content with simply robbing the tenant, the owner, in the dual capacity of landlord and employer, reduces him to virtual serfdom by making his becoming his tenant, on such terms as he sees fit to make, the condition of employment at wages likewise of his own making. It does not help the case that this landlord employer, almost always a Jew, is frequently of the thrifty Polish race just described.

Perhaps the Bohemian quarter is hardling the proper name to give to the colony, for though it has distinct boundaries it is scattered over a wide area on the East Side, in wedge-like streaks that relieve the monotony of the solid German population by their strong contrasts. The two races mingle no more on this side of the Atlantic than on the rugged slopes of the Bohemian mountains; the echoes of the thirty years' war ring in New York, after two centuries and a half, with as fierce a hatred as the gigantic com-

From *How the Other Half Lives:* Studies Among the Tenements in New York, 1890.

bat bred among the vanquished Czechs. A chief reason for this is doubt-less the complete isolation of the Bohemian immigrant. Several causes operate to bring this about: his singularly harsh and unattractive language, which he can neither easily himself unlearn nor impart to others, his stub-born pride of race, and a popular prejudice which has forced upon him the unjust stigma of a disturber of the public peace and an enemy of organized labor. I greatly mistrust that the Bohemian on our shores is a much-abused man. To his traducer, who cast up anarchism against him, he replies that the last census (1880) shows his people to have the fewest criminals of all in proportion to numbers. In New York a Bohemian crim-inal is such a rarity that the case of two firebugs of several years ago is re-member with damaging distinctness. The accusation that he lives like the "rat" he is, cutting down wages by this underpaid labor, he throws back in the teeth of the trades unions with the counter-charge that they are the first cause of his attitude to the labor question.

A little way above Houston Street the first of his colonies is encoun-tered, in Fifth Street and thereabouts. Then for a mile and a half scarce a Bohemian is to be found, until Thirty-eighth Street is reached. Fifty-fourth and Seventy-third Streets in their turn are the centres of populous Bohemian settlements. The location of the cigar factories, upon which he depends for a living, determines his choice of home, though there is less choice about it than with any other class in the community, save perhaps the colored people. Probably more than half of all the Bohemians in this city are cigarmakers, and it is the herding of these in great numbers in the so-called tenement factories, where the cheapest grade of work is done at the lowest wages, that constitutes at once their greatest hardship and the chief grudge of other workmen against them. The manufacturer who owns, say, from three to four to a dozen or more tenements continuous to his shop, fills them up with these people, charging them outrageous rents, and demanding often even a preliminary deposit of five dollars "key money"; deals them out tobacco by the week, and devotes the rest of his energies to the paring down of wages to within the peg or two of the point where the tenant rebels in desperation. When he does rebel, he is given the alternative of submission, or eviction with entire loss of employment. His needs determine the issue. Usually he is not in a position to hesitate long. Unlike the Polish Jew, whose example of untiring industry he emulates, he has seldom much laid up against a rainy day. He is fond of a glass of beer, and likes to live as well as his means will permit. The shop triumphs, and fetters more galling than ever are forged for the tenant. In the oppo-site case, the newspapers have to record the throwing upon the street of a small army of people, with pitiful cases of destitution and family misery.

Men, women and children work together seven days in the week in these cheerless tenements to make a living for the family, from the break of day till far into the night. Often the wife is the original cigarmaker from the old home, the husband having adopted her trade here as a matter of necessity, because, knowing no word of English, he could get no other work. As they state the cause of the bitter hostility of the trades unions, she was the primary bone of contention in the day of the early Bohemian immigration. The unions refused to admit the women, and, as the support of the family depended upon her to a large extent, such terms as were offered had to be accepted. The manufacturer has ever since industriously fanned the antagonism between the unions and his hands, for his own advantage. The victory rests with him, since the Court of Appeals decided that the law, passed a few years ago, to prohibit cigarmaking in tenements was unconstitutional, and thus put an end to the struggle. While it lasted, all sorts of frightful stories were told of the shocking conditions under which people lived and worked in these tenements, from a sanitary point of view especially, and a general impression survives to this day that they are particularly desperate. The Board of Health, after a careful canvass, did not find them so then. I am satisfied from personal inspection, at much a later day, guided in a number of instances by the union cigarmakers themselves to the tenements which they considered the worst, that the accounts were greatly exaggerated. Doubtless the people were poor, in many cases very poor; but they are not uncleanly, rather the reverse; they live much better than the clothing-makers in the Tenth Ward, and in spite of their sallow look, that may be due to the all-pervading smell of tobacco, they do not appear to be less healthy than other in-door workers. I found on my tours of investigation several cases of consumption, of which one at least was said by the doctor to be due to the constant inhalation of tobacco fumes. But an examination of the death records in the Health Department does not support the claim that the Bohemian cigarmakers are peculiarly prone to that disease. On the contrary, the Bohemian percentage of deaths from consumption appears quite low. This, however, is a line of scientific inquiry which I leave to others to pursue, along with the more involved problem whether the falling off in the number of children, sometimes quite noticeable in the Bohemian settlements, is, as has been suggested, depend upon the character of the parent's work. The sore grievances I found were the miserable wages and the enormous rents exacted for the minimum of accommodation. And surely these stand for enough of suffering.

Take a row of houses in East Tenth Street as an instance. They contained thirty-five families of cigarmakers, with probably not half a dozen persons in the whole lot of them, outside of the children, who could speak a word of English, though many had been in the country half a lifetime. This room with two windows giving on the street, and a rear attachment without windows, called a bedroom by courtesy, is rented at $12.25 a month. In the front room man and wife work at the bench from six in the morning till nine at night. They make a team, stripping the tobacco leaves together; then he makes the filler, and she rolls the wrapper on and finishes the cigar. For a thousand they receive $3.75, and can turn out together three thousand cigars a week. The point has been reached where the rebellion comes in, and the workers in these tenements are just now on a strike, demanding $5.00 and $5.50 for their work. The manufacturer having refused, they are expecting hourly to be served with notice to quit their homes, and the going of a stranger among them excite their resentment, until his errand is explained,. While we are in the house, the ultimatum of the "boss" is received. He will give $3.75 a thousand, not another cent. Our host is a man of seeming intelligence, yet he has been nine years in New York and know neither English nor German. Three bright little children play about the floor.

His neighbor on the same floor has been here fifteen years, but shakes his head when asked if he can speak English. He answers in a few broken syllables when addressed in German. With $11.75 rent to pay for like accommodation, he has the advantage of his oldest boy's work besides his wife's at the bench. Three properly make a team, and these three can turn out four thousand cigars a week, at $3.75. This Bohemian has a large family; there are four children, too small to work, to be cared for. A comparison of the domestic bills of fare in Tenth and in Ludlow Streets results in the discovery that this Bohemian's butcher's bill for the week, with meat at twelve cents a pounds as in Ludlow Street, is from two dollars and a half to three dollars. The Polish Jew fed as big a family one pound of meat a day. The difference proves to by typical. Here is a suite of three rooms, two dark, three flights up. The ceiling is partly down in one of the rooms. "It is three months since we asked the landlord to fix it," says the oldest son, a very intelligent lad who has learned English in the evening school. His father has not had that advantage, and has sat at his bench, deaf and dumb to the world about him except his own, for six years. He has improved his time and become an expert at his trade. Father, mother and son together, a full team, make from fifteen to sixteen dollars a week.

A man with venerable beard and keen eyes answers our questions through an interpreter, in the next house. Very few brighter faces would be met in a day's walk among American mechanics, yet he has in nine years learned no syllable of English. German he probably does not want to learn. His story supplies the explanation, as did the stories of the others. In all that time he has been at work grubbing to earn bread. Wife and he by constant labor make three thousand cigars a week, earning $11.25 when there is no lack of material; when in winter they receive from the manufacturer tobacco for only two thousand, the rent of $10 for two rooms practically one with a dark alcove, has nevertheless to be paid in full, and six mouths to be fed. He was a blacksmith in the old country, but cannot work at his trade here because he does not understand "Engliska." If he could, he says, with a bright look, he could do better work than he sees done here. It would seem happiness to him to knock off at 6 o'clock instead of working, as he now often has to do, till midnight. But how? He knows of no Bohemian blacksmith who can understand him; he should stave. Here, with his wife, he can make a living at least. "Aye, says she, turning, from listening, to her household duties, "it would be nice for sure to have father work at his trade." Then what a home she could make for them, and how happy they would be. Here is an unattainable ideal, indeed , of a workman in the most prosperous city in the world! There is genuine, if unspoken, pathos in the soft tap she gives her husband's hand as she goes about her work with a half-suppressed little sigh.

The very ash-barrels that stand in front of the big rows of tenements in Seventy-first and Seventy-third Streets advertise the business that is carried on within. They are filled to the brim with the stems of stripped tobacco leaves. The rank smell that waited for us on the corner of the block follows us into the hallways, penetrates every nook and cranny of the houses. As in the settlement farther down town, every room here has its work-bench with its stumpy knife and queer pouch of bed-tick, worn brown and greasy, fastened in front the whole length of the bench to receive the scraps of waste. This landlord-employer at all events gives three rooms for $12.50, if two be dark, one wholly and the other getting some light from the front room. The mother of the three bare-footed little children we met on the stairs was taken to the hospital the other day when she could no longer work. She will never come out alive. There is not waste in these tenements. Lives, like clothes, are worn through and out before put aside. Her place at the bench is taken already by another who divides with the head of the household his earning of $15.50 a week. He has just come out successful of a strike that brought the pay of these tenements up to $4.50 per thousand cigars. Notice to quite had already been served on them, when the employer decided to give in, frightened by the prospective loss of rent. Asked how long he works, the man says: "from they can see till bed-time." Bed-time proves to be eleven o'clock. Seventeen hours a day, seven days in the week, at thirteen cents an hour for the two, six cents and a half for each! Good average earning for a tenement-house cigarmaker in summer. In winter it is at least one-fourth less. In spite of it all, the rooms are cleanly kept. From the bedroom farthest back the woman brings out a pile of moist tobacco-leaves to be stripped. They are kept there, under cover lest they dry and crack, from Friday to Friday, when an accounting is made and fresh supplies given out. The people sleep there too, but the smell, offensive to the unfamiliar nose, does not bother them. They are used to it.

In a house around the corner that is not a factory-tenement, lives now the cigarmaker I spoke of as suffering from consumption which the doctor said was due to the tobacco-fumes. Perhaps the lack of healthy exercise has as much to do with it. His case is interesting from its own stand-point. He too is one with a—for a Bohemian—large family. Six children sit at his table. By trade a shoemaker, for thirteen years he helped his wife make cigars in the manufacturer's tenement. She was a very good hand, and until his health gave out two years ago they were able to make from $17 to $25 a week, by lengthening the day at both ends. Now that he can work no more, and the family under the doctor's orders has moved away from the smell of tobacco, the burden of its support has fallen upon her alone, for none of the children is old enough to help. She has work in the shop at eight dollars a week, and this must go round; it is all there is. Happily, this being a tenement for revenue only, unmixed with cigars, the rent is cheaper: seven dollars for two bright rooms on the top floor. No housekeeping is attempted. A woman in Seventy-second Street supplies their meals, which the wife and mother fetches in a basket, her husband being too weak. Breakfast of coffee and hard-tack, or black bread, at twenty cents for the whole eight; a good many, the little woman says with a brave, patient smile, and there is seldom anything to spare, but—. The invalid is listening, and the sentence remains unfinished. What of dinner? One of the children brings it from the cook. Oh! It is a good dinner, meat, soup, greens and bread, all for thirty cents. It is the principal family meal. Does she come home for dinner? No; she cannot leave the shop, but gets a bite at her bench. The question: A bite of what? Seems as merciless as the surgeon's knife, and she winces under it as one shrinks from physical pain. Bread, then. But at night they all have supper together—sausage and bread. For ten cents they can eat all they want. Can they not? She says, stroking the hair of the little boy at her knee; his eyes glisten hungrily at the thought, as he nods stoutly in support of his mother. Only, she adds, the week the rent is due, they have to shorten rations to pay the landlord.

But what of his being an Anarchist, this Bohemian—an infidel—I hear somebody say. Almost one might be persuaded by such facts as these— and they are everyday facts, not fancy—to retort: what more natural? With every hand raised against him in the old land the new, in the land of his hoped-for freedom, what more logical than that his should be turned against society that seems to exist only for his oppression? But the charge is not half true. Naturally the Bohemian loves peace, as he loves music and song. As someone has said: He does not seek war, but when attacked knows better how to die than how to surrender. The Czech is the Irishman of Central Europe, with all his genius and his strong passions, with the same bitter traditions of landlord-robbery, perpetuated here where he thought to forget them; like him ever and on principle in the opposition, "agin the government" wherever he goes. Among such a people, ground by poverty until their songs have died in curses upon their oppressors, hopelessly isolated and ignorant of our language and our laws it would not be hard for bad men at any time to lead a few astray. And this is what has been done. Yet, even with the occasional noise made by the few, the criminal statistics already alluded to quite dispose of the charge that they incline to turbulence and riot. So it is with the infidel propaganda, the legacy perhaps of the fierce contention through hundreds of years between Catholics and Protestants on Bohemia's soil, of bad faith and savage persecutions in the name of the Christian's God that disgrace its history. The Bohemian clergyman who spoke for his people at the Christian Conference held in Chickering Hall two years ago, took even stronger ground. "They are Roman Catholics by birth, infidels by necessity, and Protestants by history and inclination," he said. Yet he added his testimony in the same breath to the fact that, though the Freethinkers had started two schools in the immediate neighborhood of his church to counteract its influence, his flock had grown in a few years from a mere handful at the start to proportions far beyond his hopes, gathering in both Anarchists and Freethinkers, and making good church members of them.

Thus the whole matter resolves itself once more into a question of education, all the more urgent because these people are poor, miserably poor almost to a man. "There is not," said one of them, who knew thoroughly what he was speaking of, "there is not one of them all, who, if he were to sell all he was worth to-morrow, would have money enough to buy a house and lot in the country."

5.2
Strangers in the Land

John Higham

Historian John Higham here discusses the hostility Americans evidenced toward the "new" immigrants from eastern and southern Europe in the decades surrounding 1900. Higham focuses on Slavs, Italians, and Jews and tries to make sense of the intense negative reactions they evoked from the American public. Were these three groups treated more similarly or disparately? Why?

Unlike the older Catholic population, the southern and eastern Europeans who had begun to arrive in considerable numbers during the 1880's lived in the American imagination only in the form of a few vague, ethnic stereotypes. They occupied, in other words, no distinctive place, either separately or collectively, in the traditions of American nationalism. In the 1890's, for the first time, they became a significant factor in the growth of nativism. An initial distrust, compounded largely out of their culture and appearance, swelled into a pressing sense of menace, into hatred, and into violence. This process went forward essentially along two lines: first and most commonly, the general anti-foreign feelings touched off by the internal and international shocks of the late nineteenth century were discharged with special force against these new targets so that each of the southeastern European groups appeared as a particularly insidious representative of the whole foreign menace; secondly and more slowly, a campaign got under way against the new immigration as a unique entity, constituting in its difference from other foreign groups the essence of the nation's peril. The first type of attack was midwife to the second. The new immigrants had the very bad luck to arrive in America en masse at a time when nativism was already running at full tilt, and when neither anarchist nor Jesuit afforded a wholly satisfactory victim for it.

The hostilities which southeastern Europeans faced depended partly on their increasing prominence on the American scene. During the early nineties, peasants and Jews poured out of southern and eastern Europe in ever larger numbers, fleeing from poverty and inhumanity to a new promised land. Cutthroat competition among the transatlantic steamship companies eased their flight; steerage rates on first-class boats dropped to $10 or even less. The depression sharply reduced all immigration, but the new current never fell below one hundred thousand persons per year—a level it had first reached in 1887. More exclusively than most older immigrant groups, the new ones swarmed into the slums, the factories, and the mines. Either urbanites or industrial workers, and usually both, they played a role in American life that lent itself to nativist interpretation. In the crowded places where they made their homes, they lived as a class apart, the least assimilated and most impoverished of the immigrants. Hence, they symbolized vividly the social and economic ills with which nativists identified the immigrants generally. Fears of developing class cleavage could easily center on them; and with less perversion of logic than anti-Catholicism required, the problems of depression and unrest could be associated with them. Above all, each of the southern and eastern European nationalities seemed to Americans in some way a disturber of the peace, thereby focalizing the fear of foreign-bred discontent.

On the other hand, the new immigrants, although vulnerable as symbols of a general foreign problem, did not yet stand out readily as a collective entity. Until 1896 the old influx from northern and western Europe surpassed the southern and eastern European current. All in all, at least 80 per cent of the European-born population of the United States in the mid-nineties still derived from those accustomed sources—Germany, Great Britain, Scandinavia, France, Switzerland, and the Low Countries. Furthermore, concentration of settlement limited the impact of the new groups. While a few coastal cities and industrial complexes felt their arrival sharply, large parts of the country hardly knew them at all. Two-thirds of the first-generation Italians for example, settled in the mid-Atlantic and New England states. Most of America was just beginning to learn of their presence, largely at secondhand. Consequently most of the hatred of Italians, Slavs, and Jews consisted of general anti-foreign attitudes refracted through specific national stereotypes.

The Slavic coal miners of Pennsylvania illustrate very well how the new immigration inherited a wider, pre-existing animus. They acquired the immigrant's standard reputation for disorder in an unusually simple, direct form. The American mind contained, apparently, no distinctive "Slavic" stereotype, comparable to Italian and Jewish stereotypes, which might have individualized the hostile response. Consequently Slavic and Magyar laborers impressed public opinion at large simply as foreigners par excellence: uncivilized, unruly, and dangerous.

The impression fed upon the Slavic coal miners' sporadic but increasing involvement in labor unrest. Ironically, while other workingmen continued to despise them as cheap and docile competitors, the general public fixed its eyes on their lapses from docility. Already the Slavs had incurred the indignation of employers for participating in the coke strike of 1886; during the greater industrial conflicts of the nineties, they encountered the hostility of the whole middle-class community. By 1891, when Henry Clay Frick precipitated a strike of fourteen thousand coke workers by posting a new wage scale, Slavic and Magyar nationalities well outnumbered the older immigrants and native Americans in the bituminous fields. Although British and Americans led the strike, it was generally interpreted as an uprising of "Huns," who, in the words of the New York *Tribune*, were "the most dangerous of labor-unionists and strikers. They fill up with liquor and cannot be reasoned with." The company brought in nonunion workers, a step which resulted in riots and vandalism on the part of the strikers. In this tense situation, a crowd of "Huns," returning from a mass meeting, passed a frightened detachment of state militia guarding a company store. Someone fired a shot, the strikers fled, and the militia fired two volleys after them. Ten dead and fifty wounded immigrants littered the road. According to the *Tribune*, the militia's action was "upheld by businessmen and all law-abiding people in the entire region."

Frick finally succeeded in breaking the strike, though he was to face a similar walkout three years later. This time an immigrant mob killed Frick's chief engineer, causing the Pittsburgh *Times* to report that the whole region was "trembling on the brink of an insurrection. Never before were the dangerous foreigners so thoroughly aroused." A sheriff's posse, equally aroused, pursued the escaping strikers, shooting several and arresting 138 for murder. No sooner was this strike defeated than a general work stoppage throughout the bituminous coal fields ensued, bringing its quota of violence and police brutalities.

The bloodiest episode occurred in 1897. While the United Mine Workers Union was leading the new immigrants to victory in the bituminous fields, an attempt to launch a strike in the anthracite country provoked disaster. About 150 Polish and Hungarian strikers, entirely unarmed, set out from Hazleton, Pennsylvania, toward a nearby town, intent on urging the men there to join the walkout. The sheriff, persuaded by the coal owners that an organized march was illegal, gathered a posse of 102 deputies to intercept it. As the strikers came in sight, the sheriff ordered them to return. Someone struck him, frightening him into commanding the deputies to fire. They poured volley after volley into the surprised and terrorized crowd as it stampeded in flight. They killed twenty-one immigrants and wounded forty more. The sheriff, a former mine foreman, explained that the crowd consisted of "infuriated foreigners...like wild beasts." Other mine foremen agreed that if the strikers had been American-born no blood would have flowed.

In the case of the Italians, a rather similar fear of "infuriated foreigners" took a different twist. Anti-foreign sentiment filtered through a specific ethnic stereotype when Italians were involved; for in American eyes they bore the mark of Cain. They suggested the stiletto, the Mafia, the deed of impassioned violence. "The disposition to assassinate in revenge for a fancied wrong," declared the Baltimore *News*, "is a marked trait in the character of this impulsive and inexorable race." Every time a simple Italian laborer resorted to his knife, the newspapers stressed the fact of his nationality; the most trivial fracas in Mulberry Street caused a headline on "Italian Vendetta." The stereotype conditioned every major outburst of anti-Italian sentiment in the 1890's. The distinctive nativism which swarthy *paesani* experienced took the guise of social discipline applied to alleged acts of homicide.

Time and again, lynching parties struck at Italians charged with murder. In 1891 a wild rumor that drunken Italian laborers had cut the throats of a whole American family in West Virginia set off further rumors of a pitched battle between a sheriff's posse and the assassins. In 1895, when the southern Colorado coal fields were gripped by violent labor strife, a group of miners and other residents systematically massacred six Italian workers implicated in the death of an American saloonkeeper. A year later a mob dragged three Italians from jail in a small Louisiana town and hanged them. The biggest incident convulsed New Orleans—and then the whole country—at the beginning of the decade. The city combined southern folkways with all of the social problems of the urban North, and as the most southerly of American ports, it was the haven of a large migration from Sicily. In 1891 the superintendent of police was murdered under conditions which pointed to the local Sicilian population. Wholesale arrests followed in an atmosphere of hysteria. The mayor issued a public appeal: "We must teach these people a lesson that they will not forget for all time."

The city council appointed a citizens' committee to suggest ways of preventing the influx of European criminals. But when some of the accused were tried, the jury (which may have been suborned) stunned the city by refusing to convict. While officials stood idly by, a mob proceeded "to remedy the failure of justice" by lynching eleven Italian suspects. With apparent unanimity local newspapers and business leaders blessed the action.

At that point jingoism intruded upon what had began as a local, internal episode, transforming it into a nation-wide commotion and a diplomatic crisis. Italy sought redress for the victims' families and punishment of the mob that murdered them. Secretary of State James G. Blaine treated the plea cavalierly, whereupon Italy abruptly recalled her minister in Washington. Internal hatred and external conflict now interacted directly, producing an explosion of feeling against Italy and enormously magnifying the fear of Italian-Americans. A belief that the Italian fleet might suddenly descend on the United States gained fairly wide credence, and patriots flexed their muscles in preparation. Italians within the country now appeared as a potential fifth column; obviously these people could not be depended upon in times of national danger. There were reports of Italian immigrants riddling an American flag with bullets; a rumor circulated that several uniformed corps of Italians were drilling in New York. In Wheeling, West Virginia, miners went on strike because their employer refused to discharge two Italians; the strikers vowed they would not work with men "allied to a nation that was trying to bring about a war with the United States." A patriotic society demanded war if Italy continued shipping criminals to the United States. The *Review of Reviews* saw two lessons in the affair: that America must have a navy to protect itself from "wanton insult," and an immigration policy to keep out "the refuse of the murder-breeds of Southern Europe."

Clearly, as the *Review* pointed out, a revival of Americanism was emerging from the New Orleans incident. Not just Italian immigration but the whole immigration question was dramatized as nothing had dramatized it since the Haymarket Affair. The press, the pulpit, and the magazines rang with demands for stringent restriction. The influential *Nation* concluded that a secure modern state rested on community of language and proposed therefore to limit immigration to English-speaking applicants. This severe idea met considerable favor.

The third major group in the new immigration, the Jews, was also buffeted by the nativism and jingoism of the nineties. They had, of course, their own unique status, fixed by the ancient Shylock stereotype; they stood for chicane rather than crime or revolution. (The American public had heard little as yet about the radical labor movements stirring in the New York ghetto.) But the Jews' supposedly unscrupulous greed now seemed as potentially subversive as the doings of bloodthirsty Italians, "furious Huns," or Irish papists. Hatred, rooted in much the same conditions, lashed them all in rather similar ways.

The Jews felt, too, the violence endemic in that period. Beginning in the late eighties, the first serious anti-Semitic demonstrations in American history occurred in parts of the lower South where Jewish supply merchants were common. In several parishes of Louisiana debt-ridden farmers stormed into town, wrecked Jewish stores, and threatened to kill any Jews who remained in the area. During the worst year, 1893, night-riders burned dozens of farmhouses belonging to Jewish landlords in southern Mississippi, and open threats drove a substantial number of Jewish businessmen from Louisiana. Persecution in northern cities generally took the form of personal taunts and assaults. Russo-Polish Jews had been stoned occasionally in the early eighties, and in the next decade this petty kind of Jew-baiting became much more common. One serious incident broke out in a New Jersey mill town in 1891. Five hundred tending boys employed in the local glass works went on a rampage when the management hired fourteen young Russian Jews. Three days of riotous demonstrations caused most of the Jewish residents to flee from the area. In one sense the Jews came off a little better than the other minorities; apparently no lives were lost in any of these episodes.

A substantial ideological onslaught accompanied the physical assaults, however. In response to the tensions of the 1890's, the Shylock stereotype—which tended to obscure distinctions between the relatively well-to-do German Jews and the newcomers from eastern Europe—assumed a new potency. To some nativists, the Jews were capable of dominating or ruining American business. Tradition connected Jews with gold, which was becoming one of the major touchstones of internal strife. After 1890 the government's determination to maintain the gold standard excited enormous discontent and defined the great political issue of the period. Since greedy, destructive forces seemed somehow at work in the government and economy, suspicion dawned that a Jewish bid for supremacy was wreaking the havoc America could not control. Agrarian radicals, absorbed in a passionate crusade for free silver, sometimes yielded to this conjecture, but the idea was not theirs alone. The patrician Henry Adams concluded that the United States lay at the mercy of the Jews, and a New York workingman vowed: "The Russian Jews and the other Jews will completely control the finances and Government of this country in ten years, or they will all be dead....The hatred with which they are regarded...ought to be a warning to them. The people of this country...won't be starved and driven to the wall by Jews who are guilty of all the crimes, tricks and wiles that have hitherto been unknown and unthought of by civilized humanity."

Here too jingoism played a part. It was not enough for jingo-inflamed nativists to see the Jews solely as an internal threat. They were a people without single national home or center of power: an *international* people. Since gold was becoming, in fact, a more and more firmly established international standard, millions of Americans associated their country's troubles with an international medium of exchange and felt themselves in the toils of a world-wide money-power. Did the Jews perhaps have an international loyalty above all governments, a quenchless resolve to rule the world themselves? For at least a few nativists, the new tendency to see America's adversaries operating on a world stage inflated the Jewish peril from one of national subversion to one of world domination. An occasional eastern conservative detected a clandestine Jewish league controlling the money markets of the world, or blamed the depression on Jewish bankers who were said to be shipping America's gold to Europe. Western agrarians not infrequently slipped into similar allusions. Minnesota's Ignatius Donnelly wrote a utopian novel, *Caesar's Column*, prophesying a totally degraded society ruled by a Jewish world oligarchy. The greatest of the silverites, William Jennings Bryan, bluntly accused President Cleveland of putting the country in the hands of the English Rothschilds.

In nineteenth century America, even so, the menace of world Jewry was undoubtedly less important than related feats of Italians and Catholics. Certainly the vision of an Italian fifth column precipitated more immediate consequences, and the expectation of a papal uprising created greater hysteria. The chief significance of the "International Jew" lay far in the future. Denationalized and universal, the symbol curiously mingled jingoism with isolationism. It was less a summons to fight than a command to withdraw, and its full impact would not come until American nationalism reverted from a strategy of belligerent intervention to one of belligerent isolation.

For understanding late nineteenth century nativism, it is not the latent possibilities of the new anti-Semitism which need emphasis, but rather the common qualities in the assaults on the various new immigrant nationalities. No longer scorned simply for "mere habits of life," each of the major groups from southern and eastern Europe stood forth as a challenge to the nation, either endangering American institutions by unruly behavior or threatening through avarice to possess them. In lashing out at each of these ethnic groups, a distraught society secured a whole set of new adversaries.

On the other hand, the discovery that the miscellaneous Slavs, Jews, and Italians constituted a collective type, a "new immigration," dawned more gradually. The concept of a new immigration would seem to have been largely the work of cultivated minds rather than a simple derivative of popular instincts. Certainly mass opinion in the nineties pictured the Italian, the Slav, and the Jew chiefly within the context of a general foreign peril. The fact of a rising influx of southern Europeans with unusually low living standards had been mentioned as early as 1884 in the discussion of the contract labor bill but did not receive much notice. Occasionally in the late eighties and with increasing frequency after 1890, a few keen observers in the East pointed to the proportional decline of northwestern European entrants. After 1890, as the comfortable belief faded that this was a mere, temporary eddy in the migratory stream, a handful of nativist intellectuals confronted the problem of defining the general threat which the whole movement from southern and eastern Europe raised to the nation's destiny.

Neither of the major traditions of nativist thought quite fitted the problem. The anti-radical theme, with its fears of imported discontent, applied to Europeans as a whole, and surely the new immigrants presented a more docile appearance than did Irish labor leaders or the German anarchists who hanged for the Haymarket Affair. Anti-Catholic nationalism, aside from failing to account for the new Jewish immigration, reeked of religious fanaticism which literate and cultured people now disavowed. On the eve of the A.P.A.'s rise to national prominence, a typical nativist intellectual rejoiced that the present movement against immigration would be free from attacks on Catholics. There was, however, a third nativist tradition— weaker than the other two but more adaptable to the purpose at hand. The old idea that America belongs peculiarly to the Anglo-Saxon race would define the special danger of the new immigration if one assumed that northern Europeans were at least first cousins to the Anglo-Saxons.

Eastern patrician intellectuals had been the keepers of the Anglo-Saxon tradition since the Civil War, and in the climate of the nineties it was not difficult for some of them to convert a doctrine that defined their own sense of nationality into censure of an immigrant throng that displayed few common traits except the indubitable fact that it was not Anglo-Saxon. Hardly had the new immigration begun to attract attention when race-conscious intellectuals discovered its hereditary taint. In 1890 the Brahmin president of the American Economic Association alerted his fellow scholars to the new tide of "races of...the very lowest stage of degradation." About the same time Henry Cabot Lodge noticed; the shift away from northwestern Europe and began to bristle at its racial consequences.

When Lodge raised the banner of race against the new immigration, it acquired its most dangerous adversary. As Massachusetts' scholar-in-politics, he dominated both the intellectual and legislative phases of nativism. To this dual role, Lodge's own interests and values imperiously summoned him; he embodied in remarkable degree some of the major forces underlying late nineteenth century xenophobia. From his precise Vandyke beard to his clipped, Boston accent, Lodge was the model of a patrician. He was steeped, in English culture—English to the last fiber of his thought, said Henry Adams—in pride of ancestry, and in nostalgia for New England's past. During the 1870's he had plunged into a study of the Anglo-Saxons; a thesis on early Anglo-Saxon law brought him the first Ph.D. that Harvard conferred in political science. Secondly, connected with Lodge's race consciousness was a morbid sensitivity to the danger of extensive social change. He had a lively repugnance for both the rising plutocracy and the restive mob, and he felt acutely the general nativist response to class conflict. By 1888, as a fledgling Congressman, he was pointing to the diminishing supply of free land in the West and the growth of unrest in the East as reasons for restricting immigration. Finally, while attacking immigration in domestic affairs, Lodge was adopting a; belligerent stance in foreign affairs. His campaign against the new immigration during the 1890's interlaced with a jingoist crusade for expansion. Lodge the jingo hated England as much as Lodge the Anglo-Saxon loved the English; accordingly, his diplomatic belligerence took the form of an assertion of American power, his pleas for restriction a defense of the English race. But these and other inconsistencies in the life of the cold, cultivated little Senator were merely logical. They were resolved at another level—in the emotions of nationalism which shaped and guided his career.

Although the Anglo-Saxon tradition in the mid-nineties still swayed few outside of an eastern elite, through Lodge and others around him that elite occupied a position of strategic influence. Both the ideological instrument and the political leadership necessary to bring into a single focus the chaotic resentments against the new immigrant were therefore at hand.

5.3
Restrictions on Chinese Immigration (1892)

One response America had to the rapidly increasing number of "new" immigrants was to try to keep them out. Congress restricted Chinese immigration in 1882, and this document provides arguments for extending those restrictions. What reasons does the author provide for shutting the doors on Chinese immigration? Why are the Chinese "a source of danger"?

There is urgent necessity for prompt legislation on the subject of Chinese immigration. The exclusion act approved May 6, 1882, and its supplement expires by limitation of time on May 6, 1892, and after that time there will be no law to prevent the Chinese hordes from invading our country in number so vast, as soon to outnumber the present population of our flourishing States on the Pacific slope....

The popular demand for legislation excluding the Chinese from this country is urgent and imperative and almost universal. Their presence here is inimical to our institutions and is deemed injurious and a source of danger. They are a distinct race, saving from their earnings a few hundred dollars and returning to China. This they succeed in doing in from five to ten years by living in the most miserable manner, when in cities and towns in crowded tenement houses, surrounded by dirt, filth, corruption, pollution, and prostitution; and gambling houses and opium joints abound. When used as cooks, farm-hands, servants, and gardeners, they are more cleanly in habits and manners. They, as a rule, have no families here; all are men, save a few women, usually prostitutes. They have no attachment to our country, its laws or its institutions, nor are they interested in its prosperity. They never assimilate with our people, our manners, tastes, religion, or ideas. With us they have nothing in common.

Living on the cheapest diet (mostly vegetable), wearing the poorest clothing, with no family to support, they enter the field of labor in competition with the American workman. In San Francisco, and in fact throughout the whole Pacific slope, we learn from the testimony heretofore alluded to, that the Chinamen have invaded almost every branch of industry; manufacturers of cigars, cigar boxes, brooms, tailors, laundrymen, cooks, servants, farmhands, fishermen, miners and all departments of manual labor, for wages and prices at which white men and women could not support themselves and those dependent upon them. Recently this was a new country, and the Chinese may have been a necessity at one time, but now our own people are fast filling up and developing this rich and highly favored land, and American citizens will not and can not afford to stand idly by and see this undesirable race carry away the fruits of the labor which justly belongs to them. A war of races would soon be inaugurated; several times it has broken out, and bloodshed has followed. The town of Tacoma, in 1887, banished some 3,000 Chinamen on twenty-four hours' notice, and no Chinaman has ever been permitted to return.

Our people are willing, however, that those now here may remain, protected by the laws which they do not appreciate or obey, provided strong provision be made that no more shall be allowed to come, and that the smuggling of Chinese across the frontiers be scrupulously guarded against, so that gradually, by voluntary departures, death by sickness, accident, or old age, this race may be eliminated from this country, and the white race fill their places without inconvenience to our own people or to the Chinese, and thus a desirable change be happily and peacefully accomplished. It was thought that the exclusion act of 1882 would bring about this result; but it now appears that although at San Francisco the departures largely exceed the arrivals, yet the business of smuggling Chinese persons across the lines from the British Possessions and Mexico has so greatly increased that the number of arrivals now exceed the departures. This must be effectually stopped.

5.4
Survival of the Unfit (1918)

Madison Grant

A leader of the "racialist" movement in the early twentieth century, Madison Grant published, to much acclaim, The Passing of the Great Race *in 1918. In it he argued that immigration from outside of western and northern Europe threatened to destroy the American "race" by introducing inferior genetic traits that would eventually swamp the superior ones perpetuated by Americans. Here Grant discusses the Social Darwinist idea of "survival of the fittest" as applied to human society; he argues that America offers a breeding ground that encourages the "survival of the unfit."*

The prosperity that followed the war [World War I] attracted hordes of newcomers who were welcomed by the native Americans to operate factories, build railroads and fill up the waste spaces—"developing the country" it was called.

These new immigrants were no longer exclusively members of the Nordic race as were the earlier ones who came of their own impulse to improve their social conditions. The transportation lines advertised America as a land flowing with milk and honey and the European governments took the opportunity to unload upon careless, wealthy and hospitable America the sweepings of their jails and asylums. The result was that the new immigration, while it still included many strong elements from the north of Europe, contained a large and increasing number of the weak, the broken and the mentally crippled of all races drawn from the lowest stratum of the Mediterranean basin and the Balkans, together with hordes of the wretched, submerged populations of the Polish Ghettos. Our jails, insane asylums and almshouses are filled with this human flotsam and the whole tone of American life, social, moral and political has been lowered and vulgarized by them.

With a pathetic and fatuous belief in the efficacy of American institutions and environment to reverse or obliterate immemorial hereditary tendencies, these newcomers were welcomed and given a share in our land and prosperity. The American taxed himself to sanitate and educate these poor helots and as soon as they could speak English, encouraged them to enter into the political life, first of municipalities and then of the nation.

The native Americans are splendid raw material, but have as yet only an imperfectly developed national consciousness. They lack the instinct of self-preservation in a racial sense. Unless such an instinct develops their race will perish, as do all organisms which disregard this primary law of nature. Nature had granted to the Americans of a century ago the greatest opportunity in recorded history to produce in the isolation of a continent a powerful and racially homogeneous people and had provided for the experiment a pure race of one of the most gifted and vigorous stocks on earth, a stock free from the diseases, physical and moral, which have again and again sapped the vigor of the older lands. Our grandfathers threw away this opportunity in the blissful ignorance of national childhood and inexperience.

The result of unlimited immigration is showing plainly in the rapid decline in the birth rate of native Americans because the poorer classes of Colonist stock, where they still exist, will not bring children into the world to compete in the labor market with the Slovak, the Italian, the Syrian and the Jew. The native American is too proud to mix socially with them and is gradually withdrawing from the scene, abandoning to these aliens the land which he conquered and developed. The man of the old stock is being crowded out of many country districts by these foreigners just as he is today being literally driven off the streets of New York City by the swarms of Polish Jews. These immigrants adopt the language of the native American, they wear his clothes, they steal his name and they are beginning to take his women, but they seldom adopt his religion or understand his ideals and while he is being elbowed out of his own home the American looks calmly abroad and urges on others the suicidal ethics which are exterminating his own race.

When the test of actual battle comes, it will, of course, be the native American who will do the fighting and suffer the losses. With him will stand the immigrants of Nordic blood, but there will be numbers of these foreigners in the large cities who will prove to be physically unfit for military duty.

As to what the future mixture will be it is evident that in large sections of the country the native American will entirely disappear. He will not intermarry with inferior races and he cannot compete in the sweat shop and in the street trench with the newcomers. Large cities from the days of Rome, Alexandria, and Byzantium have always been gathering points of diverse races, but New York is becoming a *cloaca gentium* which will produce many amazing racial hybrids and some ethnic horrors that will be beyond the powers of future anthropologists to unravel.

One thing is certain: in any such mixture, the surviving traits will be determined by competition between the lowest and most primitive elements and the specialized traits of Nordic man; his stature, his light colored eyes, his fair skin and light colored hair, his straight nose and his splendid fighting and moral qualities, will have little part in the resultant mixture.

The "survival of the fittest" means the survival of the type best adapted to existing conditions of environment, which to-day are the tenement and factory, as in Colonial times they were the clearing of forests, fighting Indians, farming the fields and sailing the Seven Seas. From the point of view of race it were better described as the "survival of the unfit."…

Success in colonization depends on the selection of new lands and climatic conditions in harmony with the immemorial requirements of the incoming race. The adjustment of each race to its own peculiar habitat is based on thousands of years of rigid selection which cannot be safely ignored. A certain isolation and freedom from competition with other races, for some centuries at least, is also important, so that the colonists may become habituated to their new surroundings.

The Americans have not been on the continent long enough to acquire this adjustment and consequently do not present as effective a resistance to competition with immigrants as did, let us say, the Italians when overrun by northern barbarians. As soon as a group of men migrate to new surroundings, climatic, social or industrial, a new form of selection arises and those not fitted to the new conditions die off at a greater rate than in their original home. This form of differential selection plays a large part in modern industrial centres and in large cities, where unsanitary conditions bear more heavily on the children of Nordics than on those of Alpines or Mediterraneans.

5.5
Our Country (1886)

Josiah Strong

The Reverend Josiah Strong was one of the most prominent advocates for an American empire in the late nineteenth century. Strong argued for the spread of Christianity and American values around the world, based on his belief that God had a great destiny in store for the United States. In this excerpt, Strong tackles a slightly different issue: the dangers of the city. He views this problem through his philosophy of Social Darwinism. What are the evils of the American city that Strong identifies? How are those problems associated with the rise of immigration?

The city is the nerve center of our civilization. It is also the storm center. The fact, therefore, that it is growing much more rapidly than the whole population is full of significance....

The city has become a serious menace to our civilization, because in it, excepting Mormonism, each of the dangers we have discussed is enhanced, and all are focalized. It has a peculiar attraction for the immigrant. Our fifty principal cities in 1880 contained 39.3 per cent of our entire German population, and 45.8 per cent of the Irish. Our ten larger cities at that time contained only nine per cent of the entire population, but 23 per cent of the foreign. While a little less than one-third of the population of the United States was foreign by birth or parentage, sixty-two per cent of the population of Cincinnati was foreign, eighty-three per cent of Cleveland, sixty-three per cent of Boston, eighty per cent of New York, and ninety-one per cent of Chicago. A census of Massachusetts, taken in 1885, showed that in 65 towns and cities of the state 65.1 per cent of the population was foreign by birth or parentage.

From *Our Country* by Josiah Strong, edited by Jurgen Herbst.

Because our cities are so largely foreign, Romanism finds in them its chief strength.

For the same reason the saloon, together with the intemperance and the liquor power which it represents, is multiplied in the city. East of the Mississippi there was, in 1880, one saloon to every 438 of the population; in Boston, one to every 329; in Cleveland, one to every 192; in Chicago, one to every 179; in New York, one to every 171; in Cincinnati, one to every 124. Of course the demoralizing and pauperizing power of the saloons and their debauching influence in politics increase with their numerical strength.

It is the city where wealth is massed; and here are the tangible evidences of it piled many stories high. Here the sway of Mammon is widest, and his worship the most constant and eager. Here are luxuries gathered—everything that dazzles the eye, or tempts the appetite; here is the most extravagant expenditure. Here, also, is the *congestion* of wealth the severest. Dives and Lazarus are brought face to face; here, in sharp contrast, are the *ennui* of surfeit and the desperation of starvation. The rich are richer, and the poor are poorer, in the city than elsewhere; and, as a rule, the greater the city, the greater are the riches of the rich and the poverty of the poor. Not only does the proportion of the poor increase with the growth of the city, but their condition becomes more wretched. The poor of a city of 8,000 inhabitants are well off compared with many in New York; and there are hardly such depths of woe, such utter and heart-wringing wretchedness in New York as in London....

Socialism centers in the city, and the materials of its growth are multiplied with the growth of the city. Here is heaped the social dynamite; here roughs, gamblers, thieves, robbers, lawless and desperate men of all sorts, congregate; men who are ready on any pretext to raise riots for the purpose of destruction and plunder, here gather foreigners and wage-workers who are especially susceptible to social arguments; here skepticism and irreligion abound; here inequality is the greatest and most obvious, and the contrast between opulence and penury the most striking; here is suffering the sorest. As the greatest wickedness in the world is to be found not among the cannibals of some far-off coast, but in Christian lands where the light of truth is diffused and rejected, so the utmost depth of wretchedness exists not among savages who have few wants, but in great cities, where, in the presence of plenty and of every luxury men starve. Let a man become the owner of a home, and he is much less susceptible to socialistic propagandism. But real estate is so high in the city that it is almost impossible for a wage-worker to become a householder....

1. In gathering up the results of the foregoing discussion of these several perils, it should be remarked that to preserve republican institutions requires a *higher average* intelligence and virtue among large populations than among small. The government of 5,000,000 people was a simple thing compared with the government of 50,000,000; and the government of 50,000,000 is a simple thing compared with that of 500,000,000. There are many men who can conduct a small business successfully, who are utterly incapable of managing large interests. In the latter there are multiplied relations whose harmony must be preserved. A mistake is farther reaching. It has, as it were, a longer leverage. This is equally true of the business of government. The man of only average ability and intelligence discharges creditably the duties of mayor in his little town; but he would fail utterly at the head of the state or the nation. If the people are to govern, they must grow more intelligent as the population and the complications of government increase. And a higher morality is even more essential. As civilization increases, as society becomes more complex, as labor-saving machinery is multiplied and the division of labor becomes more minute, the individual becomes more fractional and dependent. Every savage possesses all the knowledge of the tribe. Throw him upon his own resources, and he is self-sufficient. A civilized man in like circumstances would perish. The savage is independent. Civilize him, and he becomes dependent; the more civilized, the more dependent. And, as men become more dependent on each other, they should be able to rely more implicitly on each other. More complicated and multiplied relations require a more delicate conscience and a stronger sense of justice. And any failure in character or conduct under such conditions is farther reaching and more disastrous in its results.

Is our progress in morals and intelligence at all comparable to the growth of population? The nation's illiteracy has not been discussed, because it is not one of the perils which peculiarly threaten the West; but any one who would calculate our political horoscope must allow it great influence in connection with the baleful stars which are in the ascendant. But the danger which arises from the corruption of popular morals is much grater. The republics of Greece and Rome, and if I mistake not, all the republics that have ever lived and died, were more intelligent at the end than at the beginning; but growing intelligence could not compensate decaying morals. What, then, is our moral progress? Are popular morals as sound as they were twenty years ago? There is, perhaps, no better index of general morality than Sabbath observance; and everybody knows there has been a great increase of Sabbath desecration in twenty years. We have seen that we are now using as a beverage 29 per cent more of alcohol per caput [per head] than we were fifty years ago. Says Dr. S. W Dike: "It is safe to say that divorce has been doubled, in proportion to marriages or population, in most of the Northern States within thirty years. Present figures indicate a still greater increase." And President Woolsey, speaking of the United States, said in 1883: "On the whole, there can be little, if any, question that the ratio of divorces to marriages or to population exceeds that of any country in the Christian world." While the population increased thirty per cent from 1870 to 1880, the number of criminals in the United States increased 82.33 per cent. It looks very much as if existing tendencies were in the direction of the deadline of. vice. Excepting Mormonism, all the perils which have been discussed seem to be increasing more rapidly than the population. *Are popular morals likely to improve under their increasing influence?*

2. The fundamental idea of popular government is the distribution of power. It has been the struggle of liberty for ages to wrest power from the hands of one or the few, and lodge it in the hands of the many. We have seen, in the foregoing discussion, that centralized power is rapidly growing. The "boss" makes his bargain, and sells his ten thousand or fifty thousand voters as if they were so many cattle. Centralized wealth is centralized power, and the capitalist and corporation find many ways to control votes. The liquor power controls thousands of votes in every considerable city. The president of the Mormon Church casts, say, sixty thousand votes. The Jesuits, it is said, are all under the command of one man in Washington. The Roman Catholic vote is more or less perfectly controlled by the priests. That means that the Pope can dictate some hundreds of thousands of votes in the United States. Is there anything unrepublican in all this? And we must remember that, if present tendencies continue, these figures will be greatly multiplied in the future. And not only is this immense power lodged in the hand of one man, which in itself is perilous, but it is wielded without the slightest reference to any policy or principle of government, solely in the interests of a church or a business, or for personal ends.

The result of a national election may depend on a single state the vote of that state may depend on a single city; the vote of that city may depend on a "boss," or a capitalist, or a corporation; or the election may be decided, and the policy of the government may be reversed, by the socialist, or liquor, or Roman Catholic or immigrant vote.

It matters not by what name we call the man who wields this centralized power—whether king, czar, pope, president, capitalist, or boss. Just so far as it is absolute and irresponsible, it is dangerous.

3. These several dangerous elements are singularly netted together, and serve to strengthen each other. It is not necessary to prove that any *one* of them is likely to destroy our national life, in order to show that it is imperiled. A man may die of wounds no one of which is fatal. No sober-minded man can look fairly at the facts, and doubt that *together* these perils constitute an array which will seriously endanger our free institutions, if the tendencies which have been pointed out continue; and especially is this true in view of the fact that these perils peculiarly confront the West, where our defense is weakest.

5.6
Opening Night at Coney Island (1904)

New York Times

*The Coney Island section of Brooklyn was a haven for bathers and
tourists before the Civil War, but its function as a site of amusement
parks dates to the 1890s, with the construction of Sea Lion Park. Soon
other parks proliferated there, Steeplechase, Luna, and Dreamland
among them. They attracted tens of thousands of visitors every year to
their bright lights, thrilling rides, weird sideshows, and devil-may-care
environment. This front-page article from the* New York Times
*reviews the opening of Dreamland Park in May 1904. What do you
think it was about Dreamland that attracted so many people, especially
those from the working class?*

They took the lid off Coney Island last night, and a quarter of a million
men and women got a glimpse of a swaying, rocking, glittering magic
city by the sea. It was Coney Island's opening day, but Coney Island never
before experienced such a bewildering opening. First of all, there were more
people there than had ever been at Coney Island at one time before. Then
there were more dazzling, wriggling, spectacular amusements offered than
had ever before been collected together at any one place at any time.

Picturesque Luna Park, with its added acres of new attractions, and
the much-talked-about Dreamland presented a bewildering mixture of
men, animals, and things that words can scarcely describe. They had been
gathered from every comer of the globe, and represented about everything
that nature and science have ever produced. Coney Island is regenerated,
and almost every trace of Old Coney has been wiped out. Frankfurters,
peanuts, and popcorn were among the few things left to represent the
place as it was in the old days.

With the new order of things came herds of elephants, genuine Nautch
girls, Indian rajahs, snake charmers, Eskimos, Indians, Japs, Russians, Chinamen, acrobats, jugglers, performing camels, pugilistic horses, and bears
that could ride a horse as well as some of the jockies of the race track.

Sixteen of the newly acquired acres of land in Luna Park were set aside for the reproduction of the glittering Durbar of Delhi. There was the Vice Royal palace in the city that had been reproduced in miniature, and a pageant of Oriental splendor was presented. There were gilded chariots and prancing horses, and trained elephants and dancing girls, regiments of soldiers, and an astonishing number of real Eastern people and animals in gay and stately trappings. The magnificence of the scene was such as to make those who witnessed it imagine they were in a genuine Oriental city. In fact, there was a charm about the streets of Delhi that kept the people spellbound until the exhibition ended. Five thousand people at a time saw this remarkable show, and then went back to see it a second time.

Outside in Luna Park proper, 20,000 or more men, women, and children gazed in wonderment at the daring feats of the acrobats, tight-rope walkers, and horsemen who appeared in connection with the three-ring circus. They saw two wonderful horses with gloves strapped on their forefeet rear up and box in a manner that would have done credit to old-time pugilists. The pugilistic horses boxed in rounds and clinched now and then with their legs about each other's neck just as prizefighters clinch.

Then came the bears that rode in jockey fashion, much to the amusement of the thousands of children who were there.

The Trip to the Moon, Twenty Thousand Leagues Under the Sea, the chutes, the scenic railway, and the other features of Luna Park were all well patronized. A new feature, known as whirl-the-whirl, proved to be a money coiner. In that boats are arranged to sail through the air in circular fashion at a height of almost a hundred feet. The newly arranged dancing platforms and the new theatres in Luna Park were as well patronized as they possibly could be, for they were crowded from the time the gates opened until closing time at midnight.

On the way out the crowd found a complete printing plant and newspaper office in operation, turning out a newspaper—The Evening Star—which will be published daily in Luna Park: The first issue contained an interview with Police Commissioner McAdoo, in which the Commissioner was quoted as saying that the new Coney Island was clean, moral, and magnificent.

There were many city and country officials among the visitors at Luna Park yesterday. Messrs. Thompson & Dundy, the proprietors of the park, entertaining them, together with a thousand other guests, after the banquet in the big dining hall over the dancing pavilion.

Dreamland, the site of which extends from Henry's Bathing Pavilion to the Iron Steamboat Company's pier, takes in the old pier and reaches from Surf Avenue far into the ocean. Dreamland opened its gates for the first time yesterday, and scarcely at any time were there less than 20,000 persons visiting its wonderful features. Illuminated at night, it resembled a city in itself. But the visitor who went there yesterday found that after getting in it contained many miniature cities. It proved to be a veritable fairyland, with its mystic palaces and Aladdin-like shows. In addition to these there was a circus in three rings, high divers, jugglers, aerial performances, and other things that are difficult to describe.

Probably one of its most interesting features is the Dwarf City, with its thousand tiny inhabitants. Storekeepers, policemen, firemen, musicians, wagon drivers, and others who live there are all dwarfs. They have a Liliputian Fire Department, with little fire engines, a miniature livery stable, a midget theatre, midget circus, diminutive horses, bantam chickens, and everything else that would go to make up a midget city, even to its midget Chinese laundrymen. Although everything there is on the smallest possible scale, it is perhaps one of the biggest features of the regenerated Coney Island.

The Incubator Building in Dreamland is designed in farmhouse style, the first story being of brick and the upper part in half timber. The tiled roof has a gable with a large storck overlooking a nest of cherubs. It is a scientific demonstration of how the lives of babies can be saved. It cost $36,000, and the building is full of babies.

The Scenic Railway Building in Dreamland has a front that expresses very successfully "l'art nouveau." The Dog and Monkey Building contains Wormwood's Dog and Monkey Show. The front of the structure symbolizes its purpose and is decorated with cocoanut trees, in which monkeys spring from branch to branch.

One of the principal attractions of Dreamland is the famous Bostock animal show.

The attraction called the "Destruction of Pompeii" is lodged in the Pompeiian Building. A painting back of the columns was executed by Charles S. Shean, a gold medalist of the Paris Salon. The subject of the work is the Bay of Naples and the surrounding neighborhood before the destruction of Pompeii.

The ballroom in Dreamland is of generous proportions, and of the style of the French Renaissance. It is reached by passing through the restaurant, the latter being 240 feet long by 100 feet wide. A movable stairway with a capacity of 7,000 persons an hour takes the visitors to the restaurant and grand ballroom, illuminated with 20,000 electric lights....

Chilkoot Pass consists of a huge proscenium arch in classic style. In ascending and descending this arch the visitors are transported by a movable stairway in a reproduction of the game of bagatelle on an enormous scale. After the visitors have ascended to the high platform, they slide down an inclined plane and roll over and strike against various obstructions which take the place of pegs, and finally reach the bottom and land in holes which are numbered, prizes being given according to the numbers entered.

Dreamland was the conception of ex-Senator William. H. Reynolds of Brooklyn, and cost more than $3,000,000 to construct. Mr. Reynolds and a number of prominent New Yorkers were present last night when it formally opened with the Fire Show. Four thousand persons were employed in producing this spectacle. Upon the ringing of the fine alarm firemen leaped from their beds in real engine houses, and slid down brass poles as they do in the New York Department. Their machines and horses were hitched in the regular way, and then they attended a real fire, which was certainly startling. A hotel appeared to burn, with scores of guests apparently trying to escape, and altogether this show proved a great success.

5.7
The Social Functions of Baseball

Steven A. Riess

Historian Steven A. Riess's Touching Base *looks at the relationship between professional baseball and American culture at the turn of the twentieth century. Here Riess discusses what he calls the "baseball creed" and what it tells us about the cultural meaning baseball had a century ago. What roles did baseball play for Americans after 1900? How did it help Americanize recent immigrants? Compare its appeal with that of Dreamland as described in Document 5.5.*

A crucial reason for baseball's expanded popularity was that the public identified it with certain basic American concepts. This resulted from owners' and sportswriters' public relations campaigns to improve the sport's image and combat competition from other amusements. Both groups cared about the success of baseball because they were fans and because their personal careers depended upon it. Proponents sought to demonstrate that besides providing entertainment, baseball was not a frivolous misuse of valuable time, but benefited the broader society.

Baseball was portrayed as a valuable vehicle to promote community integration because it supposedly instilled civic pride in fans. Club owners took advantage of traditional urban rivalries and the booster spirit to generate attention and affection for hometown teams. This localism was especially ardent if the team succeeded in a league deemed appropriate for the city's perceived status. Fans equated the team's fate on the diamond with their own success or failure. Furthermore, they rooted for the local stalwarts to defeat out-of-town opponents, or, in large metropolises, teams from different sections of town, to defend their community's honor. This was a highly satisfactory, albeit temporary, way to resolve interurban and intraurban rivalries. When teams were composed of amateurs who lived in the regions they represented, localism was a reasonable emotion, but after the demise of the National Association of Professional Base Ball Players, which lasted from 1871 to 1875, and the loosely organized Interstate League (1877–79), few professionals came from the towns in which they played.

Dispassionate commentators argued that it was irrational for spectators to get overly excited about a team composed of mercenaries from elsewhere who might be traded at any moment to a rival and thus transformed overnight from hero to villain. *New York Times* editorials repeatedly decried the principle of localism:

> It has often enough been pointed out that it is quite absurd that there should be any local patriotism around about baseball. The players are mercenaries who make no pretense of playing for anything but money, and who play where they are paid best. So that the team which local patriotism requires the local patriot to cheer for one season may require him to execrate the next. Nevertheless, local patriotism is at the bottom of the business which baseball has come to be, and is the sentiment to which the managers appeal.

Yet the *New York Times* could decide that it was worthwhile to solicit local pride for local ball clubs: "We hold that anything whatsoever that can excite local pride of New York is so far a good thing. For local pride is much the same as public spirit, which at least cannot exist without it, and there is no city in the world that is more deficient in public spirit than New York, or that ought to welcome anything that tends to stimulate that quality." The editors felt that sports fans were about the only enthusiastic, civic-minded people around, but unfortunately fans wasted their energies yelling at mercenary athletes instead of seeking municipal improvements.

The local baseball franchise was regarded by the public as a reliable index of a town's status. A city was not seen as much of an urban area unless it had a professional nine, and furthermore, it should be in the best league possible. If the team was in an association with larger cities, that was taken as a sign of its progressive and growing character. However, if the club was in a league that included smaller cities, then the town might be seen as stagnant and backward.

Smaller cities with few notable attractions relied on their baseball teams, often their only readily identifiable local institutions, to publicize their communities. Results of local games were reported in national sports weeklies and occasionally in the sports pages of leading newspapers across the country. For example, the *San Antonio News* recommended that local folk support the ball club: "Purely as a matter of advertising...whether one has any love for base ball or not,...a base ball team is the cheapest advertisement any city can have.... Reports of...games are telegraphed all over the country, and the constant keeping of a city's name before the people of a nation, as is done by a ball team, has an effect that can scarcely be estimated." The publicity a franchise obtained for the hometown was important because it was expected to attract business and trade, lure new inhabitants, and consequently raise property values....

The prestige and reputation of leading metropolitan areas were also affected by their professional clubs, although less so than those of smaller towns were, since large cities had more well-known institutions and accomplishments. Detroit had no major league franchise from 1889 until 1901, and many local folk felt that hurt its prestige. The absence of major league teams in Baltimore, Buffalo, and Milwaukee after 1902 was considered a bad reflection on those cities as well. Between 1903 and 1952, however, only ten cities had major league clubs. Boston, Chicago, Philadelphia, and St. Louis had two major league teams each, but only New York had three, which certified its stature as the leading American city.

Journalists writing in general circulation periodicals contributed to the baseball mythology by trying to convince their middle-class readership of the social functions of baseball. At a time when professional baseball was at its zenith, they wanted to explain and justify the sudden surging interest in the game. As Allen Sangree wrote in 1907, "A tonic, an exercise, a safety valve, baseball is second only to death as a leveler. So long as it remains our national game, America will abide no monarchy, and anarchy will be slow." Six years later, *American Magazine* asserted, "Baseball has given our public a fine lesson in commercial morals. It is a well paying business...for it must be above suspicion. Nobody dreams of crookedness or shadiness in baseball....Some day all business will be reorganized and conducted by baseball standards."

The baseball creed was a product of the ideology of sport that emerged in the Jacksonian era, which justified sport and physical culture as useful and moral activities that promoted good health, sound morals, and an honorable character. Prior to the Civil War, the *Detroit Free Press* described baseball as a "healthy exercise counteracting the growing tendency to visit saloons and other places of resort with which [Detroit] abounds, thus saving them [fans] from early immorality." By the late 1860s, the game's ability to teach such Victorian values as thrift, sobriety, virtue, and hard work was widely recognized, and this realization encouraged business leaders to organize company teams and give players time off for practice and matches. Bosses also expected the formation of teams would improve worker loyalty and publicize their companies.

The typical middle-class Victorian man worked hard, remained faithful to his wife, and provided well for his family. In antebellum America, most middle-income men were independent farmers, small business owners, or artisans. However, as society bureaucratized in the late nineteenth century and middle-class workers lost their autonomy and feelings of accomplishment, they often turned to sport to demonstrate their physical prowess and masculinity and to escape Victorian confinement. They were concerned about their courage, loss of sexual identity, and the perception of the feminization of mass culture. Baseball provided a means for middle-class men to prove their masculinity, which they could not demonstrate by working at physically demanding jobs. Baseball had been recognized as a manly sport since the 1860s, when rule changes had made playing more difficult (particularly the fly out rule of 1863 that required fly balls to be caught before bouncing to count as an out). Furthermore, as baseball became increasing competitive, it required considerable courage to bat against a hard-throwing pitcher or to guard a base against a speedy runner bearing down with sharpened spikes. In the 1880s, Henry Chadwick described the game in the military grammar of the post-Civil War era (pitcher and catcher constituted the "battery"; the team captain was "the commander of the field") and identified it with martial characteristics. At the turn of the century, however, the more violent game of football was recognized as the moral equivalent of war and thus *the* manly game.

The most penetrating and comprehensive essay of this period analyzing baseball was H. Addington Bruce's "Baseball and the National Life," published in *Outlook* in 1913. A nationally renowned journalist who had authored several books on psychology and other subjects, Bruce discussed with considerable clarity and insight most of baseball's alleged latent functions. Bruce was primarily concerned with identifying the sport as a source of tension management—the widely accepted concept that baseball was a safety valve dated back at least to the 1880s—and as a factor in molding youngsters.

Bruce argued that since most city dwellers worked long and arduous hours in boring, repetitive jobs, they needed an opportunity to relax and relieve themselves of built-up aggressions that might otherwise be directed toward their families or employers:

> An instinctive resort to sport [was] a method of gaining momentary relief from the strain of an intolerable burden, and at the same time finding a harmless outlet for pent-up emotions, which unless

thus gaining expression, might discharge themselves in a dangerous way....

Baseball, then, from the spectator's standpoint, is to be regarded as a means of catharsis, or perhaps better, as a safety-valve. And
it performs this service the more readily because of the appeal it
makes to the basic instincts, with resultant removal of the inhibi-
tions that ordinarily cause tenseness and restraint.

Bruce and his contemporaries believed that baseball helped fans relax and
forget about the rigors of daily life and relieved the pressures attending
great public crises. During World War 1, baseball's proponents argued that
play should continue so that stress and strain on the home front could be
alleviated. Frederick C. Lane, editor of *Baseball Magazine,* and others such
as William Lyon Phelps, a literary critic and Yale professor, wrote that the
country was tired of war news and that readers usually turned first to the
sports pages to help them forget the calamities of the day.

A second function Bruce attributed to baseball was its improvement
of players' and spectators' character. He argued that baseball developed
traits that would be important in the business of life, including fairmind-
edness, honesty, judgment, patience, quick thinking, self-control, and temperance. Furthermore, the sport encouraged the development of traits that
would eventually benefit the entire nation, such as respect for authority,
self-sacrifice, and teamwork. These sentiments were echoed by Henry S.
Curtis, a playground movement leader, in the *Journal of Education* (1916)
and in the report of the 1920 Chicago grand jury investigating the connections between baseball and gambling. Baseball became closely identified with the idea of team spirit, a concept that was vitally important in
an increasingly bureaucratic society. The sport was often used as a
metaphor by people discussing cooperation. For instance, when Warren
G. Harding was campaigning for the presidency in 1920, he delivered a
speech on 2 September entitled "Team Play" that castigated President
Woodrow Wilson's individualistic handling of foreign affairs, promising
that if elected to employ collective methods instead.

Young men were supposedly taught to become better people by watching and playing baseball and by emulating the conduct of professionals.
Ballplayers encountered a myriad of situations requiring quick decisions,
learned to sacrifice to help their team win, and were taught to accept the
authority of the umpire. Boys and other spectators learned to be competitive but also to be good sports. The historian Neil Harris argues that spectators' ability to learn to subordinate their intense desire for victory "into

a regularized code of behavior, indicated the possibilities of self-restraint in a divided society." While umpires were often the target of abuse from disgruntled fans, the crowds seldom interfered with games, especially by the late 1900s.

Boys were fed a pabulum about baseball in the formula-ridden juvenile baseball fiction that was enormously popular at the turn of the century. These texts, like many other children's books, taught the importance of such values as pluck, "clean living" (no smoking or drinking), loyalty, fair play, modesty, hard work, and resiliency. The big breakthrough for baseball in boy's literature began in 1896 when Gilbert Patten's Frank Merriwell stories first appeared in the 5-cent *Tip Top Weekly* that sold over 500,000 copies a week. Merriwell was an all-around superstar at Yale, who stood up for the right of the weak, led a virtuous life, was always an honorable sportsman, and invariably led his team to victory with an extraordinary play in the bottom of the ninth or the last minute of the fourth quarter. Over 200 Merriwell books were eventually published, and 125 million copies circulated. Nearly as successful in this genre as Patten was Ralph Henry Barbour, whose 150 titles emphasized physical prowess, morality, and fair play. Barbour's vision of future success depended upon traditional values learned on the playing field.

Boys were encouraged to imitate the play and behavior of their idols. The progressive *Outlook* reported in 1912 that professionals had a "thoroughly wholesome" influence on boys, who were inspired to play "proficiently." The pros were reportedly clean-living men since such deportment was indispensable for continued success. Naive youths were misled by pulp novelists and an obsequious press into believing that all players upheld traditional Christian values, while in reality some—like Bugs Raymond, Rube Waddell, and, later, Babe Ruth—were remarkable cases of dissipation. Ty Cobb was a crude misanthrope who fought with players, fans, and friends. Giants pitcher Bugs Raymond used his time in the bullpen to trade balls with fans for beer. When Manager John McGraw placed guards there to prevent this, Raymond lowered a rope and bucket from the clubhouse to a waiting confederate, who filled it at a nearby saloon. It was not unusual for players to suffer from venereal disease—one team alone had five players with gonorrhea—but newspapers would report that the players had been stricken by other ailments, such as malaria or rheumatism.

Babe Ruth was the outstanding hero of the 1920s and perhaps the greatest player of all time. His success came naturally, unlike Cobb, a fierce competitor who worked hard and thought fast. Ruth grew up as a wayward child in Baltimore, and his parents sent him off at seven to St. Mary's Industrial School for Boys, a combination orphanage and reformatory. He developed into a great athlete and made his first appearance in the majors as a pitcher for the Boston Red Sox at age nineteen in 1914. Belying our image of him from later in his career, the young Ruth was 6'2", slender, and muscular at 198 pounds. He went 65-33 with a 2.02 ERA during his first three full years in the majors (1915–17), including 9 shutouts in 1916 (setting an AL record for lefthanders) and led the AL with a 1.75 ERA. But his skills were hardly limited to pitching. He was one of the fastest men on the Red Sox and their most powerful batter. In 1919 when Ruth played the outfield full-time, he hit a record 29 homers. Ruth was traded one year later to the Yankees and hit 54 homers, more than any entire major league club during the season. During his tenure with the Yankees he was a man of legendary accomplishments and consumption. In an era of low taxes, he earned about $3 million from baseball and outside endeavors. Ruth epitomized anti-Victorian standards of behavior, enjoying immediate gratification and excesses with food, liquor, and women.

In contrast to these dissolute ballplayers, the athlete who especially represented Victorian ideals was tall, blond, college-educated Christy Mathewson of the New York Giants, winner of 373 games, the most in NL history up to that time. Matty was an outstanding moral hero and the model for Lester Chadwick's Baseball Joe stories. Considered the ideal Christian gentleman, Mathewson was often called upon to speak to youth organizations on clean living and fair play. "Big Six" was extremely competitive and successful at everything he tried, ranging from checkers to poker. Mathewson started playing baseball at the YMCA and never pitched on the sabbath because of his strong religious beliefs. Matty first gained athletic fame at Bucknell College, where he played baseball and football, was president of his class, and married his college sweetheart.

When Mathewson got to the majors he did not fit in with his working-class teammates, who found him conceited and morally overbearing. However, he soon won them over. Catcher Chief Meyers remembered: "How we loved to play for him! We'd break our necks for that guy. If you made an error behind him or anything of that sort, he'd never get mad or sulk. He'd come over and pat you on the back." Mathewson won 20 games in his first full season in 1901, and then 94 over the next three seasons. In the 1905 World Series he won 3 games, all shutouts. Matty was renowned for his "fade-away" (screwball) and exceptional control. He once pitched 68 straight innings without a single walk. When Mathewson's playing days ended, he managed the Cincinnati Reds for 2.5 years, resigning during World War I to become a captain in the army's Chemical Warfare Division. Mathewson's lungs were severely injured after the armistice, when he inhaled poison gas while inspecting German trenches, and subsequently contracted tuberculosis. John McGraw appointed him assistant manager of the Giants, and in 1923 he was appointed president of the Boston Braves. When he died two years later, Matty was eulogized in newspapers and magazines across the country. *Commonweal* remembered him thus: "Certainly no other pitcher ever loomed so majestically in young minds, quite overshadowing George Washington and his cherry tree or even the transcendent model of boyhood, Frank Merriwell.... Such men have a very real value above and beyond the achievements of brawn and sporting skill. They realize and typify in a fashion the ideal of sport—clean power in the hands of a clean and vigorous personality."

According to conventional wisdom, baseball was a panacea for the problems of American youths. Yet there were a few critics. Norman W. Bingham argued in *The Book of Athletics and Out-of-Door Sports* (1895) that boys overemphasized sports while neglecting academics and intellectual and moral abilities and he singled out baseball for promoting trickery and dishonesty. He was seconded by the noted progressive educator George Counts, who blamed baseball for a decline in morality and criticized it for teaching that stealing was good. Finally the psychologist Mary Brownell astutely pointed out in 1925 that "there is nothing inherent in the activity of baseball which *in itself* would make a participant develop along social, physical or mental lines. One can be made a cheat and a poor sport just as well as one can develop the desirable character traits." According to these critics, making juvenile delinquents into avid baseball fans and players did not automatically produce better citizens with improved characters.

The third theme Bruce discussed was the democratizing value of baseball. The sport was regarded as a wonderful leveler of people. "The spectator at a ball game is no longer a statesman, lawyer, broker, doctor, merchant, or artisan," Bruce explained, "but just a plain everyday man." Sportswriters were continually pointing out that ballplayers and fans were drawn from all levels of society and that spectators mingled together on equal terms. Edward B. Moss, sports editor of the *New York Sun*, wrote in *Harper's Weekly*, "Businessmen and professional men forget their standing in the community and shoulder to shoulder with the street urchin 'root' frantically for the hit needed to win the game." Hugh Fullerton examined crowds in the nation's capital and found "the Cabinet, Supreme Court, and Senate touch elbows with department clerks and discuss plays with porters and bartenders. "

The democratic character of the baseball crowd at ballparks and sand-lots was considered a means to promote a sense of community in the dis-tended cities. Jane Addams applauded the popularity of Saturday sandlot ball games in Chicago when it seemed that all the menfolk were enjoying themselves watching baseball and forgetting about their problems:

> The enormous crowd of cheering men and boys are talkative, good-natured, full of the holiday spirit, and absolutely released from the grind of life. They are lifted out of their individual affairs and so fused together that a man cannot tell whether it is his own shout or another's that fills his ears; whether it is his own coat or another's that he is wildly waving to celebrate a victory. He does not call the stranger who sits next to him his "brother" but he un-consciously embraces him in an overwhelming outburst of kindly feeling when the favorite player makes a home run. Does not this contain a suggestion of the undoubted power of public recreation to bring together all classes of a community in the modern city un-happily so full of devices for keeping men apart?

The fourth and final latent function Bruce analyzed was baseball's con-tribution to public health. Theodore Roosevelt's strenuous life theory struck a chord with progressive reformers at the turn of the century. They promoted physical culture through the small parks and playground movements, offering clean, healthy, adult-supervised recreation to inner-city youths. Playing baseball was considered an ameliorative activity and a sound alternative to escapist entertainment at saloons, amusement parks, and cheap theaters. Participants would learn discipline and respect for fig-ures of authority and be kept out of trouble.

But how could professional baseball, a spectator sport, contribute to the physical well-being of fans, who sat in the stands watching players work? Baseball's proponents claimed that "a fairly large proportion of the people who pay for the support of the professional clubs play the game themselves to the benefit of the national health and the development of the national muscle." Furthermore, they contended that the mere presence of fans at ball games contributed to health. As Bruce indicated, "it is a psychological commonplace that pleasurable emotions, especially if they find expression in laughter, shouts, cheers, and other muscle expanding noises, have a tonic value to the whole bodily system. So that it is quite possible to get exercise vicariously as it were; and the more stimulating the spectacle that excites feelings of happiness and enjoyment, the greater will be the resultant good.

Most decidedly baseball is a game well-designed to render this excellent service." This weak logic was supported by a 1914 report in the *New York Medical Journal* indicating that many physicians believed a man's health was improved merely by sitting out in the fresh air, shouting at the top of his lungs, and waving his arms in excitement. These doctors found such exercise sufficient for the typical male adult and doubted that his well-being could be significantly affected by participating in sports, since that merely developed his inherited capacities without creating new ones.

Another social function journalists frequently attributed to professional baseball was its ability to acculturate the children of new immigrants. Baseball was said to be second only to the public schools as a teacher of American mores to immigrant children. Young boys were far more interested in American customs and habits than their parents, and observers rightly believed that they were receptive to baseball's appeal. It was a common sight to see kids playing stickball on city streets, using a rubber ball and a broomstick for their equipment. The respected sportswriter Hugh Fullerton wrote, "Baseball, to my way of thinking, is the greatest single force working for Americanization. No other game appeals so much to the foreign-born youngsters and nothing, not even the schools, teaches the American spirit so quickly, or inculcates the idea of sportsmanship or fair play as thoroughly." Fullerton cited correspondence from Chicago settlement house workers in a Czech-Jewish neighborhood: "We consider baseball one of the best means of teaching our boys American ideas and ideals." Schools, YMCAs, and other youth agencies used baseball to ameliorate urban problems. In 1904, for example, the Chicago public schools made adult-supervised ballplaying a centerpiece of elementary physical education.

Merely playing baseball, however, did not necessarily promote structural assimilation because youths often played on teams sponsored by church groups, fraternal organizations, and single ethnic associations like Chicago's Polish League, founded in 1913 to promote ethnic identification and counter assimilationist trends. When French Canadians in the predominantly francophone industrial town of Woonsocket, Rhode Island, became baseball fans in the 1890s, their ethnic identification did not weaken. They read box scores in the local French-language newspaper to follow their hero, Napoleon Lajoie, the premier second baseman of the early 1900s, and when local francophone teams played Anglo nines, players often gave signals in French. Baseball could be as much a means of promoting ethnic pride and cultural pluralism as Americanization.

The theory of baseball's latent functions strongly appealed to mainstream, middle-class Americans because it touched base with their own beliefs, values, and social needs. Playing and watching the game seemed to provide a progressive education, enabling children to learn from life experiences and not merely from rote memorization. Furthermore, as Kuklick points out, contests provided many fans with "their only experience of physical contest and victory, of valor and endurance, of grace under pressure and dignity in defeat." Professional baseball was welcomed as a moral, healthful recreation for hard-working men. The sport demonstrated the apparent reality of the fundamental American ideal of democracy and reassured old stock Americans of the relevance of their rural-based value system in a modern world. The national pastime purportedly taught traditional qualities such as individualism, yet simultaneously instructed participants and audiences in the newer trait of teamwork, a quality vital for success in a bureaucratized society. Baseball resolved for many Americans the apparent paradox of team play and individualism by showing that winning squads got their nine players to work together as a unit—exemplified by the hit and run, the sacrifice bunt, and the double play—while taking advantage of individual talents to achieve the collective goal of victory.

CHAPTER 6

The Progressive Era, 1880-1920

6.1 Jane Addams, "The Subjective Necessity for Social Settlements" (1892)

6.2 John Dewey, "A Democrat Schoolroom" (1900)

6.3 Jane Addams, "Why the Ward Boss Rules" (1898)

6.4 *Muller v. Oregon* (1908)

6.5 Judge Benjamin B. Lindsey, "The Dangerous Life" (1931)

6.6 Maureen A. Flanagan, "Gender and Urban Political Reform: The City Club and the Woman's City Club of Chicago in the Progressive Era"

6.1
The Subjective Necessity for Social Settlements (1892)

Jane Addams

The founder of the Hull House settlement in Chicago, Jane Addams is considered by many to be the archetypal Progressive. Here, in a piece from her book Twenty Years at Hull-House (1910), *Addams defines the purpose of the settlement house movement, and in so doing defines an important aspect of Progressivism. What role should settlement houses play in American society? What purpose does Christian morality play as a motive force in this movement?*

This paper is an attempt to analyze the motives which underlie a movement based, not only upon conviction, but upon genuine emotion, wherever educated young people are seeking an outlet for that sentiment of universal brotherhood, which the best spirit of our times is forcing from an emotion into a motive. These young people accomplish little toward the solution of this social problem, and bear the brunt of being cultivated into unnourished, oversensitive lives. They have been shut off from the common labor by which they live which is a great source of moral and physical health. They feel a fatal want of harmony between their theory and their lives, a lack of coördination between thought and action. I think it is hard for us to realize how seriously many of them are taking to the notion of human brotherhood, how eagerly they long to give tangible expression to the democratic ideal. These young men and women, longing to socialize their democracy, are animated by certain hopes which may be thus loosely formulated; that if in a democratic country nothing can be permanently achieved save through the masses of the people, it will be impossible to establish a higher political life than the people themselves crave; that it is difficult to see how the notion of a higher civic life can be fostered save through common intercourse; that the blessings which we associate with a life of refinement and cultivation can be made universal and must be made universal if they are to be permanent; that the good we secure for ourselves is precarious and uncertain, is floating in mid-air, until it is secured for all of us and incorporated into our common life. It is easier to state these hopes than to formulate the line of motives, which I believe to constitute the trend of the subjective pressure toward the Settlement. There is something primordial about these motives, but I am perhaps overbold in designating them as a great desire to share the race life. We all bear traces of the starvation struggle which for so long made up the life of the race. Our very organism holds memories and glimpses of that long life of our ancestors which still goes on among so many of our contemporaries. Nothing so deadens the sympathies and shrivels the power of enjoyment as the persistent keeping away from the great opportunities for helpfulness and a continual ignoring of the starvation struggle which makes up the life of at least half the race. To shut one's self away from that half of the race life is to shut one's self away from the most vital part of it; it is to live out but half the humanity to which we have been born heir and to use but half our faculties. We have all had longings for a fuller life which should include the use of these faculties. These longings are the physical complement of the "Intimations of Immortality," on which no ode has yet been written. To portray these would be the work of a poet, and it is hazardous for any but a poet to attempt it.

You may remember the forlorn feeling which occasionally seizes you when you arrive early in the morning a stranger in a great city: the stream of laboring people goes past you as you gaze through the plate-glass window of your hotel; you see hard workingmen lifting great burdens; you hear the driving and jostling of huge carts and your heart sinks with a sudden sense of futility. The door opens behind you and you turn to the man who brings you in your breakfast with a quick sense of human fellowship. You find yourself praying that you may never lose your hold on it all. A more poetic prayer would be that the great mother breasts of our common humanity, with its labor and suffering and its homely comforts, may never be withheld from you. You turn helplessly to the waiter and feel that it would be almost grotesque to claim from him the sympathy you crave because civilization has placed you apart, but you resent your position with a sudden sense of snobbery. Literature is full of portrayals of these glimpses: they come to shipwrecked men on rafts; they overcome the differences of an incongruous multitude when in the presence of a great danger or when moved by a common enthusiasm. They are not, however, confined to such moments, and if we were in the habit of telling them to each other, the recital would be as long as the tales of children are, when they sit down on the green grass and confide to each other how many times they have remembered that they lived once before. If these childish tales are the stirring of inherited impressions, just so surely is the other the striving of inherited powers.

"It is true that there is nothing after disease, indigence and a sense of guilt, so fatal to health and to life itself as the want of a proper outlet for active faculties." I have seen young girls suffer and grow sensibly lowered in vitality in the first years after they leave school. In our attempt then to give a girl pleasure and freedom from care we succeed, for the most part, in making her pitifully miserable. She finds "life" so different from what she expected it to be. She is besotted with innocent little ambitions, and does not understand this apparent waste of herself, this elaborate preparation, if no work is provided for her. There is a heritage of noble obligation which young people accept and long to perpetuate. The desire for action, the wish to right wrong and alleviate suffering haunts them daily. Society smiles at it indulgently instead of making it of value to itself. The wrong to them begins even farther back, when we restrain the first childish desires for "doing good" and tell them that they must wait until they are older and better fitted. We intimate that social obligation begins at a fixed date, forgetting that it begins with birth itself. We treat them as children who, with strong-growing limbs, are allowed to use their legs but not their arms, or whose legs are daily carefully exercised that after a while their arms may be put to high use. We do this in spite of the protest of the best educators, Locke and Pestalozzi. We are fortunate in the meantime if their unused members do not weaken and disappear. They do sometimes. There are a few girls who, by the time they are "educated," forget their old childish desires to help the world and to play with poor little girls "who haven't play things." Parents are often inconsistent: they deliberately expose their daughters to knowledge of the distress in the world; they send them to hear missionary addresses on famines in India and China; they accompany them to lectures on the suffering in Siberia; they agitate together over the forgotten region of East London. In addition to this, from babyhood the altruistic tendencies of these daughters are persistently cultivated. They are taught to be self-forgetting and self-sacrificing, to consider the good of the whole before the good of the ego. But when all this information and culture show results, when the daughter comes back from college and begins to recognize her social claim to the "submerged tenth," and to evince a disposition to fulfill it, the family claim is strenuously asserted; she is told that she is unjustified, ill-advised in her efforts. If she persists, the family too often are injured and unhappy unless the efforts are called missionary and the religious zeal of the family carry them over their sense of abuse. When this zeal does not exist; the result is perplexing. It is a curious violation of what we would fain believe a fundamental law—that the final return of the deed is upon the head of the doer. The deed is that of exclusiveness and caution, but the return, instead of falling upon the head of the exclusive and cautious, falls upon a young head full of generous and unselfish plans. The girl loses something vital out of her life to which she is entitled. She is restricted and unhappy; her elders, meanwhile, are unconscious of the situation and we have all the elements of a tragedy.

We have in America a fast-growing number of cultivated young people who have no recognized outlet for their active faculties. They hear constantly of the great social maladjustment, but no way is provided for them to change it, and, their uselessness hangs about them heavily. Huxley declares that the sense of uselessness is the severest shock which the human system can sustain, and that if persistently sustained, it results in atrophy of function. These young people have had advantages of college, of European travel, and of economic study, but they are sustaining this shock of inaction. They have pet phrases, and they tell you that the things that make us all alike are stronger than the things that make us different. They say, that all men are united by needs and sympathies far more permanent and radical than anything that temporarily divides them and sets them in opposition to each other. If they affect art, they say that the decay in artistic expression is due to the decay in ethics, that art when shut away from the human interests and from the great mass of humanity is self-destructive. They tell their elders with all the bitterness of youth if they expect success from them in business or politics or in whatever lines their ambition for them has run, they must let them consult all of humanity; that they must let them find out what the people want and how they want it. It is only the stronger young people, however, who formulate this. Many of them dissipate their energies in so-called enjoyment. Others not content with that, go on studying and go back to college for their second degrees; not that they are especially fond of study, but because they want something definite to do, and their powers have been trained in the direction of mental accumulation. Many are buried beneath this mental accumulation which lowered vitality and discontent. Walter Besant says they have had the vision that Peter had when he saw the great sheet let down from heaven, wherein was neither clean nor unclean. He calls it the sense of humanity. It is not philanthropy nor benevolence, but a thing fuller and wider than either of these.

This young life, so sincere in its emotion and good phrase and yet so undirected, seems to me as pitiful as the other great mass of destitute lives. One is supplementary to the other, and some method of communication can surely be devised. Mr. Barnett, who urged the first Settlement—Toynbee Hall, in East London—recognized this need of outlet for the young men of Oxford and Cambridge, and hoped that the Settlement would supply the communication. It is easy to see why the Settlement movement originated in England, where the years of education are more constrained and definite than they are here, where class distinctions are more rigid. The necessity of it was greater there, but we are fast feeling the pressure of the need and meeting the necessity for Settlements in America. Our young people feel nervously the need of putting theory into action, and respond quickly to the Settlement form of activity.

Other motives which I believe make toward the Settlement are the result of a certain renaissance going forward in Christianity. The impulse to share the lives of the poor, the desire to make social service, irrespective of propaganda, express the spirit of Christ, is as old as Christianity itself. We have no proof from the records themselves that the early Roman Christians, who strained their simple art to the point of grotesqueness in their eagerness to record a "good news" on the walls of the catacombs, considered this good news a religion. Jesus had no set of truths labeled Religious. On the contrary, his doctrine was that all truth is one, that the appropriation of it is freedom. His teaching had no dogma to mark it off from truth and action in general. He himself called it a revelation—a life. These early Roman Christians received the Gospel message, a command to love all men, with a certain joyous simplicity. The image of the Good Shepherd is blithe and gay beyond the gentlest shepherd of Greek mythology; the hart no longer pants, but rushes to the water brooks. The Christians looked for the continuous revelation, but believed what Jesus said, that this revelation, to be retained and made manifest, must be put into terms of action; that action is the only medium man has for receiving and appropriating truth; that the doctrine must be known through the will.

That Christianity has to be revealed and embodied in the line of social progress is a corollary to the simple proposition that man's action is found in his social relationships in the way in which he connects with his fellows; that his motives for action are the zeal and affection with which he regards his fellows. By this simple process was created a deep enthusiasm for humanity, which regarded man as at once the organ and the object of revelation; and by this process came about the wonderful fellowship, the true democracy of the early Church, that so captivates the imagination. The early Christians were pre-eminently nonresistant. They believed in love as a cosmic force. There was no iconoclasm during the minor peace of the Church. They did not yet denounce nor tear down temples, nor preach the end of the world. They grew to a mighty number but it never occurred to them, either in their weakness or in their strength, to regard other men for an instant as their foes or as aliens. The spectacle of the Christians loving all men was the most astounding Rome had ever seen. They were eager to sacrifice themselves for the weak, for children, and for the aged; they identified themselves with slaves and did not avoid the plague; they longed to share the common lot that they might receive the constant revelation. It was a new treasure which the early Christians added to the sum of all treasures, a joy hitherto unknown in the world—the joy of finding the Christ which lieth in each man, but which no man can unfold save in fellowship. A happiness ranging from the heroic to the pastoral enveloped them. They were to possess a revelation as long as life had new meaning to unfold, new action to propose.

I believe that there is a distinct turning among many young men and women toward this simple acceptance of Christ's message. They resent the assumption that Christianity is a set of ideas which belong to the religious consciousness, whatever that may be. They insist that it cannot be proclaimed and instituted apart from the social life of the community and that it must seek a simple and natural expression in the social organism itself. The Settlement movement is only one manifestation of that wider humanitarian movement which throughout Christendom, put pre-eminently in England, is endeavoring to embody itself, not in a sect, but in society itself.

I believe that this turning, this renaissance of the early Christian humanitarianism, is going on in America, in Chicago, if you please, without leaders who write or philosophize, without much speaking, but with a bent to express in social service and in terms of action the spirit of Christ. Certain it is that spiritual force is found in the Settlement movement, and it is also true that this force must be evoked and must be called into play before the success of any Settlement is assured. There must be the over-mastering belief that all that is noblest in life is common to men as men, in order to accentuate the likenesses and ignore the differences which are found among the people whom the Settlement constantly brings into juxtaposition. It may be true, as the Positivists insist, that the very religious fervor of man can be turned into love for his race, and his desire for a future life into content to live in the echo of his deeds; Paul's formula of seeking for the Christ which lieth in each man and founding our likenesses on him, seems a simpler formula to many of us.

In a thousand voices singing the Hallelujah Chorus in Handel's "Messiah," it is possible to distinguish the leading voices, but the differences of training and cultivation between them and the voices of the chorus, are lost in the unity of purpose and in the fact that they are all human voices lifted by a high motive. This is a weak illustration of what a Settlement attempts to do. It aims, in a measure, to develop whatever of social life its neighborhood may afford, to focus and give form to that life, to bring to bear upon it the results of cultivation and training; but it receives in exchange for the music of isolated voices the volume and strength of the chorus. It is quite impossible for me to say in what proportion or degree the subjective necessity which led to the opening of Hull-House combined the three trends: first, the desire to interpret democracy in social terms; secondly, the impulse beating at the very source of our lives, urging us to aid in the race progress; and, thirdly, the Christian movement toward humanitarianism. It is difficult to analyze a living thing; the analysis is at best imperfect. Many more motives may blend with the three trends; possibly the desire for a new form of social success due to the nicety of imagination, which refuses worldly pleasures unmixed with the joys of self-sacrifice; possibly, a love of approbation, so vast that it is not content with the treble clapping of delicate hands, but wishes also to hear the brass notes from toughened palms, may mingle with these.

The Settlement, then, is an experimental effort to aid in the solution of the social and industrial problems which are engendered by the modern conditions of life in a great city. It insists that these problems are not confined to any one portion of a city. It is an attempt to relieve, at the same time, the overaccumulation at one end of society and the destitution at the other; but it assumes that this overaccumulation and destitution is most sorely felt in the things that pertain to social and educational privileges. From its very nature it can stand for no political or social propaganda. It must, in a sense, give the warm welcome of an inn to all such propaganda, if perchance one of them be found an angel. The one thing to be dreaded in the Settlement is that it lose its flexibility, its power of quick adaptation, its readiness to change its methods as its environment may demand. It must be open to conviction and must have a deep and abiding sense of tolerance. It must be hospitable and ready for experiment. It should demand from its residents a scientific patience in the accumulation of facts and the steady holding of their sympathies as one of the best instruments for that accumulation. It must be grounded in a philosophy whose foundation is on the solidarity of the human race, a philosophy which will not waver when the race happens to be represented by a drunken woman or an idiot boy. Its residents must be emptied of all conceit of opinion and all self-assertion, and ready to arouse and interpret the public opinion of their neighborhood. They must be content to live quietly side by side with their neighbors, until they grow into a sense of relationship and mutual interests. Their neighbors are held apart by differences of race and language which the residents can more easily overcome. They are bound to see the needs of their neighborhood as a whole, to furnish data for legislation, and to use their influence to secure it. In short, residents are pledged to devote themselves to the duties of good citizenship and to the arousing of the social energies which too largely lie dormant in every neighborhood given over to industrialism. They are bound to regard the entire life of their city as organic, to make an effort to unify it, and to protest against its over differentiation.

It is always easy to make all philosophy point one particular moral and all history adorn one particular tale; but I may be forgiven the reminder that the best speculative philosophy sets forth the solidarity of the human race; that the highest moralists have taught that without the advance and improvement of the whole, no man can hope for any lasting improvement in his own moral or material individual condition; and that the subjective necessity for Social Settlements is therefore identical with that necessity, which urges us on toward social and individual salvation.

6.2
A Democratic Schoolroom (1900)

John Dewey

The father of modern American education, John Dewey uses a story about searching for school equipment as the means to lay out his educational philosophy. What does Dewey think should be the focus of education? How does that translate into an improved, more effectively democratic society? In what way does Dewey represent Progressive ideals?

S ome few years ago I was looking about the school supply stores in the city, trying to find desks and chairs which seemed thoroughly suitable from all points of view—artistic, hygienic, and educational—to the needs of the children. We had a great deal of difficulty in finding what we needed, and finally one dealer, more intelligent than the rest, made this remark: " I am afraid we have not what you want. You want something at which the children may work; these are all for listening." That tells the story of the traditional education. Just as the biologist can take a bone or two and reconstruct the whole animal, so, if we put before the mind's eye the ordinary schoolroom, with its rows of ugly desks placed in geometrical order, crowded together so that there shall be as little moving room as possible, desks almost all of the same size, with just space enough to hold books, pencils, and paper, and add a table, some chairs, the bare walls, and possibly a few pictures, we can reconstruct the only educational activity that can possibly go on in such a place. It is all made "for listening"—because simply studying lessons out of a book is only another kind of listening; it marks the dependency of one mind upon another. The attitude of listening means, comparatively speaking, passivity, absorption; that there are certain ready-made materials which are there, which have been prepared by the school superintendent, the board, the teacher, and of which the child is to take in as much as possible in the least possible time....

Another thing that is suggested by these schoolrooms, with their set desks, is that everything is arranged for handling as large numbers of children as possible; for dealing with children *en masse*, as an aggregate of units; involving, again, that they be treated passively. The moment children act they individualize themselves; they cease to be a mass and become the intensely distinctive beings that we are acquainted with out of school, in the home, the family, on the playground, and in the neighborhood.

On the same basis is explicable the uniformity of method and curriculum. If everything is on a "listening" basis, you can have uniformity of material and method. The ear, and the book which reflects the ear, constitute the medium which is alike for all. There is next to no opportunity for adjustment to varying capacities and demands. There is a certain amount—a fixed quantity—of ready-made results and accomplishments to be acquired by all children alike in a given time. It is in response to this demand that the curriculum has been developed from the elementary school up through the college. There is just so much desirable knowledge, and there are just so many needed technical accomplishments in the world. Then comes the mathematical problem of dividing this by the six, twelve, or sixteen years of school life. Now give the children every year just the proportionate fraction of the total, and by the time they have finished they will have mastered the whole. By covering so much ground during this hour or day or week or year, everything comes out with perfect evenness at the end—provided the children have not forgotten what they have previously learned. The outcome of all this is Matthew Arnold's report of the statement, proudly made to him by an educational authority in France, that so many thousands of children were studying at a given hour, say eleven o'clock, just such a lesson in geography; and in one of our own western cities this proud boast used to be repeated to successive visitors by its superintendent....

The real child, it hardly need be said, lives in the world of imaginative values and ideas which find only imperfect outward embodiment. We hear much nowadays about the cultivation of the child's "imagination." Then we undo much of our own talk and work by a belief that the imagination is some social part of the child that finds its satisfaction in some one particular direction—generally speaking, that of the unreal and make-believe, of the myth and made-up story. Why are we so hard of heart and so slow to believe? The imagination is the medium in which the child lives. To him there is everywhere and in everything which occupies his mind and activity at all a surplusage of value and significance. The question of the relation of the school to the child's life is at bottom simply this: Shall we ignore this native setting and tendency, dealing, not with the living child at all, but with the dead image we have erected, or shall we give it play and satisfaction? If we once believe in life and in the life of the child, then will all the occupations and uses spoken of, then will all history and science, become instruments of appeal and materials of culture to his imagination, and through that to the richness and the orderliness of his life. Where we now see only the outward doing and the outward product, there, behind all visible results, is the readjustment of mental attitude, the enlarged and sympathetic vision, the sense of growing power, and the willing ability to identify both insight and capacity with the interests of the world and man. Unless culture be a superficial polish, a veneering of mahogany over common wood, it surely is this—the growth of the imagination in flexibility, in scope, and in sympathy, till the life which the individual lives is informed with the life of nature and of society. When nature and society can live in the schoolroom, when the forms and tools of learning are subordinated to the substance of experience, then shall there be an opportunity for this identification, and culture shall be the democratic password.

6.3
Why the Ward Boss Rules (1898)

Jane Addams

In this selection Addams describes how "machine" politicians acquire power in major American cities like New York (see Documents 4.1 and 4.2) and Chicago. How do they do it? One important Progressive goal was to lessen the influence and control "ward bosses" had over voters. What prescription does Addams offer here, and what characterizes that prescription as "progressive"?

Primitive people, such as the South Italian peasants who live in the Nineteenth Ward, deep down in their hearts admire nothing so much as the good man. The successful candidate must be a good man according to the standards of his constituents. He must not attempt to hold up a morality beyond them, nor must he attempt to reform or change the standard. If he believes what they believe, and does what they are all cherishing a secret ambition to do, he will dazzle them by his success and win their confidence. Any one who has lived among poorer people cannot fail to be impressed with their constant kindness to each other; that unfailing response to the needs and distresses of their neighbors, even when in danger of bankruptcy themselves. This is their reward for living in the midst of poverty. They have constant opportunities for self-sacrifice and generosity, to which, as a rule, they respond. A man stands by his friend when he gets too drunk to take care of himself, when he loses his wife or child, when he is evicted for non-payment of rent, when he is arrested for a petty crime. It seems to such a man entirely fitting that his Alderman should do the same thing on a larger scale—that he should help a constituent out of trouble just because he is in trouble, irrespective of the justice involved.

The Alderman, therefore, bails out his constituents when they are arrested, or says a good word to the police justice when they appear before

From Jane Addams, "Why the Ward Boss Rules," *The Outlook*, April 2, 1898.

him for trial; uses his "pull" with the magistrate when they are likely to be fined for a civil misdemeanor, or sees what he can do to "fix up matters" with the State's attorney when the charge is really a serious one.

Because of simple friendliness, the Alderman is expected to pay rent for the hard-pressed tenant when no rent is forthcoming, to find jobs when work is hard to get, to procure and divide among his constituents all the places which he can seize from the City Hall. The Alderman of the Nineteenth Ward at one time made the proud boast that he had two thousand six hundred people in his ward upon the public pay-roll. This, of course, included day-laborers, but each one felt under distinct obligations to him for getting the job.

If we recollect, further, that the franchise-seeking companies pay respectful heed to the applicants backed by the Alderman, the question of voting for the successful man becomes as much an industrial as a political one. An Italian laborer wants a job more than anything else, and quite simply votes for the man who promises him one.

The Alderman may himself be quite sincere in his acts of kindness. In certain stages of moral evolution, a man is incapable of unselfish action the results of which will not benefit some one of his acquaintances; still more, of conduct that does not aim to assist any individual whatsoever; and it is a long step in moral progress to appreciate the work done by the individual for the community.

The Alderman gives presents at weddings and christenings. He seizes these days of family festivities for making friends. It is easiest to reach people in the holiday mood of expansive good will, but on their side it seems natural and kindly that he should do it. The Alderman procures passes from the railroads when his constituents wish to visit friends or to attend the funerals of distant relatives; he buys tickets galore for benefit entertainments given for a widow or a consumptive in peculiar distress; he contributes to prizes which are awarded to the handsomest lady or the most popular man. At a church bazaar, for instance, the Alderman finds the stage all set for his dramatic performance. When others are spending pennies he is spending dollars. Where anxious relatives are canvassing to secure votes for the two most beautiful children who are being voted upon, he recklessly buys votes from both sides, and laughingly declines to say which one he likes the best, buying off the young lady who is persistently determined to find out, with five dollars for the flower bazaar, the posies, of course, to be sent to the sick of the parish. The moral atmosphere of a bazaar suits him exactly. He murmurs many times, "Never mind; the money all goes to the poor," or, "It is all straight enough if the church gets it."

There is something archaic in a community of simple people in their attitude towards death and burial. Nothing so easy to collect money for as a funeral. If the Alderman seizes upon festivities for expressions of his good will, much more does he seize upon periods of sorrow. At a funeral he has the double advantage of ministering to a genuine craving for comfort and solace, and at the same time of assisting at an important social function.

In addition to this, there is among the poor, who have few social occasions, a great desire for a well-arranged funeral, the grade of which almost determines their social standing in the neighborhood. The Alderman saves the very poorest of his constituents from that awful horror of burial by the county; he provides carriages for the poor, who otherwise could not have them; for the more prosperous he sends extra carriages, so that they may invite more friends and have a longer procession; for the most prosperous of all there will be probably only a large "flower-piece." It may be too much to say that all the relatives and friends who ride in the carriages provided by the Alderman's bounty vote for him, but they are certainly influenced by his kindness, and talk of his virtues during the long hours of the ride back and forth from the suburban cemetery. A man who would ask at such a time where all this money comes from would be considered sinister. Many a man at such a time has formulated a lenient judgment of political corruption and has heard kindly speeches which he has remembered on election day. "Ah, well, he has a big Irish heart. He is good to the widow and the fatherless." "He knows the poor better than the big guns who are always about talking civil service and reform."

Indeed, what headway can the notion of civic purity, of honesty of administration, make against this big manifestation of human friendliness, this stalking survival of village kindness? The notions of the civic reformer are negative and impotent before it. The reformers give themselves over largely to criticisms of the present state of affairs, to writing and talking of what the future must be; but their goodness is not dramatic; it is not even concrete and human.

Such an Alderman will keep a standing account with an undertaker, and telephone every week, and sometimes more than once, the kind of outfit he wishes provided for a bereaved constituent, until the sum may roll up into hundreds a year. Such a man understands what the people want, and ministers just as truly to a great human need as the musician or the artist does. I recall an attempt to substitute what we might call a later standard.

A delicate little child was deserted in the Hull House nursery. An investigation showed that it had been born ten days previously in the Cook

County Hospital, but no trace could be found of the unfortunate mother. The little thing lived for several weeks, and then, in spite of every care, died. We decided to have it buried by the county, and the wagon was to arrive by eleven o'clock. About nine o'clock in the morning the rumor of this awful deed reached the neighbors. A half-dozen of them came, in a very excited state of mind, to protest. They took up a collection out of their poverty with which to defray a funeral. We were then comparatively new in the neighborhood. We did not realize that we were really shocking a genuine moral sentiment of the community. In our crudeness, we instanced the care and tenderness which had been expended upon the little creature while it was alive; that it had had every attention from a skilled physician and trained nurse; we even intimated that the excited members of the group had not taken part in this, and that it now lay with us to decide that the child should be buried, as it had been born, at the county's expense. It is doubtful whether Hull House has ever done anything which injured it so deeply in the minds of some of its neighbors. We were only forgiven by the most indulgent on the ground that we were spinsters and could not know a mother's heart. No one born and reared in the community could possibly have made a mistake like that. No one who had studied the ethical standards with any care could have bungled so completely.

Last Christmas our Alderman distributed six tons of turkeys, and four or more tons of ducks and geese; but each luckless biped was handed out either by himself or one of his friends with a "Merry Christmas." Inevitably, some families got three or four apiece, but what of that? He had none of the nagging rules of the charitable societies, nor was he ready to declare that, because a man wanted two turkeys for Christmas, he was a scoundrel, who should never be allowed to eat turkey again.

The Alderman's wisdom was again displayed in procuring from downtown friends the sum of three thousand dollars wherewith to uniform and equip a boys' temperance brigade which had been formed in the ward a few months before his campaign. Is it strange that the good leader, whose heart was filled with innocent pride as he looked upon these promising young scions of virtue, should decline to enter into a reform campaign?

The question does, of course, occur to many minds, Where does the money come from with which to dramatize so successfully? The more primitive people accept the truthful statement of its sources without any shock to their moral sense. To their simple minds he gets it "from the rich," and so long as he again gives it out to the poor, as a true Robin Hood, with open hand, they have no objections to offer. Their ethics are quite honestly those of the merry-making foresters. The next less primitive people of the vicinage are quite willing to admit that he leads "the gang" in the City Council, and sells out the city franchises; that he makes deals with the franchise-seeking companies; that he guarantees to steel dubious measures though the Council, for which he demands liberal pay; that he is, in short, a successful boodler. But when there is intellect enough to get this point of view, there is also enough to make the contention that this is universally done; that all the Aldermen do it more or less successfully, but that the Alderman of the Nineteenth Ward is unique in being so generous; that such a state of affairs is to be deplored, of course, but that that is the way business is run, and we are fortunate when a kind-hearted man who is close to the people gets a large share of the boodle; that he serves these franchised companies who employ men in the building and construction of their enterprises, and that they are bound in return to give jobs to his constituency. Even when they are intelligent enough to complete the circle, and to see that the money comes, not from the pockets of the companies' agents, but from the street-car fares of people like themselves, it almost seems as if they would rather pay two cents more each time they ride than give up the consciousness that they have a big, warm-hearted friend at court who will stand by them in an emergency. The sense of just dealing comes apparently much later than the desire for protection and kindness. The Alderman is really elected because he is a good friend and neighbor.

During a campaign a year and a half ago, when a reform league put up a candidate against our corrupt Alderman, and when Hull House worked hard to rally the moral sentiment of the ward in favor of the new man, we encountered another and unexpected difficulty. Finding that it was hard to secure enough local speakers of the moral tone which we desired, we imported orators from other parts of the town, from the "better element," so to speak. Suddenly we heard it rumored on all sides that, while the money and speakers for the reform candidate were coming from the swells, the money which was backing our corrupt Alderman also came from a swell source; it was rumored that the president of a street-car combination, for whom he performed constant offices in the City Council, was ready to back him to the extent of fifty thousand dollars; that he, too, was a good man, and sat in high places; that he had recently given a large sum of money to an educational institution, and was, therefore, as philanthropic, not to say good and upright, as any man in town; that our Alderman had the sanction of the highest authorities, and that the lecturers who were talking against corruption, and the selling and buying of franchises, were only the cranks, and not the solid business men who had developed and built up Chicago.

All parts of the community are bound together in ethical development. If the so-called more enlightened members of the community accept public gifts from the man who buys up the Council, and the so-called less enlightened members accept individual gifts from the man who sells out the Council, we surely must take our punishment together.

Another curious experience during that campaign was the difference of standards between the imported speakers and the audience. One man, high in the council of the "better element," one evening used as an example of the philanthropic politician an Alderman of the vicinity, recently dead, who was devotedly loved and mourned by his constituents. When the audience caught the familiar name in the midst of the platitudes, they brightened up wonderfully. But, as the speaker went on, they first looked puzzled, then astounded, and gradually their astonishment turned to indignation. The speaker, all unconscious of the situation, went on, imagining, perhaps, that he was addressing his usual audience, and totally unaware that he was perpetrating an outrage upon the finest feelings of the people who were sitting before him. He certainly succeeded in irrevocably injuring the chances of the candidate for whom he was speaking. The speaker's standard of ethics was upright dealing in positions of public trust. The standard of ethics held by his audience was, being good to the poor and speaking gently of the dead. If he considered them corrupt and illiterate voters, they quite honestly held him blackguard.

If we would hold to our political democracy, some pains must be taken to keep on common ground in our human experiences, and to some solidarity in our ethical conceptions. And if we discover that men of low ideals and corrupt practice are forming popular political standards simply because such men stand by and for and with the people, then nothing remains but to obtain a like sense of identification before we can hope to modify ethical standards.

6.4
Muller v. Oregon (1908)

In one of the most important Supreme Court rulings of the earlier twentieth century, Justice David Brewer wrote an opinion, excerpted below, defending an Oregon law which restricted the number of hours women could work for wages. A key part of Progressive Era reform, such laws were intended to serve the greater good of society, rather than specifically look out for the interests of women. What was that "greater good"? What reasons does Brewer give for upholding this law? Do you agree with them? Are they echoes here of more contemporary arguments regarding the place of women in American society?

Mr. Justice Brewer delivered the opinion of the court:

On February 19, 1903, the legislature of the state of Oregon passed an act the first section of which is in these words:

'Sec. 1. That no female (shall) be employed in any mechanical establishment, or factory, or laundry in this state more than ten hours during any one day. The hours of work may be so arranged as to permit the employment of females at any time so that they shall not work more than ten hours during the twenty-four hours of any one day.'

Sec. 3 made a violation of the provisions of the prior sections a misdemeanor subject to a fine of not less than $10 nor more than $25. On September 18, 1905, an information was filed in the circuit court of the state for the county of Multanomah, charging that the defendant' on the 4th day of September, A. D. 1905, in the county of Multnomah and state of Oregon, then and there being the owner of a laundry, known as the Grand Laundry, in the city of Portland, and the employer of females therein, did then and there unlawfully permit and suffer one Joe Haselbock, he, the

U S Supreme Court, 208 .S. 415

said Joe Haselbock, then and there being an overseer, superintendent, and agent of said Curt Muller, in the said Grant Laundry, to require a female, to wit, one Mrs. E. Gotcher, to work more than ten hours in said laundry on said 4th day of September, A. D. 1905, contrary to the statutes in such cases made and provided, and against the peace and dignity of the state of Oregon.'

A trial resulted in a verdict against the defendant, who was sentenced to pay a fine of $10. The supreme court of the state affirmed the conviction whereupon the case was brought here on writ of error.

The single question is the constitutionality of the statute under which the defendant was convicted, so far as it affects the work of a female in a laundry. That it does not conflict with any provisions of the state Constitution is settled by the decision of the supreme court of the state. The contentions of the defendant, now plaintiff in error, are thus stated in his brief:

'(1) Because the statute attempts to prevent persons sui juris from making their own contracts and thus violates the provisions of the 14 Amendment, as follows:

'No state shall make or enforce any law which shall abridge the privileges or immunities of citizens of the United States; nor shall any state deprive any person of life, liberty, or property, without due process of law; nor deny to any person within its jurisdiction the equal protection of the laws.'

'(2) Because the statute does not apply equally to all persons similarly situated, and is class legislation.

'(3) The statute is not a valid exercise of the police power. The kinds of work prescribed are not lawful, nor are they declared to be immoral or dangerous to the public health; nor can such a law be sustained on the ground that it is designed to protect women on account of their sex. There is no necessary or reasonable connection between the limitation prescribed by the act and the public health, safety, or welfare.'

It is the law of Oregon that women, whether married or single, have equal contractual and personal rights with men....

It thus appears that, putting to one side the elective franchise, in the matter of personal and contractual rights they stand on the same plane as the other sex. Their rights in these respects can no more be infringed than the equal rights of their brothers. We held in Lochner v. New York, a law providing that no laborer shall be required or permitted to work in bakeries more than sixty hours in a week or ten hours in a day was not as to men a legitimate exercise of the police power of the state, but an unreasonable, unnecessary, and arbitrary interference with the right and liberty of the individual to contract in relation to his labor, and as such was in conflict with, and void under, the Federal Constitution. That decision is invoked by plaintiff in error as decisive of the question before us. But this assumes that the difference between the sexes does not justify a different rule respecting a restriction of the hours of labor....

It is undoubtedly true, as more than once declared by this court, that the general right to contract in relation to one's business is part of the liberty of the individual, protected by the 14th Amendment to the Federal Constitution; yet is equally well settled that this liberty is not absolute and extending to all contracts, and that a state may, without conflicting with the provisions of the 14th Amendment, restrict in many respects the individual's power of contract....

That woman's physical structure and the performance of maternal functions place her at a disadvantage in the struggle for subsistence is obvious. This is especially true when the burdens of motherhood are upon her. Even when they are not, by abundant testimony of the medical fraternity continuance for a long time on her feet at work, repeating this from day to day, tends to injurious effects upon the body, and, as healthy mothers are essential to vigorous offspring, the physical well-being of woman becomes an object of public interest and care in order to preserve the strength and vigor of the race.

Still again, history discloses the fact that woman has always been dependent upon man. He established his control at the outset by superior physical strength, may, without conflicting with the provisions and this control in various forms, with diminished intensity, has continued to the present. As minors, thought not to the same extent, she has been looked upon in the courts as needing especial care that her rights may be preserved. Education was long denied her, and while now the doors of the schoolroom are opened and her opportunities for acquiring knowledge are great, yet even with that and the consequent subsistence she is not an equal competitor with her brother. Though limitations upon personal and contractual rights may be removed by legislation, there is that in her disposition and habits of life which will operate against a full assertion of those rights. She will still be where some legislation to protect her seems necessary to secure a real equality of right. Doubtless there are individual exceptions, and there are many respects in which she has an advantage over him; but looking at it from the viewpoint of the effort to maintain an independent position in life, she is not upon an equality. Differentiated by these matters from the other sex, she is properly placed in a class by herself, and legislation designed for her protection may be sustained, even when like legislation is not necessary for her protection may be sustained. It is impossible to close one's eyes to the fact that she still looks to her brother and depends upon him. Even though all restrictions on political, personal, and contractual rights were taken away, and she stood, so far as statutes are concerned, upon an absolutely equal plane with him, it would still be true that she is so constituted that she will rest upon and look to him for protection; that her physical structure and a proper discharge of her maternal functions-having in view not merely her own health, but the well-being of the race-justify legislation to protect her from the greed as well as the passion of man. The limitations which this statute places upon her contractual powers, upon her right to agree with her employer as to the time she shall labor, are not imposed solely for her benefit, but also largely for the benefit of all. Many words cannot make this plainer. The two sexes differ in structure of body, in the functions to be performed by each, in the amount of physical strength, in the capacity for long continued labor, particularly when done standing, the influence of vigorous health upon the future well-being of the race, the self-reliance which enables one to assert full rights, and in the capacity to maintain the struggle for subsistence. This difference justifies a difference in legislation, and upholds that which is designed to compensate for some for the burdens which rest upon her.

We have not referred in this discussion to the denial of the elective franchise in the state of Oregon, for while that may disclose a lack of political equality in all things with her brother, that is not of itself decisive. The reason runs deeper, and rests in the inherent difference between the two sexes, and in the different functions in life which they perform.

For these reasons, and without questioning in any respect the decision in Lochner v. New York, we are of the opinion that it cannot be adjudged that the act in question is in conflict with the Federal Constitution, so far as it respects the work of a female in a laundry, and the judgment of the Supreme Court of Oregon is affirmed.

6.5
The Dangerous Life (1931)

Benjamin B. Lindsey

Known as one of the founders of the juvenile court movement during the Progressive Era, Lindsey began his career as a lawyer. Here he recounts the story of his first case as a defense attorney representing youthful offenders. In this account Lindsey indicates some reasons why he believed that the legal system should treat youth differently than adults who find themselves accused of crimes. What are those reasons? Are you persuaded by them?

The clerk gave me the numbers of the cases. I got the pleadings [court case paperwork] and went into the old West Side jail to see my clients. The Warden smiled when I told him their names. I followed him through clanging iron doors with their rating rattling bolts and bars to the back part of the building.

At the end of a corridor I came in front of a cage on the floor of which were two small boys engaged in gambling with two grown men who had been brought in from some outlying section of Arapahoe county, a sparsely settled empire that then ran clear to the eastern state line.

I found that these boys had already been in jail more than 60 days and had learned to play poker from their older cell mates, a safe cracker and a horse thief, upon whom they had come to look as great heroes.

My first thought was that the judge in assigning me to defend two such men from serious crimes had given me a pretty tough job but my concern was soon relieved as the Warden explained: "It's the kids the judge wants you to look after. He was over here the other day and he didn't like it very much that they're still here. He said he knew a young fellow who was just the one to look after the case. I guess it must be you."

"Then," I asked, to make doubly sure, "it's not those two men who are my clients?"

"No," he drawled. "Those guys have got two real lawyers to defend 'em."

"But," I persisted, "I am appointed to defend two burglars."

The kids looked like such real boys that in my confusion I had been unable to visualize them as criminals—my mind just refused to work that way.

"Sure you are," said the Warden, "but them's the burglars."

A number of things shot through my mind as this first step in my difficulties cleared up. One was that it, perhaps, took "two burglars" like these boys to make "one burglar." And so my pride that had soared from the flattery of two assignments when any young fellow would have been tickled to death with one was a bit humbled.

My first task—that was afterward to become my task in so many thousands of cases that I then little knew were to follow—was to get acquainted with the prisoners. It was my first appearance before the bench of youth but its lesson was to stay with me even in the days when I had long ceased to be a lawyer and had become a judge. For there by those bars that would have shamed the King Tiger of the Jungle I was able to begin a lasting friendship with the little prisoners.

They were typical boys from the realm of Gangville, as I was to come to know it so well. They were about twelve years of age.

The one that impressed me most was a little freckle-faced Irish lad with a sense of humor. He was charged with having gone into a railroad section house and taken a lot of tools.

"Sonny," I said, "you are charged with burglary."

"I ain't no burglary," he countered.

"I guess you don't know what burglary means," I ventured. And I explained to him that the long rigamarole in the complaint papers meant to charge him with breaking and entering a tool house and *that* constituted burglary.

"I never stole 'em, I just took 'em," he answered heatedly. "So I ain't done no burglary—I ain't done nothing'."

"Well, one thing you can't deny," I went on, getting chummy with my client. "You've got the dirtiest face I ever saw on a kid."

"Tain't my fault," he shot back with a grin. "A guy threw water on me and the dust settled on it."

When I protested to the Warden against this good-natured boy being held in jail with two hardened old criminals, he admitted it was "a damned outrage."

"How many boys are there in jail?" I asked.

"Oh, quite a number," he answered. "Most of them don't stay so long as these two boys—they're waiting for the fall term of court. Their families couldn't afford to put up bonds."

"But why do you put them in with that horse thief and safe cracker?"

"The jail is crowded," he said. And he gave various other excuses.

Well, in answering the charge against those kids, I did a thing that was perhaps purely artless, the direct reaction from my rage complexes, my indignation at injustice.

I prepared an answer that was an indictment against the state of Colorado for its crime against those two boys. The thing got a lot of public discussion and raised quite a furor.

Here were two boys, neither of them serious enemies of society, who were about to be convicted of burglary and have felony records standing against them for the remainder of their lives. And, pending the decision of their cases, they were associating generally with criminals and particularly with a horse thief and a safe cracker. The state was sending them to a school for crime—deliberately teaching them to be horse thieves and safe crackers. It was outrageous—and absurd.

My first fight then was with the state of Colorado. I was determined that those boys should have their chance. I saw only vaguely then what afterward became clearer to me—that my first fight with the state was not just for those two boys but for millions like them. Even then, however,—before I had formulated any plan to change the things that were or had written any of the hundreds of laws I afterward wrote for my own and other states and foreign countries—I had made up my mind to smash the system that meant so much injustice.

6.6

Gender and Urban Political Reform: The City Club and the Woman's City Club of Chicago in the Progressive Era

Maureen A. Flanagan

Maureen Flanagan here compares the activities of two important Progressive organizations in Chicago, one comprised of men, the other of women. How did the goals of each group differ? What about the means of achieving those goals? According to Flanagan, were the differences in the organizations and their activities largely a function of gender differences, or can they be explained by other factors as well?

To bring together...as many as possible of those men ...who sincerely desire to meet the full measure of their responsibility as citizens, who are genuinely interested in the improvement, by non-partisans and disinterested methods, of the political, social, and economic conditions of the community in which we live ...[who] are united in the sincerity of their desire to promote the public welfare.

—City Club of Chicago Statement of Purpose[1]

To bring together women interested in promoting the welfare of the city; to coordinate and render more effective the scattered social and civic activities in which they are engaged; to extend a knowledge of public affairs; to aid in improving civic conditions and to assist in arousing an increased sense of social responsibility for the safeguarding of the home, the maintenance of good government, and the ennobling of that large home of all—the city.

—Woman's City Club of Chicago Statement of Purpose[2]

From *American Historical Review,* Vol. 95, No. 4, October 1990 by Marueen A. Flanagan. Reprinted by permission of the author.

On one political reform issue after another, the men and women of the Chicago City Clubs disagreed over the means and ends of Progressive Era reform. In the second decade of the twentieth century, the men of the City Club of Chicago, a civic reform organization, were working with businessmen's clubs to implement a vocational education curriculum in the public schools designed to train workers for the benefit of industry. Simultaneously, the female counterpart of the City Club, the Woman's City Club of Chicago, was cooperating with the Chicago Federation of Labor, the Chicago Federation of Teachers, the Women's Trade Union League, the Woman's party, and the Socialist party of Illinois in sponsoring a talk in Chicago by Congressman David L. Lewis advocating government ownership of the telephones. The men of the City Club strongly opposed any attempt to implement government ownership of utilities as anticapitalist; they also would never have dreamed of cooperating with workers' organizations or the Socialist party on any issue.

It is commonly accepted that male and female reformers in the first two decades of the twentieth century had different agendas for reform; that these differences stemmed primarily from gender concerns is also assumed. Yet historians have rarely compared the political activities of men and women of the same class. Most works on Progressive Era politics and reform concentrate on men, ignoring women's roles, viewing them only as partners with their husbands or assigning them to the periphery of charity and church work. The idea that women were actively concerned with politics is ignored in favor of seeing them as interested in social, not political, causes and reforms. By ignoring women as political reformers, historians assume that women have little or no political history, at least until we can count their votes. As a result, the processes that led women to pursue political activity and political goals in the first place, and the reasons why their political goals differed from men of their own class, have not been examined.

The members of both the Woman's City Club and the City Club were deeply engaged in political action of the sort Eric Foner has characterized as concerned with "how power in civil society is ordered and exercised [and] the way in which power was wielded and conceptualized." Feeling assaulted by numerous and vexatious municipal problems, they sought to solve them by changing the structure of government, reorganizing the urban environment, and reallocating power within it. Streets and sidewalks in Chicago were in constant disrepair; the public utilities provided abysmal service; the sewer and garbage collection and disposal systems could not handle the volume of waste produced every day in the city; the public school system was overcrowded, understaffed, and underfunded; the smoke, fumes, and waste from industrial plants polluted the air and ground; a large percentage of the populace lived in crowded, rickety, unsanitary tenement houses that flourished in the face of minimal building regulations; and the city's police force neither controlled crime nor kept the peace. Moreover, in the early twentieth century, municipal governments in the United States often lacked institutional authority for attacking these and other urban problems. Chicago's municipal government was structurally weak, the locus of political power was diffuse and decentralized, and no consensus existed on who should wield power and to what purposes. Such issues as how to collect and dispose of municipal garbage and waste, how to restructure and run the system of public education, and how, and to what ends, to regulate the use of police power within the city were controversial, and no consensus existed among the citizenry about the appropriate solutions. Because of their different relationships to the urban power structure, to daily life within the city, and to other individuals, when the members of the Woman's City Club confronted these problems, they came to a vision of a good city and specific proposals of how best to provide for the welfare of its residents that were very different from those of their male counterparts in the City Club.

The contrasting approaches of the two City Clubs is particularly significant because in other respects the groups resembled each other. Both were founded as municipal reform organizations, the men's club in 1903 and the women's club in 1910, on the principle that the citizens of a city were responsible for the welfare of the community in which they lived. The two clubs drew their membership largely from the same class of upper-middle-class white men and women within the city. The men were generally businessmen or professionals; often, husbands in the City Club had wives who belonged to the Woman's City Club. Of the 909 married women who joined the Woman's City Club in its inaugural year of 1910-11, almost 10 percent were married to men who were members of the City Club; five years later, the total percentage had risen to 16. A smaller percentage of women who joined the Woman's City Club were the sisters, mothers, and daughters of men in the City Club. During this same period, 1910-15, more women joined the Woman's City Club whose husbands had previously been in the City Club and who had either died or dropped membership for other reasons, a circumstance that adds to the picture of a membership drawn from a similar pool of people within the city. Among the leadership of the Woman's City Club, the correlation between husbands and wives belonging to their respective clubs is higher:

55 percent of the married women serving as officers and directors of the Woman's City Club in 1915-16, for example, were married to men in the City Club; one other officer was the widow of a former City Club member. Of the married women who chaired the club's standing and civic committees, 75 percent had husbands as members of the City Club; and 33 percent of the married women who headed the ward organization committees were married to men in the City Club.

Some of the founding members of the City Club were from the prominent, wealthy Chicago families who had built industrial Chicago: Medill McCormick, John V. Farwell, Jr., Charles R. Crane, Murry Nelson, Jr., and Kellogg Fairbank, for example. But the majority of the membership came from the newer business and professional ranks, which furnished most of the city's middle-class reformers. Among them were real estate developer Arthur Aldis, manufacturer T. K. Webster, and stationer George Cole; lawyers Walter L. Fisher, Victor Elting, and Hoyt King; university professor Charles Merriam and newspaper editor Slason Thompson. At the Woman's City Club, first-year members included the wives of some of these men—Ruth McCormick, Mabel Fisher, Emma Webster, Mary Nelson, Julia Thompson, and Mary Aldis; the wives of other prominent Chicago business and professional men—Ellen Henrotin, Mary Emily Blatchford, Harriet McCormick, Edith Rockefeller McCormick, Anita McCormick Blaine, Paulette Palmer, and Julie Wolf; and settlement house workers—Jane Addams, Mary McDowell, Anna Nicoles, and Harriet Vittum.

A goodly number of unmarried professional women, including some social workers, belonged to the Woman's City Club. It would be a mistake to assume, however, that the settlement house workers wielded a disproportionate influence over the policies pursued by the club. Of the 1,243 members of the Woman's City Club in 1910-11, twenty-three listed one of five settlement houses as their residence; two other women were married to male settlement house workers. Five years later, 2,789 members, forty-three gave their residence as a settlement house with another three married to male settlement house workers. In no year between 1910 and 1916 did settlement house workers occupy more than five of the twenty-eight positions of officers and directors of the Woman's City Club, nor did they hold a higher percentage of chairs of standing, civic, and ward committees. Solidly middle to upper-class women—either married or widowed—were considerably more numerous than settlement house workers. In 1915, for instance, 388 members listed a residence in the city's affluent twenty-first ward; eighty of these women had husbands or fathers in the City

Club. Such prominent Chicago women as Ruth Hanna (Mrs. Medill) Mc-Cormick, Ellen (Mrs. Charles) Henrotin, Louise DeKoven (Mrs. Joseph) Bowen, and Elizabeth (Mrs. Charles E.) Merriam, for example, served as vice presidents, directors, and as chairs of standing, civic, and ward committees during the years covered by this study. During the club's first six years, its presidency was held by three prominent Chicago women: Mary (Mrs. H. W.) Wilmarth, Louise DeKoven Bown, and University of Chicago Professor Sophonisba Breckenridge; and two settlement house workers: Harriet Vittum and Mary McDowell.

It is more difficult to determine how many male settlements house workers may have belonged to the City Club because its membership lists do not give addresses or professions. Raymond Robins and Graham Taylor, two of the city's most prominent settlement house workers, joined the club in early 1904. One or the other of these two men were among the club's thirteen directors during its first four years; neither held a higher position but both men were consistently active in club affairs and programs and in attempting to influence club policies.

Despite the similar constituencies and statements of purpose of the two City Clubs, they took opposing positions on several current municipal issues in a way that reveals profound differences in their conceptions of city government and its responsibility of the general welfare of its residents. For example, the two clubs took very different approaches to the noxious problem of municipal sanitation when the city's contract with the Chicago Reduction Company expired in 1913. Following standard municipal policy at the time, the city had contracted out to this private business most of the task of municipal garbage and waste disposal. The city itself only collected garbage from houses and small buildings, and it hired private contractors to collect from apartment buildings, hotels, hospitals, and other large establishments. It then paid the Chicago Reduction Company $47,500 per year to dispose of the garbage, and the company made profits from selling the by-products produced from the garbage. On the whole, the citizens of Chicago were unhappy with the system. They complained of infrequent garbage collection, of unsanitary and rickety wagons used for collection that leaked garbage and refuse onto the streets and alleys through which they traveled, of having to separate garbage from other types of waste, and of the reeking fumes emanating from the Reduction Company's plant on the city's near southwest side. When the contract expired, the city had several options to improve service. It could sign a new contract with the Chicago Reduction Company requiring the company to provide better services, it could seek a new company with which to contract, or it could assume direct municipal ownership and operation of all garbage and waste disposal.

The problem of how best to dispose of garbage was part of a larger dilemma faced by U.S. cities during the early twentieth century over the provision of vital municipal services. It was a dilemma not simply because it involved choosing the best possible means but because there was no agreement among urban residents about what criteria defined the best means. One group wished to replace the system of contracting out (franchising) with municipal ownership and operation of municipal services. Another wanted to retain the present system, albeit more tightly regulated. As everyone involved realized, there was a critical difference between these two positions: with municipal ownership and operation of municipal services, the city government would assume far more power than it currently possessed. It would also deprive private enterprise and the city's businessmen of an arena for profit.

In 1913, both the City Club and the Woman's City Club considered the garbage issue in ways that suggest significant differences between the members of the two clubs. The City Club's approach typified its method of investigating municipal problems. The club constituted a committee and charged it to study the problem, consult with "experts" in the field, and make recommendations to the club as a whole. The club also scheduled meetings to which it invited various people concerned with the problem to present their ideas and recommendations to the general membership. It directed the committee to collect all possible information on garbage dumps, refuse loading stations, ward dump yards, and any and all real property used for the purpose of garbage disposal. The committee was also to visit and inspect the plant used by the Chicago Reduction Company. Most important, the City Club instructed the committee to gain all the information it could about the "financial details of the reduction business."

On the basis of the committee's findings and reports, and a competing bid offered by the Illinois Rendering Company, the City Club firmly supported the option of keeping the system in private hands for financial reasons. The only question in the club member's minds was how to secure the most favorable contract arrangement from one of the two reduction companies. In all its deliberations, the City Club rejected outright the option of municipal ownership and operation would be more financially rewarding than private ownership. Under the club's calculations, if the city retained its system of private contractors, it would continue to pay costs of collection and reduction, estimated at nearly $500,000 per year, but would avoid the costs of purchasing and operating a reduction plant. This approach, the City club argued, would be more fiscally efficient. The City Club also proposed that the one costly item for the city, its collection from private residences, be reduced by making the garbage wagon drivers civil servants.

The City Club carried forward its opposition to municipal ownership when it recommended that its membership oppose an ordinance before the City Council in 1914 to appropriate money for city purchase of the reduction plant, which would then be operated by the city's department of health. Even when the ordinance passed, the club refused to withdraw its opposition. In early 1915, it grudgingly supported a bond issue of $700,000 for the health department, saying that, since the money had already been spent (for the purchase and renovation of the plant), the bonds had to be approved. The City Club, however, never ceased fighting municipal ownership of this and other public utilities.

It was not just its cost-benefit analysis of municipal ownership that motivated the City Club. The debate over garbage disposal also concerned whether to continue with reduction—the disposal method used by both the companies bidding for the city contract—or to shift to the incineration method. When Willis Nance, an alderman and a member of the City Waste commission, spoke to the City Club, he emphasized that reduction "has proven in certain cities to be of immense value from a commercial standpoint." In Chicago, for example, the profit realized from reduction (a process that rendered an oil product used in the manufacture of soaps) had reached as high as $150,000 per year. "It is a question worth considering if in burning all our waste [that is, incineration] we will not become a bit extravagant in our method." Nance admitted that incineration plants were virtually odorless, that because the extreme heat destroyed almost everything this method was certainly sanitary, and that the heat generated by burning refuse could be used to create electricity for the city. Yet Nance, and the City Club, rejected these considerations in favor of reduction. In its refusal to consider creating a municipally owned and operated garbage system, and its support of reduction over incineration, the City Club remained solidly on the side of private profit and limited municipal power over city services. The club did not even investigate possible long-term savings to the city of buying and operating the disposal equipment. Implicit in its stance was the notion that the good of the city lay in maximizing private profits from the provision of municipal services and minimizing governmental involvement.

The Woman's City Club, on the other hand, favored both municipal control over and incineration of garbage on the grounds that they would maximize the healthiness of the urban environment. The Woman's City Club did not concentrate on fiscal details but directed Mary McDowell to explore the variety of sanitation methods used in the United States and in Europe. McDowell, a settlement house worker and chair of the club's Committee on City Waste, undertook an extensive tour of waste disposal operations on both continents in 1913. On her return, she addressed the men's club about her findings. Her tour had convinced her that incineration was a more efficient and sanitary way to dispose of garbage. All the incineration plants she had visited, she told her audience, were free of noxious fumes, the heat from incineration went to generate electricity, and the hardened ash left as a by-product was being used in Europe for street paving. She could see little to recommend in reduction and told the men of the City Club that is was wrong to think of garbage removal as a business rather than a question of health and sanitation. By thinking of it as a business, they failed to consider for instance that, because a reduction plant could only handle pure garbage, citizens had to perform the unhealthy task of sorting pure garbage from unreducible refuse before it could be collected. Reduction, she bluntly told them, "fascinates the business man in America because you can extract money out of the garbage."

Incineration was only one facet of the overall program for garbage collection and disposal reform favored by the members of the Woman's City Club. These women wanted to centralize power through the municipal ownership and operation of waste facilities, the same system specifically rejected by their male counterparts. After the city purchased the reduction plant in 1914, the men continued to decry the lack of facts and figures available to show whether municipal ownership could be profitable. The women responded by showing that it was indeed profitable. In contrast to the men of the City Club, who advocated maximizing private profits—as high as $150,000—while minimizing municipal expenditures, the women showed that the city had made a profit of almost $6,000 in the year after it purchased the reduction plant. According to their calculations, once the initial outlay had been made to purchase equipment, the possibilities of small yearly profit for the city existed. Moreover, while they never advocated waste or careless expenditure of municipal finances, they did not see profit as the primary issue. As debate continued during 1915, the Woman's City Club's Committee on City Waste stressed the primacy of health over economics. Where garbage disposal was concerned, announced the club, "the true measure of its efficiency in such work is not the financial returns to be received, but the character of the service given."

In 1916, the Woman's City Club made municipal ownership and operation of all garbage and waste collection and disposal a provision of its Woman's Municipal Platform for Reform. later that year, the club proposed additionally that the city institutionalize garbage collection and disposal in a new municipal bureau, opposing a new bond issue of $2 million that neither provided for purchase and development of collection equipment nor established this municipal bureau. Unlike the men of the City Club, these women believed that service and the good health and sanitation of the city should be the priority for settling this issue. They rejected claims that municipal garbage disposal would not work, wondering aloud "why a municipality should not use the same sense in running their business that a packing plant does."

On the issue of public education, the differences between the City Club and the Woman's City Club were, if anything, even more pronounced. For a number of years, the City Club had been seeking to increase the business efficiency of the school system by implementing a type of education "more in accordance with the demands of modern society and business conditions" In 1908, in response to the statement of Superintendent of Schools Cooley that "instruction in the elementary grades of the city schools was hopelessly academic and unable to fit the mass of the children for the vocation upon which they were to enter," the City Club constituted a subcommittee to investigate the possibilities of instituting a curriculum stressing vocational education. The club followed its general operating premise that every issue should be scientifically investigated—a task made easier by its wealth—and hired an outside investigator. E. A. Wreidt of the University of Chicago, to pursue this issue for them.

The City Club was seeking a system of vocational education that would better train students for industrial jobs. This system, the club decided after some consideration, could best be established by businessmen and the board of education working together to design a program "directing school children toward proper occupations, and securing additional training for these children in the occupations themselves," while they were still in school. To secure the requisite funding and administration, the City Club supported various measures in the state legislature. It especially liked a bill introduced by the Illinois Bankers' Association to give state support to schools providing vocational education within the general school curriculum.

As was true of the City Club's attitude toward garbage and waste disposal, its proposals for vocational education, intended to create a dependable industrial work force, reflected members' preoccupations with financial reward for business. The subcommittee on vocational education declared industrial education "urgent if not imperative if we are to attain a place in the world's commerce commensurate with out possibilities and opportunities." Whether children or parents wanted this innovation did not concern the City Club. If anyone objected, he or she was accused of selfishness. The club's resolution in support of vocational education declared that "the nurture of intelligent skill in our hand workers is but increasing our effectiveness in industrial production. Certainly any measure looking to this end should have the hearty support of all classes of our citizens. What is good for the whole people can not possibly work harm to any section of our country."

The Woman's City Club also supported vocational education but of a different type and for different means and ends. These women used no rhetoric about the productivity and advancement of industrial society. They were concerned instead with the fate of the individual child within the school and industrial work systems. The Woman's City Club did not establish a new subcommittee to study the problems, and they could not afford outside experts. Working jointly with more than two hundred women from thirty women's clubs across the city, the Woman's City Club approached the issue of vocational education with two goas in mind. The first was to find ways to keep children in school beyond age fourteen (the mandatory age limit for schooling) in order to educate and prepare them for better paying jobs. These women believed it a social and personal tragedy that thousands of children left school every year to enter low-grade industries, untrained, unguided and unguarded." They wanted children to understand "that the earning capacity of those who have had a technical or commercial training is much greater than those who have completed only the eighth grade." Their second goals was to provide advice and guidance to schoolchildren once they were ready to leave school and seek work. Children, the Woman's City Club believed, needed "help in choosing a job so as to prevent the wastage that comes to them and the employers from their own haphazard choice."

To help carry out both these goals, in 1911 the Woman's City Club, along with the Chicago Woman's Club and the Association of Collegiate Alumnae, formed the Bureau for Vocational Supervision. The bureau took a personal interest in schoolchildren, working directly to place them in appropriate jobs when they left school and then to follow their subsequent progress. It also established a scholarship committee to raise funds to keep needy children between the ages of fourteen and sixteen in school "until they have acquired enough education, training and physical strength to guarantee them some chance of success in the industrial work." Scholarship money could be used for books, carfare, or as a stipend to replace the income a needy family could have earned from having a child leave school at fourteen; a book-loan fund was also established. The women's organizations, unlike their male counterparts, were always low on funds. The bureau raised the scholarship and book-loan monies through pledges of $1 a month from their memberships.

The positions of the City Club and the Woman's City Club on two additional aspects of educational reform also invite comparison. One is the question of whether to establish a system of vocational education separate from general education. Both groups opposed this proposition—which had been introduced into the state legislature with the avid support of the Commercial Club of Chicago—but for different reasons. The City Club thought a dual system would make it difficult to attract students into vocational education. Fearing that vocational education was viewed negatively by much of U.S. society, the club preferred that it be offered within the common schools as a separate curriculum. The Woman's City Club, on the other hand, emphatically rejected a separate system of vocational education as discriminatory. Speaking before the club, Agnes Nestor, a glove worker who at the age of eighteen had led her fellow women workers in a successful strike, and who was both a labor organizer with the Women's Trade Union League and member of the Woman's City Club, urged her audience to reject a separate system of education. She reminded club members that while children might be trained for work in school, they deserved the privilege of cultural training as well as the practical. The women agreed. They passed a resolution stating, "All the children of the community, whether rich or poor are entitled ... to the benefits of general education for citizenship...[and] the children who are to become efficient workmen must comprehend their work in relation to science, art, and to society in general."

The second aspect of education reform over which the two clubs differed was that the maximum classroom size. After visiting public schools and talking to teachers, the Woman's City Club insisted that there be no more than thirty children to a classroom and urged the City Club to support this goal, or at the very least, some definite limit to classroom size. The women further declared that they would "insist that Chicago can afford and must have adequate facilities and a sufficient teaching force to insure a maximum of thirty in high-school courses." In other words, the principle of reduced class size demanded the municipality find and allocate the money to implement the changes. The City Club, for its part, refused to support any specific limits on class size, either the thirty initially proposed or the limits of forty-two and twenty-eight in elementary and secondary classrooms that the Woman's City Club later suggested as alternatives. In a letter to the women, the City Club sympathized with the idea of reducing the size of classrooms, It preferred, however, "to go into the question of the proper number of children under each teacher …with some care" and to make a future recommendation "based on the best evidence which can be obtained through the country after a rather careful search as to the maximum number of children that can be efficiently taught by a single teacher."

The two organizations also clashed over the issue of police power in the city, especially police activities during labor strikes. Although the men of the City Club, unlike the members of the more ardent antilabor business clubs such as the Commercial Club, did not advocate or condone police violence against strikers, they were loath to condemn it when it happened. After a controversial strike in February 1914 by waitresses from the restaurant workers' union against the Henrici restaurant, the club confined itself to "investigating" both sides of the issue. During the strike, more than one hundred of the striking waitresses had been arrested on the picket line, and the restaurant owners had secured a court injunction against picketing. On both issues—the injunction and the arrests—the chairman of the club's Committee on Labor Conditions, Frederick S. Deibler, presented a noncommittal report to the general membership. It acknowledged that the courts recognized the right to peaceful picketing and conceded that, in general, this was good for labor relations, but is also pointed out that courts could rule against picketing on the grounds that such activity "threatened irreparable injury to property." How to determine whether to issue an injunction was best left to the courts. If in this particular case a judge had found just cause in enjoining the Henrici strike, Deibler implied, that decision out to be accepted by the club and all citizens. He neither challenged the court's ruling nor questioned the prevailing idea that workers' rights to picket should be restricted to peaceful actions that casued no harm to property. The latter limitation was particularly important. Implicit in that notion was the protection of companies from the loss of any business or trade as a result of picketing.

Deibler did show more doubt about the propriety of the arrests of the striking waitresses and their treatment by the police. "When all the circumstances surrounding the dispute are concerned," he told the club members, "it is difficult to account for the necessity of 119 or more arrests." It looked, he reported, as if the police had been determined to halt the picketing, whatever the legal rights of the waitresses. He expressed doubts about the validity of the restaurant's claim that it had to employ private detectives, who were used against the strikers, in order to protect its property. However, he refused to condemn either the police or the owners for their actions. Deibler's report merely suggested that police violence during strikes and the restaurant's use of private police during this particular strike did not help labor-business relations. The Henrici strike provoked no sentiment within the City Club to modify the exercise of police powers, at least as far as these affected labor activities.

By contrast, members of the Woman's City Club were actively involved in the strike itself trying to resolve it and promoting reform of police powers. Several of these women, including Ruth Hanna McCormick (the wife of Medill McCormick, congressman, former publisher of the Chicago Tribune, and founding member of the City Club), had walked the picket lines with the striking waitresses. Based on its experiences, the Woman's City Club accused the police and businessmen of brutality, demanded that policewomen be assigned to protect the picketers, and asked that all private guards be withdrawn.

That police violence seemed endemic to labor situations in Chicago appalled the members of the Woman's City Club. At the mass meeting of the club called to consider the Woman's Municipal Platform in March 1916, they roundly condemned the 1,800 arrests made by police and private guards during the garment workers' strike of 1915. "It is time we challenged such things," Agnes Nestor told the assembly. "[The strikers] have come to this country because it holds out a promise to them. They come seeking freedom ... and instead of that, they find they are exploited, and when they go on strike to protest against conditions, they are arrested. ... They are arrested at the suggestion of the employer." The women attending the meeting agreed with Nestor; they adopted a plank opposing the extraordinary use of police power against workers. "We condemn the practice of giving police power to private guards whose employment during industrial disputes we believe increases disorder," read the plank. "We protest against the illegal arrest of persons engaged in patrolling the district where a strike is in progress." This last referred to the police practice of arresting private citizens who were walking the picket lines in order to protect the striking workers from police brutality.

Nestor was a working-class woman. The vast majority of women attending the meeting were not, and many were married to men who were employers. This did not keep them from sharing Nestor's sentiments, nor had it in the past. Six years earlier during a strike by the garment workers, Louise DeKoven Bowen, the wealthy Chicago reformer who chaired the meeting in 1916, had declared her sympathies to be on the side of the workers and their right to organize and protest.

As part of their municipal platform, the Woman's City Club also demanded that the city create a municipal strike bureau. This bureau would require the office of chief of police to act as mediator in strikes, instead of acting on the behalf of employers, and would ban the use of private guards. The club declared that, while injustices or wrong-headedness might exist on the part of both employer and employee in labor disagreements, the workers' actions were quite often valid and justified. It advocated mediation, negotiation, and police protection of strikers rather than police power to arrest and abuse them. The men of the City Club, by contrast, were oriented to the needs and desires of businessmen on this issue as on most others. At a discussion meeting held to consider the proposed strike bureau, they listened to the attorney for the Illinois Manufacturers' Assocation speak against the measure as an infringement on the rights of business. There is no evidence that the City Club held a different opinion or that it ever seriously considered supporting a municipal strike bureau.

It has been a prevailing idea of Progressive Era historiography that middle-class business and professional men, such as the members of the City Club, became municipal reformers because they had developed a citywide vision. This vision resulted from their realization that, as business affairs were conducted increasingly on a citywide basis, they need to reform the entire urban structure in order to protect these affairs. In Chicago, the men of the City Club viewed the city primarily as an arena in which to do business, and they advocated municipal reforms intended to protect and further the aims of business. If business and businessmen prospered, they argued, the city and the rest of its inhabitants would ultimately prosper. Thus, while they designed solutions for municipal problems that would, in practice, most directly profit one class, they argued that the benefits would spread through the remainder of the city. On one issue after another, they made fiscal efficiency and financial profitability the criteria for evaluating proposals for change.

I have argued elsewhere that, by the turn of the century, a broad range of urban residents, not just elite white males, had developed often-conflicting visions of the city as a whole. The vision pursued by the members of the Woman's City Club has not been studied, in large part because of the tendency in Progressive Era political history to study men. That the women of the Woman's City Club had a citywide vision is apparent in their arguments and proposals for garbage disposal, public education, and the uses of police power. For them, municipal problems required solutions that guaranteed the well-being of everyone within the city, regardless of their immediate implications for business. The Woman's Municipal Platform of 1916 laid out the club's position on franchises, schools, housing, public health and sanitation, police and crime, among others. Underlying it was the belief that all municipal problems had to be solved before the city would be a good place in which to live.

One must, however, ask why the members of the Woman's City Club took strikingly different positions on municipal issues from the men of the City Club. As mentioned earlier, the different vision of the women of the Woman's City Club cannot be explained simple as one that the settlement house workers imposed on the rest of the membership. No one, we assume, forced Ruth McCormick to march the picket lines with the striking waitresses in 1914 in the company of Hull House resident Ellen Gates Starr. As president of the club, Louise DeKoven Bowen willingly took the lead in designing and promoting the woman's Municipal Platform. Where the settlement house workers may well have made an impact on the Woman's City Club was in their skill in political organizing. Kathryn Kish Sklar's recent work on the activities of the women at Hull House suggests that the settlement house milieu gave women "a means of bypassing the control of male associations and institutions," one in which "women reformers were able to develop their capacity for political leadership free from many if not all of the constraint that otherwise might have been imposed on their power by the male-dominated parties or groups." The activities of the Woman's City Club were the next step in the progression of building political leadership. Twenty-five years after the founding of Hull House, these Chicago women had gained more in the political arena than just the right to vote.

In explaining why middle-class men and women had such different views of the city, and of political reform, it is also not sufficient to attribute the Woman's City Club positions to a received female culture both traditional and limited. Paula Baker has argued for the influence of a female culture, the basic tenets of which were shaped in the early nineteenth century. This female culture, emanating from a belief in the "special moral nature of women," compelled women to work to "ensure the moral and social order" of their surroundings, first through voluntary organizations and then government agencies. Women's efforts in the Progressive Era were thus, according to Baker, an extension of the pursuit of a morality-based social reform in which women passed "on to the state the work of social policy that they found increasingly unmanageable." But the Woman's City Club did not speak about the higher morality of women. Mary McDowell described the club's work as " a constructive fight for better things, for higher standards, for a sense of collective responsibility for public safety and public morals....Civic patriotism with a living daily sacrifice is the need of the hour." Louise DeKoven Bowen, during her term as president of the Woman's City Club, proclaimed that the club "should act not only as a spotlight turned on our community...but it should also serve as an agency to correct the evils depicted and to guide women in their efforts to make of their citizenship a constructive force in the city's life."

Further, even if Woman's City Club members may have learned from their mothers to concern themselves with the welfare of the poor, these received ideas do not explain the political strategies and the specific municipal proposals they developed in response to the problems of early twentieth-century Chicago. There is a crucial distinction between ideas received from previous generations and those that individuals create out of their own experiences. Received ideas had nothing to say about labor unions, for example, or municipal efficiency and municipal ownership. We know that businessmen, working out of their personal experiences of life and business in the city, changed their conception of politics and municipal government over the course of a generation. Women went through the same process. But, as women's daily experiences were different from men's, they came to different conclusions about the direction political reform should take in Chicago.

The majority of men in the City Club were businessmen who drew on their professional experiences to design urban reform agendas. They were accustomed to thinking in terms of profitability and fiscal efficiency, of assessing a problem through the slow but steady accumulation of facts, and of seeking solutions that were best for themselves and their businesses. Their proposals for solving the problems of garbage disposal, public education, and police power make clear that they came easily to see as best for the city what was best for business and businessmen.

The primary daily experience for most middle-class women, on the other hand, was the home. Women were used to organizing a home environment that ensured the well-being of everyone in the family. When they entered the political arena, they sought to achieve the same objective. "The struggle within the city is a fight for the welfare of all the children of all the people," declared Mary McDowell. The Bulletin decreed that women "must form a citywide organization. We must unite forces for the common good and act together." Suppose we had a system of municipal relief," asked DeKoven Bowen, "which is built upon the principle that the community is one great family and that each member of it is bound to help the other, the burden of support falling on all alike?" Thus women applied their experience of how the home worked to what a city government should try to achieve.

The different gender experiences of the members of the City Club and Woman's City Club also shaped the recruitment and activities of the club. To begin with, members of the City Club established more rigorous membership requirements than did the Woman's City Club. Before joining the City Club, any proposed member had to have his name submitted along with "facts and references indicating his fitness for membership and facilitating corroborative inquiry among the members." One negative vote was enough to blackball a prospective member. The admission requirements were strict, not because the purpose of the club was to make business contacts (as was the case with the Commercial Club) but to ensure that men whose opinions might differ dramatically from the majority did not have access to the club. "The chief function of the club," read an early circular, "is to promote the acquaintance, the friendly intercourse, and the accurate information and personal co-operation of those who are sincerely interested in practical methods of improving the public life and affairs of the community in which we live." This sentiment was echoed by founding member Walter Fisher, who wrote that membership was "confined to those who are sincerely interested in practical methods of improving public conditions." Careful admission requirements gave the City Club the leeway to define sincere interest and practical methods as it wished and to keep out those with whom its members might disagree. Entry into the Woman's City Club was easier. The club seems to have assumed that most women could contribute to its work, for all that was needed was nomination by one club member who believed that the nominee sympathized with the objectives of the organization. Without records of who was proposed for membership, or who was turned down, no definitive statement can be made about the City Club's membership practices. It is clear, however, that the City Club grew more slowly than did the Woman's City Club. From an initial membership of 335 in 1903-04, the City Club reached approximately 2,400 members in 1916; the members of the Woman's City Club numbered around 1,250 in its inaugural year of 1910-11 and stood at approximately 2,800 for 1915-16.64

Similarly reflective of their different experiences are the methods by which the two clubs investigated municipal problems. As businessmen, the members of the City Club were accustomed to experiencing firsthand only parts of the problem they were investigating. Employees often gathered facts and figures for the employer. Although social workers were members of the City Club, it is doubtful that the majority of the club members ever saw the places social workers lived and worked because the City club carried on much of its work within its own quarters.65 In contrast, the women focus on grass-roots activities out in the city itself. The Woman's City Club leader directed members to organize according to their city ward (in its membership list, the club provides the ward each woman lived in). They also instructed them to go out into the wards to investigate street, alley, and sidewalk conditions; housing, schools, and churches; infant mortality rates, numbers of children, and juvenile delinquency: parks, playgrounds, dance halls, saloons, hotels, jails, and courts.66 A personal investigation of the garbage problem convinced the female reformers that only municipal ownership and operation of the means of garbage disposal would work well enough. Whether municipal ownership was the most financially profitable way to dispose of garbage was not their first concern; they asked whether it was the best way to promote the health and sanitation of the individuals whose neighborhoods they visited. When the answer seemed to be yes, they demanded municipal ownership.67

Gender experiences, finally, help explain why the Woman's City Club, and women involved in municipal reform movements throughout the country, used the term "municipal housekeeping" to describe their activities—a more complicated, metaphor than has previously been acknowledged. The women of the Woman's City Club were not just attempting to keep the city clean, as they did their homes. They had tried that approach years earlier, for example, in 1894-95 when Jane Addams had organized women to go out and clean the streets themselves when the city was doing little about the problem. Rather, from their recognition of what it took to keep a home running, and running for the benefit of all is members, they developed ideas about how a good city should be run for the benefit of all its members. To characterize its work, the club talked in terms of "the Links that Bind the Home to the City Hall," with city hall in the middle, linked by chains to fourteen pair of squares describing municipal activities and bureaus that affected life in the city.

The home and all life within the city, they argued, were inextricably "chained" to city hall. As one might expect, their illustration of these links includes the "traditional" female concerns about food inspection, factory safety, and clean air. But the two squares that depict the power of the city to license marriage and register birth showed that these women had become conscious of the power of the state to regulate and control their lives.

"Whether she [the club member] likes it or not, the city government invades the privacy of her family life in the interests of the whole city," pointedly noted an essayist in the club's bulletin.[68] Marriage and birth may be viewed as primarily female concerns, but, without a political agenda to organize, investigate, and promote political municipal reforms in these and other areas, women had no say in that city government or over how it affected the home.

Using a term such as "municipal housekeeping" enabled women to become involved in every facet of urban affairs without arousing opposition from those who believed woman's only place was in the home.[69] Moreover, by depicting the city as the larger home, the women were asserting their right to involve themselves in every decision made by the Chicago city government, even to restructure that government. They supported the creation of a municipal strike bureau, for instance, in order to institutionalize within government protection for workers from businessmen.[70] When the club sought to institutionalize municipal ownership and operation of garbage disposal, it was advocating a radical change in Chicago's city government, for municipal ownership would dramatically change the political purposes and structures of city governments. In attempting to redefine what was economic in the political system, it came into direct conflict with established, male-dominated institutions.[71] In its positions on these issues, the Woman's City Club had thus moved beyond reliance on moral suasion to sophisticated participation in the political system.[72]

I do not to mean to suggest that gender was the only point of reference for these women or that they were political radicals. They wished to have the city control certain public services, but they did not vote for socialists; they belonged to the Women's Trade Union League but not the Industrial Workers of the World. They also tended to believe that theirs was the only appropriate municipal vision for women and that part of their task was to educate women of other classes to their point of view. Undoubtedly, there were people in the neighborhoods and institutions they visited who did not always welcome their presence. But, because of their gender experiences, the Woman's City Club members were more open to the possibilities of cross-class alliances than were most of their male counterparts.[75] These experiences also brought them to a different vision of good city government. Woman's City Club member seldom quoted the good of the business community with the good of the citizenry as a whole. Instead, member of the Woman's City Club viewed the city as they had viewed their homes, a place where the health wand welfare of all members should be sought.

CHAPTER 7

Imperialism and World War I, 1880–1920

7.1 Alfred Thayer Mahan, "The Influence of Sea Power upon History" (1890)

7.2 Albert J. Beveridge, "The Command of the Pacific "(1902)

7.3 Joseph Henry Crooker, "The Menace to America" (1900)

7.4 Woodrow Wilson, "War Message to Congress" (1917)

7.5 George Norris, "Opposition to U.S. Involvement in World War I" (1917)

7.6 J. William T. Youngs, "The Lafayette Escadrille"

7.7 *Schenck v. U.S.* (1919)

7.1

The Influence of Sea Power upon History (1890)

Alfred Thayer Mahan

Few Americans had more influence in urging the government to become an imperial power in the late nineteenth century than Alfred Thayer Mahan. His classic book, excerpted here, argued forcefully for radical growth in the American navy—and Congress listened, greatly increasing the size and quality of the Navy during the 1890s to a point where the United States handily beat the Spanish navy during the Spanish-American War. What importance does Mahan attach to naval power, and how has it shaped history? Why does Mahan think America should cobble together an empire based on naval power?

As the practical object of this inquiry is to draw from the lessons of history inferences applicable to one's own country and service, it is proper now to ask how far the conditions of the United States involve serious danger, and call for action on the part of the government, in order to build again her sea power. It will not be too much to say that the action of the government since the Civil War, and up to this day, has been effectively directed solely to what has been called the first link in the chain which makes sea power. Internal development, great production, with the accompanying aim and boast of self-sufficingness, such has been the object, such to some extent the result. In this the government has faithfully reflected the bent of the controlling elements of the country, though it is not always easy to feel that such controlling elements are truly representative, even in a free country. However that may be, there is no doubt that, besides having no colonies, the intermediate link of a peaceful shipping, and

---

From Alfred Thayer Mahan, *The Influence of Sea Power upon History, 1660–1783*, 12th ed. (Boston: Little, Brown and Company, 1st ed, 1890), pp. 83–89.

the interests involved in it, are now likewise lacking. In short, the United States has only one link of the three.

The circumstances of naval war have changed so much within the last hundred years, that it may be doubted whether such disastrous effects on the one hand, or such brilliant prosperity on the other, as were seen in the wars between England and France, could now recur. In her secure and haughty sway of the seas England imposed a yoke on neutrals which will never again be borne; and the principle that the flag covers the goods is forever secured. The commerce of a belligerent can therefore now be safely carried on in neutral ships, except when contraband of war or to blockaded ports; and as regards the latter, it is also certain that there will be no more paper blockades. Putting aside therefore the question of defending her seaports from capture or contribution, as to which there is practical unanimity in theory and entire indifference in practice, what need has the United States of sea power? Her commerce is even now carried on by others; why should her people desire that which, if possessed, must be defended at great cost? So far as this question is economical, it is outside the scope of this work; but conditions which may entail suffering and loss on the country by war are directly pertinent to it. Granting therefore that the foreign trade of the United States, going and coming, is on board ships which an enemy cannot touch except when bound to a blockaded port, what will constitute an efficient blockade? The present definition is, that it is such as to constitute a manifest danger to a vessel seeking to enter or leave the port. This is evidently very elastic. Many can remember that during the Civil War, after a night attack on the United States fleet off Charleston, the Confederates next morning sent out a steamer with some foreign consuls on board, who so far satisfied themselves that no blockading vessel was in sight that they issued a declaration to that effect. On the strength of this declaration some Southern authorities claimed that the blockade was technically broken, and could not be technically re-established without a new notification. Is it necessary, to constitute a real danger to blockade runners, that the blockading fleet should be in sight? Half a dozen fast steamers, cruising twenty miles off-shore between the New Jersey and Long Island coast, would be a very real danger to ships seeking to go in or out by the principal entrance to New York; and similar positions might effectively blockade Boston, the Delaware, and the Chesapeake. The main body of the blockading fleet, prepared not only to capture merchant-ships but to resist military attempts to break the blockade, need not be within sight, nor in a position known to the shore. The bulk of Nelson's fleet was fifty miles from Cadiz two days before Trafalgar, with a small detachment watching close to the harbor. The allied fleet began to get under way at 7 A.M., and Nelson, even under the conditions of those days, knew it by 9.30. The English fleet at that distance was a very real danger to its enemy. It seems possible, in these days of submarine telegraphs, that the blockading forces in-shore and off-shore, and from one port to another, might be in telegraphic communication with one another along the whole coast of the United States, readily giving mutual support; and if, by some fortunate military combination, one detachment were attacked in force, it could warn the others and retreat upon them. Granting that such a blockade off one port were broken on one day, by fairly driving away the ships maintaining it, the notification of its being re-established could be cabled all over the world the next. To avoid such blockades there must be a military force afloat that will at all times so endanger a blockading fleet that it can by no means keep its place. Then neutral ships, except those laden with contraband of war, can come and go freely, and maintain the commercial relations of the country with the world outside.

It may be urged that, with the extensive sea-coast of the United States, a blockade of the whole line cannot be effectively kept up. No one will more readily concede this than officers who remember how the blockade of the Southern coast alone was maintained. But in the present condition of the navy, and, it may be added, with any additions not exceeding those so far proposed by the government, the attempt to blockade Boston, New York, the Delaware, the Chesapeake, and the Mississippi, in other words, the great centres of export and import, would not entail upon one of the large maritime nations efforts greater than have been made before. England has at the same time blockaded Brest, the Biscay coast, Toulon, and Cadiz, when there were powerful squadrons lying within the harbors. It is true that commerce in neutral ships can then enter other ports of the United States than those named; but what a dislocation of the carrying traffic of the country, what failure of supplies at times, what inadequate means of transport by rail or water, of dockage, of lighter-age, of warehousing, will be involved in such an enforced change of the ports of entry Will there be no money loss, no suffering, consequent upon this? And when with much pain and expense these evils have been partially remedied, the enemy may be led to stop the new inlets as he did the old. The people of the United States will certainly not starve, but they may suffer grievously. As for supplies which are contraband of war, is there not reason to fear that the United States is not now able to go alone if an emergency should arise?

The question is eminently one in which the influence of the government should make itself felt, to build up for the nation a navy which, if not capable of reaching distant countries, shall at least be able to keep clear the chief approaches to its own. The eyes of the country have for a quarter of a century been turned from the sea; the results of such a policy and of its opposite will be shown in the instance of France and of England. Without asserting a narrow parallelism between the case of the United States and either of these, it may safely be said that it is essential to the welfare of the whole country that the conditions of trade and commerce should remain, as far as possible, unaffected by an external war. In order to do this, the enemy must be kept not only out of our ports, but far away from our coasts.

Can this navy be had without restoring the merchant shipping? It is doubtful. History has proved that such a purely military sea power can be built up by a despot, as was done by Louis XIV, but though so fair seeming, experience showed that his navy was like a growth which having no root soon withers away. But in a representative government any military expenditure must have a strongly represented interest behind it, convinced of its necessity. Such an interest in sea power does not exist, cannot exist here without action by the government. How such a merchant shipping should be built up, whether by subsidies or by free trade, by constant administration of tonics or by free movement in the open air, is not a military but an economical question. Even had the United States a great national shipping, it may be doubted whether a sufficient navy would follow; the distance which separates her from other great powers, in one way a protection, is also a snare. The motive, if any there be, which will give the United States a navy, is probably now quickening in the Central American Isthmus. Let us hope it will not come to the birth too late.

Here concludes the general discussion of the principal elements which affect, favorably or unfavorably, the growth of sea power in nations. The aim has been, first to consider those elements in their natural tendency for or against, and then to illustrate by particular examples and by the experience of the past. Such discussions, while undoubtedly embracing a wider field, yet fall mainly within the province of strategy, as distinguished from tactics. The considerations and principles which enter into them belong to the unchangeable, or unchanging, order of things, remaining the same, in cause and effect, from age to age. They belong, as it were, to the Order of Nature, of whose stability so much is heard in our day; whereas tactics, using as its instruments the weapons made by man, shares in the change and progress of the race from generation to generation. From time to time the superstructure of tactics has to be altered or wholly torn down; but the old foundations of strategy so far remain, as though laid upon a rock. There will next be examined the general history of Europe and America, with particular reference to the effect exercised upon that history, and upon the welfare of the people, by sea power in its broad sense. From time to time, as occasion offers, the aim will be to recall and reinforce the general teaching, already elicited, by particular illustrations. The general tenor of the study will therefore be strategical, in that broad definition of naval strategy which has before been quoted and accepted. "Naval strategy has for its end to found, support, and increase, as well in peace as in war, the sea power of a country." In the matter of particular battles, while freely admitting that the change of details has made obsolete much of their teaching, the attempt will be made to point out where the application or neglect of true general principles has produced decisive effects; and, other things being equal, those actions will be preferred which, from their association with the names of the most distinguished officers, may be presumed to show how far just tactical ideas obtained in a particular age or a particular service. It will also be desirable, where analogies between ancient and modern weapons appear on the surface, to derive such probable lessons as they offer, without laying undue stress upon the points of resemblance. Finally, it must be remembered that, among all changes, the nature of man remains much the same; the personal equation, though uncertain in quantity and quality in the particular instance, is sure always to be found.

7.2
The Command of the Pacific (1902)

Albert J. Beveridge

*Historian and Indiana Senator Albert Beveridge was, like Mahan, a
leading spokesman for the acquisition of an American empire at the
turn of the century. Here he focuses on his argument for American
control of the Pacific as the centerpiece of that budding empire. What
advantages will accrue to America should it take Beveridge's advice?
What attitudes about Americans and other ethnic groups does
Beveridge display?*

*F*ellow Americans of California and the Pacific Slope:

The Pacific is the ocean of the future; and the Pacific is yours. The markets of the Orient are the Republic's future commercial salvation; and the Orient's commercial future is yours. Important as other questions are, the one great question that covers seas, and islands, and continents; that will last when other questions have been answered and forgotten; that will determine your present prosperity and the greatness of your children's children in their day, is the mastery of the Pacific and the commercial conquest of the eastern world.

That question is peculiarly your question, people of the Pacific slope. If your wealth is to increase you must produce a surplus; and if you produce a surplus, you must sell it. And where will you sell it, people of the Pacific slope, save over the seas of sunset? If your laboring-men are to be employed, you must have commerce; and where will commerce great enough for your ever increasing population be found, save in your supply of the ever increasing demands of the millions of the Orient?...

Mark now the historic conjunction of the elements of national growth, national duty and national necessity. First, the time had come when the Republic was prepared to do its part in governing peoples and lands not ready to govern themselves. Second, at this hour of our preparation for this duty, war gave us the Philippines and our possessions in the Gulf [of Mexico].

And, third, at that very time our commerce was crying aloud for new markets where we might sell the surplus products of our factories and farms—and the only remaining markets on the globe were those surrounding the lands which war had given us. American duty, American preparedness, American commercial necessity came in the same great hour of fate.

Let us consider the argument of advantage to ourselves, flowing from the Philippines, the Orient and from American mastery of the Pacific. What is the great commercial necessity of the Republic? It is markets—foreign markets. At one time we needed to build up our industries here and for that purpose to save for them our home markets. Protection did that; and to-day our home market is supplied. Now we have invaded the markets of Europe and filled them almost to their capacity with American goods. Our great combinations of capital devoted to manufacturing and transportation compete successfully with foreign manufacturers in their own countries.

But still we have a surplus; and an unsold surplus is commercial peril. Every unsold bushel of wheat reduces the price of every other one of the millions of bushels of wheat produced. If our manufacturers produce more than they can sell, that surplus product causes the mills to shut down until they produce no more than they can sell. And after we supply our own market, after we sell all we can to the markets of Europe, we still have an unsold surplus. If our prosperity continues this must be sold.

Where shall the Republic sell its surplus? Where shall the Pacific coast sell its surplus? And your surplus unsold means your commerce paralyzed, your laboring-men starving. Expansion answers that question....

If it is not true that her possessions help England's commerce, why does not England give them up? Why does not Germany give up her possession in Northern China? Why is she spending tens of millions of dollars there, building German railways, German docks and vast plants for future German commerce? Why does Russia spend a hundred million dollars of Russian gold building Russian railways through Manchuria and binding that territory, vast in extent as all the states of the Pacific slope combined, to the Russian empire with bands of steel? Why is Japan now preparing to take Manchuria from Russia as she has already taken Formosa from China?

The Philippines not help us in Oriental commerce! They have helped us even now by making the American name known throughout the East, and our commerce with the islands and countries influenced by the Philippines has in two short years leaped from $43,000,000 to $120,000,000.

If an American manufacturer established a great storehouse in London believing that it would help his business and then found his sales in

London increasing 300 per cent, in less than three years, would he give away that branch establishment because some theorist told him that branch houses did not help trade and that he could sell as much and more if he shipped direct from his factory to the English purchaser?

And yet this practically is what the Opposition asks the American people to believe about and do with the Philippines. From every English and German possession in the East English and German goods are shipped in bulk and then reshipped as quick orders near at hand call for them. And these possessions influence the entire population of the countries where they are located.

If this is true of English and German possessions, will it not be true of America's possessions at the very door of this mighty market? If it is not true, it will be because American energy, American sagacity, American enterprise are not equal to the commercial opportunity which the Philippines give us in the Orient. Americans never yet found an obstacle which they did not overcome, an opportunity they did not make their own.

Has the decay of American energy begun with you, men of the West? Who says so is infidel to American character. Answer these slanders of your energy and power, people of the Pacific states—answer them with our ballots! Tell the world that, of all this masterful Nation, none more vital than the men and women who hold aloft the Republic's flag on our Pacific shores!

If we need this Oriental market—and we can not dispose of our surplus without it—what American farmer is willing for us to give the Philippines to America's competitors? What American manufacturer is willing to surrender this permanent commercial advantage to the nations who are striving for those very markets? Yet, that is what the Opposition asks you to do. For if we quit them certainly Germany or England or Japan will take them.

And these markets, great as they are, are hardly yet opened to the modern world. They are like a gold mine worked by ancient methods and yielding only a fraction of its wealth. Apply to that gold mine modern machinery, modern science, modern methods and its stream of gold swells in volume. This illustration applies to Oriental markets. For example, China buys from all the world at the present time $250,000,000 worth of foreign products. These are consumed by less than 75,000,000 of the Chinese people. The reason of this is that foreign goods can not penetrate the interior. There are no railways, no roads; merchandise must be transported on human backs, and corrupt officials lay heavy transportation taxes at every stage. But now all this begins to change. All over China railroads are projected, surveyed and even now are building.

And wherever they have gone Chinese commerce has increased, just as our own commerce increases here wherever a railroad goes. And wherever railways go wagon roads branch from them. Thus the methods of modern civilization are weaving a network of modern conditions among this most ancient of peoples. And if China now buys $250,000,000 worth of products from the rest of the world, what will she buy when all this change that is now taking place brings her 400,000,000 as purchasers to the markets of the world? The most conservative experts estimate that China alone will buy at last one thousand million dollars worth of the products of other countries every year....

The Philippines and the Orient are your commercial opportunity. Does our duty as a Nation forbid you to accept it? Does our fitness for the work prevent us from doing it? Or does the Nation's preparedness, the Republic's duty and the commercial necessity of the American people unite in demanding of American statesmanship the holding of the Philippines and the commercial conquest of the Oriental world?

Do they say that it is a wrong to any people to govern them without their consent? Consider Hayti [sic] and read in her awful decline since French government there was overthrown the answer to that theory. Remember that English administration in Egypt has in less than twenty years made fertile her fields and redeemed her people, debased by a thousand years of decline, and read in that miracle the answer to that theory.

Examine every example of administration of government in the Orient or Africa by a superior power and find the answer to that theory. Come nearer home. Analyze the three years of American administration in Porto [sic] Rico—American schools for the humblest, just laws, honest government, prosperous commerce. Now sail for less than a day to the sister island of San [sic] Domingo and behold commerce extinguished, justice unknown, government and law a whim, religion degenerated to voodoo rites, and answer whether American administration in Porto Rico, even if it had been without the consent of the governed, is not better for that people than San Domingo's independent savagery.

Let us trust the American people! The most fervent belief in their purity, their power and their destiny is feeble, after all, compared with the reality on which that faith is founded. Great as our fathers were, the citizens of this Republic, on the whole, are greater still to-day, with broader education, loftier outlook. And if this were not so, we should not be worthy of our fathers; for, to do as well as they we must do better. Over the entire Republic the people's common schools increase, churches multiply, culture spreads, the poorest have privileges impossible to the wealthiest fifty years ago.

When any man fears the decay of American institutions, he ignores the elemental forces around him which are building future generations of Americans, stronger, nobler than ourselves. And those who ask you to believe that administration of orderly government in the Philippines will poison the fountain of Americanism here at home, ask you to believe that your children are a mockery, your schools a myth, your churches a dream.

American soldiers, American teachers, American administrators—all are the instruments of the Nation in discharging the Nation's high duty to the ancient and yet infant people which circumstance has placed in our keeping. If it is said that our duty is to teach the world by example, I ask if our duty ends with that? Does any man's duty to his children end with mere example? Does organized society owe no duty to the orphan and the abandoned save that of example? Why, then, are our schools, our asylums, our benevolent institutions, which force physical and mental training upon the neglected youth of the Republic? And does the parent or does organized society refrain from discharging this duty if the child resists?

And just so nations can not escape the larger duties to senile or infant peoples. Nations can not escape the charge laid upon them to develop the world's neglected resources, to snake the wilderness, the fields, the mines and countries inhabited by barbarous peoples useful to civilized man. No nation lives to itself alone. It can not if it would. Even the great powers influence one another, not only by example, but by tariffs, by trade arrangements, by armies, by navies. How much greater should be this influence when circumstance gives to the keeping of a great power the destiny of an undeveloped race and the fortunes of an undeveloped country?

7.3
The Menace to America (1900)

Joseph Henry Crooker

The Reverend Joseph Henry Crooker was one of the founders of the American Anti-Imperialist League (1898). In this document Crooker lays out an argument against American control of the Philippines after our victory in the Spanish-American War. Compare Crooker's position to that of Beveridge in Document 6.3. Which is more persuasive and why?

A political doctrine is now preached in our midst that is the most alarming evidence of oral decay that ever appeared in American history. Its baleful significance consists, not simply in its moral hatefulness, but in the fact that its advocates are so numerous and so prominent.

It is this: A powerful nation, representative of civilization, has the right, for the general good of humanity, to buy, conquer, subjugate, control, and govern feeble and backward races and peoples, without reference to their wishes or opinions.

This is preached from pulpits as the gospel of Christ. It is proclaimed in executive documents as American statesmanship. It is defended in legislative halls as the beginning of a more glorious chapter in human history. It is boastfully declaimed from the platform as the first great act in the regeneration of mankind It is published in innumerable editorials, red with cries for blood and hot with lust for gold, as the call of God to the American people.

But how came these men to know so clearly the mind of the Almighty? Was the cant of piety ever more infamously used? Was selfishness ever more wantonly arrayed in the vestments of sanctity? Is this the modern chivalry of the strong to the weak? Then let us surrender all our fair ideals

From Joseph Henry Crooker, *The Menace to America* (Chicago: American Anti-Imperialist League, 1900).

and admit that might alone makes right. Is this the duty of great nations to small peoples? Then morality is a fiction. Is this the gospel of Jesus? Then let us repudiate the Golden Rule. Is this the crowning lesson of America to the world? Then let us renounce our democracy.

This doctrine is the maxim of bigotry, "The end justifies the means," reshaped by the ambition of reckless politicians and enforced by the greed of selfish speculators. It is infinitely worse than the policy of the old ecclesiastics, for they had in view the salvation of others, while the advocates of this seek the subjugation of others. The colonial motive, now stirring among us, is not love for others. The mask is too thin and too black to deceive even a savage Filipino.

A similar motive and policy piled the fagots about every burning martyr. It turned every thumbscrew that tortured heretics. It laid on the lash that drew blood from the back of every suffering slave. This teaching unbars the bottomless pit and lets loose upon the world every demon that ever vexed the human race. It unchains every wild passion that has lingered in man's blood since it flowed upward from the brute. It prepares the path by which the despot will reach his throne of tyranny and it arms him with instruments of oppression....

To banish this theory of human affairs from the new world Washington suffered at Valley Forge and contended at Yorktown. To destroy the last vestige of this hateful policy, Grant conquered at Appomattox. This is not true Americanism, but the contradiction of every principle for which we have contended and in which we have gloried for over a century. This is not the upward way of civilization, but the backward descent to barbarism....

Something more than the welfare of distant peoples is at stake. We condemn this teaching and policy, not simply to secure justice for the brown man, but to insure justice and freedom for ourselves. The motive of our protest is more than friendship for him: it is devotion to principles of liberty that are the necessary conditions of universal human progress. The feelings of sympathy and justice ought to rule us in these relations. But every advocate of our present national policy outrages these sentiments whenever he makes his defense. His words ring false. And yet, the heart of the matter lies far deeper. The true glory of America is imperiled. The happiness of our descendants is assailed. The mission of America as the representative and guardian of Liberty is in question. The perpetuity of free institutions hangs in the balance.

We cannot worship this golden calf and go unscourged. We cannot violate the principles of our government and enjoy the blessings of those principles. We cannot deny freedom across the ocean and maintain it at home. This Nation cannot endure with part of its people citizens and part colonists. The flag will lose all its glory if it floats at once over freemen and subjects. We cannot long rule other men and keep our own liberty. In the high and holy name of humanity, we are trampling upon the rights of men. But Nemesis will wake. The mask will fall; our joy will turn to bitterness; we shall find ourselves in chains.

Most of all, we lament the stain that has come to our flag, not from the soldier carrying it, but from the policy that has compelled him to carry it in an unjust cause. On executive hands falls, not only the blood of the hunted islander, but the blood of the American murdered by the ambition that sent him to invade distant lands. What we most deplore is the surrender that we as a nation have made of our leadership in the world's great work of human emancipation. What we most bitterly mourn is that we, by our selfish dreams of mere commercialism, have piled obstacles mountain high in the way of progress.

What is most surprising and most alarming is the fact that large numbers of our people still call this national ambition for conquest and dominion a form of exalted patriotism. But we are surely under the spell of a malign influence. A false Americanism has captivated our reason and corrupted our conscience.

May this hypnotic lethargy, induced by the glittering but deceptive bauble of imperialism, speedily pass away; and may these fellow citizens become again true Americans, free to labor for the liberty of all men and intent on helping the lowly of all lands to independence.

It is time that all American citizens should look more carefully into the conditions and tendencies which constitute what may well be called, "The Menace to America." Let me discuss briefly certain phases of what rises ominously before us as the Philippine problem. It is a problem of vast importance, and yet it has not been treated as fully as its great magnitude and inherent difficulties deserve. One of the alarming indications of the hour is the popular unwillingness to admit that these new policies present any serious problem. There seems to be no general recognition that anything strange or dangerous is happening. Those who raise a cry of warning are denounced as pessimists; those who enter criticism are branded as traitors. We are told in a jaunty manner to have faith in the American people. This blind trust in "destiny" makes the triumph of the demagogue easy. This indifference to political discussion is the symptom of the paralysis of true patriotism.

The following is one phase of the popular argument in justification of our oriental aggressions: The obligations of humanity demanded that we take possession of the Philippine Islands in order to prevent the anarchy which would certainly have followed had we taken any other course than that which we did.

But would a little native-grown anarchy have been as bad as the slaughter and destruction which we have intruded? Let us remember that we ourselves have already killed and wounded thousands of the inhabitants. We have arrayed tribe against tribe; we have desolated homes and burned villages; agriculture and commerce have been prostrated; and finally, we have created hatred of ourselves in the breasts of millions of people to remain for years to plague us and them. It is not likely that if left to themselves anything half so serious would have occurred. It is perfectly clear that some other attitude towards those Islands besides that of domination, which this Nation most unfortunately took, would have prevented these results.

And we are not yet at the end. Recurring outbreaks against us as intruders, by people desirous of independence, will undoubtedly produce more distress and disorder in the next ten years (if our present policy is maintained) than would have resulted from native incapacity. Moreover, there are no facts in evidence that warrant the assertion that anarchy would have followed had we left them more to themselves. This is wholly an unfounded assumption. It would certainly have been well to have waited and given them a chance before interfering. That we did not wait, that we did not give them a chance, is proof positive that our national policy was not shaped by considerations of humanity or a reasonable desire to benefit them, but by a spirit of selfish aggrandizement....

It is pitiful that our people, and especially the common people, should be so carried away by wild and baseless dreams of the commercial advantage of these Islands. It is bad enough to sacrifice patriotism upon the altar of Mammon; but it is clear that in this case the sacrifice will be made without securing any benefit, even from Mammon.

The annual expense our Nation will incur by the military and naval establishment in the Philippines will be at least $100,000,000. This the taxpayer of America must pay. On the other hand, the trade profits from these Islands—from the very nature of the case—will go directly into the pockets of millionaire monopolists, the few speculators who will get possession of the business interests there, in the line of hemp, sugar, tobacco and lumber.

The proposition is a plain one. These Islands will cost us, the common people, a hundred million dollars a year. The profits from them, possibly an equal sum, will go directly to a few very rich men. This is a very sleek speculative scheme for transferring vast sums of money from the people at large to the bank accounts of a few monopolists. Can any one see anything very helpful to the common taxpayer in such a policy? This is a serious problem for consideration, in addition to the competition of American labor with cheap Asiatic workmen—in itself sufficiently serious.

The question I press is this: Can such a policy work anything but financial harm to the average American citizen? For one, I do not care to pay this tribute money every time I draw a check or buy a bottle of medicine, tribute money that means oppression to those distant islanders, unnecessary burdens to our own people, and a still larger store for speculators to be used in corrupting American politics!

A passionate demand for expansion has taken possession of the American imagination. It is contended, We must come out of our little corner and take our place on the worldstage of the nations.

But what has been the real expansion of our Nation for over a century? It has been two-fold. (1) The extension of our free institutions westward across the continent to the Pacific coast; (2) the powerful influence of our republican principles throughout the world. Our political ideals have modified the sentiments of great nations; our people have flowed over contiguous territories and planted there the same civic, social, religious and educational institutions that they possessed in their Eastern home. All this has been a normal and natural growth of true Americanism.

The policy that now popularly bears the name "expansion" is something radically different; and it is in no sense the expansion of America. Our people have been sadly deceived by something far worse than an optical illusion—a deceptive phrase has lured them into danger and toward despotism. To buy 10,000,000 distant islanders is the expansion of Jefferson Davis, not the expansion of Abraham Lincoln. To tax far-off colonists without their consent is the expansion of the policy of George III, not the expansion of the patriotism of George Washington. To rule without representation subject peoples is not the expansion of Americanism, but the triumph of imperialism.

The policy advocated is the suppression of American principles, the surrender of our sublime ideals, and the end of our beneficent ministry of liberty among the nations. Just because I want to see America expand I condemn the policy as unpatriotic. Let us not deceive ourselves; the expansion of military rule and sordid commercialism is not the expansion of our real strength or true glory. Let us not mistake the renunciation of American ideals for the expansion of American institutions.

Wherever the flag goes, there the constitution must go. Wherever the flag waves, there the whole of the flag must be present. Wherever the constitution is extended, there the entire constitution must rule. If any one does not wish to accept these consequences, then let the flag be brought back to the spot where it can represent true Americanism, and Americanism in its entirety. What shall our banner be to the Filipino? A symbol of his own liberty or the hated emblem of a foreign oppressor? Shall it float over him in Manila as a mere subject and say to him when he lands in San Francisco that he is an alien? Then that flag will become the object of the world's derision!

If it does not symbolize American institutions in their fulness wherever it floats, then our starry banner becomes false to America and oppressive to those who may fear its authority, but do not share its freedom. Disgrace and harm will not come from taking the flag down, but rather from keeping it where it loses all that our statesmen, prophets and soldiers have put into it. The only way to keep "Old Glory" from becoming a falsehood is to give all under it the liberty that it represents. Nowhere must it remain simply to represent a power to be dreaded, but everywhere it must symbolize rights and privileges shared by all.

Among the many bad things bound up with this unfortunate business none is worse than the degradation of America, sure to follow in more ways than one, if we persist in the course that we are now following. No stronger or sadder proof of the unwise and harmful character of this policy is needed than the fact that its defenders are led so quickly to part company with sober argument and truthful statement and rush into virulent abuse and deceptive sophistries. Who would have believed two years ago that any sane man would have appealed to Washington in support of a policy so abhorrent to the Father of his Country? What ignoble unveracity in twisting his words into the approval of foreign conquest! Who would have thought it possible that scholars and statesmen would so soon become mere jugglers with words, pretending that our previous territorial expansion furnishes analogy and warrant for a colonial system far across the ocean, entered upon by warfare and maintained by Congress without constitutional safeguards! These facts show how virulent a poison is at work upon the national mind. We have here already a perversion of patriotism and a loss of political sagacity and veracity.

It is bad enough to hear men exclaim: "There is money in it and that is sufficient"—but a national venture that leads men to scoff at the Declaration of Independence, to ridicule the constitution as outgrown, to denounce the wisdom of the fathers as foolishness, and to declare that

American glory dates from Manila bay: Is there not something ominous in such talk? If a brief experience in the expansion of America that scoffs at American principles produces such results, is it not time to sound the alarm? If the defense of a policy compels men to take such positions, there is something infinitely dangerous in that policy.

7.4
War Message to Congress (1917)

Woodrow Wilson

*One potential consequence of becoming a world power is the difficulty
of avoiding conflicts involving other nations. Despite its involvement
in the world as an economic giant and an imperial newcomer, the
United States tried hard to stay out of World War I when it began in
1914. Eventually, German aggression on the high seas forced President
Woodrow Wilson's hand, and on April 2, 1917, Wilson gave this
address before Congress, asking it to declare war on Germany. What are
the reasons Wilson gives for U.S. participation in the war? What values
does he claim the U.S. and Germany represent in this conflict?*

Gentlemen of the Congress:

I have called the Congress into extraordinary session because there are
serious, very serious, choices of policy to be made, and made immediately, which it was neither right nor constitutionally permissible that I should
assume the responsibility of making.

On the 3d of February last I officially laid before you the extraordinary
announcement of the Imperial German Government that on and after the
1st day of February it was its purpose to put aside all restraints of law or of
humanity and use its submarines to sink every vessel that sought to approach either the ports of Great Britain and Ireland or the western coasts of
Europe or any of the ports controlled by the enemies of Germany within
the Mediterranean. That had seemed to be the object of the German submarine warfare earlier in the war, but since April of last year the Imperial
Government had somewhat restrained the commanders of its undersea
craft in conformity with its promise then given to us that passenger boats
should not be sunk and that due warning would be given to all other vessels which its submarines might seek to destroy, when no resistance was
offered or escape attempted, and care taken that their crews were given at
least a fair chance to save their lives in their open boats. The precautions

taken were meagre and haphazard enough, as was proved in distressing instance after instance in the progress of the cruel and unmanly business, but a certain degree of restraint was observed. The new policy has swept every restriction aside. Vessels of every kind, whatever their flag, their character, their cargo, their destination, their errand, have been ruthlessly sent to the bottom without warning and without thought of help or mercy for those on board, the vessels of friendly neutrals along with those of belligerents. Even hospital ships and ships carrying relief to the sorely bereaved and stricken people of Belgium, though the latter were provided with safe-conduct through the proscribed areas by the German Government itself and were distinguished by unmistakable marks of identity, have been sunk with the same reckless lack of compassion or of principle.

I was for a little while unable to believe that such things would in fact be done by any government that had hitherto subscribed to the humane practices of civilized nations. International law had its origin in the attempt to set up some law which would be respected and observed upon the seas, where no nation had right of dominion and where lay the free highways of the world. By painful stage after stage has that law been built up, with meagre enough results, indeed, after all was accomplished that could be accomplished, but always with a clear view, at least, of what the heart and conscience of mankind demanded. This minimum of right the German Government has swept aside under the plea of retaliation and necessity and because it had no weapons which it could use at sea except these which it is impossible to employ as it is employing them without throwing to the winds all scruples of humanity or of respect for the understandings that were supposed to underlie the intercourse of the world. I am not now thinking of the loss of property involved, immense and serious as that is, but only of the wanton and wholesale destruction of the lives of noncombatants, men, women, and children, engaged in pursuits which have always, even in the darkest periods of modern history, been deemed innocent and legitimate. Property can be paid for; the lives of peaceful and innocent people can not be. The present German submarine warfare against commerce is a warfare against mankind.

It is a war against all nations. American ships have been sunk, American lives taken, in ways which it has stirred us very deeply to learn of, but the ships and people of other neutral and friendly nations have been sunk and overwhelmed in the waters in the same way. There has been no discrimination. The challenge is to all mankind. Each nation must decide for itself how it will meet it. The choice we make for ourselves must be made with a moderation of counsel and a temperateness of judgment befitting our character and our motives as a nation. We must put excited feeling away. Our motive will not be revenge or the victorious assertion of the physical might of the nation, but only the vindication of right, of human right, of which we are only a single champion.

When I addressed the Congress on the 26th of February last, I thought that it would suffice to assert our neutral rights with arms, our right to use the seas against unlawful interference, our right to keep our people safe against unlawful violence. But armed neutrality, it now appears, is impracticable. Because submarines are in effect outlaws when used as the German submarines have been used against merchant shipping, it is impossible to defend ships against their attacks as the law of nations has assumed that merchantmen would defend themselves against privateers or cruisers, visible craft giving chase upon the open sea. It is common prudence in such circumstances, grim necessity indeed, to endeavour to destroy them before they have shown their own intention. They must be dealt with upon sight, if dealt with at all. The German Government denies the right of neutrals to use arms at all within the areas of the sea which it has proscribed, even in the defense of rights which no modem publicist has ever before questioned their right to defend. The intimation is conveyed that the armed guards which we have placed on our merchant ships will be treated as beyond the pale of law and subject to be dealt with as pirates would be. Armed neutrality is ineffectual enough at best; in such circumstances and in the face of such pretensions it is worse than ineffectual; it is likely only to produce what it was meant to prevent; it is practically certain to draw us into the war without either the rights or the effectiveness of belligerents. There is one choice we can not make, we are incapable of making: we will not choose the path of submission and suffer the most sacred rights of our nation and our people to be ignored or violated. The wrongs against which we now array ourselves are no common wrongs; they cut to the very roots of human life.

With a profound sense of the solemn and even tragical character of the step I am taking and of the grave responsibilities which it involves, but in unhesitating obedience to what I deem my constitutional duty, I advise that the Congress declare the recent course of the Imperial German Government to be in fact nothing less than war against the Government and people of the United States; that it formally accept the status of belligerent which has thus been thrust upon it, and that it take immediate steps not only to put the country in a more thorough state of defense but also to exert all its power and employ all its resources to bring the Government of the German Empire to terms and end the war.

What this will involve is clear. It will involve the utmost practicable co-operation in counsel and action with the governments now at war with Germany, and, as incident to that, the extension to those governments of the most liberal financial credits, in order that our resources may so far as possible be added to theirs. It will involve the organization and mobilization of all the material resources of the country to supply the materials of war and serve the incidental needs of the nation in the most abundant and yet the most economical and efficient way possible. It will involve the immediate full equipment of the Navy in all respects but particularly in supplying it with the best means of dealing with the enemy's submarines. It will involve the immediate addition to the armed forces of the United States already provided for by law in case of war at least 500,000 men, who should, in my opinion, be chosen upon the principle of universal liability to service, and also the authorization of subsequent additional increments of equal force so soon as they may be needed and can be handled in training. It will involve also, of course, the granting of adequate credits to the Government, sustained, I hope, so far as they can equitably be sustained by the present generation, by well conceived taxation....

While we do these things, these deeply momentous things, let us be very clear, and make very clear to all the world what our motives and our objects are. My own thought has not been driven from its habitual and normal course by the unhappy events of the last two months, and I do not believe that the thought of the nation has been altered or clouded by them I have exactly the same things in mind now that I had in mind when I addressed the Senate on the 22d of January last; the same that I had in mind when I addressed the Congress on the 3d of February and on the 26th of February. Our object now, as then, is to vindicate the principles of peace and justice in the life of the world as against selfish and autocratic power and to set up amongst the really free and self-governed peoples of the world such a concert of purpose and of action as will henceforth ensure the observance of those principles. Neutrality is no longer feasible or desirable where the peace of the world is involved and the freedom of its peoples, and the menace to that peace and freedom lies in the existence of autocratic governments backed by organized force which is controlled wholly by their will, not by the will of their people. We have seen the last of neutrality in such circumstances. We are at the beginning of an age in which it will be insisted that the same standards of conduct and of responsibility for wrong done shall be observed among nations and their governments that are observed among the individual citizens of civilized states.

We have no quarrel with the German people. We have no feeling towards them but one of sympathy and friendship. It was not upon their impulse that their Government acted in entering this war. It was not with their previous knowledge or approval. It was a war determined upon as wars used to be determined upon in the old, unhappy days when peoples were nowhere consulted by their rulers and wars were provoked and waged in the interest of dynasties or of little groups of ambitious men who were accustomed to use their fellow men as pawns and tools. Self-governed nations do not fill their neighbour states with spies or set the course of intrigue to bring about some critical posture of affairs which will give them an opportunity to strike and make conquest. Such designs can be successfully worked out only under cover and where no one has the right to ask questions. Cunningly contrived plans of deception or aggression, carried, it may be, from generation to generation, can be worked out and kept from the light only within the privacy of courts or behind the carefully guarded confidences of a narrow and privileged class. They are happily impossible where public opinion commands and insists upon full information concerning all the nation's affairs.

A steadfast concern for peace can never be maintained except by a partnership of democratic nations. No autocratic government could be trusted to keep faith within it or observe its covenants. It must be a league of honour, a partnership of opinion. Intrigue would eat its vitals away; the plottings of inner circles who could plan what they would and render account to no one would be a corruption seated at its very heart. Only free peoples can hold their purpose and their honour steady to a common end and prefer the interests of mankind to any narrow interest of their own.

Does not every American feel that assurance has been added to our hope for the future peace of the world by the wonderful and heartening things that have been happening within the last few weeks in Russia? Russia was known by those who knew it best to have been always in fact democratic at heart, in all the vital habits of her thought, in all the intimate relationships of her people that spoke their natural instinct, their habitual attitude towards life. The autocracy that crowned the summit of her political structure, long as it had stood and terrible as was the reality of its power, was not in fact Russian in origin, character, or purpose; and now it has been shaken off and the great, generous Russian people have been added in all their naive majesty and might to the forces that are fighting for freedom in the world, for justice, and for peace. Here is a fit partner for a league of honour....

We are glad, now that we see the facts with no veil of false pretence about them, to fight thus for the ultimate peace of the world and for the liberation of its peoples, the German peoples included: for the rights of nations great and small and the privilege of men everywhere to choose their way of life and of obedience. The world must be made safe for democracy. Its peace must be planted upon the tested foundations of political liberty. We have no selfish ends to serve. We desire no conquest, no dominion. We seek no indemnities for ourselves, no material compensation for the sacrifices we shall freely make. We are but one of the champions of the rights of mankind. We shall be satisfied when those rights have been made as secure as the faith and the freedom of nations can make them.

Just because we fight without rancour and without selfish object, seeking nothing for ourselves but what we shall wish to share with all free peoples, we shall, I feel confident, conduct our operations as belligerents without passion and ourselves observe with proud punctilio the principles of right and of fair play we profess to be fighting for....

It will be all the easier for us to conduct ourselves as belligerents in a high spirit of right and fairness because we act without animus, not in enmity towards a people or with the desire to bring any injury or disadvantage upon them, but only in armed opposition to an irresponsible government which has thrown aside all considerations of humanity and of right and is running amuck. We are, let me say again, the sincere friends of the German people, and shall desire nothing so much as the early reestablishment of intimate relations of mutual advantage between us—however hard it may be for them, for the time being, to believe that this is spoken from our hearts. We have borne with their present government through all these bitter months because of that friendship—exercising a patience and forbearance which would otherwise have been impossible. We shall, happily, still have an opportunity to prove that friendship in our daily attitude and actions towards the millions of men and women of German birth and native sympathy, who live amongst us and share our life, and we shall be proud to prove it towards all who are in fact loyal to their neighbours and to the Government in the hour of test. They are, most of them, as true and loyal Americans as if they had never known any other fealty or allegiance. They will be prompt to stand with us in rebuking and restraining the few who may be of a different mind and purpose. If there should be disloyalty, it will be dealt with with a firm hand of stern repression; but, if it lifts its head at all, it will lift it only here and there and without countenance except from a lawless and malignant few.

It is a distressing and oppressive duty, gentlemen of the Congress, which I have performed in thus addressing you. There are, it may be, many months of fiery trial and sacrifice ahead of us. It is a fearful thing to lead this great peaceful people into war, into the most terrible and disastrous of all wars, civilization itself seeming to be in the balance. But the right is more precious than peace, and we shall fight for the things which we have always carried nearest our hearts—for democracy, for the right of those who submit to authority to have a voice in their own governments for the rights and liberties of small nations, for a universal dominion of right by such a concert of free peoples as shall bring peace and safety to all nations and make the world itself at last free. To such a task we can dedicate our lives and our fortunes, everything that we are and everything that we have, with the pride of those who know that the day has come when America is privileged to spend her blood and her might for the principles that gave her birth and happiness and the peace which she has treasured. God helping her, she can do no other.

7.5

Opposition to U.S. Involvement in World War I (1917)

George Norris

Nebraska Senator George Norris was one of only a handful of Congressmen to vote against the declaration of war bill. In this excerpt from a speech given just two days after Wilson's (see Document 6.5), Norris outlines the reasons for his opposition.

There are a great many American citizens who feel that we owe it as a duty to humanity to take part in this war. Many instances of cruelty and inhumanity can be found on both sides. Men are often biased in their judgment on account of their sympathy and their interests. To my mind, what we ought to have maintained from the beginning was the strictest neutrality. If we had done this I do not believe we would have been on the verge of war at the present time. We had a right as a nation, if we desired, to cease at any time to be neutral. We had a technical right to respect the English war zone and to disregard the German war zone, but we could not do that and be neutral. I have no quarrel to find with the man who does not desire our country to remain neutral. While many such people are moved by selfish motives and hopes of gain, I have no doubt but that in a great many instances, through what I believe to be a misunderstanding of the real condition, there are many honest, patriotic citizens who think we ought to engage in this war and who are behind the President in his demand that we should declare war against Germany. I think such people err in judgment and to a great extent have been misled as to the real history and the true facts by the almost unanimous demand of the great combination of wealth that has a direct financial interest in our participation in the war.

From George Norris, speech before the Senate, April 4, 1917; U.S. 65th Congress, 1st Session.

We have loaned many hundreds of millions of dollars to the allies in this controversy. While such action was legal and countenanced by international law, there is no doubt in my mind but the enormous amount of money loaned to the allies in this country has been instrumental in bringing about a public sentiment in favor of our country taking a course that would make every bond worth a hundred cents on the dollar and making the payment of every debt certain and sure. Through this instrumentality and also through the instrumentality of others who have not only made millions out of the war in the manufacture of munitions, etc., and who would expect to make millions more if our country can be drawn into the catastrophe, a large number of the great newspapers and news agencies of the country have been controlled and enlisted in the greatest propaganda that the world has ever known, to manufacture sentiment in favor of war. It is now demanded that the American citizens shall be used as insurance policies to guarantee the safe delivery of munitions of war to belligerent nations. The enormous profits of munition manufacturers, stockbrokers, and bond dealers must be still further increased by our entrance into the war. This has brought us to the present moment, when Congress, urged by the President and backed by the artificial sentiment, is about to declare war and engulf our country in the greatest holocaust that the world has ever known....

To whom does the war bring prosperity? Not to the soldier who for the munificent compensation of $16 per month shoulders his musket and goes into the trench, there to shed his blood and to die if necessary; not to the broken-hearted widow who waits for the return of the mangled body of her husband; not to the mother who weeps at the death of her brave boy; not to the little children who shiver with cold; not to the babe who suffers from hunger; nor to the millions of mothers and daughters who carry broken hearts to their graves. War brings no prosperity to the great mass of common and patriotic citizens. It increases the cost of living of those who toil and those who already must strain every effort to keep soul and body together. War brings prosperity to the stock gambler on Wall street—to those who are already in possession of more wealth than can be realized or enjoyed. [A Wall Street broker] says if we can not get war, "it is nevertheless good opinion that the preparedness program will compensate in good measure for the loss of the stimulus of actual war." That is, if we can not get war, let us go as far in that direction as possible. If we can not get war, let us cry for additional ships, additional guns, additional munitions, and everything else that will have a tendency to bring us as near as possible to the verge of war. And if war comes do such men as these shoulder the musket and go into the trenches?

Their object in having war and in preparing for war is to make money. Human suffering and the sacrifice of human life are necessary, but Wall Street considers only the dollars and the cents. The men who do the fighting, the people who make the sacrifices, are the ones who will not be counted in the measure of this great prosperity he depicts. The stock brokers would not, of course, go to war, because the very object they have in bringing on the war is profit, and therefore they must remain in their Wall Street offices in order to share in that great prosperity which they say war will bring. The volunteer officer, even the drafting officer, will not find them. They will be concealed in their palatial offices on Wall Street, sitting behind mahogany desks, covered up with clipped coupons—coupons soiled with the sweat of honest toil, coupons stained with mothers' tears, coupons dyed in the lifeblood of their fellow men.

We are taking a step today that is fraught with untold danger. We are going into war upon the command of gold. We are going to run the risk of sacrificing millions of our countrymen's lives in order that other countrymen may coin their lifeblood into money. And even if we do not cross the Atlantic and go into the trenches, we are going to pile up a debt that the toiling masses that shall come many generations after us will have to pay. Unborn millions will bend their backs in toil in order to pay for the terrible step we are now about to take. We are about to do the bidding of wealth's terrible mandate. By our act we will make millions of our countrymen suffer, and the consequences of it may well be that millions of our brethren must shed their lifeblood, millions of broken-hearted women must weep, millions of children must suffer with cold, and millions of babes must die from hunger, and all because we want to preserve the commercial right of American citizens to deliver munitions of war to belligerent nations.

7.6
The Lafayette Escadrille

J. William T. Youngs

*This entry tells the remarkable, and almost unknown, story of
American pilots during World War I. Relatively new in 1914,
airplanes became "the third dimension of combat," and American
volunteers helped pave the way for using them for a variety of
purposes. Youngs describes the difficulties and the heroics of these
young men, flying for the French in a unit that came to be known
as the "Lafayette Escadrille."*

Mildred Aldrich, an elderly American expatriate, arose each morning
at dawn during the summer of 1914, wrapped herself in a cloak, and
went to her lawn to gaze over the French countryside. Each morning the
sun illuminated the same lovely valley: "miles and miles of laughing country, little white towns just smiling in the early lights, a thin strip of river
here and there, dimpling and dancing, stretches of fields of all colors."

For years Aldrich had lived in Paris as a theater critic for the *New York
Times*. But age and declining health had changed her. She moved to the
country to find "a quiet refuge" and "the simple life." In retirement Mildred Aldrich liked to look over the countryside as she worked in her garden. Winding through the fields and villages, the Marne River made a
"wonderful loop" to within a mile of her hilltop house. Aldrich's American
friends chided her for abandoning her native land, but even while gazing
at the French countryside, she had not forgotten the United States. She reported: "I turn my eyes to the west often with a queer sort of amazed

Ch. 7, "American Volunteers in World War I," pp. 123-147 from *American
Realities*, vol. II, 5th ed. By J. William T. Youngs, Copyright © 2001 by
J. William T. Youngs. Reprinted by permission of Pearson Education, Inc.

pride." The United States was, however, a country for "the young, the energetic, and the ambitious." Aldrich had once been all of those, but now she cherished the calm life of rural France.

From her dreamlike locale, the world itself seemed a kind of dream. One morning a paper arrived with the news that the crown prince of Austria had been assassinated at Sarajevo, Serbia. Considering the event from her hilltop, Aldrich reasoned that "Austria will not grieve much'" because Archduke Franz Ferdinand was "none too popular" with his people.

If Mildred Aldrich had been an active political reporter rather than a retired drama critic, she might have sensed that the assassination in Sarajevo would not be so easily forgotten. Within a few weeks there were a series of threats, first by Austria against Serbia, then by Russia against Austria, then by the other major powers of Europe, including England and France, against each other. These threats, once acted upon, would drive Europe into World War I, the most bloody conflict in history. And the first great battle of that war would soon take place along the Marne River, in the very countryside that Mildred Aldrich viewed from her front yard.

A few weeks after her first mention of Sarajevo, Aldrich was writing home, "It is a nasty outlook. We are simply holding our breaths here." On July 30, 1914, she envisioned the looming warfare: "It will be the bloodiest affair the world has ever seen—a war in the air, a war under the sea as well as on it, and carried out with the most effective manslaughtering machines ever used in battle." A few days later a man walked up and down the rural lanes near her farmhouse beating a drum and calling on the men to mobilize. All day long Aldrich could watch airplanes flying from Paris to the frontier to observe the German movements. Airplanes! She had attended an exhibition just fourteen years before where a model of an airplane was on display; it had never flown nor had any other heavier-than-air machine gone aloft at that time. Two years later, in 1903, Wilbur and Orville Wright flew a plane a few hundred yards at Kitty Hawk, North Carolina. The progress in flight during the next decade had been astonishing. Sitting in her garden, where she watched airplanes flying overhead, "so steady and so sure," Aldrich reflected, "It is awe-compelling to remember how these cars in the air change all military tactics." No longer would an army be able to move unobserved.

With war imminent, friends urged Mildred Aldrich to retire from her country home to a safer distance from the German border, to Paris or better still the United States. But she chose to stay in her new home. The German armies moved quickly during the first weeks of the war, through Belgium and across the French border, Still Aldrich stayed. One morning

Aldrich heard a tremendous explosion and learned the bridges over the Marne River were being dynamited to delay the Germans. French and British troops began moving past the farmhouse headed for the front, and Aldrich served up tea an biscuidts to some of the soldiers. Officers surveyed the countryside from her front yard.

The contending armies—Germany invading and England and France resisting—came over the horizon, and Aldrich could hear the cannon and see smoke in the distance. She wrote: "To my imagination every shot meant awful slaughter, and between me and the terrible thing stretched a beautiful country, as calm in the sunshine as if horrors were not." That night the Germans came closer. With their artillery they set fire to grain stacks and buildings visible from the farm house. These fires "stood like a procession of huge torches across my beloved panorama."

From her hilltop Mildred Aldrich was witnessing a portion of the Battle of the Marne, one of the most important fights of the war. If the French and English failed to hold, the Germans would likely occupy Paris. But the Allies did hold. On September 7, 1914, Aldrich noticed that the cannon fire seemed more distant. An English soldier on a bicycle wheeled up to her house and told her, "Everything is all right. Germans been as near you as they will ever get. Close shave." She learned that the Germans had come within four miles of her hilltop, where they were stopped and retreated back a few miles to defensive positions. Aldrich had endured the sound of cannon for three days—pounding "on every nerve in my body"—but she realized that others had sacrificed much more: "Out there on the plain, almost within my sight, lay the men who had paid with their lives—each dear to someone—to hold back the battle from Pairs."

Three months after the Battle of the Marne, Mildred Aldrich toured the war zone by car. She passed through village after village where houses had been shelled to rubble and through forests where huge trees had been snapped like twigs by cannon fire. She came to a broad field where some of the dead were buried all the graves marked by French flags, floating "like fine flowers in the landscape. They made tiny spots against the far-off horizon line, and groups like beds of flowers in the foreground, and we knew that, behind the skyline, there were more."

Tens of thousands of soldiers fell at the Battle of the Marne. Millions more would die before the end of the war. Mildred Aldrich would continue to observe the conflict from her hilltop and send reports in letters to friends—the basis eventually for three books. Other Americans, young men driven by idealism or the thirst for adventure, would become more actively engaged in the fighting.

With the opening of World War I the United States began a policy of neutrality that was to last into 1917. At the onset of the war President Woodrow Wilson urged Americans to remain "neutral in fact as well as in name, impartial in thought as well as action." Wilson believed that Americans could set a standard for world peace by remaining above the conflict. But other citizens identified from the start with the Allied cause: they thought of England and France as fellow democracies and read with horror stories of the German army sweeping across Belgium toward Paris. Hundreds of individual Americans served as volunteers, driving ambulances and fighting in combat units. The most famous of the volunteers, Ernest Hemingway, was wounded while engaged as an ambulance driver for the Italian army. His *Farewell to Arms,* while fiction, draws on his actual experiences on the Italian front. Most American volunteers served with the Allies—France, Britain, and Italy. But a few served as ambulance drivers for the Germans. Many of these Americans went to war to take part in what they considered a righteous cause. An American volunteer named Alan Seeger, who would die in 1916 at the Battle of the Somme, wrote a poem in which he thanked France for giving him and his fellows "that rare privilege of dying well." Another American volunteer was described as devoted to "the cause of Liberty and Righteousness throughout the world."

Most of the Americans who served in France joined the Foreign Legion and helped defend a line of trenches that ran from the North Sea four hundred miles to Switzerland. Other trenches, occupied by Germans, ran parallel to the Allied line, sometimes several hundred yards distant, sometimes much closer. In these trenches millions of men served during World War I. After the early engagements in the war, including the Battle of the Marne, armies on the western front seldom moved more than a few hundred yards in an attack. Sometimes one side would attempt a breakthrough, gaining a few miles of the other's territory. But on the whole, both sides were literally bogged down for most of the war.

The men in the trenches lived in mud, exposed to rain, cold, and enemy bombardments. During the night they made excursions into "no man's land," the dangerous ground between the lines. In larger attacks, the soldiers were called upon to make near-suicidal frontal assault, walking across open ground toward the enemy trenches. Such maneuvers had been dangerous enough for troops during the eighteenth century, when an enemy soldier could barely fire one bullet per minute. Against modern rapid-firing machine guns frontal assaults were murderous. In a single attack at the Somme River the British suffered 60,000 casualties in one day.

In and around the line of trenches between 1914 and 1918 millions of men died.

For a few thousand soldiers World War I opened a new field of combat, a war waged above the trenches in airplanes. In a sense, the third dimension of warfare had been introduced more than a century before with the use of observation balloons in the Napoleonic Wars and later in the U.S. Civil War. By 1914 armies regularly employed such balloons to provide information about the enemy's position for the artillery—on the western front gunners were firing shells so far that often they could not even see their targets. The Zeppelin also made its appearance in the war. Named after a German count who produced the first effective models, these lighter-than-air craft could carry bombs far behind the enemies lines. But the most important innovation of the war was the use of the airplane for collecting intelligence, conducting bombing runs, strafing enemy troops, and engaging other aircraft.

The Italians had pioneered air warfare in 1911 by using nine planes in a war against the Turks in Libya. Their firsts included intelligence gathering, a bombing run, and the wounding of one of their pilots by a bullet fired from the ground. The United States used planes for reconnaissance during a short-lived occupation of Vera Cruz, Mexico, in 1914. With these exceptions and a few others, the airplane was largely untested as a military weapon at the beginning of World War I.

The planes that Mildred Aldrich saw flying above her farmhouse near the Marne had been gathering intelligence on German movements—the one activity that would obviously benefit from air power. At first observation planes from opposite sides simply flew past each other, their pilots sometimes even waving cheerfully, invoking a kind of fraternity of the air. But it was soon apparent that enemy planes were helping to kill one's own countrymen, and tactics were developed to enable pilots to destroy enemy observers. Initially these consisted of arming pilots with pistols, but small arms had little effect in aerial combat. Other early suggestions for the military pilot's arsenal included hand grenades, harpoons, and hooks. Machine guns were at first too heavy to be useful in early aircraft, but in 1911 an American army officer, Isaac N. Lewis, developed a machine gun weighing only twenty-five pounds. Lewis guns were subsequently mounted on the planes, making aerial combat deadly.

Pilots were provided various tactical assignments and appropriate planes. Fast, maneuverable chasse (hunting) planes guarded slower observation planes. Bombers were designed to carry increasingly large payloads, and chasse planes were assigned to protect them. Methods of aerial combat included elaborate formations in which one plane protect another, and maneuvers in which planes turned, climbed, and swooped in death-defying maneuvers in order to shoot down an enemy plane or avoid being shot down themselves. In 1903 Wilbur and Orville Wright had flown only a few dozen yards above the ground. By 1918 combat pilots could reach heights of twenty thousand feet. The planes themselves added to the risk of combat. Made mainly of wood, canvas, and wire, they could easily break apart or be set afire in combat. Moreover, the pilots in World War I went aloft without parachutes.

Despite the dangers of combat flight, many young men were intrigued by the idea of becoming pilots. In addition to the Americans who served in the French infantry, a few enlisted in the French Flying Corps. One young American, Norman Prince, hoped not simply to fly for France but to fly for France in a distinct American squadron. Prince hailed from Massachusetts but had spent many vacations at Pau in southern France, where he hunted, made friends, and earned to speak French. A polo-playing Harvard graduate, he was born to wealth, like many other future American volunteers in the French Flying Corps. During autumn 1914, at the beginning of the war, Prince was enrolled in a flight school in Marblehead, Massachusetts. There he developed the idea of creating a separate unit within the French Flying Corps composed of Americans. A few months later he set sail for France aboard the Rochambeau, an ocean liner named appropriately for a Frenchman who had served in America during the Revolution. On shore at Le Havre, Norman Prince wrote his mother, "I believe I can find a place to do some efficient and useful work for the cause to which I am so deeply devoted."

At first it was difficult for American volunteers to find places in the French Flying Corps at all, to say nothing of creating a separate unit. The chance to pilot one of a relatively small number of planes went first to Frenchmen. Eventually, however, many of these plots were killed and more planes were built, making room for American volunteers. Norman Prince was one of those airmen. In May 1915 he went to the front to replace a disabled pilot. He wrote home, "I saw the battle lines and heard for the first time the never-ending boom of guns. This is war in dead earnest and right at hand." Prince flew for several months and was then given leave with two other American airmen to return to the United States and tour the country on a kind of goodwill mission for France. The German embassy demanded that these Americans in French uniforms be interred for the duration of the war, but Prince and his comrades slipped aboard a ship and returned to France in winter 1916.

By then the idea of a separate American unit within the French Flying Corps was bearing fruit. An American expatriate doctor, Edmund L. Gros, who was already working for the American Ambulance Corps in France, helped persuade acquaintances within the French Ministry of Foreign Affairs that they could gain propaganda benefits by creating a unique American unit within the French Flying Corps. Gros was part of the Franco-American Committee, a collection of French and American citizens devoted to bringing Americans and ultimately America itself into the war. While Gros and his colleagues politicked, American pilots such as Norman Prince had fought well in French units. Before leaving for America Prine had been cited as an "excellent military pilot who has consistently displayed great audacity and presence of mind." Another American, William Thaw, stayed aloft over the front during one especially serious mission, guiding French artillery fire despite taking so many hits that when his plane landed it was beyond repair. Such American exploits proved that the volunteer could actually contribute to the war effort as well as create favorable publicity in the United States. Finally on March 14, 1916, a separate American escadrille (squadron) was created within the French Flying Corps. It began with nine members, one of whom was Norman Prince.

Many of the American volunteers in the Flying Corps were the sons of wealthy families and graduates of prestigious colleges, but at the training camps not all the men fit that description. As one volunteer noted: "There is a fine crew in this school. Men from all colleges and men who don't know the name of a college,…men sticky with money in the same barracks with others who worked their way over on ships." He went on to describe an African American in the barracks—most likely Edward Bullard of Columbus, Georgia. At the time the American army was segregated, but that was not the case with the French forces. Although the American pilot described his African American compatriot in terms that today would be considered racial stereotypes, he still demonstrated a healthy respect for this fellow pilot:

> This democracy is a fine thing in the army and makes better men of all hands. For instance, the corporal of our room in an American, as black as the ace of spades, but a mighty white fellow at that. The next two bunks to his are occupied by Princeton men of old Southern families. They talk more like a darky than he does and are best of friends with him…This black brother has been in the Foreign Legion, wounded four times, covered with medals for his bravery in the trenches, and now uses his experiences and knowledge of

French for the benefit of our room.

The American volunteers, along with other airmen in World War I, were pioneers in a new kind of warfare. As one trainee wrote, "I am now in a French aviation school and learning how to imitate the birds." Among the pilots who would join the flying Corps was a young American who would become one f the most famous writers of his time, James Norman Hall. Along with another American pilot, Charles Nordhoff, Hall would author *Mutiny on the Bounty*. In 1917 and 1918 Hall wrote a series of articles for the *Atlantic Monthly* based on his experience as an airman. The articles formed the basis for his book about the air war, *High Adventure*. A good writer as well as a skilled pilot, Hall was able to capture the experience of flight in the early years.

On his first day of flight training, James Hall listened carefully to the advice of fellow Americans: wear all your flight gear including goggles and fur-lined boots—it's cold up there. Eager to get it right, Hall dressed for high altitude and made his way to the airfield, where he saw his first "airplane." Called a Penguin, this class of planes had clipped wings, a twenty-five-horsepower engine, and was incapable of even leaving the ground. Seasoned aviators, French and American, laughed at the joke on Hall and left the overdressed novice to his education.

The Penguin, James Hall learned, could build up just enough speed for the tail to lift, giving the pilot practice in steering with a rudder. "Never have I seen a stranger sight than that of a swarm of Penguins at work," wrote Hall. "They ran along the ground at an amazing speed, zigzagged this way and that, and whirled about as if trying to catch their own tails." As Hall watched, two of the Penguins rushed at each other "as though driven by the hand of fate" and crashed head-on. Hall's turn came and he charged down the field at full speed, lifted the Penguin's tail, seemed about to flip over, cut his engine, and spun around in a circle. Later in the day, he was able to steer a straight course with the rudder, and he sped down the field to a flag marking the end of the course. There a man turned his machine 180 degrees, and Hall headed back, having mastered the Penguin—"compelled it to do my bidding."

James Hall taxied proudly to the starting point, anticipating congratulations. But instead the other airmen were looking up at a plane high overhead. As they watched, it turned straight up into the sky, hung for a moment, then dropped into a nosedive, turning as it fell "like a scrap of paper." The French called this maneuver a *vrille*, "their prettiest piece of aerial acrobatics that one could wish to see." After seven or eight runs, the pilot came out of his dive, gathered speed and made two quick loops, followed by a *retournement*—turning over in the air and reversing his direction. He then spiraled down over the onlookers and landed so perfectly that it was "impossible to know when the machine touched the ground." The "birdman" removed his helmet and goggles and was recognized at once as a former instructor, taking the afternoon off from the front to visit old friends. For him those death-defying maneuvers were more than aerial sport—under other circumstances they might save his life or enable him to shoot down an enemy. Mounted on the hood of his plane was a machine gun with a long belt of cartridges—a reminder of the war.

After the pilot went off with his friends, James Hall examined his plan carefully, looking into the cockpit. He noted that the gun was mounted so that it would fire directly through the propeller, which rotated at speed of up to 1,900 revolutions per minute. Hall looked back at his little Penguin and realized how much he had to learn.

The French course in military aviation undertaken by most Americans usually consisted of a sequence of increasingly complex solar flights, unlike modern flight training where the instructor goes aloft with the pupil. At first trainees flew up and down the runway barely leaving the ground; then they mounted to about one hundred feet, shut off their engines, and glided back to earth. Next they added a turn to their flights, climbing above the airdrome, and circling around to land. Still close to the training field, a student then flew to 3,000 feet, shut off his engine, and glided down to a predetermined spot. Another test required the trainee to climb above 6,500 feet and remain there for a full hour. Finally, he would make several cross-country flights.

The program made good sense, but every stage brought surprises—some troublesome and some deadly. The commandant at Avord, where most Americans were trained, was killed when a student flew into his plane, knocking off a wing. The commandant's plane crashed to the ground, but the student managed to land safely, although the wing of the other plane stuck to his machine. Another pilot crashed into the roof of the camp bakery, ending up hanging from the ceiling, uninjured. Others were less fortunate; about 1 percent of all student pilots died in flight training.

The first real flight by the novice, beyond simply cruising down the runway, was called the *tour de piste*. The solo trainee had to climb high over the airdrome, make his first-ever turn, and land. If he failed to coordinate hands and feet on the controls, he could easily crash into a hanger or the runway. One American took off from Avord, flew over a row of haystacks indicating where he should turn, and dipped his left wing according to instructions. But he was unprepared for the sensation: he felt as if he were falling out of the open-cockpit plane. Distracted, he misjudged the turn and went sailing across the space of another class and toward a nearby village. By the time he managed to turn again, his landing field was in the "dim distance." The novice barely skimmed a row of tress, "trespassed" through the air space of another class, and landed.

"What did you do?" said the instructor.

"God only knows," the student replied.

Told to try again, he managed two good tours. But on the second he learned another lesson about flight: "I struck a bump and received an awful jolt, which to say the least startled me considerably." Seasoned pilots knew, and beginners soon learned, that unseen air currents could unexpectedly lift or drop a plane a hundred feet or more. "My machine we seized and turned sideways," one pilot recounted:

> Then, as though tossed by a giant who had instantly changed his mind, it was dropped into a hole, perhaps 100 feet deep. Gusts strike you in front, sideways, behind; up you go over a mountainous wave; then down, falling over the other side. So it goes, gently easing each bump with the controls, sideways, forwards or backwards, with a delicate touch that comes by instinct.

James Hall's instructor explained that the air could be turbulent at one level and yet calm at another—a fact known to any modern air traveler—but the young trainee was "incredulous" until he actually experienced the change in winds. Hall had not until then lost his "boyhood belief that the wind went all the way up."

After developing a feeling for air currents, trainees practiced more complex maneuvers including flying spirals and landing without an engine—"a very difficult thing to do," one pilot recounted, "as the field from 3,400 feet appears as small as your back yard." After this test the trainee would be required to pass the high altitude test. One pilot, who held his plane at 8,000 feet for the required hour, regretted that he had taken only a sweater for warmth. He "nearly froze" during the flight and even after landing he was "chilled through for a long time afterwards."

In the classroom the trainees received instruction in navigation by map and by compass. Then came their brevet flights, journeys of about two hundred miles. The trainee flew to an assigned destination, landed, and flew home. James Hall's flight papers included a list of prices to be paid to farmers in case of forced landings on their crops. Hall particularly treasured the official orders telling him to proceed "by the route of the air" from Avord to Châteauroux and Romorantin. He read this "with feelings which must have been nearly akin to those of Columbus on a memorable day in 1492 when he received his clearance papers from Cadiz. 'By the route of air!' How the imagination lingered over that phrase!"

Hall donned a fur-lined flight suit, climbed into his craft, and took off. His plane was at first buffeted by the winds. Then he reached 2,500 feet and smooth air. As he flew on he saw with wonder the land from the open cockpit of his airplane. Beneath was a cathedral he had often visited in a town near the airdrome:

> Looking down on it now, it seemed no larger than a toy cathedral in a toy town, such as one sees in the shops of Paris. The streets were empty, for it was not yet seven o'clock. Strips of shadow crossed them where taller roofs cut off the sunshine. A toy train, which I could have put nicely into my fountain-pen case, was pulling into a station no larger than a wren's house.

James Hall climbed to 6,000 feet: "It seemed a tremendous altitude." He could see scores of villages and châteaus, forests and farmland: "It looked like a world planned and laid out by the best of Santa Clauses ...For untold generations only the birds have had the privilege of seeing and enjoying it from the wing. Small wonder that they sing." Hall followed a straight road, heading southwest toward Châteauroux. His motor ran smoothly and for a while he reflected that flying was "the simplest thing in the world." But the young pilot would soon learn to be more respectful of the dangers of flight.

Hall's trip into Châteauroux went well. In the distance he could see the spires and roofs of the town; nearby were barracks, hangers, and a landing field. Hall reduced speed. His motor purring gently, the landscape coming closer: "shining threads of silver became rivers and canals, tiny green shrubs became tress." He saw people in the street and then spotted a mother spanking a small boy in her yard. She stopped spanking to look up at the approaching plane, and the boy escaped. Hall was pleased to have done the child an unintentional favor.

After refueling, he continued on toward Romorantin, the second point in his triangular route. He was following the correct compass course, when suddenly he realized that something was wrong. Glancing at his map Hall discovered that he had been blown far off course. His instructors had cautioned against being "certain about anything while in the air." But Hall had failed to take into account the unseen, unfelt force of a sidewind. He flew on, looking for landmarks, but he was soon flying over an unbroken bank of clouds. He later wrote, there is "no isolation so complete as that of the airman who has above him only the blue sky, and below, a level floor of pure white cloud." Hall was still confident, however, that he could use his compass to correct his course to Romorantin. But now the clouds came upon him in "heaped" masses, soon surrounding him on all sides. "I made a hasty revision of my opinion as to the calm and tranquil joys of aviation, thinking what fools men are who willingly leave the good green earth and trust themselves to all the winds of heaven in a frail box of cloth-covered sticks." James Hall could no longer avoid flying into the clouds, and in a moment he was "hopelessly lost in a blanket of cold drenching mist." He could not even see his own wings and lost all sense of direction.

Then Hall fell into a dive while thinking he was flying level, an illusion common in low visibility flight—one that killed John Kennedy Jr. on a flight near Cape Cod in 1999. The air screaming through the wires of James Hall's plane may have saved his life. Startled by the sound, he looked at his "speed-dial," saw that he was flying too fast, and knew that he must be falling earthward "at a terrific pace." Suddenly dropping out of the clouds he saw the world tilted at such a crazy angle that he half expected to see "dogs and dishpans, baby carriages and ash-barrels roll out of every house in France, and go clattering off into space."

Hall pulled desperately at the "broom-stick" and brought his plane level with the horizon. Relieved to be alive, and not wanting to fly over "half of France" looking for Romorantin, he chose one of a dozen villages within view—one surrounded by wide level fields—shut off his engine, and glided toward the ground. Barely clearing a row of fruit trees, he touched down. Hall's plane rolled down a hill and stopped a few feet short of a small stream. He decided to wait by his plane, hoping someone had seen his descent. Soon a small boy appeared shouting triumphantly to friends that he had found the downed biplane. "*Bonjour, mon petit,*" said Hall, but the shy youngster said nothing. Soon several score children appeared along with women and old men. As in other villages throughout France, the young men were dead or fighting at the front.

The crowd made a circle around the machine, waiting politely for Hall to speak. He in turn pretended to be attending to his plane while in reality he was trying to "screw up my courage" to say something in French. The mayor of the town arrive and Hall tried without success to communicate. Unable to express himself in words, Hall invited each of the boys to sit in the cockpit. Eventually, despite the language problem, Hall learned the correct direction to Romorantin. Then with the help of the boys, he pushed his biplane to level ground and took off.

After a short flight, Hall landed safely in Romorantin, completing the second phase of his triangle. Soon he climbed again into the sky for his final flight. The weather had improved and Hall enjoyed skimming through broken clouds, sometimes skirting them so closely that the current of air from his propeller "reveled out fragments of shining vapor, which streamed into the clear spaces like wisps of filmy silk." Suddenly Hall saw a "Fantastically painted" twin-engine plane going in the opposite direction:

> The thing startled me, not so much because of its weird appearance as by the mere fact of its being there. Strangely enough, for a moment it seemed impossible that I should meet another avion. Despite a long apprenticeship in aviation, in these days when one's mind has only begun to grasp the fact that the mastery of the air has been accomplished, the sudden presentation of a bit of evidence sometimes shocks it into a moment of amazement bordering on incredulity.

The brief appearance of the other plane set Hall thinking about the reality of flight and of his own vulnerability. Listening to the "swish of the wind through wires and struts" he reflected that if only "a few frail wires should part" his ingenious biplan would tumble to the ground.

Then in the distance he saw the barracks, hangars, and machine shops of Avord. Feeling as if he had been away for many years instead of just a few hours, he brought the plan to a halt and greeted a "monitor," the man who would confirm that James Hall had completed his triangle. That night he sat at a rickety table and wrote by candlelight his account of the day's adventure. In the distance he could hear the sound of heavy guns: "the very ghost of sound, as faint as the beating of the pulses in one's ears." Many of the men whose absence had been so conspicuous in the village of Hall's forced landing would have been fighting among those cannon— or dead already in combat along the western front.

James Hall's preliminary flight had been an adventure, made memorable by his own skill in capturing in words the wonder and terror of flight. Other pilots tackled these brevet flights with varying degrees of success. One American, a man named Millard, made three attempts at his brevet flight, crashing each time. James Hall noted that the man "could never find the towns where he was supposed to land, so he would keep on going until his gas gave out. Then the machine would come down of itself, and Millard would crawl out from under the wreckage and come back by train." Eager as they were to train American pilots, the French finally gave up on Millard.

Forced landings were more common than crashes, and many a pilot, like Hall, came to ground in a framer's field. One American lost power during a brevet flight and landed several kilometers from the nearest town. A suspicious farmer "collared" him as a possible German spy and took him to a nearby chateau. There the owner, speaking English, learned that the pilot was an American. He treated the airman to a meal and lodged him in an elegant chamber. Pilots sometimes returned to their planes after forced landings to find them covered with flowers. At least one American, returning to his craft after a forced landing, discovered that young girls of the village had written amorous messages on the wings.

Some pilots were less fortunate than James Hall when it came to taking off after a forced landing. An American persuaded a group of boys to hold his plane while turning the propeller by hand to start the engine. The motor roared to life, frightening the boys into letting go before the pilot could scramble into the cockpit. The plane sped across a field with the pilot running behind. He caught up after the plane came to rest ignobly nose down in ta ditch, looking "like a duck hunting bugs in the mud."

Other pilots were, like Hall, struck by the sheer beauty of the earth and clouds, seen for the first time from high in the sky. Their sense of wonder was not unlike that of the astronauts about a half century later, looking down on the earth from outer space. In letters and articles pilots tried to find words to described the new element. The subject could be as simple as the clouds: "the view ahead and on the east side was like snow-fields of soft wet snow, with here and there hillocks rising in it with blue shadows." And the subject could be as grand as a flight into the mountains. One American pilot wrote this account of a flight into the Pyrenees in southern France:

> Turning eastward, I passed over some of the outer peaks which, snowcapped and bare of all foliage, were scarcely three hundred meters below me. I saw no one moving above the snow-line. It looked bleak, but very splendid in the sunlight....I drank in the chilling, pure air with delight and fixed the picture so firmly in my mind that I shall never forget it.

Eventually these training flights came to an end. Soon after this difficult first triangle, James Hall made a second brevet flight, this one in three hours and without problems. That exercise completed the first stage of his training, and Hall was advanced to the rank of corporal. At a local tailor shop he had wings and a star sewn to his collar, designating him a *pilot aviateur*. He was now a brevetted military pilot. But before he could fly in combat he needs to complete another level of training to prepare him to fly among enemy pilots, whose purpose would be to destroy him and his craft. Most Americans learned marksmanship at Cazaux, which they called "Kazoo," where they began by firing shotguns at clay pigeons and balloons. Next they fired machine guns at a target pulled by speedboat across a nearby lake and fired rockets from the air at silhouette targets on the ground. The course in "acrobacy' —learning the maneuvers for aerial combat—involved moves that would have been thought impossible at the beginning of the war. These included the barrel turn, "a series of rapid, horizontal, corkscrew turns," and the *vrille*, a spinning nose dive that killed more than one novice pilot "for the reasons that one could not know, beforehand whether he would be able to keep his head, with the earth gone mad spinning like top, standing on one rim, turning upside down."

After learning these maneuvers and others James Hall flew practice fighter missions with fellow pilots. Sometimes three planes would fly in a mock attack on a village or a train. They were forbidden to fly over Paris during these outings, and so, Hall remarks, "we took all the more delight in doing it." Hall saw Paris "in all its moods: in the haze of early morning, at midday when the air had been washed clean by spring rains, in the soft light of afternoon." Such flights may have seemed all the more satisfying at that time because they came before the real work of being Word War I pilot. Soon enough James Hall would join other pilots in a new exercise where the scenery would include not only landscapes and clouds, but also enemy pilots bent on their destruction.

American volunteers would serve in many French units during the war, but they were best known for their participation in the one distinctively American squadron, Escadrille N-124, called originally the Escadrille Américaine. When Germany protested the Squadron's name was a violation of American neutrality, the name was changed to the Lafayette Escadrille in honor of the Marquis de LaFayette, a young Frenchman who had won distinction leading French troops in the American Revolution. These pilots and a larger group of Americans fighting in French units were known collectively as the Lafayette Flying Corps. The members of the Lafayette Escadrille would eventually adopt as their insignia the head of a Sioux Indian, resplendent in feathers, copied from the picture on a box of Remington rifles.

The initial member of the unit gathered at Luxeuil-les-Baines in the northeastern France in April 1916. This was a quiet sector of the front where they formed themselves into a combat squadron, complete with administrative personnel and mechanics. They also began to accumulate a collection of pets that would eventually include cats, a dog, foxes, and two lion cubs whom they named Whiskey and Soda. Their planes arrived from Paris, Nieuport 11 scouts with a wingspan of twenty-seven feet, maximum speed of just over 100 miles per hour, and armament consisting of Lewis machine guns. The leader of the squadron was a Frenchman named Bapt. Georges Thenault, an early supporter of the idea of a distinct American unit. Among the original members of the escadrille was Norman Prince, who had at first proposed such a squadron, and Victor Chapman, a descendent of John Jay, first chief justice of the U.S. Supreme Court.

On May 13, 1916, five planes of the Lafayette Escadrille climbed into the sky, formed in to a V, and flew the squadron's first mission. They headed over a section of Switzerland and into Germany, where they encountered antiaircraft fire and buzzed a German airdrome but found no enemy planes. Five days later Kiffin Rockwell, a North Carolinian, was flying alone when he encountered an enemy aircraft. Taking it by surprise, he brought the plan down with four well-placed bullets. His comrades, having heard of the kill before he landed, hoisted Rockwell in triumph from his cockpit. At the height of the celebration that night, Rockwell pulled out an eighty-year-old bottle of bourbon, given him by his brother, and took a drink. Rather than finish the bottle then and there, the pilots decided to keep it in readiness for other Americans to drink after they downed enemy planes—one drink per kill. Many of the pilots who took that drought later died themselves in aerial combat, and so the flask came to be known as and "The Bottle of Death."

A few days later the Lafayette Escadrille was transferred to Behomme in the Verdun region of the front, where Germany was attempting to break through the Allied lines. The French would hold on at Verdun throughout 1916, but before the German offensive ended, roughly one million soldiers would die. Soon the American pilots found themselves in daily combat with German planes above the battlefield, and several Americans were almost killed. Kiffin Rockwell took a direct hit on his windshield and was half blinded, but managed to bring down an enemy aircraft and land safely. One of the bravest of the pilots, Victor Chapman, attacked two observation planes and their three escorts. He shot down one of the planes, but the others then turned on Chapman. One bullet grazed his skull and another shattered the control for the right aileron. Chapman's plane dropped like a stone while he struggled to fix the broken mechanism. Finally he regained control and glided to a safe landing.

At Behomme the squadron gained several more pilots including Clyde Balsley, a shy Texan, and Raoul Lufbery, who would become the squadron's ace with seventeen kills. In the air Lufbery was a fierce and innovative fighter; on the ground he liked to roam the local forests in search of mushrooms. In time it was inevitable that one of the American pilots would be killed in combat. Clyde Balsley was almost the first: his machine gun jammed when he attacked a German plane. The German then turned his guns on Balsley and sent bullets into his pelvis and legs. Balsley managed to crash land behind the French lines. He was hospitalized and retired from the air corps as an invalid.

While Balsley was in the hospital, Victor Chapman flew to visit him, bringing along a basket of fruit. At the last moment Chapman, though recently wounded himself, decided to join three comrades on a morning patrol. He fell behind the others and four Germans attacked him, damaging his plane so badly that it fell apart as it plummeted toward the ground. This first death in the ranks of the Lafayette Escadrille shocked the other pilots. "We could read the pain in one another's eyes," wrote one. At a ceremony on July 4, 1916, the French prime minster took note of Chapman's death, calling him and his squadron "the living symbol of American idealism." The prime minister was aware of the value of Victor Chapman's sacrifice as an example to other Americans, perhaps to the United States as a whole. "France will never forget this new comradeship," he said, "this evidence of a devotion to a common ideal." After the funeral ceremony, most of the American airmen went to Lafayette's grave for a July Fourth commemoration of the Frenchman's contribution to the American Revolution.

More deaths soon followed. September 1916, Kiffin Rockwell, who had recorded the squadron's first kill, took a bullet in the throat and died before his plane hit the ground friends called him the "soul" of the escadrille, and Captain Thenault shed tears as he proclaimed that the "best and bravest of us all" is no more. Soon afterward the squadron took part in a raid on the German arms works at Oberndorf-am-Neckar. On the way back Norman Prince, who had first suggested the creation of an American squadron, tried to land at dusk at an unfamiliar airfield. His plane struck a high tension wire, catapulting Prince to the ground. Raoul Lufbery, who had landed just before Prince, rushed to his side. Although both of his legs were broken and he had suffered from massive internal injuries, Prince was still conscious. "Hurry up and light the flares, " he said, "so that another fellow won't come down and break himself up as I have." Lufbery reported:

> I placed him in an ambulance, urging the driver to hurry him to the hospital at Gerardmer. Throughout the trip, Norman did not

cease to talk and chat with the good humor that was on of his charming characteristics....He spoke of his desire to be back with the squadron soon. But in the meantime, he began to suffer horribly and at times his face would be distorted with pain. His hand, which I was holding between my own, was wet with sweat. His endurance was remarkable and when the pain became so intense that he grew faint, he sang to keep from losing consciousness. My own heart was torn to see the struggle within him.

Norman Prince died the next day.

Death was a constant companion in the French Flying Corps; cots were cleared regularly of one man's gear for another to replace him. When the specter of death was not too overwhelming, the pilots sometimes sang a grim song, "The Dying Aviator," as they attempted to laugh in the face of death:

The young aviator lay dying
And as 'neath the wreckage he lay,
To the mechanics assembled around him,
These last parting words he did say:
"Two valve springs you'll find in my stomach,
Three spark plugs are safe in my lung,
The prop is in splinters inside me,
To my fingers the joy stick has clung.
Take the cylinders out of my kidneys,
The connecting rods out of my brain;
From the small of my back get the crankshaft,
And assemble the engine again."

Soon after Norman Prince's death the Lafayette Escadrille was transferred to Cachy, near a great battle by the Somme River. This engagement, like the Battle of Verdun, would take roughly one million lives. But during their three months at the Somme, bad weather kept the planes on the ground most of the time: one American described the visibility as so poor that "even the ducks were walking." The squadron lost no more members, and their Nieuports were replaced by the SPADs, tougher, faster aircraft, the equal of any planes the Germans could bring against them. In view of the new aircraft, the unit's official name gained a SPAD designation: SPA-124.

James Hall completed his training and joined the Lafayette Escadrille after it had become a seasoned squadron. Veteran pilots warned him that he would soon be exhausted by the work: he should plan on getting ten or twelve hours of sleep per night when he could. He discovered that many of the pilots' waking hours were spent scanning maps of the sector over which they would be flying and swapping tales with fellow aviators. Almost always there was the drone of motors overhead as planes took off or landed in a series of patrols lasting from dawn till dark.

Then came the morning of James Hall's first patrol. An elderly man known as the "messroom steward" came to his cot with a lighted candle. *"Beau temps, monsieur,"* he said, and left the candle on the bed table. Through the oiled cloth that served as a window, Hall saw no light at all outside. In the messroom, where he would eat breakfast, there was a fire. The mingled aesthetics of French and American pilots appeared in the music from the phonograph: *"Chansons sans Paroles"* followed by "Oh, movin' man, don't take ma baby grand."

Outside there were clouds at about ten thousand feet with stars shining though the gaps. Hall learned that his squadron would be flying over the sector on high patrol, as much as three miles above the front. He finished his hot chocolate and waited anxiously for departure time. In *High Adventure* he describes the scene: "The canvas hangars billowed and flapped, and the wooden supports creaked with the quiet sound made by ships at sea. And there was almost the peace of the sea there, intensified, if anything, by the distant rumble of heavy cannonading." mechanics clustered around the machines, arming the machine guns, polishing the windshields, and starting the engines. "In a moment every machine was turning over." The pilots wore a variety of gear including woolen helmets, leather helmets, fur helmets; one pilot even wore for a helmet a silk bonnet that made him look like a "dear old lady."

Finally the machines rolled out onto the field, a mechanic running beside each one, every plane in the formation sporting an Indian head. One by one the pilots turned into the wind, gathered speed, and climbed over the airdrome. They rose together with the lead planes diving and climbing to keep James Hall, whose craft lagged behind, in the formation. "Sometimes we seemed, all of us, to be hanging motionless, then rising and falling like small boats riding a heavy swell." Then the sun crested the horizon, bathing the clouds in "shades of rose and amethyst and gold." Beneath the beauty of the clouds, Hall saw the killing grounds of the front:

> It was till dusk on the ground and my first view was that of thousands of winking lights, the flashes of guns and of bursting shells....The lights soon faded and the long, winding battle-front emerged from the shadow, a broad strip of desert land through a fair, green country....I knew that shells of enormous caliber were wrecking trenches, blasting out huge craters; and yet not a sound,

not the faintest reverberation of a gun....To look down from a height of more than two miles, on an endless panorama of suffering and horror, is to have the sense of one's littleness....The best the airman can do is to repeat, "We're here and we look at it like blind men."

Until now Hall had been in sight of the other members of the escadrille, but suddenly they were gone. Eventually he learned that such was the nature of aerial combat, with planes appearing and disappearing suddenly and fights often over in a few seconds. Hall spotted one of the squadron diving sharply and pointed his own plane down. A seasoned pilot in a hurry to lose altitude would fall into a vertical dive; Hall had not yet developed the confidence for that maneuver and dropped more slowly, falling farther behind his comrades. Suddenly an artillery shell passed close by his plane, reached the top of its arc and dropped downward. Then bombs began exploding around him, jolting his craft with their concussions. The explosions came closer, bursting "in clouds of coal-black smoke." One seemed to have ruined his tail: "my feeling was not that of fear exactly. It was more like despair." He knew he should head for home, but couldn't get a compass reading without flying straight for at least thirty seconds, which would have made him a perfect target for the Germans gunning for him from the ground.

Then a plane piloted by a friend came into sight and guided the novice Hall back to the airdrome.

Back on the ground the other pilot chided Hall: "If I had been a Hun! Oh, man! You were fruit salad! Fruit salad, I tell you! I could have speared you with my eyes shut."

Hall protested that he would have been able to fight his way out of the jam. The man shot back,

"Tell me this: did you see me?"

"Yes."

"When?"

"When you passed over my head."

"And twenty seconds before that you would have been a sieve, if either of us had been a *Boche* (a German)."

During the next few months, James Hall made forced landings—twice. Late one afternoon he was flying over Germany, delayed to watch a pretty sunset, and lost track of the rest of his squadron. As night fell he flew in the direction he thought would bring him back into France. In the distance he saw a large building, well lit, and decided to land near it. He glided down, barely missing a huge factory chimney and a line of telegraph wires before landing in a field of sugar beets. He was safely on the ground, but was he in France? The first words he heard were German, and soon his plane was surrounded by Germans. As casually as possible he reached for matches, hoping to set his plane afire so that the enemy could not use it. Then a voice rang out in French, *"Qu'est-ce-que vous faites la? Allez! Vite!"* ("What are you doing there? Go Quickly!") The Germans moved away from the plane, and a Frenchman approached. Soon Hall learned that the Germans were war prisoners, harvesting French sugar beets. He had landed in friendly territory.

The next time he was forced down Hall was not so fortunate. On patrol over Germany, the cloth fabric began ripping away from his right wing, and soon afterward he was hit by an antiaircraft shell. His engine dropped forward in its mounts and the plan fell quickly toward the earth. On impact the motor and landing gear dropped away and the fuselage skidded along the ground. The crash broke one of Hall's ankles, sprained the other, and injured his nose. This time the voices he heard were not French.

During his imprisonment, the Germans treated Hall well. Shortly after the crash he was invited to join German aviators at lunch. One had been in Hall's gunsights when his wing started to give way. Hall found himself "heartily glad" he had not killed the man. In prison he and other Allied pilots could indulge themselves on a "splendid little library" of history, biography, essays, and novels. Hall's time in the hospital, before being sent to prison, may have encouraged him to reflect on the war as a whole. At any rate, in a historical novel he later authored with Charles Nordhoff, there is a revealing scene. In *Falcons of France* an American pilot crashes behind enemy lines and suffers injuries very like Hall's. In the hospital the airman is given a private room but not so remote as to shield him from the screams of badly wounded German soldiers. The narrator reflects on these men and on the injured men he had encountered at Neuilly, France, where he had received treatment for injuries from a previous crash:

> Their moans and cries, echoing and reechoing along the hallway, froze my blood. There is a quality scarcely human in the screams of a man crying out in sheer animal terror and pain. Once again, as at the American hospital at Neuilly, was stripped for me of all its romance and glory. Many a time I wished that politicians, munitions makers, breeders and abettors of war of whatever sort, might be forced to make the rounds of such hospitals so that they might see with their own eyes the horrible suffering they had brought to pass.

James Hall concludes his autobiographical account of the war by noting that in Germany, although individual Americans were treated well, "bitterness towards America there certainly is everywhere, and an intense hatred for President Wilson." By then America had entered the war on the side of the Allies, following Woodrow Wilson's war proclamation in which he promised to make the world "safe for democracy." The United States proclaimed war on Germany in 1917, but did not engage in any large-scale operations until 1918. In the meantime the Lafayette Escadrille continued to function as a unit of the French Flying Corps, and other Americans fought in other French air squadrons.

Edmund Genet was one of the escadrille pilots who watched with enthusiasm the entry of the United States into the war. Genet was the great-great grandson and namesake of Edmond "Citizen" Genet, who had served as minister from France to the United States when George Washington was president. This Genet had gone far beyond the traditional role of diplomat in the United States, giving speeches to large crowds in which he encouraged Americans to support the French Revolution. He married an American woman and settled in the United States. His great-great grandson was equally idealistic in his support for France—so much so that he deserted the U.S. Navy at the outbreak of the war in order to fight for France. At first Edmund Genet fought in the trenches along with Kiffin Rockwell, another future pilot.

Genet joined the Lafayette Escadrille in January 1917. A fellow pilot described him as a youth who "didn't look a day over fourteen. His peach-bloom complexion showed no traces of ever having met a razor socially." Genet quickly distinguished himself as one of the escadrille's most aggressive pilots, going out in weather that keep other airmen on the ground and finding Germans. When he heard on April 4, 1917, that the United States had entered the war and that "Paris is decorated with Old Glory everywhere," he was at first elated and pinned a small American flag on his coat. "I wish we could fling out in sight of all the Germans the glorious stars and stipes to defy them," he wrote in his diary. Later that night his humor changed to depression—he had recently lost one of his best friends, who died flying for the escadrille, and in addition he had just learned that his girlfriend back in the United States had fallen in love with another man. In this dark mood, Edmund Genet wrote these lines in his diary:

> Somehow I've given away completely this evening. I feel sure there is something very serious going to happen to me very soon. It doesn't seem any less than Death itself. I've never had such a

feeling or been so saddened since coming over to battle for this glorious France. I tore into shreds a little silken American flag which I've carried since the beginning of my enlistment. Somehow it seems a mockery to rejoice over the entrance of our country into the conflict with the Entente when we have been over here so long giving our all for the right while our country has been holding back.

A few days later on April 16 1917, Genet went out on patrol with Raoul Lufbery, the ace of the Lafayette Escadrille. Lufbery saw antiaircraft fire exploding near Genet's plane and saw him bank as if to return home. Thinking his friend was all right, Lufbery headed back to the airdrome. But Genet did not return. Reports from French soldiers and an investigation of his remains told the story. At 4,000 feet Edmund Genet was severely wounded by shell fire. His plane dropped into a violent spin, losing one of the wings. The plane hit a road at full speed. One of Genet's fellow pilots visited the scene of the wreck and reported, "I have never seen so complete a crash."

Edmund Genet thus became the first American to die in France after the United States entered the war. At his funeral service, Captain Thenault, the leader of the escadrille, spoke of Genet and America:" Respectfully I salute our memory which we shall cherish, and before the grave of the first soldier fallen for the two flags—the Stars and Stripes and the Tricolor—in the great war, we say, Thanks to America for having given sons such as thou. Farewell."

Soon afterward Genet's mother received letters of condolence from President Wilson and Secretary of the Navy Josephus Daniels. Daniels told her that since her son had died fighting for an ally, his service with the U.S. Navy would be "considered in every respect an honorable one.

The Lafayette Escadrille continued as a distinct squadron until February 18, 1918, when it was transferred to the American Expeditionary Force as part of the 103rd Aero Pursuit Squadron. During its existence it had grown from a showcase squadron, viewed by the French as most valuable for its propaganda value, into tough-fighting escadrille playing an important part in the war. Including the Americans who fought for other French squadrons, 180 American flew for France during World War I. They undertook thousands of sorties and shot down 199 German planes. Fifteen of the volunteers were captured and fifty-one died in action.

The Lafayette Escadrille's top pilot was Raoul Lufbery, who brought down seventeen German planes. In 1918 after the squadron had been absorbed by the United States, the government decided that Lufbery was too important as a living war hero to be risked in combat. He was assigned to a desk job, but he persuaded his superiors to allow him to return to combat. On May 18, 1918, he attacked a German plane at about 2,000 feet in sight of his own aerodrome Lufbery was close to brining down the enemy when a bullet struck his own fuel tank, and his plane burst into flames. Lufbery was only slightly wounded and might have parachuted to safety—if he had a parachute.

Parachutes had been in existence for more than a century, ever since a French inventor had tested one from a balloon—first on his dog and then on himself. And parachutes were routinely issued to men in observation balloons on the front. But during World War I, pilots went aloft without parachutes. Some authorities said that they were too bulky to be worn in fighter cockpits; some said that would encourage pilots to desert craft that might be brought down safely; some said that only a coward would want one. To a pilot in a burning plane thousands of feet above the ground none of these reasons made much sense. For that reason an Italian instructor told his students that if their plane caught fire, "Shut off the gas and commend your soul to God." In quarters Raoul Lufbery had debated with fellow pilots about what to do in a flaming aircraft: he advocated staying with the plane. But now as other pilots watched Lufbery from the ground, they could see him pull himself from the cockpit of his burning craft and jump. Later some speculated that he had hoped to hit a stream far below, with some slight chance for survival. But instead he landed in a garden behind a French house and died instantly.

With the United States fully engaged in the war, other American heroes—notably Billy Mitchell and Eddie Rickenbacker—came to the fore as the great aces of the conflict. But although they appear in the record books with more kills than Raoul Lufbery, the escadrille pilot likely shot down more Germans. Differences between French and American methods of confirming victories diminished Lufbery's total. Pilots who knew all three said that Lufbery was the best of the American airmen.

Raoul Lufbery and other American volunteers who flew for France were forerunners of the larger American participation of World War I. In fact, soon after the American declaration of war pilots in the Lafayette Escadrille were allowed to fly the American flag, making them the first airmen to fight in Word War I under Old Glory. Like the millions of U.S. soldiers who eventually enlisted, the early volunteer thought of themselves as taking part in a great adventure and offering their lives for a glorious cause.

During one of his early flights, when he made a forced landing outside a French village, James Hall had sensed the larger meaning of his fighting for France. *"Vous etes Anglais, monsieur?"* (You are English, Sir?), a Frenchman had asked. *"Non, Monsieur,"* Hall replied, "American." The reaction was impressive.

> That magic word! What potency it had in France....I might have had the village for the asking. I willingly accepted the role of ambassador of the American people. Had it not been for the language barrier, I think I would have made a speech, for I felt the generous spirit of Uncle Sam prompting me to give those fathers and mothers, whose husbands and sons were at the front, the promise of our unqualified support.

With America's entry into the war, that "unqualified support" had arrived.

7.7
Schenck v. U.S. (1919)

In 1917, Congress passed legislation making it a crime to criticize publicly the war effort, soldiers, the draft, the President, Congress, and the military. Many Americans believed that such laws violated the First Amendment's protection of free speech. One was Charles Schenck, general secretary of the Socialist Party of America. Schenck oversaw the production of a pamphlet urging men of draft age to "assert your rights" and to refuse to be drafted. The government arrested Schenck and charged him with violating the Espionage Act. Schenck's appeal of his conviction reached the Supreme Court in 1919; here is an excerpt of the Court's decision upholding Schenck's conviction. What reasoning does Justice Oliver Wendell Holmes Jr. use in his ruling? Are you persuaded by it?

Mr. Justice HOLMES delivered the opinion of the Court.

This is an indictment in three counts.... The defendants were found guilty on all the counts. They set up the First Amendment to the Constitution forbidding Congress to make any law abridging the freedom of speech, or of the press, and bringing the case here on that ground have argued some other points also of which we must dispose.

It is argued that the evidence, if admissible, was not sufficient to prove that the defendant Schenck was concerned in sending the documents. According to the testimony Schenck said he was general secretary of the Socialist party and had charge of the Socialist headquarters from which the documents were sent. He identified a book found there as the minutes of the Executive Committee of the party. The book showed a resolution of August 13, 1917, that 15,000 leaflets should be printed on the other side of one of them in use, to be mailed to men who had passed exemption boards, and for distribution. Schenck personally attended to the printing. On August 20 the general secretary's report said "Obtained new leaflets from printer and started work addressing envelopes" &c; and there was a resolve that Comrade Schenck be allowed $125 for sending leaflets through the mail. He said that he had about fifteen or sixteen thousand printed. There were files of the circular in question in the inner office which he said were printed on the other side of the one sided circular and were there for distribution. Other copies were proved to have been sent through the mails to drafted men. Without going into confirmatory details that were proved, no reasonable man could doubt that the defendant Schenck was largely instrumental in sending the circulars about....

The document in question upon its first printed side recited the first section of the Thirteenth Amendment, said that the idea embodied in it was violated by the conscription act and that a conscript is little better than a convict. In impassioned language it intimated that conscription was despotism in its worst form and a monstrous wrong against humanity in the interest of Wall Street's chosen few. It said, "Do not submit to intimidation," but in form at least confined itself to peaceful measures such as a petition for the repeal of the act. The other and later printed side of the sheet was headed "Assert Your Rights." It stated reasons for alleging that any one violated the Constitution when he refused to recognize "your right to assert your opposition to the draft," and went on, "If you do not assert and support your rights, you are helping to deny or disparage rights which it is the solemn duty of all citizens and residents of the United States to retain." It described the arguments on the other side as coming from cunning politicians and a mercenary capitalist press, and even silent consent to the conscription law as helping to support an infamous conspiracy. It denied the power to send our citizens away to foreign shores to shoot up the people of other lands, and added that words could not express the condemnation such cold-blooded ruthlessness deserves, &c., &c., winding up, "You must do your share to maintain, support and uphold the rights of the people of this country." Of course the document would not have been sent unless it had been intended to have some effect, and we do not see what effect it could be expected to have upon persons subject to the draft except to influence them to obstruct the carrying of it out. The defendants do not deny that the jury might find against them on this point.

But it is said, suppose that that was the tendency of this circular, it is protected by the First Amendment to the Constitution. Two of the strongest expressions are said to be quoted respectively from well-known public men.... We admit that in many places and in ordinary times the defendants in saying all that was said in the circular would have been within their constitutional rights. But the character of every act depends upon the circumstances in which it is done.... The most stringent protection of free speech would not protect a man in falsely shouting fire in a theatre and causing a panic.... The question in every case is whether the words used are used in such circumstances and are of such a nature as to create a clear and present danger that they will bring about the substantive evils that Congress has a right to prevent. It is a question of proximity and degree. When a nation is at war many things that might be said in time of peace are such a hindrance to its effort that their utterance will not be endured so long as men fight and that no Court could regard them as protected by any constitutional right....

Judgments affirmed.

CHAPTER 8

America in the 1920s

8.1   Frederick Lewis Allen, "Prelude: May, 1919" (1930)

8.2   Lynn Dumenil, "The Modern Temper"

8.3   John D'Emilio and Estelle Friedman, "The Sexual Revolution of the 1920s"

8.4   Jules Tygiel, "Unreconciled Strivings: Baseball in Jim Crow America"

8.5   Langston Hughes, "The Negro Artist and the Racial Mountain" (1926)

8.6   Poets of the Harlem Renaissance: Claude McKay and Sterling Brown

8.1
Prelude: May, 1919 (1930)

Frederick Lewis Allen

Journalist Frederick Lewis Allen wrote Only Yesterday: An Informal History of the 1920s *as soon as the decade ended. This, the first chapter of that book, sets the stage for the Twenties by detailing the experiences of a fictional Smith family in 1919. How might you characterize the Smiths' behavior and attitudes at the dawn of this decade? What kinds of things did each member of the family care about?*

If time were suddenly to turn back to the earliest days of the Post-war Decade, and you were to look about you, what would seem strange to you? Since 1919 the circumstances of American life have been transformed—yes, but exactly how?

Let us refresh our memories by following a moderately well-to do young couple of Cleveland or Boston or Seattle or Baltimore—it hardly matters which—through the routine of an ordinary day in May, 1919. (I select that particular date, six months after the Armistice of 1918, because by then the United States had largely succeeded in turning from the ways of war to those of peace, yet the profound alterations wrought by the Post-war Decade had hardly begun to take place.) There is no better way of suggesting what the passage of a few years has done to change you and me and the environment in which we live.

From the appearance of Mr. Smith as he comes to the breakfast table on this May morning in 1919, you would hardly know that you are not in

---

the nineteen-thirties (though you might, perhaps, be struck by the narrowness of his trousers). The movement of men's fashions is glacial. It is different, however, with Mrs. Smith.

She comes to breakfast in a suit, the skirt of which—rather tight at the ankles—hangs just six inches from the ground. She has read in *Vogue* the alarming news that skirts may become even shorter, and that "not since the days of the Bourbons has the woman of fashion been visible so far above the ankle"; but six inches is still the orthodox clearance. She wears low shoes now, for spring has come; but all last winter she protected her ankles either with spats or with high laced "walking-boots," or with high patent-leather shoes with contrasting buckskin tops. Her stockings are black (or tan, perhaps, if she wears tan shoes); the idea of flesh-colored stockings would appall her. A few minutes ago Mrs. Smith was surrounding herself with an "envelope chemise" and a petticoat; and from the thick ruffles on her undergarments it was apparent that she was not disposed to make herself more boyish in form than ample nature intended.

Mrs. Smith may use powder, but she probably draws the line at paint. Although the use of cosmetics is no longer, in 1919, considered *prima facie* evidence of a scarlet career, and sophisticated young girls have already begun to apply them with some bravado, most well-brought-up women still frown upon rouge. The beauty-parlor industry is in its infancy; there are a dozen hair-dressing parlors for every beauty parlor, and Mrs. Smith has never heard of such dark arts as that of face-lifting. When she puts on her hat to go shopping she will add a veil pinned neatly together behind her head. In the shops she will perhaps buy a bathing-suit for use in the summer; it will consist of an outer tunic of silk or cretonne over a tight knitted undergarment—worn, of course, with long stockings.

Her hair is long, and the idea of a woman ever frequenting a barber shop would never occur to her. If you have forgotten what the general public thought of short hair in those days, listen to the remark of the manager of the Palm Garden in New York when reporters asked him, one night in November, 1918, how he happened to rent his hall for a pro-Bolshevist meeting which had led to a riot. Explaining that a well-dressed woman had come in a fine automobile to make arrangements for the use of the auditorium, he added, "Had we noticed then, as we do now, that she had short hair, we would have refused to rent the hall." In Mrs. Smith's mind, as in that of the manager of the Palm Garden, short-haired women, like long-haired men, are associated with radicalism, if not with free love.

The breakfast to which Mr. and Mrs. Smith sit down may have been arranged with a view to the provision of a sufficient number of calories—

they need only to go to Childs' to learn about calories—but in all probability neither of them has ever heard of a vitamin.

As Mr. Smith eats, he opens the morning paper. It is almost certainly not a tabloid, no matter how rudimentary Mr. Smith's journalistic tastes may be: for although Mr. Hearst has already experimented with small-sized picture papers, the first conspicuously successful tabloid is yet to be born. Not until June 26, 1919, will the *New York Daily News* reach the newsstands, beginning a career that will bring its daily circulation in one year to nearly a quarter of a million, in five years to over four-fifths of a million, and in ten years to the amazing total of over one million three hundred thousand.

Strung across the front page of Mr. Smith's paper are headlines telling of the progress of the American Navy seaplane, the NC-4, on its flight across the Atlantic *via* the Azores. That flight is the most sensational news story of May, 1919. (Alcock and Brown have not yet crossed the ocean in a single hop; they will do it a few weeks hence, eight long years ahead of Lindbergh.) But there is other news, too: of the Peace Conference at Paris, where the Treaty is now in its later stages of preparation; of the successful oversubscription of the Victory Loan ("Sure, we'll finish the job!" the campaign posters have been shouting); of the arrival of another transport with soldiers from overseas; of the threat of a new strike; of a speech by Mayor Ole Hanson of Seattle denouncing that scourge of the times, the I.W.W.; of the prospects for the passage of the Suffrage Amendment, which it is predicted will enable women to take "a finer place in the national life"; and of Henry Ford's libel suit against the *Chicago Tribune*—in the course of which he will call Benedict Arnold a writer, and in reply to the question, "Have there been any revolutions in this country?" will answer, "Yes, in 1812."

If Mr. Smith attends closely to the sporting news, he may find obscure mention of a young pitcher and outfielder for the Boston Red Sox named Ruth. But he will hardly find the Babe's name in the headlines. (In April, 1919, Ruth made one home run; in May, two; but the season was much further advanced before sporting writers began to notice that he was running up a new record for swatting—twenty-nine home runs for the year; the season had closed before the New York Yankees, seeing gold in the hills, bought him for $125,000; and the summer of 1920 had arrived before a man died of excitement when he saw Ruth smash a ball into the bleachers, and it became clear that the mob had found a new idol. In 1919, the veteran Ty Cobb, not Ruth, led the American League in batting.)

The sporting pages inform Mr. Smith that Rickard has selected Toledo as the scene of a forthcoming encounter between the heavyweight champion, Jess Willard, and another future idol of the mob, Jack Dempsey. (They met, you may recall, on the Fourth of July, 1919, and sober citizens were horrified to read that 19,650 people were so depraved as to sit in a broiling sun to watch Dempsey knock out the six-foot-six-inch champion in the third round. How would the sober citizens have felt if they had known that eight years later a Dempsey-Tunney fight would bring in more than five times as much money in gate receipts as this battle of Toledo?) In the sporting pages there may be news of Bobby Jones, the seventeen-year-old Southern golf champion, or of William T. Tilden, Jr., who is winning tennis tournaments here and there, but neither of them is yet a national champion. And even if Jones were to win this year he would hardly become a great popular hero; for although golf is gaining every day in popularity, it has not yet become an inevitable part of the weekly ritual of the American business man. Mr. Smith very likely still scoffs at "grown men who spend their time knocking a little white ball along the ground"; it is quite certain that he has never heard of plus fours; and if he should happen to play golf he had better not show his knickerbockers in the city streets, or small boys will shout to him, "Hey, get some men's pants!"

Did I say that by May, 1919, the war was a thing of the past? There are still reminders of it in Mr. Smith's paper. Not only the news from the Peace Conference, not only the item about Sergeant Alvin York being on his way home; there is still that ugliest reminder of all, the daily casualty list.

Mr. and Mrs. Smith discuss a burning subject, the High Cost of Living. Mr. Smith is hoping for an increase in salary, but meanwhile the family income seems to be dwindling as prices rise. Everything is going up—food, rent, clothing, and taxes. These are the days when people remark that even the man without a dollar is fifty cents better off than he once was, and that if we coined seven-cent pieces for meet-car fares, in another year we should have to discontinue them and begin to coin fourteen-cent pieces. Mrs. Smith, confronted with an appeal from Mr. Smith for economy, reminds him that milk has jumped since 1914 from nine to fifteen cents a quart, sirloin steak from twenty-seven to forty-two cents a pound, butter from thirty-two to sixty-one cents a pound, and fresh eggs from thirty-four to sixty-two cents a dozen. No wonder people on fixed salaries are suffering, and colleges are beginning to talk of applying the money-raising methods learned during the Liberty Loan campaigns to the increasing of college endowments. Rents are almost worse than food prices, for that matter; since the Armistice there has been an increasing shortage of houses and apartments, and the profiteering landlord has become an object of popular hate along with the profiteering middleman. Mr. Smith tells his wife that "these profiteers are about as bad as the I.W.W.'s." He could make no stronger statement.

Breakfast over, Mr. Smith gets into his automobile to drive to the office. The car is as likely to be a Lexington, a Maxwell, a Briscoe, or a Templar as to be a Dodge, Buick, Chevrolet, Cadillac, or Hudson, and it surely will not be a Chrysler; Mr. Chrysler has just been elected first vice-president of the General Motors Corporation. Whatever the make of the car, it stands higher than the cars of the nineteen thirties; the passengers look down upon their surroundings from an imposing altitude. The chances are nine to one that Mr. Smith's automobile is open (only 10.3 per cent of the cars manufactured in 1919 were closed). The vogue of the sedan is just beginning. Closed cars are still associated in the public mind with wealth; the hated profiteer of the newspaper cartoon rides in a limousine.

If Mr. Smith's car is one of the high, hideous, but efficient model T Fords of the day, let us watch him for a minute. He climbs in by the right-hand door (for there is no left-hand door by the front seat), reaches over to the wheel, and sets the spark and throttle levers in a position like that of the hands of a dock at ten minutes to three. Then, unless he has paid extra for a self-starter, he gets out to crank. Seizing the crank in his right hand carefully (for a friend of his once broke his arm cranking), he slips his left forefinger through a loop of wire that controls the choke. He pulls the loop of wire, he revolves the crank mightily, and as the engine at last roars, he leaps to the trembling running-board, leans in, and moves the spark and throttle to twenty-five minutes of two. Perhaps he reaches the throttle before the engine falters into silence, but if it is a cold morning perhaps he does not. In that case, back to the crank again and the loop of wire. Mr. Smith wishes Mrs. Smith would come out and sit in the driver's seat and pull that spark lever down before the engine has time to die.

Finally he is at the wheel with the engine roaring as it should. He releases the emergency hand-brake, shoves his left foot against the low-speed pedal, and as the car sweeps loudly out into the street, he releases his left foot, lets the car into high gear, and is off. Now his only care is for that long hill down the street; yesterday he burned his brake on it, and this morning he must remember to brake with the reverse pedal, or the low-speed pedal, or both, or all three in alternation. (Jam your foot down on any of the three pedals and you slow the car.)

Mr. Smith is on the open road—a good deal more open than it will be a decade hence. On his way to work he passes hardly a third as many cars as he will pass in 1929; there are less than seven million passenger cars registered in the United States in 1919, as against over twenty-three million cars only ten years later. He is unlikely to find many concrete roads in his vicinity, and the lack of them is reflected in the speed regulations. A few states like California and New York permit a rate of thirty miles an hour in 1919, but the average limit is twenty (as against thirty-five or forty in 1931). The Illinois rate of 1919 is characteristic of the day; it limits the driver to fifteen miles in residential parts of cities, ten miles in built-up sections, and six miles on curves. The idea of making a hundred-mile trip in two and a half hours—as will constantly be done in the nineteen-thirties by drivers who consider themselves conservative—would seem to Mr. Smith perilous, and with the roads of 1919 to drive on he would be right.

In the course of his day at the office, Mr. Smith discusses business conditions. It appears that things are looking up. There was a period of uncertainty and falling stock prices after the Armistice, as huge government contracts were canceled and plants which had been running overtime on war work began to throw off men by the thousand, but since then conditions have been better. Everybody is talking about the bright prospects for international trade and American shipping. The shipyards are running full tilt. There are too many strikes going on, to be sure; it seems as if the demands of labor for higher and higher wages would never be satisfied, although Mr. Smith admits that in a way you can't blame the men, with prices still mounting week by week. But there is so much business activity that the men being turned out of army camps to look for jobs are being absorbed better than Mr. Smith ever thought they would be. It was back in the winter and early spring that there was so much talk about the ex-service men walking the streets without work; it was then that *Life* ran a cartoon which represented Uncle Sam saying to a soldier, "Nothing is too good for you, my boy! What would you like?" and the soldier answering, "A job." Now the boys seem to be sifting slowly but surely into the ranks of the employed, and the only clouds on the business horizon are strikes and Bolshevism and the dangerous wave of speculation in the stock market.

"Bull Market Taxes Nerves of Brokers," cry the headlines in the financial pages, and they speak of "Long Hours for Clerks." Is there a familiar ring to those phrases? Does it seem natural to you, remembering as you do the Big Bull Market of 1928 and 1929, that the decision to keep the Stock Exchange closed over the 31st of May, 1919, should elicit such newspaper comments as this: "The highly specialized machine which handles the purchase and sales of stocks and bonds in the New York market is fairly well exhausted and needs a rest"? Then listen; in May, 1919, it was a long series of *million-and-a-half-share* days which was causing financiers to worry and the Federal Reserve Board to consider issuing a warning against speculation. During that year a new record of six two-million-share days was set up, and on only 145 days did the trading amount to over a million shares. What would Mr. Smith and his associates think if they were to be told that within eleven years there would occur a sixteen-million-share day; and that they would see the time when three-million-share days would be referred to as "virtual stagnation" or as "listless trading by professionals only, with the general public refusing to become interested"? The price of a seat on the New York Stock Exchange in 1919 ranged between $60,000 and a new high record of $110,000; it would be hard for Mr. Smith to believe that before the end of the decade seats on the Exchange would fetch a half million.

In those days of May, 1919, the record of daily Stock Exchange transactions occupied hardly a newspaper column. The Curb Market record referred to trading on a real curb—to that extraordinary outdoor market in Broad Street, New York, where boys with telephone receivers clamped to their heads hung out of windows high above the street and grimaced and wigwagged through the din to traders clustered on the pavement below. And if there was anything Mrs. Smith was certain not to have on her mind as she went shopping, it was the price of stocks. Yet the "unprecedented bull market" of 1919 brought fat profits to those who participated in it. Between February 15th and May 14th, Baldwin Locomotive rose from 72 to 93, General Motors from 130 to 191, United States Steel from 90 to 104½, and International Mercantile Marine common (to which traders were attracted on account of the apparently boundless possibilities of shipping) from 23 to 47⅝.

When Mr. Smith goes out to luncheon, he has to proceed to his club in a roundabout way, for a regiment of soldiers just returned from Europe is on parade and the central thoroughfares of the city are blocked with crowds. It is a great season for parades, this spring of 1919. As the transports from Brest swing up New York Harbor, the men packed solid on the decks are greeted by Mayor Hylan's Committee of Welcome, represented sometimes by the Mayor's spruce young secretary, Grover Whalen, who in later years is to reduce welcoming to a science and raise it to an art. New York City has built in honor of the homecoming troops a huge plaster arch in Fifth Avenue at Madison Square, toward the design of which forty artists are said to have contributed. ("But the result," comments the *New York Tribune*, sadly, "suggests four hundred rather than forty. It holds everything that was ever on an arch anywhere, the lay mind suspects, not forgetting the horses on top of a certain justly celebrated Brandenburg Gate.") Farther up the Avenue, before the Public library, there is a shrine of pylons and palms called the Court of the Heroic Dead, of whose decorative effect the *Tribune* says, curtly, "Add perils of death." A few blocks to the north an arch of jewels is suspended above the Avenue "like a net of precious stones, between two white pillars surmounted by stars"; on this arch colored searchlights play at night with superb effect. The Avenue is hung with flags from end to end; and as the Twenty-seventh Division parades under the arches the air is white with confetti and ticker tape, and the sidewalks are jammed with cheering crowds. Nor is New York alone in its enthusiasm for the returning soldiers; every other city has its victory parade, with the city elders on the reviewing stand and flags waving and the bayonets of the troops glistening in the spring sunlight and the bands playing "The Long, Long Trail." Not yet disillusioned, the nation welcomes its heroes—and the heroes only wish the fuss were all over and they could get into civilian clothes and sleep late in the mornings and do what they please, and try to forget.

Mr. and Mrs. Smith have been invited to a tea dance at one of the local hotels, and Mr. Smith hurries from his office to the scene of revelry. If the hotel is up to the latest wrinkles, it has a jazz-band instead of the traditional orchestra for dancing, but not yet does a saxophone player stand out in the foreground and contort from his instrument that piercing music, "endlessly sorrowful yet endlessly unsentimental, with no past, no memory, no future, no hope," which William Bolitho called the *Zeitgeist* of the Post-war Age. The jazz-band plays "I'm Always Chasing Rainbows," the tune which Harry Carroll wrote in wartime after Harrison Fisher persuaded him that Chopin's "Fantasie Impromptu" had the makings of a good ragtime tune. It plays, too, "Smiles" and "Dardanella" and "Hindustan" and "Japanese Sandman" and "I Love You Sunday," and that other song which is to give the Post-war Decade one of its most persistent and wearisome slang phases, "I'll Say She Does." There are a good many military uniforms among the fox-trotting dancers. There is one French officer in blue; the days are not past when a foreign uniform adds the zest of war-time romance to any party. In the more dimly lighted palm-room there may be a juvenile petting party or two going on, but of this Mr. and Mrs. Smith are doubtless oblivious. F. Scott Fitzgerald has yet to confront a horrified republic with the Problem of the Younger Generation.

After a few dances, Mr. Smith wanders out to the bar (if this is not a dry state). He finds there a group of men downing Bronxes and Scotch highballs, and discussing with dismay the approach of prohibition. On the 1st of July the so-called Wartime Prohibition Law is to take effect (designed as a war measure, but not signed by the President until after the

Armistice), and already the ratification of the Eighteenth Amendment has made it certain that prohibition is to be permanent. Even now, distilling and brewing are forbidden. liquor is therefore expensive, as the frequenters of midnight cabarets are learning to their cost. Yet here is the bar, still quite legally doing business. Of course there is not a woman within eyeshot of it; drinking by women is unusual in 1919, and drinking at a bar is an exclusively masculine prerogative. Although Mr. and Mrs. Smith's hosts may perhaps serve cocktails before dinner this evening, Mr. and Mrs. Smith have never heard of cocktail parties as a substitute for tea parties.

As Mr. Smith stands with his foot on the brass rail, he listens to the comments on the coming of prohibition. There is some indignant talk about it, but even here the indignation is by no means unanimous. One man, as he tosses off his Bronx, says that he'll miss his liquor for a time, he supposes, but he thinks "his boys will be better off for living in a world where there is no alcohol"; and two or three others agree with him. Prohibition has an overwhelming majority behind it throughout the United States; the Spartan fervor of wartime has not yet cooled. Nor is there anything ironical in the expressed assumption of these men that when the Eighteenth Amendment goes into effect, alcohol will be banished from the land. They look forward vaguely to an endless era of actual drought.

At the dinner party to which Mr. and Mrs. Smith go that evening, some of the younger women may be bold enough to smoke, but they probably puff their cigarettes self-consciously, even defiantly. (The national consumption of cigarettes in 1919, excluding the very large sizes, is less than half of what it will be by 1930.)

After dinner the company may possibly go to the movies to see Charlie Chaplin in "Shoulder Arms" or Douglas Fairbanks in "The Knickerbocker Buckaroo" or Mary Pickford in "Daddy Long Legs," or Theda Bara, or Pearl White, or Griffith's much touted and much wept-at "Broken Blossoms." Or they may play auction bridge (not contract, of course). Mah Jong, which a few years hence will be almost obligatory, is still over the horizon. They may discuss such best sellers of the day as *The Four Horsemen of the Apocalypse,* Tarkington's *The Magnificent Ambersons,* Conrad's *Arrow of Gold,* Brand Whitlock's *Belgium,* and Wells's *The Undying Fire.* (The *Outline of History* is still unwritten.) They may go to the theater: the New York successes of May, 1919, include "Friendly Enemies," "Three Faces East," and "The Better 'Ole," which have been running ever since war-time and are still going strong, and also "Listen, Lester," Gillette in "Dear Brutus," Frances Starr in "Tiger! Tiger!" and—to satisfy a growing taste for bedroom farce—such tidbits as "Up in Mabel's Room." The Theater Guild is about to launch its first drama, Ervine's "John Ferguson." The members of the senior class at Princeton have just voted "Lightnin'" their favorite play (after "Macbeth" and "Hamlet," for which they cast the votes expected of educated men), and their favorite actresses, in order of preference, are Norma Talmadge, Elsie Ferguson, Marguerite Clark, Constance Talmadge, and Madge Kennedy.

One thing the Smiths certainly will not do this evening. They will not listen to the radio.

For there is no such thing as radio broadcasting. Here and there a mechanically inclined boy has a wireless set, with which, if he knows the Morse code, he may listen to messages from ships at sea and from land stations equipped with sending apparatus. The radiophone has been so far developed that men flying in an airplane over Manhattan have talked with other men in an office-building below. But the broadcasting of speeches and music—well, it was tried years ago by DeForest, and "nothing came of it." Not until the spring of 1920 will Frank Conrad of the Westinghouse Company of East Pittsburgh, who has been sending out phonograph music and baseball scores from the barn which he has rigged up as a spare-time research station, find that so many amateur wireless operators arc listening to them that a Pittsburgh newspaper has had the bright idea of advertising radio equipment "which may be used by those who listen to Dr. Conrad's programs." And not until this advertisement appears will the Westinghouse officials decide to open the first broadcasting station in history in order to stimulate the sale of their supplies.

One more word about Mr. and Mrs. Smith and we may dismiss them for the night. Not only have they never heard of radio broadcasting; they have never heard of Coué, the Dayton Trial, cross-word puzzles, bathing-beauty contests, John J. Raskob, racketeers, Teapot Dome, Coral Gables, the *American Mercury*, Sacco and Vanzetti, companionate marriage, brokers' loan statistics, Michael Arlen, the Wall Street explosion, confession magazines, the Hall-Mills case, radio stock, speakeasies, Al Capone, automatic traffic lights, or Charles A. Lindbergh.

The Post-war Decade lies before them.

8.2
The Modern Temper

Lynn Dumenil

Cultural historian Lynn Dumenil provides another view of the culture of the 1920s, arguing here that the Twenties saw the birth of "modern" American society. What does Dumenil mean by "modern," and how does her perspective compare to Frederick Lewis Allen's (Document 8.1)? Are they more alike or different? Does the fact that Dumenil writes about the decade sixty-five years after it ended, and Allen only one year, matter in their depictions of that period?

"The world broke in two in 1922 or thereabouts," announced novelist Willa Cather. Journalist Mark Sullivan picked 1914, the beginning of World War I, as the point "of fundamental alteration, from which we would never go back." That these astute observers were joined by many others in offering different dates to mark the watershed of the twentieth century should call into question the historian's penchant for precise periodization. U.S. history covering the last hundred years has tended to fall into neat divisions by decade, a fate especially true of the 1920s. World War I's end in 1918 seemed a natural break, signifying the close of one era and the beginning of a new one that in turn was closed by the stock market crash in 1929. The war's timing encouraged contemporaries and historians to see a sharp break between prewar and postwar America. Moreover, it contributed to a sense that the war had been causal in transforming American cultural and intellectual life by bringing about the alienated, lost generation of intellectuals, creating the new woman, and pushing Americans into hedonism. Recent scholarship has challenged this vision; social historians in particular have made it increasingly clear that many of the changes so evident in the 1920s predated the war. The thrust of social history has been to challenge conventional periodization and to emphasize as well the unevenness of social change and the continuities that characterized the private worlds of individuals.

Why have historians persisted in viewing the period as so distinctive? Is it perhaps that historians cannot escape the fascination for the decade's drama any more than their students can lose their romantic vision of the twenties filtered through the lens of *The Great Gatsby?* In part. It is also because the richness of the newer research—on women, ethnicity, and leisure, for example—makes an attempt at a new synthesis almost irresistible. And it is because an analysis of the decade's events and concerns reveals so clearly the transformation of American culture as it emerged as a "modern" society.

In characterizing the 1920s as modern, I recognize that the essential transformations began in the late nineteenth century, with the triad of rapid industrialization, sprawling urbanization, and massive immigration. Industrial development changed the nature of work and daily life and gave rise to an extensive network of corporations that integrated the country into a national economy. The result, as Robert Wiebe has suggested in *The Search for Order, 1877–1920,* was to erode the isolation of "island communities"—the towns of antebellum America that while part of a market economy had nonetheless maintained a degree of local autonomy and order based on "modesty in women, rectitude in men, and thrift, sobriety, and hard work in both." But the spread of railroads and national corporations after the Civil War transformed American communities. The multiplication of national bureaucratic structures—of voluntary associations, professional organizations, and corporations—led to an organized society in which both individuals and communities found themselves powerfully affected by forces outside their control and increasingly removed from the locus of economic and political power.

The growth of cities added to the complexity of life, as urban dwellers experienced impersonal relationships that replaced the intimate nature of smaller communities. Skyscrapers, elevators, streetcars, and the noise of the metropolis also contributed to a more mechanized, regimented life. And despite the nationalizing trends in the economy that had a certain homogenizing effect, the cities also became bastions of cultural pluralism. A highly visible working class increasingly subjected to the power of corporate employers made urban areas the site of notable episodes of class conflict, such as the Chicago Haymarket Riot of 1886. These tensions invaded the arena of culture as well when working-class saloons, dance halls, and other leisure-time venues became the focus of middle- and upper-class elites' fears about declining morality and disintegrating social order.

These fears were closely associated with the pervasive presence of immigrants in the city. By 1900, "new" immigrants from Southern and Eastern Europe were the target of intense nativism, and in the early twentieth century, two other groups joined the streams of people migrating to American cities. Mexican immigration into the Southwest and Midwest dramatically increased in the teens, and African American migration from the South to the cities of the North accelerated with the beginning of World War I, adding still further diversity to the urban matrix.

The late nineteenth century witnessed other significant transformations. The massacre at Wounded Knee in 1890 signaled the final military conquest of Native Americans. With the displacement of indigenous people and the extension of the railroad, settlement and corporations moved west, leading historian Frederick Jackson Turner to reflect in 1893 on the meaning of the closing of the frontier. At the same time, the trajectory of conquest moved beyond the continent. Through diplomatic negotiations and the Spanish-American War, the United States had acquired an empire and become an international power, a position confirmed by its role in World War I.

Other changes stemmed from the challenges to traditional religious faith embodied in Darwinian science and the new biblical criticism that resulted in denominational upheavals for the churches and spiritual crises for individuals. Assaults on an older order emerged on the gender front as well, as working-class women increasingly entered paid employment and middle-class women began a campaign for women's rights that coalesced in the suffrage amendment of 1919. Both were harbingers of major changes in women's role and the family itself.

Many Americans were of two minds about these transformations. On the one hand, they were fearful about urban poverty, decay, and disorder. The decline in individual and community autonomy and the hardening of class lines prompted anxieties about social mobility and democratic politics. Pluralism threatened the nineteenth-century Victorian worldview that valued hierarchy, order, and a single standard of culture, morality, and values. On the other hand, many people were excited about progress. Breakthroughs in technology, the increase in material wealth, and the beginning of an empire seemingly heralded the upward march of civilization, with America in the forefront. Thus despite prevailing fears about challenges to their ordered world, for the most part Victorians remained optimistic.

In the 1920s, the same broad forces that had so powerfully transformed the nineteenth century continued the process of making America
more "modern"—more organized, more bureaucratic, more complex.
These continuities will be made evident as most chapters reach back a few
years, sometimes a few decades, to set the stage and demonstrate that history resists clear-cut periodization. But despite strong links with the past,
we can identify distinctive qualities as well. For example, the sense of unprecedented prosperity—made all the more striking by its dramatic collapse in the stock market crash of 1929—helped to give the decade its
singular tone. By 1922 the country had recovered from a debilitating
postwar depression and entered a period of stunning industrial productivity, neatly symbolized by auto manufacturer Henry Ford, whose use
of mechanization and innovative management helped him to churn out
affordable cars at such a spectacular rate that his success earned the label
"The Ford Miracle." This productivity, coupled with war-inflicted devas-
tation of European economies, made the United States the dominant
world economic power. At home, most Americans enjoyed a higher standard of living. Not everyone shared in the fabled prosperity, however.
Many sectors of the economy, especially farming, never truly recovered
from the postwar depression, and African Americans and other minorities continued to live in poverty. In general, the aura of wealth obscured
a highly skewed distribution of income that placed the bulk of the country's assets in the hands of a few. Nonetheless, the 1920s were marked by
a sense of prosperity and a get-rich-quick mentality, evident not only in
the stock market but also in giddy land booms in Florida and Los Angeles that reflected prosperous Americans' sense of a new era of unlimited
material progress.

The faith in prosperity powerfully shaped the politics of the decade.
The Progressive reform era (1900–14) that had preceded World War I gave
way in the 1920s to a period of conservatism in which politicians and pun-
dits alike celebrated Big Business as the savior of American democracy
and enterprise. The period's Presidents—Warren Harding (1921–23), who
died in office, Calvin Coolidge (1923–29), and Herbert Hoover (1929–33)—
were Republicans who successfully identified their party with the promise
of peace and prosperity. Differing dramatically in temperament and skill,
they shared a commitment to promoting strong business/government co-
operation that led to almost unbridled corporate power. Their approach
to what they called the "New Era" underwrote a sense of complacency
and preoccupation with material progress that is one facet of the characteristic tone of the 1920s.

But another key image, and perhaps the most enduring, is that of the roaring twenties—of a fast life, propelled by riches and rapidly changing social values. Dubious get-rich-quick schemes and fads like flagpole sitting contributed to a tone of feverish frivolity. Flappers dancing the Charleston and participating in a sexual revolution, movie stars in already decadent Los Angeles setting the pace for the rest of the country, and speakeasies trafficking in illegal liquor, all suggested a world far removed from Victorian restraint.

One group that contributed to this stereotype was the Lost Generation, a term used to describe the young artists and writers of the decade whose works embodied so much of the spirit of the times. Poets like Edna St. Vincent Millay celebrated the new—and sexually liberated—woman. Novelists like F. Scott Fitzgerald and Ernest Hemingway depicted a generation's cynicism and disillusionment which seemed to explain the escapism that fueled the excesses of the jazz age. Somewhat older writers like Sinclair Lewis also figured importantly in creating the literary portrait of the twenties. Lewis's *Babbitt* serves as such an enduring critique of middle-class life that "Babbitt" entered dictionaries as a term connoting a businessman caught up in almost ritualistic consumerism and conformity. These writers made a lasting mark, shaping a scenario of the twenties for generations to come. While there is some truth to these images—especially among the urban, white, prosperous middle and upper classes—they overshadow the average Americans who led far more quiet lives and ignore those excluded from the prosperity of the times.

This depiction of the roaring twenties also obscures the complexities lying beneath the surface, especially the considerable social tensions that permeated the culture. After a major period of industrial unrest in 1919–20, in which corporations ruthlessly repressed strikes, labor was for the most part quiescent in the twenties and subject to increased regimentation. But if class conflict for the most part was muted, ethnic and racial tensions came roiling to the surface. Race riots in Chicago and other cities in 1919 signified new dynamics in urban areas that had experienced significant African American migration during the war years. Migration to the North as well as wartime military service helped to create a militant spirit among African Americans. Both the artistic movement termed the Harlem Renaissance and the black nationalism of Marcus Garvey and his Universal Negro Improvement Association symbolized what was popularly called the New Negro. Empowering for African Americans, the new spirit was unsettling to whites who wished to maintain a repressive racial order.

White Anglo-Saxon Protestants also continued to resent the rising influence of immigrants, Catholics, and Jews, and the 1920s were a particularly virulent period of nativism. The decade had been ushered in by the 1919–20 Red Scare, a product of Americans' fears that the 1919 Bolshevik Revolution in Russia might spread to the United States. That fear, coupled with the postwar wave of strikes, unspent wartime nationalism, and longstanding hostility to immigrants, led to a widespread hysteria about radicals and dissenters, with much of the focus on aliens. After a witch hunt marked by massive violations of civil liberties, the extremes of the Red Scare died down, but the animus toward immigrants did not, and Congress passed a series of laws that severely restricted European and Asian immigration. A new Ku Klux Klan modeled after the southern Reconstruction Klan contributed to the nativist furor. Targeting African Americans, immigrants, Catholics, and Jews, it spread its racist and xenophobic ideology and became a potent force in local and national politics until its demise in the mid-twenties.

Nativism also figured in another distinctive facet of the 1920s: prohibition. The Eighteenth Amendment outlawing the sale of intoxicating beverages had passed in 1919, but it continued to be a highly contested issue until its repeal in 1933. Supporters viewed prohibition not only as a means of promoting morality and sobriety but as a symbol of the dominance of white Anglo-Saxon Protestant cultural values. Critics assailed it for violating personal liberties while ethnic groups resented its cultural imperialism. Prohibition persisted as a disruptive issue in politics, most notably in the 1928 presidential contest between Hoover and Al Smith, where Smith's immigrant background, Catholicism, and opposition to prohibition figured prominently in the campaign.

Specific events, people, and social movements helped to define the 1920s, but the decade was also distinguished by Americans' growing consciousness of change, a perception that a yawning gulf separated them from the world of only a decade before. World War I set the stage for this shift in tone. Older interpretations of the impact of war centered on the way it crushed the progressive reform movement that had sought to ameliorate problems of industrial, urban society. The war allegedly left in its wake disillusionment and reaction, as indicated by the Red Scare's repression of aliens and radicals. Disillusionment with war and a concomitant search for escape in amusements also suggested an explanation for the nation's retreat from world politics and the Senate's failure to ratify the Covenant of the League of Nations, Woodrow Wilson's cherished plan for an international organization to prevent future wars. In this view, Americans in the

1920s appear to be reactionary, hedonistic, and self-centered, and the stock market crash brings to an end a morality play, with the Great Depression the nation's punishment for its sins of excess and selfishness.

Revisionist historians have long since corrected this image of the jazz age (although it seems quite resilient in popular culture and memory and thus worth addressing here). The 1920s were not a period of unrelieved hedonism, nor did reform completely disappear. Partisan politics, Wilson's intransigence, and the public's ambivalence about internationalism had as much to do with killing the League as did disillusionment. Nor does World War I account for the tremendous social forces transforming American life—industrialization, immigration, urbanization, and changing patterns in work, politics, religion, leisure, and the family were in place well before 1914–18.

Yet, if the impact of the war has been misstated, it was nonetheless a major watershed that is central to understanding the decade. It contributed to the economic boom that made the prosperity of the twenties possible, and also promoted significant population movement—especially the rural-to-urban migration of African Americans, Mexicans, and native whites—thus underscoring the ethnic and racial heterogeneity of the society. Many contemporaries were also convinced that the war, by giving women opportunities in formerly male jobs, had created the liberated woman. Other popular views held that war undermined religious faith and set in motion the secular trends that many observers noted in the 1920s. Although both of these perceptions greatly overstated the impact of the war, nonetheless they point to the way in which the public viewed the war as undermining traditional values, religious faith, and sexual mores.

Indeed, "since the war" emerged as a persistent refrain that people invoked to describe a wide range of changes in dally life and cultural values. Everything from rising divorce rates, "flaming youth," African American militancy, increased standardization and regimentation, and the vogue for fads like crossword puzzles was chalked up to the war. Most commonly, Americans used it to try to pin down a troubling change in mood. From the pages of *Presbyterian Magazine* came the announcement: "The world has been convulsed ... and every field of thought and action has been disturbed. ... The most settled principles and laws of society ... have been attacked." In the popular journal *World's Work*, one author announced that "the World War has accentuated all our differences. It has not created those differences, but it has revealed and emphasized them." The war, in short, became a key metaphor for major changes transforming modern civilization: a marker that helped to explain and thus make more manageable the emergence of a modern society.

A watershed of a different kind was reflected in the U.S. Census Bureau's findings that marked 1920 as the turning point of the country's urbanization: fully one-half of America's 105 million people now lived in cities. To some extent, this was a dubious statistic, since the Census Bureau used a population of 2,500 people as the cutoff for "urban," not a very meaningful measure of urbanization. But the census data formed part of the contemporary assessment of the growth and influence of cities. Observers in the 1920s had a sense—at times oversimplified—that they were witnessing an urban/rural conflict, a battle between the forces of change and the forces of reaction. Prohibition, the Ku Klux Klan, and immigration restriction were just the most well-known manifestations of this tension, and signified native white Protestants' anxious concern that the cities and the culture itself risked being dominated by immigrants and African Americans. For their part, more than ever before, African Americans and other minorities were challenging the status quo, and were demanding a pluralistic vision of American identity that would accord them cultural influence and political power.

In addition to pluralism, the cities also embodied the power of large corporations, their economic influence, and the continued transformation of work. The metropolis was also the home of mass culture—of popular magazines, newspaper syndications, advertising, and the movies. Leisure and consumption provided some of the most visible, modern changes of the 1920s. An urban, cosmopolitan culture, shaped by its pluralism and the agencies of mass culture, spread to the hinterlands and helped to promote new social values. Technology and mass production resulted in a flood of consumer products. Automobiles, electric irons, refrigerators, and radios, a fraction of the goods available to increasingly more Americans, helped to transform daily life dramatically.

The new values and new products signaled the clear emergence of a consumer culture characterized by an emphasis on leisure, purchasing, sociability, expressiveness, and personal pleasure. Changing sexual morality, modified ideas about success and how to achieve it, and mounting secularism merged with the values of consumerism to form a major challenge to the Victorian ethos of restraint, frugality, and order. All of these changes were contested, as some Americans embraced the freedom implied in the new social order while others bemoaned the corruption of the old culture. And for many, both sentiments played a part. As Lawrence W. Levine has suggested, Americans in the twenties harbored feelings of both "progress and nostalgia."

8.3
The Sexual Revolution of the 1920s

John D'Emilio and Estelle Friedman

*One of the significant changes in American culture during the 1920s
was the spread of a much more liberal attitude toward sexuality and
sexual behavior. Historians D'Emilio and Friedman identify several
factors that help explain that change. What were those factors? Were
some Americans more affected by this cultural shift than others? Why?*

In the winter of 1924, the sociologists Robert and Helen Lynd arrived in
Muncie, Indiana, to embark upon an intensive investigation of life in a
small American city. The study that resulted, *Middletown*, became an American classic. Casting their net widely, the Lynds examined work, home,
youth, leisure, religious beliefs, and civic institutions in an effort to draw
a complex picture of life in the modern age. In the process, *Middletown* had
much to say about the social context that was shaping sexuality in the
1920s and that would continue to affect American mores.

In order to emphasize the rapidly changing nature of social life in an
industrial era, the Lynds offered 1890 as a counterpoint to the 1920s. Reflecting the small-town values that still survived at the turn of the century
in parts of the country, males and females moved in different spheres;
daughters remained at home with their mothers, and adolescent boys entered the public world of work which their fathers inhabited. Young men
and women rarely mingled without the careful chaperonage of adults. Socializing continued to take place in public settings that brought families
and community residents together. Once a couple had embarked upon a
serious courtship, they gained the permission to be alone together, but
most often in the family parlor or on the front porch, not far from parental

From *Intimate Matters: A History of Sexuality in America*, pp. 239–242 and 256–265
by D'Emilio and Freedman. Reprinted by permission of The University of
Chicago Press.

supervision. A heavy taboo hung over sexual relations outside of marriage. Sex was an intensely private matter that came into public view only occasionally, when Muncie's small red-light district overstepped its boundaries, angering the citizenry.

Even as the Lynds described it, contemporary readers would have recognized this as the portrait of a world irrevocably lost. Indeed, the youth of Muncie, for whom change had been most dramatic, would not even have remembered what that earlier world was like. Instead, by the 1920s, adolescents moved in a youth-centered world, based in the high schools that most now attended. School had become, according to the Lynds, "a place from which they go home to eat and sleep." Males and females met in classes, at after-school activities and evening socials. Cars provided privacy, and marked the end of the "gentleman caller" who sat in the parlor. A majority of the students went out with friends four or more evenings a week. Youth patronized movies together, drove to nearby towns for weekend dances, and parked in lovers' lanes on the way home. Almost half of Muncie's male high school students, and a third of its female students, had participated in the recent vogue of the "petting" party; girls who did not were decidedly less popular. After graduation, boys and girls alike left home to work. Increasing economic independence led to less parental supervision over premarital behavior, at the same time that work allowed the young to continue to meet away from home.

This new autonomy and mobility of youth came at a time when Muncie society, through many of the items and activities of a consumer economy, was focused more and more on sexuality. The newspaper advice columns of Dorothy Dix and other syndicated writers instructed female readers in how to catch a man, the thrill and magic of love, and the nature of modern marriage at the same time that relationships were being redefined in romantic, erotic terms. Popular songs of the decade, such as "It Had to Be You," taught that love was a mysterious experience that occurred in a flash when the "chemistry" was right. Sex adventure magazines had become big sellers with stories titled "The Primitive Lover" ("She wanted a caveman husband") and "Indolent Kisses." Muncie's nine movie theaters, open daily and offering twenty-two programs a week, filled their houses by offering such fare as *Married Flirts, Rouged Lips,* and *Alimony.* One popular film of the decade, *Flaming Youth,* attracted audiences by promising images of "neckers, petters, white kisses, red kisses, pleasure-mad daughters, sensation-craving mothers."

The world that the Lynds described, of autonomous youth coming of age in a social environment where erotic images beckoned, has remained fixed in the popular view of the 1920s as a time of new sexual freedoms. Frederick Lewis Allen, in his best-selling account of the decade, *Only Yesterday*, looked at the cultural landscape and detected a "revolution in manners and morals." Images from the 1920s abound to sustain his assessment—flappers and jazz babies; rumble seats and raccoon coats; F. Scott Fitzgerald novels and speakeasies; petting parties and Hollywood sex symbols. And, in fact, despite the evidence of change in sexual mores in the years before World War I, the 1920s do stand out as a time when something in the sexual landscape decisively altered and new patterns clearly emerged. The decade was recognizably modern in a way that previous ones were not. The values, attitudes, and activities of the pre-Depression years unmistakably point to the future rather than the past.

One reason, perhaps, why the twenties have loomed so large as a critical turning point is that patterns of behavior and sexual norms formerly associated with other groups in the population had, by then, spread to the white middle class. The more lavish cabaret appropriated the music and dancing of black and white working-class youth. Movie palaces replaced storefront theaters, and Hollywood directors churned out feature-length films that attracted youths and adults of every class. Bohemian radicals relinquished their proprietorship over the work of modern sexual theorists such as Ellis and Freud, whose ideas received wide currency. Purity crusaders lost the momentum of the prewar years and found themselves rapidly left behind by a culture that scoffed at the sexual prudery of its ancestors. Although each of these developments had roots in the prewar era, not until the 1920s did they experience a full flowering.

The sexual issues that preoccupied the 1920s—the freedom of middle-class youth, the continuing agitation over birth control, debates about the future of marriage, the commercial manipulation of the erotic—suggest the direction in which American values were heading. Sexual expression was moving beyond the confines of marriage, not as the deviant behavior of prostitutes and their customers, but as the normative behavior of many Americans. The heterosocial world in which youth matured encouraged the trend, and the growing availability of contraceptives removed some of the danger attached to nonmarital heterosexuality. New ideas about the essential healthfulness of sexual expression reshaped marriage, too, as couples approached conjugal life with the expectation that erotic enjoyment, and not simply spiritual union, was an integral part of a successful marital relationship. To be sure, resistance to these modern norms surfaced. Some supporters of a new "companionate" marriage advocated it as a way of containing the excesses of youthful libido, while the new visibility of the erotic in popular culture antagonized some and spawned opposition. But, in general, American society was moving by the 1920s toward a view of erotic expression that can be defined as sexual liberalism—an overlapping set of beliefs that detached sexual activity from the instrumental goal of procreation, affirmed heterosexual pleasure as a value in itself, defined sexual satisfaction as a critical component of personal happiness and successful marriage, and weakened the connections between sexual expression and marriage by providing youth with room for some experimentation as preparation for adult status.

At times during the succeeding generation, the crises that punctuated mid-twentieth-century American life seemed to obscure this trend. Under the pressure of the Depression of the 1930s, for instance, the consumerism and commercialized amusements that gave play to sexual adventure temporarily withered. Sobriety and gloom replaced the buoyant exuberance of the previous decade. Dating became a simpler affair, while the anxieties of unemployment and hard times created sexual tensions in many marriages. Birth control became less an issue of freedom for women, and more a method of regulating the poor. After World War II, the impulse to conform and settle down after years of depression, war, and cold war encouraged a rush to early marriage and saw the birth rate zoom upward. Sexual experimentation appeared lost in a maze on suburban housing developments as a new generation took on family responsibilities and raised more children than their parents had. The erotic seemed to disappear under a wave of innocent domesticity, captured in television shows like *Father Knows Best* or the Hollywood comedies of Rock Hudson and Doris Day. A resurgent purity, impulse attacked symbols of sexual permissiveness such as pornography and imposed penalties on those who deviated too sharply from family values.

Despite these appearances, however, the forces that fed sexual liberalism developed apace. The availability and accessibility of reliable contraceptives highlighted the divorce of sexual activity from the procreative consequences that inhibited erotic enthusiasm. Sexual imagery gradually became an integral feature of the public realm, legitimate and aboveground. A youth culture that encouraged heterosexual expressiveness became ubiquitous. Couples looked to marriage as a source of continuing erotic pleasures. By the mid-1960s, sexual liberalism had become the dominant ethic, as powerful in its way as was the civilized morality of the late nineteenth century....

Birth control offers perhaps the most dramatic example of the change that occurred in American sexual mores during the middle of the twentieth century. At the start of the 1920s, it still bore the mark of radicalism, and the birth control movement appeared to many as a threat to moral order. The federal Comstock law, with its prohibition on the importation, mailing, and interstate shipment of contraceptive information and devices, remained in effect, and almost half of the states, including most of the populous ones of the Northeast and Midwest, had their own anti-contraceptive statutes. To agitate for birth control placed one outside the law. By the late 1960s, however, virtually all legal impediments to access had collapsed, and the federal government was actively promoting it. Advances in technology and shifts in values made reliable contraceptives an integral feature of married life as well as widely available to the unmarried.

For most of the 1920s and 1930s Margaret Sanger remained the key figure in the birth control movement and the individual most responsible for the changes that occurred. Though her leadership and visibility provided continuity with the pre-World War I agitation, the politics of the movement was undergoing an important shift. Government repression of radicalism and the decline of organized feminism after suffrage altered the context in which the fight for birth control was occurring. Sanger adapted to the new circumstances by detaching the question of contraception from larger social issues and movements. Throughout the twenties and thirties, she campaigned solely to make contraception freely available to women.

Even with a narrowed focus, however, Sanger remained a militant fighter, willing to use any means necessary to achieve her goals. She continued to risk arrest, believing as she did that "agitation through violation of the law was the key to the public." She also propagandized widely, through the pages of her journal (the *Birth Control Review*), through the books that she authored, and through her extensive speaking tours and public conferences. With the backing of her organization, the American Birth Control League, Sanger lobbied for legislative change and embarked once again on a venture in clinical services when she established the Clinical Research Bureau in 1923.

Sanger's lobbying efforts and the clinic that she supported point to an important way in which her strategy was evolving. In New York State in the 1920s, she campaigned for a "doctors only" bill, designed to allow physicians to provide contraceptives, but restricting that right to licensed practitioners. The Clinical Research Bureau, though it provided female clients with contraceptive devices, existed mainly to gather data that would persuade a science-conscious profession that safe, reliable methods of fertility control were available. Both initiatives aimed at enlisting the medical profession as allies in her cause, since its hostility to contraception constituted a major obstacle to success. In the process, however, the politics of birth control tilted in a more conservative direction. From a key issue in the struggle for female emancipation, contraception was gradually becoming a matter of professional health care....

As one might expect, the contraceptive revolution moved hand in hand with changes in both sexual behavior and attitudes. Historians of twentieth-century mores have tended to underplay this shift, by emphasizing instead the stability of one important index of sexual behavior, the female premarital coital rate. For women coming of age in the 1920s, the incidence of premarital intercourse jumped sharply, to roughly fifty percent of the cohort, and thereafter remained relatively constant until the late 1960s. Yet hidden behind the stability of these figures lay a whole world of sexual change. Activity that provoked guilt in the 1920s had become integrated by the 1960s into a new code of sexual ethics that made it morally acceptable. What was daring and nonconformist in the earlier period appeared commonplace a generation later. And, as attitudes and ideals altered, so too did aspects of sexual activity. Dating, necking, and petting among peers became part and parcel of the experience of American youth, providing an initiatory stage, uncommon for their elders, leading to the coital experience of adulthood and marriage. To marriage itself, couples brought new expectations of pleasure, satisfaction, and mutual enjoyment, encouraged by a more explicit advice literature that emphasized the sexual component of conjugal life. The integration of contraception into middle-class married life also meant that the reproductive requirement for marital intimacy had receded far into the background. Though experience might not always live up to these new standards, men and women in the mid-twentieth century were approaching marriage with heightened anticipation of physical pleasure.

Evidence abounds of shifts in both standards and patterns of behavior among American youth in the decades after World War I. During the 1920s, white college youth captured the lion's share of attention of contemporaries seeking to chart the society's changing values. Although less than thirteen percent of the eighteen- to twenty-one-year-old population were enrolled in colleges at the end of the 1920s, the numbers had more than tripled since 1890. For the first time, a distinctive subculture took shape among the middle-class young, with values and activities that set them apart from their parents' generation.

Sexual innovation played a key role in this new world of youth. Particularly in coeducational institutions, heterosocial mixing became the norm. Young men and women mixed casually in classes, extracurricular activities, and social spaces, with a great deal of freedom from adult supervision. Dating in pairs, unlike the informal group socializing of the nineteenth century, permitted sexual liberties that formerly were sanctioned only for couples who were courting. College youth flaunted their new freedoms. As one male editor of a campus paper provocatively expressed it, "there are only two kinds of co-eds, those who have been kissed, and those who are sorry they haven't been kissed." Magazines debated the implications of "petting parties," an increasingly common feature of college life. One study of college youth during the 1920s found that ninety-two percent of coeds had engaged in petting, and that those "rejecting all sex play feel that they are on the defensive."

What a relatively small percentage of middle-class youth were experiencing in college, much larger numbers tasted in high school. By the 1920s, high school had become a mass experience, with almost three-quarters of the young enrolled. Here, too, adolescent boys and girls encountered one another daily, with casual interaction throughout the day that often continued into evening social activities. One observer of youth mores estimated that a large majority of high school youth engaged in hugging and kissing and that a significant minority "do not restrict themselves to that, but go further, and indulge in other sex liberties which, by all the conventions, are outrageously improper." Automobiles allowed young people still living at home greater freedom of movement than ever before. Groups of teenagers might drive to the next town for a Saturday-night dance; on weeknights, too, it became easier to escape parental supervision. So quickly and widely did cars become an essential part of this heterosocial world of youth that one commentator labeled the auto "a house of prostitution on wheels." Assessing these changes, Ben Lindsey, a Colorado juvenile court judge who had dealt with the young for a generation, considered them to be reflective of a historic transformation in American life. "Not only is this revolt from the old standards of conduct taking place," he wrote, "but it is unlike any revolt that has ever taken place before. Youth has always been rebellious. ... But this is different. It has the whole weight and momentum of a new scientific and economic order behind it"

Although the innovations in sexual behavior among middle-class youth were real, they nonetheless operated within certain peer-defined limits. Young men took liberties with women of their own class that their parents would have considered improper, but the sexual freedom of the 1920s was hardly a promiscuous one. The kissing and petting that occurred among couples who dated casually did not often progress beyond that.

Surveys of sexual behavior among white middle-class women revealed that the generation coming of age in the 1920s had a significantly higher incidence of premarital intercourse than women born in the preceding decades. But the evidence also suggests that, for the most part, young women generally restricted coitus to a single partner, the man they expected to marry. "Going all the way" was permissible, but only in the context of love and commitment. For men, the changes in female sexual behavior had important implications. Beginning in the 1920s, the frequency of recourse to prostitution began to decline. As Lindsey noted, "with the breaking up of those districts, [boys] turned to girls of their own class, a thing they had seldom done in the past."

As young people adopted the novel practice of dating, they shaped, learned, and refashioned its rules. Newspaper advice columns in the years after World War I printed letters from confused youth who wondered whether a good-night kiss was an appropriate ending for an evening date, and who searched for words to define the feelings aroused by the dating relationship. By the 1930s, the elaboration of this teenage ritual had produced words other than "love" to describe the emotions, and had differentiated "courting" and "keeping company" from the more casual, and common, practices of "going out" an going steady." When the Lynds returned to Muncie in the 1930s, one young man reported to them that "the fellows regard necking as a taken-for-granted part of a date. We fellows used occasionally to get slapped for things, but the girls don't do that much any more. ... Our high school students of both sexes...know everything and do everything—openly." Although he likely exaggerated in his claims about "everything," numerous surveys of American youth confirm the widening boundaries of permissible sexual activity. The rapid acceptance of this peer-directed system of dating, as well as the quick demise of its predecessor, can be inferred from changes in that reliable arbiter of social behavior, Emily Post's *Etiquette*. A chapter which, in the 1923 edition, was titled "Chaperons and Other Conventions" became "The Vanishing Chaperon and Other New Conventions" four years later; the passing of another decade brought the wistful heading "The Vanished Chaperon and Other Lost Conventions." One study of high school students in St. Louis on the eve of World War 11 found dating to be ubiquitous, with most couples returning home after one in the morning. Freed from parental supervision for long hours, boys and girls alike exhibited "a fairly general acceptance of the naturalness" of kisses and light petting as part of a date. Indeed, St. Louis's high school students proved far more tolerant about sexual matters than about other kinds of behavior such as smoking and drinking.

The system of dating, at least as it evolved between the two world wars, did not extend to all youth. Its adoption depended upon surplus income for clothes and entertainment, access to automobiles outside major cities, school attendance to enforce peer-based norms, and sufficient population density to sustain a range of commercialized amusements. Its contours thus mark it as a ritual of white middle-class youth in the cities and suburbs.

Among poor blacks in the rural South, for instance, older patterns of sociability persisted as young people experienced both traditional freedoms and constraints. With few sanctions against premarital intercourse, "sex play," according to one observer, "becomes matter-of-fact behavior for youth." As one young girl explained it, "I ain't never thought of there being anything wrong about it." Denied access because of segregation, poverty, and rural isolation from most of the places where formal dating took place, young rural blacks met at church, harvest festivals, picnics, and while working in the fields, much as they had in the past. Yet, an awareness of the world beyond the small rural community also generated a "longing for pleasures like those of the city." One young man expressed his discontent by telling an interviewer, "there ain't no decent place to take a girl....If you ain't got a car, you just ain't nowhere." Meanwhile, black parents of moderate wealth and status, in an effort to differentiate themselves from the rural masses and to provide education and mobility for the next generation, socialized their children into strict moral codes. In his study of youth in the Black Belt before World War II, Charles Johnson found that among the elite, even young men accepted rigid standards of chastity. Parents kept close rein on their daughters, as the testimony of one North Carolina girl made clear: "Yes, I have a boy friend. He calls on me and takes me to socials. Sometimes mama lets me go to movies with him in the afternoon, but if he goes with me at night papa and mama go too."

For white youth as well, rural and small-town residence affected patterns of sexual interaction. In rural communities many young people lacked mobility. "I had no car," explained one youth who bemoaned his inability to date. "We lived 20 miles from town and to get to town I had to ride with my father or some other adult." Then, too, in smaller communities adults were able to watch the behavior of the young more closely. "I'll tell you, it's really tough getting it in a small town," one young man complained. "Everyone has their eyes on you and especially on the girl. You can hardly get away with anything." A young man who moved to the city when he was seventeen noted the difference it made. He had never felt much sexual desire during his years in the country, he commented, but city life with its abundant opportunities suddenly seemed to generate "much more interest in it."

Although urban working-class youth did not share in the sexual culture of the middle class, this by no means implied a sentence of chastity. In some cases it could translate into freedom from the constraints of peer-enforced norms. In cities and towns, white and black youth who dropped out of high school or who did not immediately marry after graduation found themselves earning wages, yet without the expense of maintaining a household. Removed from the web of daily gossip that shaped the behavior of high school and college students, they were more likely to move beyond petting in their sexual relationships. Dance halls, bowling alleys, skating rinks, and, after prohibition, bars provided settings for young men and women to meet; automobiles, bought with hard-earned wages, offered privacy. One high school dropout embarked upon her first sexual affair with a dance-hall partner. "I made up my mind at the dance Oscar could have it," she recalled. "Oh, it was wonderful. That night, I thought, 'I don't care if I have a baby.'" Several more relationships ensued before she married in her late teens. The thriving business in condoms that Malcolm X operated at a Boston dance hall suggests the ease with which sexual favors could be exchanged among working-class youth in the city. So, too, does evidence of prenuptial conceptions and illegitimacy among the poor and the working class. In one Illinois town, over half of the girls who did not graduate from high school gave birth within eight months of their wedding. And almost a quarter of the births in the lowest social class of whites occurred outside of marriage.

By accelerating the shift to city living, and by providing youth with more economic autonomy and freedom from adult supervision, World War II brought unprecedented opportunities for premarital experience. The war released millions of youth from the social environments that inhibited erotic expression, and threw them into circumstances that opened up new sexual possibilities. Millions of young men left home to join the military, while many young women migrated in search of employment. The demands of wartime drew teenagers into the paid labor force while weakening the influence that family and community held over their behavior.

Ample testimony from the war years confirms the sexual expressiveness of youth. For many young women, men in uniform held erotic appeal. "When I was 16," one college student recalled,

> I let a sailor pick me up and go all the way with me. I had intercourse with him partly because he had a strong personal appeal for me, but mainly because I had a feeling of high adventure and because I wanted to please a member of the armed forces.

Another, rebuffed by a sailor boyfriend who felt she was too young, went on to have affairs with fifteen others by war's end. Civilian men, too, partook of the sexual freedom of the war years. One teenager described his life then as "a real sex paradise. The plant and the town were just full of working girls who were on the make. Where I was, a male war worker became the center of loose morality. It was a sex paradise." A high school student lost his virginity with a woman of thirty whose husband was overseas. "We weren't in love," he recalled, "although we were very fond of each other. The times were conducive for this sort of thing. Otherwise, nothing would ever have happened between us."

The response of moral reformers points to the changes that had occurred since the previous generation. Whereas those of the First World War focused on the dangers of prostitution, by the 1940s it was the behavior of "amateur girls"—popularly known as khaki-wackies, victory girls, and good-time Charlottes—that concerned moralists. "The old time prostitute in a house or formal prostitute on the street is sinking into second place," wrote one venereal-disease expert. "The new type is the young girl in her late teens and early twenties, the young woman in every field of life who is determined to have one fling or better." Efforts to scare GIs into continence by emphasizing the danger of disease had little impact on men who, according to one officer, "think as little of a gonorrheal infection as they do of the ordinary common cold." Or, as another phrased it, "the sex act cannot be made unpopular." local law-enforcement officials worked overtime to contain the sexual behavior of young women, yet their efforts only seemed to confirm the perception that prostitution was not the issue. Arrests for selling sexual favors rose less than twenty percent during the war years, but charges of disorderly conduct increased almost two hundred percent, and those for other morals offenses, such as promiscuous behavior or patronizing bars too frequently, increased nearly as much....

8.4

Unreconciled Strivings

Baseball in Jim Crow America

Jules Tygiel

Historian Jules Tygiel here discusses the function of black baseball in the first half of the twentieth century. He argues that black baseball embodied a "dualism" in its role in society. What does Tygiel mean by "dualism," and how does he describe it in this essay? Does the document persuade you that a discussion of sports history can shed light on the larger historical questions we ask about a society?

Andrew "Rube" Foster epitomized African-American pride. A tall, imposing, right-handed pitcher, he had migrated from his native Texas to Chicago in 1902 to play for the Chicago Union Giants. When warned that he might face "the best clubs in the land, white clubs," he announced, "I fear nobody." Over the next decade he established himself as perhaps the outstanding pitcher in all of baseball. In 1911 he formed his own team, the Chicago American Giants, and won a reputation as a managerial genius equal to his friend, John McGraw. Nine years later Foster, seeking to "keep colored baseball from control of the whites" and "to do something concrete for the loyalty of the Race," created the Negro National League. Foster criticized white owners for not letting African Americans "count a ticket [or] learn anything about the business," and called for a league dominated by black men. "There can be no such thing as [a black baseball league] with four or five of the directors white any more than you can call a streetcar a steamship," he asserted. Foster urged black fans: "It is your

---

From *Past Time: Baseball as History* by Jules Tygiel, pages 116-143. Reprinted by permission of Oxford University Press, Inc.

league. Nurse it! Help it! Keep it!" yet Foster's intense racial pride notwithstanding, he also made his ultimate goal clear. "We have to be ready," he proclaimed, "when the time comes for integration."

Rube Foster—and indeed, the entire experience of blacks in baseball in early twentieth-century American—exemplifies elements of Booker T. Washington's call for the development of separate economic spheres so that his race might prepare itself for ultimate inclusion in American life. Yet black baseball also captured what Washington's rival, W.E.B. Du Bois, labeled the "twoness" of the African-American experience. "One ever feels his twoness—an American, a Negro," wrote Du Bois, "two souls, two thoughts, two unreconciled strivings; two warring ideals in one dark body, whose dogged strength alone keeps it from being torn asunder." The architects of black baseball embodied this dualism. They strove to create viable enterprises that served their communities and simultaneously might wins a measure of respectability in the broader society. These ventures would prepare them for the day on which, according to Du Bois's vision, it would be "possible for a man to be both a Negro and American, without being cursed and spit upon by his fellows, without having the doors of Opportunity closed roughly in his face."

The essence of black professional baseball is far more elusive than that of its white counterpart. The major leagues always constituted the epitome and cultural core of mainstream baseball, but the formal Negro Leagues represented no more than a segment of the black baseball experience. No leagues existed until 1920, and even during their halcyon days official contests never constituted more than perhaps a third of the games played. Some of the strongest black teams and best players performed outside the league structure. Top teams often boasted names like the Homestead Grays, Bachrach Giants, or the Hilldale Club, reflecting affiliations not to major cities but to people and small communities. The most popular attractions often involved exhibitions against white semiprofessional and professional teams. In all of these many guises and varieties, black baseball constituted a vital element of African-American culture, while also dramatizing the contradictions and challenges of survival in ta world dominated by whites.

Within the African-American community, the officials, players, and teams of black baseball symbolized pride and achievement while creating a sphere of style and excitement that overlapped with the worlds of black business, politics, religion, and entertainment. During the baseball season Negro League teams constituted a constant presence in the black community. Placards announcing the games appeared in the windows of local businesses, along with advertisements featuring player endorsements and commands to "get those pretty clothes" for the "opening day…Fashion Parade." In Kansas City fans could purchase tickets in a number of locales where African Americans congregated, including the Monarch Billiard Parlor, Stark's Newspaper Stand, the Panama Taxi Stand, and McCampbell's and Hueston's Drug Store. The Elbon and Lincoln movie theaters would show pictures of the players, advertisements for the games and newsreel footage of the lavish opening day ceremonies.

Local businesses rallied around the teams. Some, like Herman Stark's clothing store in Detroit, offered prizes to the first player to hit a home run or get a hit in a Sunday or opening day contest. Several cities featured booster clubs, like the Hilldale Royal Rooters and Baltimore's Frontiers Club, that supported their teams. The Kansas City Booster Club, the most lavish of these organizations, included both black and white merchants whose stores served the black community. Formed in 1926, the Kansas City Boosters organized the opening day parade, sponsored banquets for the players, and stage beauty contests at the ball game. These businesses profited, in turn, from black baseball. "The cafes, beer joints, and rooming houses of the Negro neighborhoods all benefitted as black baseball monies sometimes trickled, sometimes rippled through the black community," writes Donn Rogosin. After the 1944 East-West all-star game in Chicago, reported Wendell Smith, "Hot spots were all loaded, and so were most of the patrons."

African-American baseball also provided one of the most popular features of black newspapers. As early as the turn of the century the *Indianapolis Freeman* had discovered that baseball coverage attracted readers. Sportswriter David Wyatt, who had played for the Cuban Giants and Chicago Union Giants from 1896 to 1902, reported on news of black baseball from all over the country. The Indianapolis ABCs and other teams would arrange matches by placing ads in the *Freeman*. Other black weeklies began covering the game more seriously after 1910. The *Philadelphia Tribune* forged a close alliance with Ed Bolden's Hilldale Club. Bolden advertised games in the *Tribune* and provided press releases and game results. Beginning in 1914 the *Tribune* began to print box scores and in 1915 published Bolden's weekly column, "Hilldale Pickups." Black newspapermen, led by Wyatt, played key roles in the creation and promotion of the Negro National League in 1920. "Behind this opening should be the concentrated support of every race man in Detroit," asserted the *Detroit Contender*. "If the league succeeds your race succeeds; if the league fails, the race fails. …Our ability to put over large projects will be measured largely by the way w handle this one."

Nonetheless, reporting in the African-American journals was frequently sketchy. Black newspapers could not afford to send writers to accompany clubs on the road and depended heavily on reports submitted by the teams. This source proved highly unreliable, as the traveling squads often failed to call in or refused to reveal losses. In addition, since many of the black weeklies appeared on Saturday, they tended to focus on previous of the following day's contests, rather than results of the previous week, making it difficult for fans to follow a team with any consistency. Nonetheless, by the 1920s and 1930s all the major black weeklies had substantial sports sections with regular coverage and standout columnists like Frank A. (Fay) Young of the *Chicago Defender,* Wendell Smith of the *Pittsburgh Courier,* and Sam Lacy of the *Baltimore Afro-American.* The black press played a critical role in promoting the East-West all-star game, the showcase event of Negro League baseball. The newspapers printed ballots and lists of eligible players and by 1939 top performers received as many as 500,000 votes. "The success of the game was made by Negro newspapers," commented Fay Young. "It was the Negro press that carried the percentages, the feats of the various stars all through the year, and it was the readers of the Negro newspapers who had knowledge of what they were going to see."

Owners and officials of black clubs often ranked among the most prominent figures in the African-American community. Club officials participated actively in local business, fraternal, and civil rights organizations. Ed Bolden, owner of the Philadelphia-based Hilldale Club in the 1920s, belonged to local black fraternal groups and the Citizen's Republican Club. Kansas City Monarchs' secretary Quincy J. Gilmore was the guiding force behind the local Elks Club and the Negro Twilight League that brought together industrial, youth, and semiprofessional teams in the Kansas City area. Homestead Grays owner Cum Posey served on the Homestead school board. Bolden, Posey, Rube Foster, and others wrote regular columns for local black newspapers.

Several team owners figured prominently in civil rights activities. Olivia Taylor, who inherited the Indianapolis ABCs from her husband, became president of the Indianapolis NAACP chapter in 1925. Newark Eagle owner Effa Manley was an indefatigable campaigner again discrimination. In the years before she and her husband Abe purchased the ball club, Manley had achieved prominence in New York City as the secretary of the Citizen's League for Fair Play, which waged successful campaigns against Harlem businesses that refused to employ African Americans. In Newark

Manley served as the treasurer of the New Jersey chapter of the NAACP and on several occasions held ballpark benefits for the organization. At one event the Eagles sold NAACP "Stop Lynching" buttons to fans. Manley also joined the "Citizen's Committee to End Jim Crow in Baseball Committee" created by the Congress of Industrial Organizations in 1942.

Black teams hosted numerous benefit games for African-American charities and causes, raising funds for churches, hospitals, youth groups, and civil rights bodies. The Kansas City Monarchs staged benefits for the Negro national Business League and the Red Cross. The Newark Eagles regularly raised money to purchase medical equipment for the Booker T. Washington Community Hospital. During World War I the Indianapolis ABCs and Chicago American Giants played games on behalf of the Red Cross, and in the 1920s Hillsdale played fund-raisers for war veterans. The first black baseball game at Yankee Stadium pitted the Lincoln Giants and Baltimore Black Sox in a 1930 benefit for the Brotherhood of Sleeping Car Porters. The outbreak of World War II prompted additional efforts.

The players themselves often had close ties to the cities in which they performed. Many teams recruited from the local sandlots and discovered some of their best players literally perched on their doorsteps. Hall of Fame outfielder Oscar Charleston, who grew upon Indianapolis's East Side, served as batboy for the ABCs before joining the squad as a player. He performed alongside Frank Warfield, "the pride of Indianapolis's West Side." The Homestead Grays discovered Josh Gibson playing semiprofessional baseball in Pittsburgh's Hill district. Memphis Blues pitching ace Verdell Mathis grew up within a short walk of Martin Field. Effa Manley's Eagles frequently found their best players—including Monte Irvin, Larry Doby, and Don Newcombe—in the Newark area. The Birmingham Black Barons snatched the fifteen-year-old Willie Mays from a local high school.

The players often made the Negro League cities their year-round homes and became fixtures in their communities. In Detroit in the 1920s players found winter jobs in the local automobile plants. Turkey Stearnes and other Detroit Stars worked in factories owned by Detroit Tigers co-owner Walter O. Briggs, glad to hire them in his legendarily grimy and unsafe paint shops, but not on his baseball team. In Pittsburgh many of the Crawfords found work as lookouts for owner Gus Greenlee's gambling operations. Some athletes stayed on in the citys where they had won their fame, opening up bars or other small businesses. John Henry "Pop" Lloyd, who had played for, among other teams, the Bachrach Giants of Atlantic City, settled there on retirement and reigned as "a sort of foster father" to the city's children. Lloyd became the commissioner of the local little league and had a neighborhood ball field named in his honor.

Those who did not have homes in the city often resided during the season at the finest black hotels. In an age when most mainstream hotels even in northern cities barred African Americans, each major city featured a showplace hotel where traveling athletes, entertainers, and members of the black elite lodged and congregated. These were the places, as poet Amiri Baraka describes Newark's Grand Hotel, where "the ballplayers and the slick people could meet." In Detroit the players stayed at the Norwood, which also housed the Plantation nightclub. In Baltimore the Black Sox lived at the Smith Hotel, owned by the city's black Democratic political boss. Street's Hotel in Kansans City, located at Eighteenth and Vine Streets, was the place, according to its manager, that "everybody that came to KC stopped at."

As a teenager in Newark, Baraka reveled in mixing with the postgame throngs at the Grand Hotel, where "Everybody's super clean and high-falutin'." Monte Irvin recalls, "To the fans, the hotel presented an opportunity to join the ballplayer' special circle." This circle often included not just ballplayers, but the entertainment royalty of black American—jazz musicians, dancers, actors and actresses, theater and movie stars, and boxers like Jack Johnson and Joe Louis. Indeed, a close bond formed between the itinerant athletes and performers. Entertainers often could be found at the ballparks, rooting for their favorite clubs and clowning around with their favorite players. The Mills Brothers loved to don Pittsburgh Crawford uniforms and work out with the club. When they appeared at team owner Gus Greenlee's Crawford Grille, Satchel Paige, a talented singer, would return the favor, joining them on stage for impromptu jazz sessions. In Memphis, where Martin Park bordered the Beale Street music district, bluesman B. B. King would set up near first base and sing as the fans filed in. Lena Horne, whose father was Gus Greenlee's right-hand man, appeared frequently at Negro League games. The New York Black Yankees, co-owned by dancer Bill "Bojangles" Robinson, attracted a parade of celebrities to games at Dyckman's Oval in Harlem. When Count Baise was in Kansas City on a Sunday, he headed out to see the Monarchs, "because that's where everyone else was going on a Sunday afternoon."

The games themselves, particularly season openers and Sunday games, were festive occasions in the black community. As the *Chicago Defender* reported in 1923, fans would turn out for the first home game "like a lot of bees hidden away all winter…getting active when the sun shines." The contests often marked the culmination of daylong celebrations. David

Wyatt, a former player turned sports reporter, described the scene in Indianapolis in 1917:

> The big noise, the mammoth street parade, swung into motion promptly at 10 o'clock upon Saturday. There were something like one hundred conveyances of the gasoline, electric or other propelling types in the line...occupied by persons of both races, some internationally know to fame. ...[We] jammed the downtown district and went on our way rejoicing.

In Kansas City the Monarchs' Booster Club organized an annual parade that snaked through the city's black district and arrived at the park in time for the opening ceremonies. These ceremonies in most cities featured high school bands, color guards, prominent black celebrities, or black and white politicians to throw out the first pitch.

Indeed, as the African-American citizenry in northern cities expanded in numbers and influence, baseball stadiums became a prime location for politicians courting the black vote. In Atlantic City in the 1920s the Bachrach Giants were named for Mayor Henry Bachrach, who had brought an African-American team up from Florida to entertain the resort town's growing population of black hotel workers. Playing at a converted dog track near the Boardwalk, the Bachrach Giants became a popular fixture and an advertisement for the mayor for the remainder of the decade. Indiana Governor Harry Leslie, hoping to rebuild black support for the Republicans in the wake of the party's flirtation with the Ku Klux Klan, threw out the first pitch at the ABCs home opener in 1930. Although attendance by governors proved rare, in the 1930s and 1940s big-city mayors routinely kicked off the local black season. When Pittsburgh Crawfords' owner Gus Greenlee unveiled his new stadium in 1932, the mayor, city council, and county commissioner all attended. In 1935 Mayor Fiorello La Guardia performed the first-pitch honors at a Brooklyn Eagles-Homestead Grays game, and Cleveland Mayor Harry L. Davis joined 8,000 fans at a match between the Crawfords and American Giants honoring Ohio State track star Jesse Owens. The mayors of Baltimore, Kansas City, and Newark all frequently appeared at opening games. The mayor of Newark, recalls Jerry Izenberg, could avoid the Eagles' home opener only "if he chose not to be re-elected."

Opening day and Sunday contests attracted a wide cross section of the African-American community, dressed in their finest clothes. A white writer who attended a Sunday game in Detroit in 1922 reported, "All the youth, beauty, and chivalry of local African artistocracy is there to see and be seen. The latest 'modes and the most advanced fashions in "nobby suit-ings for young men" are on view'....Gallons of perfumery and tons of powder are expended on this great social event." The tradition continued into the 1940s. Memphis blues/soul singer Rufus Thomas recalls: "They put on their best frocks, the best suits, the best everything they had an went to the ballgame and when they would sit up there watching the game, it looked like a fashion parade." For rookie pitcher, like Newark's James Walker, the intimidating scene "looked like a big cloud of flowers of different colors."

The Sunday spectacle, according to Newark resident Connie Woodruff, represented "a combination of two things, an opportunity for all women to show off their Sunday finery" and " once a week family affair." People would arrive, according to Woodruff, "with big baskets of chicken, potato salad, all the things you would have on a picnic...it was the thrill of being there, being seen, seeing who they could see." For recent arrivals from the South, Sunday games often served as reunions. Lena Cox, the sister of Homestead Grays' star Buck Leonard, had immigrated from Rocky Mount, North Carolina, to Washington, D.C. "You would see everyone from home when you went to the ball game," she recalled. Many people went direct-ly from church to the ballpark. Clubs often played benefit games for churches and gave free passes to ministers, who, in return, urged their flocks to accompany them to the games. In Washington, D.C., where Elder Michaux operated a popular church across the street from Griffith Stadi-um, his parishioners would cross Georgia Avenue to catch the Homestead Grays in action during the 1940s after the service.

The Sunday games, asserted Black Yankees outfielder Charlie Biot, "were THE event of the week."Teams capitalized on the popularity of these contests by throwing their star pitchers and scheduling four-team doubleheaders. According to an intimate of Rube Foster, Foster com-mended Negro National League affiliates in the 1920s that "no star twirler was used to the limit before a small Saturday crowd with the prospects of a good Sunday attendance." In Memphis in the 1940s ace Verdell Mathis became known as the "Sunday Feature," because he almost always hurled the first game of the scheduled doubleheader.

This emphasis on Sunday games, however, also revealed the limita-tions of black baseball. The black professional game depended, as Janet Bruce has written, "on an impoverished people who had too little discre-tionary money and too little leisure time." As most blacks who could af-ford to attend games worked or searched for casual work six days a week, Sunday was often the only day they could attend games. Sunday matchups usually attracted between 4,000 and 8,000 fans; weekday contests drew a few hundred. As Foster noted, "There are only twenty seven Sundays and holidays in the playing season. It is a proven fact that on Sundays only have clubs been able to play at a profit. The weekdays have on many occasions been a complete loss." Since several states, most notably Pennsylvania, had "blue laws" prohibiting Sunday games, teams like the Hilldale Club lost these lucrative home dates. Teams that shared facilities with white major and minor league squads could only schedule home Sunday dates when the host club was on the road. A few Sunday rainouts could devastate a team's narrow profit margin.

Attempts to stage a World Series between the champions of the Negro National League and the Eastern Colored League in 1924 illustrated the problem. Since black fans in any city could not be expected to afford tickets for more than a few consecutive games, the ten-game series pitting the Hillsdale Club against the Monarchs was played not just in Philadelphia and Kansas City, but in Baltimore and Chicago as well. Three Sunday dates attracted an average of almost 7,000 fans a game. Two Monday games, including the finale to a tightly contested series, attracted crowds of 534 and 1,549. This pattern continued into the 1930s and 1940s. The Newark Eagles, for example, averaged 4,293 Sunday admissions in 1940, but only 870 on other days.

These realities of black baseball exposed a great deal about the complex racial dynamics of America. As early as 1911 David Wyatt pointed out that "baseball can not live or thrive upon the attendance of colored only," and noted the necessity of scheduling weekday games against white teams. As Neil Lanctot demonstrates, the success of the Hilldale Club in the early 1920s stemmed from the availability of white opponents. Hilldale played almost two-thirds of its games against white semiprofessional and industrial teams.

White baseball fans across the nation attended games that pitted black teams against white semiprofessional and professional squads, but most whites had minimal exposure to top-level competition between black athletes. The daily press in most cities rarely covered constructive black activities of any kind. When several white papers deigned to mention the 1924 Negro World Series, the *Kansas City Call* observed, "Negro sport has done what Negro Churches, Negro lodges, Negro business could not do...shown that Negro can get attention for a good deed well done, and that publicity is no longer the exclusive mark of our criminals." In the 1930s and 1940s Effa Manley discovered that "it was next to impossible to get much space in the white metropolitan dailies." Reports of games that

found their way into the white press often lampooned the fans and festivities or referred to the players as "duskies" and other racist terms.

White fans appear to have been more likely to attend all-black games
in the early years of the century. In 1907 a three-game series in Chicago between the Indianapolis ABCs and Lincoln Giants attracted 30,0000 fans of
both races. "There was no color line anywhere; our white brethren outnumbered us by a few hundred, and bumped elbows in the grand-
stands...the box seats and bleachers," reported Wyatt. The ABCs,
Monarchs, Hilldales, and Lincoln Giants (who played in Harlem) all reported substantial white attendance during these years. During the 1920s,
however, perhaps due to the more rigid segregation arising in response to
the Great Migration and 1919 race riots, white attendance dropped to 10
percent or less. Efforts to bolster protest by attracting more whites inevitably proved unsuccessful. In 1939 Effa Manley made a strong effort to
lure white to Newark Eagles' games, but the *Philadelphia Tribune* reported
in 1940 that "up in Newark...[one] would have seen 95 colored faces for
every five white ones." Chicago reporter Fay Young frequently criticized
attempts to get more whites to the games. Although the leagues had employed white promoters to bolster attendance at all-star games in Chicago and New York in 1939, observed Young, the 32,000 fans in Chicago
included only 1,500 whites, and "the white people in New York didn't give
a tinker's damn about Negro baseball." Two years later, young noted, the
crowd of 50,000 people who attended the East-West game" didn't have
5,000 white people out."

Although whites rarely attended Negro League games, blacks in many
cities frequented major and minor league ballparks. Many African Americans, particularly those who read only mainstream newspapers, were
more aware of white baseball than the black alternative. "Scores of people
in Harlem...do not know there is a colored baseball club in the city," alleged the *Amsterdam News* in 1929. The *Philadelphia Tribune* reported that
black children attending a Hilldale game in the 1920s "had heard of Cobb,
Speaker, Hornsby and Babe Ruth and other pale-faced stars, but know not
that they had players of their own group who could hold their own with
any stars of any league." Buck O'Neil recalled that as children in Florida he
and his friends, unfamiliar with black baseball, emulated the intensely
racist Ty Cobb and other major league players in their imaginary games.

African-American newspapermen repeatedly chided blacks for supporting organized baseball. "It is bad enough to ride on Jim Crow cars, but
to go into ecstasies over a Jim Crow sport is unforgivable," admonished
the *Chicago Whip* in 1921. Two years later a sportswriter in Washington,

D.C., where African Americans avidly rooted for the Senators, asked, "Why then should we continue to support, foster and fill the coffers of a national enterprise that has no place or future for men of color, although they have the ability to make the grade?" Wendell Smith offered a scathing critique of black fans in 1938:

> Why we continue to flock to major league ball parks, spending our hard earned dough, screaming and hollering, stamping our feet and clapping our hands, begging and pleading for some white batter to knock some white pitcher's ears off, almost having fits if the home team loses and crying for joy when they win, is a question that will probably never be settled satisfactorily. What in the world are we thinking about anyway?
>
> The fact that major league baseball refuses to admit Negro players within its folds makes the question just that much more perplexing. Surely, it's sufficient reason for us to quit spending our money and time in their ball parks. Major league baseball doesn't want us. It never has. Still we continue to help support this institution that places a bold "Not Welcome" sign over its thriving portal and refuse to patronize the very place that has shown that it is more than welcome to have us. We black folks are a strange tribe!

The presence of black fans at white games grated for many reasons. As a Kansas City minister commented about the patronage of white-owned businesses, "All of that money goes into the white man's pocket and then out of our neighborhood." The prevalence of segregated seating provoked additional irritation. In St. Louis, where fans had to sit in a separate area behind a screen, a black newspaper condemned fans who ignored th St. Louis Stars, but chose to "fork over six bits to see a game at Sportsman's Park...and get Jim Crow in the bargain." In Kansas City blacks faced segregated seating at minor league Blues games throughout the 1920s. When former major league catcher Johnny Kling bought the team in the 1930s, he ended this policy, but when the Yankees purchased the club in 1938, the organization reinstituted Jim Crow. Other ballparks, like Griffith Stadium in Washington, had no formal policy dividing the races, but African Americans always sat in specific areas of the outfield. "There were no signs," remembered one black Senators fan. "You just knew that was where you should sit."

Many of these same ballparks regularly hosted Negro League and other black contests. After 50,000 fans attended the all-star extravaganza at Comiskey Park in 1941, Fay Young protested, "The East versus West game ought to make Chicago folk get busy and have a ballyard of their own. Why is it we have to 'rent' the other fellows belongings?" But the cost of constructing a stadium fell beyond the limited resources of most team owners. Only a handful of teams—the Memphis Red Sox, the Pittsburgh Crawfords in the 1930s, and the Nashville Elite Giants—owned the stadiums they played in. Most leased or rented facilities usually controlled by white, often in white neighborhoods, and governed by the unpredictable racial mores of the era.

The thorny issue of acquiring a place for black teams to play further illustrated the complex American racial dynamics. For the independent clubs of the early twentieth century, the ability to secure reliable access to a playing field often elevated the team from sandlot to professional level. After 1907 the Indianapolis ABCs held a lease to play at Northwestern Park, a small black-owned stadium in the city's African-American district. The club advertised itself as one of the few black teams to "own their own park" and its ability to guarantee playing dates attracted a steady stream of frontline opponents. In the 1910s Ed Bolden obtained the use of Hilldale Park in Darby, Pennsylvania, just outside Philadelphia. Connected by trolley to Philadelphia's African-American area, Hilldale Park seated 8,000 fans, providing Bolden's Hilldale Club with a steady following.

Hilldale Park was a curious affair, with several trees and tree stumps scattered through the outfield and a hazardous depression that ran across center field. Indeed, many of the ballparks left much to be desired as playing fields. Early teams in Newark performed at Sprague Stadium, hemmed in on one side by a laundry building so close to the infield that balls hit on its roof became ground-rule doubles. The Baltimore Black Sox played in what the *Afro-American* called "a sewer known as Maryland park, which featured broken seats, holes in the roof, nonworking toilets and weeds on the field."

As the popularity of black baseball increased, however, teams began renting larger and better white-owned facilities from recreation entrepreneurs or major and minor League teams. Some parks were located in black neighborhoods, but others brought players and fans across town into white districts. When the White Sox abandoned 18,000-seat South Side park in Chicago's Black Belt for the new Comiskey Stadium, Charles Comiskey's brother-in-law, John Scholing, refurbished the arena and offered it to Rube Foster's American Giants. After 1923 the Kansas City Monarchs leased Muehlebach Stadium, home of the Kansas City blues of the American Association, another ballpark located in the black section. The Detroit

Stars, on the other hand, played at Mack Park, situated amid a German working-class neighborhood. After Mack Park burned down in 1929 the Stars moved to a field in Hamtramck, a Polish community.

Playing in a white-owned facility raised numerous problems for black teams and players. Many stadiums refused to allow African-American players to use the locker rooms. When the Pittsburgh Crawfords or Homestead Grays played at Ammons Field or Forbes Field, the players had to dress and shower at the local YMCA. Some ballparks, like American Association Park in Kansas City, where the Monarchs played form 1920 to 1922, insisted on segregated easing, even for Negro League games. The shift from a small black-owned arena to a larger white-owned one also raised the specter of racial betrayal. The 1916 move by the ABCs from Northwestern Park to Federal League park posed a familiar dilemma. Switching to the new park placed the ABCs in a modern facility, comparable to many major league fields. However, as the *Indianapolis Freeman* complained, the relocation would transfer rent and concession money as well as jobs from blacks to whites. When the Lincoln Giants moved their games from Olympic Stadium in Harlem to the more distant, but attractive protectory Oval, the *New York Amsterdam News* protested, "To see a good baseball game in which colored men engage you now have to travel miles out of the district."

By the late 1930s and early 1040s several major and minor league teams had discovered that renting their stadiums for Sunday Negro League doubleheaders could be a lucrative proposition. In 1932 the New York Yankees began scheduling four-team doubleheaders at Yankee Stadium when the Yankees were on the road. In 1939 the Yankees even donated a "Jacob Ruppert Memorial Cup," named after the team's late owner, to the black club that own the most games at the stadium that year. By the end of the decade the Yankees also rented out the ballparks of their Kansas City and Newark affiliates to the Monarchs and Eagles. In 1939 the Baltimore Orioles, who had previously refused to allow the Elite Giants to use Oriole Park, accepted several Sunday dates. The Homestead Grays played regular Sunday dates at Griffith Stadium starting in 1940, averaging better than 10,000 fans a game. Even Shibe park in Philadelphia, where blacks had rarely played previously, began scheduling Negro League games in the 1940s.

These bookings marked important breakthroughs. They demonstrated the economic potential of black baseball fans and their respectability as well. As the *Kansas City Call* commented in a 1949 editorial, "From a sociological point of view, the Monarchs have done more than any other single agent to break the damnable outrage of prejudice that exists in this city. White fans, the thinking class at least, can not have watched the orderly crowds at Association Park…and not concede that we are humans at least, and worthy of consideration as such."

Perhaps the most significant area of racial controversy revolved around the white owners and booking agents who profited from black baseball. In 1917 David Wyatt derided "the white man who has now and in the past secured grounds and induced some one in the role of the 'good old Nigger' to gather a lot of athletes and then used circus methods to drag a bunch of our best citizens out, only to undergo humiliation, with all kinds of indignities flaunted in their faces, while he sits back and grows rich off a percentage of the proceeds." Yet, as Wyatt well knew, few African Americans in the early twentieth century had the resources to underwrite a baseball enterprise. As *Pittsburgh Courier* columnist Rollo Wilson observed in 1933: "Might few teams have been entirely financed by Negro capital…There have been many instances of so-called Negro 'owners' being nothing but a 'front' for the white interest behind him." Before the 1930s, when the urban "numbers kings" began bankrolling Negro League franchises, economic survival almost always required either partial or complete white ownership or an alliance with white booking agents who controlled access to playing fields.

Both contemporaries and historians have frequently portrayed white booking agents as the Shylockian villains of black baseball. Operating in a universe in which few African-American teams owned playing fields, these baseball entrepreneurs controlled access to the best ballparks and many of the most popular opponents. Nat Strong personified these individuals. A former sporting goods salesman, Strong, like the men who founded vaudeville, had glimpsed an opportunity to profit along the fringes of American entertainment. Recognizing the broad interest in semiprofessional baseball in the 1890s, Strong gained control of New York-area ball fields like Dexter Park in Queens that hosted these games. He rented out these facilities to white an black teams like and gradually expanded his empire to include a substantial portion of the East coast. In 1905 Strong formed the National Association of Colored Professional Clubs of the United States and Cuba, which booked games for the Philadelphia Giants, Cuban X Giants, Brooklyn Royal Giants, and other top eastern black squads.

Any team hoping to schedule lucrative Sunday dates at a profitable site had to deal with Strong, who systematically attempted to secure a monopoly over black professional baseball. Teams that defied Strong found themselves barred from the best bookings. When John Connors, the black owner of the Royal Giants, obtained a playing field in 1911 and attempted to arrange his own games, Strong blacklisted teams that dealt with Connors. Within two years Strong had wrested control of the rebellious franchise from Connors. Black teams also resented the fact that Strong paid a flat guarantee rather than a percentage of the gate, allowing him to reap the profits from large crowds. Behavior like this led former player and organizer Sol White to remark in 1929, "There is not a man in the country who has made as much money from colored ballplaying as Nat Strong, and yet he is the least interested in its welfare."

The creation of the original Negro Leagues in the 1920s occurred against this backdrop. Historians have usually accepted Rube Foster's descriptions of his Negro National League (NNL) as a purer circuit than the rival Eastern Colored League (ECL). Black owners predominated thin the NNL; white owners, particularly Strong, prevailed in the ECL. Foster vehemently dismissed the ECL as a tool of Strong. Yet, the reality of the two leagues was more complex.

As Neil Lanctot has demonstrated, the key figure of the ECL was not Strong, but its president, Ed Bolden. Bolden, a black Philadelphia-area postal worker, had elevated the Hilldale Club of Darby, Pennsylvania, from a sandlot team into a frontline independent competitor. In 1918, when Strong had attempted to gain control of the Hilldale Club, Bolden sent an open letter to the *Philadelphia Tribune,* proclaiming, "The race people of Philadelphia and vicinity are proud to proclaim Hilldale the biggest thing in the baseball world owned fostered and controlled by race men....To affiliate ourselves with other than race men would be a mark against our name that could never be eradicated." Yet, five years later Bolden allied with Strong to form the ECL. Bolden, heavily dependent on scheduling nonleague games at locales like Dexter park, owned or controlled by Strong, recognized the benefits of amalgamation. "Close analysis will prove that only where the color line fades and co-operation instituted are our business advances gratified," wrote Bolden in 1925.

If, as Foster and black sportswriters alleged, Strong "was the league and ran the league," his conduct certainly belied this accusation. The ECL failed, in no small measure, because Strong's Brooklyn Royal Giants refused to adhere to the league schedule. A traveling team with no home base, the Royal Giants frequently bypassed games with league opponents if offered more lucrative bookings. In 1924 the league commissioners voted the Royal Giants out of the ECL, but relented when Strong promised his team would play all scheduled games. His failure to adhere to this pledge greatly weakened the league.

As Bolden noted, however, the Negro National League also had a "few [white] skeletons lurking in the closet." The most visible white presence in the NNL was league secretary J. L. Wilkinson, the owner of the Kansas City Monarchs. Wilkinson represented the best in Negro League ownership, white or black. As Wendell Smith later saluted, he "not only invested his money, but his very heart and soul" in black baseball. But Wilkinson always remained conscious of the need to portray the Monarchs as a black institution. African Americans Dr. Howard Smith and Quincy J. Gilmore became the public faces of the Monarchs, attending league meetings and riding in the lead care at the opening game festivities. In Detroit, first Tenny Blunt and later Mose Walker fronted for white businessman John Roesink as owner of the Stars. Most significantly, Foster himself was not the sole owner of the Chicago American Giants. John Schorling, owner of Schorling Stadium, the team's home grounds, underwrote the American Giants and split all profits evenly with Foster. After the *Chicago Broad Ax* protested in 1912 that Schorling received proceeds that "should be received by the Race to whom the patrons of the game belong," Foster concealed Schorling's role. Nonetheless, other N.L. owners remained suspicious of Schorling's influence and, when Foster became ill in 1926 Schorling assumed sole ownership of the team.

Nor was the N.L. free from the tyranny of booking agents. In this instance, however, the key figure was Foster. As early as 1917 Foster had seized control of scheduling in the Midwest. As president of N.L., Foster booked all league games and received 5 percent of the gate. Critics leveled charges against Foster's domination similar to those directed at Nat Strong in the East St. Louis Giants secretary W. S. Ferrance protested Foster's profits, noting, "There was not a man connected [with the league] that was not in a position to book his own club and had been doing so for years." Others charged that Foster guaranteed lucrative Sunday games for his American Giants. One black writer charged that Foster's "Race baseball league" was designed to "extend his booking agency," just as Foster accused Strong of manipulating the ECL.

Racial controversies also arose in the operations of both leagues, most notably over the issue of employing white umpires. Fay Young protested in 1922, "It isn't necessary for us to sit by the thousands watching eighteen men perform in the national pastime, using every bit of strategy and brain work to have it all spoiled by thinking it is impossible to have any other man officiating but pale faces." Many owners believed that white arbiters could exercise more authority and better control player rowdiness.

They also argued that few blacks had the requisite experience to offer competent officiating. "The colored umpire does not have the advantage that the white umpire has, in passing from sandlot ball to the minor leagues and then to the majors," contended Baltimore Black Sox owner George Rossiter. "As a result of his inexperience he is not able to deliver the goods." Nonetheless, many fans and sportswriters agreed with the verdict of the *Philadelphia Tribune*, which argued, "Regardless of the reason for colored ball games having white umpires it is a disgusting and indefensible practice" and "a reflection on the ability and intelligence of colored people."

The very presence of white owners also continued to rankle many in the African-American community. After a tragic fire injured 219 black fans at Mack Park in Detroit in1929, some blacks organized a boycott protesting white owner John Roesink's "failure to advertise in 'shine' newspapers, his arrogant, insulting attitude toward patrons of the game" and "his failure to compensate, or visit or even speak kindly to any of the persons inured in the catastrophe at Mack Park." The boycott reportedly "brought Roesink down from his 'high horse'" and elicited a promise that he would stay away from the park and allow his black assistant Mose Walker to operate the Stars. That same year the *Baltimore Afro-American* attacked the local Black Sox on the umpire issue. Ignoring the fact that both white-owned and black-owned teams employed whites, the *Afro-American* maintained, "If the Sox management were colored, we'd have colored umpires tomorrow."

Both the NNL and ECL collapsed with the onset of the Great Depression. By this time a group of unorthodox, but highly successful, black businessmen wealthy enough to finance black professional baseball had arisen in many cities. Cuban Stars' impresario Alessandro (Alex) Pompez pioneered this new breed of owner in the 1920s. Pompez, a Cuban American born in Florida, reigned as the numbers king of Harlem. The numbers game was a poor man's lottery. For as little as a nickel, individuals could gamble on hitting a lucky combination of three numbers and winning a payoff of 600 to 1. Since the true odds of winning were 999 to 1, considerable profits awaited a resourceful and reliable man who could oversee the operation. Pompez reportedly grossed as much as $7,000 to $8,000 a day from his organization. In the 1920s Pompez purchased Dyckman's Oval, a park and stadium in Harlem, and staged a variety of sports events including boxing, wrestling, and motorcycle racing. Pompez, who had strong connections in Cuba and a keen eye for baseball talent, formed the Cuban Stars to play at Dyckman's Oval. In 1923 they joined the ECL, one of only two black-owned clubs in the league. During the 1930s he owned the New York Cubans. Pompez imported top Cuban players like Martin Dihigo and Luis Tiant, Sr., to perform for his teams.

The numbers operations run by Pompez and others were illegal but widely accepted in black America. In a world in which African Americans had few legitimate business opportunities, many of the most talented and resourceful entrepreneurs, men who, according to novelist Richard Wright, "would have been steel tycoons, Wall street brokers, auto moguls had they been white," entered the numbers racket. Some, like Jim "Soldier Boy" Semler of New York or Dick Kent of St. Louis, were ruthless gangsters, prone to violence and intimidation. Others like Pompez and Gus Green-lee of Pittsburgh, although not avers to using strong-arm methods to ex-pand the defend their empires, won reputations as community benefactors. Often these numbers kings turned a portion of their profits back into the black community through loans, charity and investments.

In the 1930s black gambling barons throughout the nation began to fol-low Pompez into baseball. In Pittsburgh Gus Greenlee, a Pompez friend and protégé whose peak income has been estimate at $20,000 to $25,000 a day, launched the Pittsburgh Crawfords. In Detroit Everett Wilson, num-bers partner of John Roxborough who managed Joe Louis, bought the De-troit Stars from John Roesink. Abe Manley, a retired numbers banker from Camden, owned first the Brooklyn and then the Newark Eagles. Semler ran the New York Black Yankees and Rufus "Sonnyman" Jackson supplied needed capital for Cum Posey's Homestead Grays. When Greenlee unit-ed the eastern teams into a new Negro National League in 1933, league meetings, according to Donn Rogosin, brought together "the most pow-erful black gangsters in the nation."

Their wealth, power, and influence within the black community notwithstanding, the numbers kings still had to make their way in a white-dominated world. Of the Negro national League teams of the 1930s and 1940s, only the Pittsburgh Crawfords owned and operated their own sta-dium. All teams still relied heavily on white booking agents for schedul-ing. Nat Strong had died in the early 1930s, but William Leuchsner who ran Nat C. Strong Baseball Enterprises in the New York area, and Eddie Gottlieb, who operated out of Philadelphia, now ruled Strong's domain. In the midwest, where a new Negro American League formed in 1937, Abe Saperstein, better known as the founder of the Harlem Globetrotters, had succeeded Rube Foster as the preeminent booking agent. Saperstein even received 5 percent of the substantial gate at the East-West showcase. These arrangements were not without benefits for Negro League teams. Gottlieb, for example, coordinated ticket sales and newspaper and poster publicity for events he booked, enabling teams to reduce their over head and maintain fewer employees. The booking agents also negotiated reduced rental, operating, and insurance fees from major and minor league ballparks. The Homestead Grays reported that Gottlieb's intervention with the New York Yankees saved league owners $10,000 in 1940.

Nonetheless, many owners bridled at the influence of white booking agents and repeatedly sought to be free of them. According to Effa Manley, who owned the Newark Eagles with her husband Abe, "[We] fought a…war against the booking agents from the first day [we] entered the picture…but [we] fought a losing battle. The tentacle-like grip of the booking agents proved impossible to break." Their resistance cost the Eagles their Yankee Stadium playing dates in 1939 and 1940. At the 1940 league meetings, the Manleys demanded the removal of Gottlieb as booking agent for Yankee Stadium. According to *Baltimore Afro-American* sports editor Art Carter, Effa Manley "assumed the position that the league was a colored organization and that wanted to see all the money kept within the group." When Posey defended Gottleib, Manley (who, although she lived as a black woman, later claimed to be white) denounced the Gray's owners as a "handkerchief head," a street-slang variation on "Uncle Tom." That same year black sportswriter at the East-West game organized the American Sportswriters Association to protest Saperstein's domination of that event and the Negro American League removed Saperstein as its official booking agent. The fact that Strong, Leuchsner, Gottlieb, and Saperstein were all Jewish injected elements of anti-Semitism into these disputes.

The race issue also reared its head in hiring decisions. On several occasions teams hired whites to handle publicity in hopes that they might be able to better attract more whites to the games, much to the chagrin of black sportswriters. In the 1920s, when Ed Bolden hired a local white sportswriter as the ECL umpire supervisor to garner attention, John Howe of the *Philadelphia Tribune* called it inappropriate to hire whites in a league "of…for…and by Negroes." Greenlee employed Saperstein to publicize the East-West game in the 1930s, but the move brought out few white fans. Even the Manleys, who demanded black control, had, in the words of sportswriter Ed Harris, "the temerity to hire a white press agent to do their work," evoking widespread criticism. One columnist noted, "Speaking of unholy alliances, how about the one between …the Negro owner of a Negro baseball team who hires a white press agent." Oliver "Butts" Brown of the *New Jersey Herald News*, protested: 'no white publicity man could be of much assistance to you in the many things you hope to do to improve the condition of Negro baseball. In fact he would be a detriment."

These conflicts and debates over the role of whites in black baseball revealed not just the racial tensions that always existed in the age segregation, but the stake of African Americans in successful black-owned and -operated institutions. "Who owns the Grays?" reflected the *Washington Afro-American* in 1943. "It is a pleasure to inform the fans of Washington that the Washington Homestead Grays are owned and operated by three colored gentleman." A scene at the opening game of the 1946 Negro League World Series captures this sense of pride. When heavyweight champion Joe Louis threw out the first pitch, he tossed a silver ball that had been awarded to the Cuban Giants, the first great black professional team, for winning a tournament in 1888. As James Overmyer writes, "With a sweep of his right arm, Louis, the greatest black athlete of his day, symbolically linked the earliest era of Negro baseball with its most recent high point."

The World Series ceremony occurred at a critical juncture in the history of black baseball. In September 1946 Jackie Robinson was completing his successful first season in Organized Baseball. The response to Robinson revealed the fragile hold that all-black baseball held on the African-American psyche. From its earliest days, the promoters of the African-American game had made its transitional nature clear. In *The History of Colored Baseball* in 1906, Sol White advised the black ballplayer to take the game "seriously…as honest efforts with his great ability will open an avenue in the near future wherein he might walk hand-in-hand with the opposite race in the greatest of all American games." In a remarkably prescient passage, White added, "There are grounds for hoping that some day the bar will drop and some good man will be chosen out of the colored profession that will be credit to all, and pave the way for others to follow." Rube Foster had another vision, wherein an all-black team would pierce the ranks of the white professional leagues, but the model of ultimate integration remained. *The Crisis,* the journal of the National Association for the Advancement of Colored People, left no doubt as to the ultimate purpose of the Negro Leagues. "It is only through the elevation of our Negro league baseball that colored ballplayers will break into white major league ball," avowed *The Crisis* in 1938. Even as strong an advocate of "Race baseball" as Fay Young who railed against white umpires, publicity men, and booking agents, joined the chorus. "We want negroes in the major leagues if they have to crawl to get there," wrote Young in 1945.

Most people involved with black baseball had few illusions as to what the impact of integration would be. Asked about the prospect of blacks in the major leagues in 1939, Homestead Grays Manager Vic Harris replied, "If they start picking them up, what are the remaining players going to do to make a living?...And suppose our stars—the fellows who do draw well—are gobbled up by the big clubs. How could the other 75 to 80% survive?" Black sportswriters like Sam Lacy "knew [that integration] would have a devastating effect on black baseball." Joe Bostic wrote in 1942:

> Today, there are two Negro organized leagues, just on the threshold of emergence as real financial factors....To kill [them] would be criminal and that's just what the entry of their players into the American and National Leagues would do.

> Nor should money from the by products be overlooked such as the printers, the Negro papers and the other advertising media, which wet their taste: the officials, storekeepers, announcers secretaries, and a host of others. These monies are coming into Negro pockets. You can rest assured that we'd get none of those jobs in other leagues, *even with a player or two in their leagues.*

In sum: From an idealist and democratic point of view, we say"yes" to Negroes in the two other leagues. From the point of practicality: "No."

But for Lacy, Bostic, and others, "the idealistic and democratic point of view" won out. Less than three years after issuing his admonition, Bostic ardently pursued the policy had had condemned confronting Branch Rickey with Negro League players Terris McDuffie and Dave Thomas and demanding a tryout with the Dodgers during spring training in 1945. Wendell Smith might criticize black fans for attending white games, but, working alongside Rickey, he became one of the key architects of baseball integration. Sam Lacy acknowledged, "After Jackie, the Negro Leagues [became] a symbol I couldn't live with anymore." For these sportswriters, as James Overmyer points out, "covering baseball integration [was] the biggest story of the lives" and they pursued it wholeheartedly.

Throughout black America the focus shifted from the Negro Leagues to the major leagues. The African-American press reduced its coverage of the Negro Leagues to make room for updates and statistics about Robinson and other black players in Organized Baseball. Advertisements appeared for special rail excursions to National League cities to see Robinson pay. Even the Negro Leagues themselves attempted to capitalize on Robinson's popularity. The cover of the 1946 Negro League yearbook featured Robinson rather than one of the established league stars. A program for the Philadelphia Stars in the late 1940s pictured Robinson in his Dodger uniform.

Negro League fans voted with their dollars decisively in favor of integration. In 1946 Effa Manley found that "our fans would go as far as Baltimore" to see Robinson play for the Montreal Royals. Once he joined the Dodgers and New York-area fans could see Robinson in eighty-eight games at Ebbets Field and the Polo Grounds, attendance plummeted for the Newark Eagles and New York Black Yankees. Other teams also felt the pinch. "People wanted to go to see the Brooklynites," recalled Monarch pitcher Hilton Smith. "Even if we were playing here in Kansas City, people wanted to go over to St. Louis to see Jackie."

Occasionally critics raised their voices to protest the abandonment of black baseball. "Around 400 players are involved in the Negro version od the national pastime," warned Dan Burley in *The Amsterdam News* in 1948. "If there are no customers out to see them, they don't earn a living. In enriching the coffers of the major league clubs, we put the cart before the horse for no purpose." But most commentators were less sympathetic. In response to Manley's complaints about declining fan support, the *Kansas City Call* cajoled, "The day of loyalty to Jim Crow anything is fast passing away. Sister, haven't you heard the news? Democracy is a-coming fast." The Manleys sold the Eagles after the 1948 season. By the early 1950s all but a handful of the Negro League clubs had disbanded.

As Burley, Manley, and others had predicted, the end of segregation would mean that fewer, rather than more, African Americans would earn their living from baseball in the latter half of the twentieth century. The failure of major league teams to hire black managers, coaches, and front-office personnel compounded this problem. The nearly universal celebration of Jackie Robinson's triumph notwithstanding, integration would produce negative as well a positive consequences.

Cultural critic Gerald Early sees the demise of the Negro Leagues as the destruction of "an important black economic and cultural institution" that encompassed many of the best and worst elements of African-American life. Blacks, writes Early, "have never gotten over the loss of the Negro Leagues because they have never completely understood the ironically compressed expression of shame and pride of degradation and achievement that those leagues represented." In the final analysis, the black baseball experience captured the "twoness" in the "souls of black folk" as well as the "dogged strength' that kept them "from being torn asunder."

8.5

The Negro Artist and the Racial Mountain (1926)

Langston Hughes

African American culture underwent a profound shift in the Twenties, too. Known as the Harlem Renaissance, this flowering of black art, literature, music, theater, and poetry revealed a sea change in the black intellectual community. Langston Hughes was among the most important artistic figures of the Harlem Renaissance, and in this essay he identifies the obstacles facing the "Negro artist" of the 1920s. What are they, and how are they to be overcome?

One of the most promising of the young Negro poets said to me once, "I want to be a poet—not a Negro poet," meaning, "I want to write like a white poet"; meaning subconsciously, "I would like to be a white poet"; meaning behind that, "I would like to be white." And I was sorry the young man said that, for no great poet has ever been afraid of being himself. And I doubted then that, with his desire to run away spiritually from his race, this boy would ever be a great poet. But this is the mountain standing in the way of true Negro art in America—this urge within the race toward whiteness, the desire to pour racial individuality into the mold of American standardization, and to be as little Negro and as much American as possible.

But let us look at the immediate background of this young poet. His family is of what I suppose one would call the Negro middle class: people who are by no means rich yet never very uncomfortable nor hungry—smug, contented, respectable folk, members of the Baptist church. The father goes to work every morning. He is a chief steward at a large white club. The mother sometimes does fancy sewing or supervises parties for the rich families of the town. The children go to a mixed school. In the home they read white papers and magazines. And the mother often says, "Don't be like niggers" when the children are bad. A frequent phrase from the father is, "Look how well a white man does things." And so the word white comes to be unconsciously a symbol of all virtues. It holds for the children beauty, morality, money. The whisper of "I want to be white" runs silently through their minds. This young poet's home is, I believe, fairly typical of the colored middle class. One sees immediately how dificult it would be for an artist born in such a home to interest himself in interpreting the beauty of his own people. He is never taught to see that beauty. He is taught rather not to see it, or if he does, to be ashamed of it when it is not according to Caucasian patterns.

For the racial culture the home of a self-styled "high-class" Negro has nothing better to offer. Instead there will perhaps be more aping of things white than in a less cultured or less wealthy home. The father is perhaps a doctor, a lawyer, landowner, or politician. The mother may be a social worker, or a teacher, or she may do nothing and have a maid. Father is often dark, but he has married the lightest woman he could find. The family attend a fashionable church where few really colored faces are to be found. And they themselves draw the color line. In the North they go to white theatres and white movies. And in the South they have at least two cars and a house, "just like white folks." Nordic manners, Nordic faces, Nordic hair, Nordic art (if any), and an Episcopal heaven. A very high mountain indeed for the would-be racial artist to climb in order to discover himself and his people....

Certainly there is, for the American Negro artist who can escape the restrictions the more advanced among his own group would put upon him, a great field of unused material for his art. Without going outside his race, and even among the better classes with their "white"culture and conscious American manners, but still Negro enough to be different, there is sufficient matter to furnish a black artist with a lifetime of creative work. And when he chooses to touch on the relations between Negroes and whites in this country with their innumerable overtones and undertones, surely, and especially for literature and the drama, there is an inexhaustible supply of themes at hand. To these the Negro artist can give his racial individuality, his heritage...and his incongruous humor that so oten, as in the Blues, becomes ironic laughter mixed with tears....

Most of my own poems are racial in theme and treatment, derived from the life I know. In many of them, I try to grasp and hold some of the meanings and rhythms of jazz. I am sincere as I know how to be in these poems, and yet after every reading I answer questions like these from my own people: Do you think Negroes should always write about Negroes? I wish you wouldn't read some of your poems to white folks. How do you find anything interesting in a place like a cabaret? Why do you write about black people? You aren't black. What makes you do so many jazz poems?

But jazz to me is one of the inherent expressions of Negro life in America: the eternal tom-tom beating in the Negro soul—the tom-tom of revolt against weariness in a white world, a world of subway trains, and work, work, work; the tom-tom of joy and laughter, and pain swallowed in a smile. Yet the Philadelphia clubwoman is ashamed to say that her race created it and she does not like me to write about it. The old subconscious "white is best" runs through her mind. Years of study under white teachers, a lifetime of white books, pictures and papers, and white manners, morals, and Puritan standards made her dislike the spirituals. And now she turns up her nose at jazz and all its manifestations—likewise anything else distinctly racial. She doesn't care for the Winold Reiss portraits of Negroes because they are "too Negro." She does not want a true picture of herself from anybody. She wants the artist to flatter her, to make the white world believe that all Negroes are as smug and near-white in soul as she wants to be. But, to my mind, it is the duty of the younger Negro artist, if he accepts any duties at all from outsiders, to change through the force of his art that old whispering "I want to be white," hidden in the aspirations of his people, to "Why should I want to be white? I am a Negro—and beautiful!"

8.6
Poets of the Harlem Renaissance

Claude McKay and Sterling Brown

Along with Langston Hughes (see Doc. 8.5), McKay and Brown are among the best-known poets of the Harlem Renaissance. Here are two poems which embody quite well the aesthetics of that African American artistic movement. In what ways do McKay's and Brown's poems satisfy the definition of "Negro art" as described by Hughes in the preceding document?

If We Must Die (1919)*

Claude McKay

If we must die, let it not be like hogs
Hunted and penned in an inglorious spot,
While round us bark the mad and hungry dogs,
Making their mock at our accursed lot.
If we must die, O let us nobly die,
So that our precious blood may not be shed
In vain; then even the monsters we defy
Shall be constrained to honor us though dead!
O kinsmen! We must meet the common foe!
Though far outnumbered let us show us brave,
And for their thousand blows deal one deathblow!
What though before us lies the open grave?
Like men we'll face the murderous, cowardly pack,
Pressed to the wall, dying, but fighting back!

*Written 1919.

He Was a Man (1932)**

Sterling Brown

It wasn't about no woman,
It wasn't about no rape,
He wasn't crazy, and he wasn't drunk,
An' it wasn't no shooting scrape,
He was a man, and they laid him down.

He wasn't no quarrelsome feller,
And he let other folks alone,
But he took a life, as a man will do,
In a fight for to save his own,
He was a man, and they laid him down.

He worked on his little homeplace
Down on the Eastern Shore;
He had his family, and he had his friends,
And he didn't expect much more,
He was a man, and they laid him down.

He wasn't nobody's great man,
He wasn't nobody's good,
Was a po'boy tried to get from life
What happiness he could,
He was a man, and they laid him down.

He didn't abuse Tom Wickley,
Said nothing when the white man curst,
But when Tom grabbed his gun, he pulled his own,
And his bullet got there first,
He was a man, and they laid him down.

Didn't catch him in no manhunt,
But they took him from a hospital bed,
Stretched on his back in the nigger ward,
With a bullet wound in his head,
He was a man, and they laid him down.

**From *The Collected Poems of Sterling A. Brown,* edited by Michael S. Harper.
Reprinted by permission of HarperCollins Publishers Inc.

It didn't come off at midnight
Nor yet at the break of day,
It was in the broad noon daylight,
When they put po' Will away,
He was a man, and they laid him down.

Didn't take him to no swampland,
Didn't take him to no woods,
Didn't hide themselves, didn't have no masks,
Didn't wear no Ku Klux hoods,
He was a man, and they laid him down.

They strung him up on Main Street,
On a tree in the Court House Square,
And people came from miles around
To enjoy a holiday there,
He was a man, and we'll lay him down.

They hung him and they shot him,
They piled packing cases around,
They burnt up Will's black body,
'Cause he shot a white man down;
"He was a man, and we'll lay him down."

It wasn't no solemn business,
Was more like a barbecue,
The crackers yelled when the fire blazed,
And the women and the children too—
"He was a man, and we laid him down."

The Coroner and the Sheriff
Said "Death by Hands Unknown."
The mob broke up by midnight,
"Another uppity Nigger gone—
He was a man, an' we laid him down."

CHAPTER 9

The Great Depression and The New Deal, 1929–1940

9.1 Magnus Alexander, "A Businessman's Reaction to the Crash" (1929)

9.2 Herbert Hoover, "Lincoln's Birthday Radio Address" (1931)

9.3 John A. Garraty, "The Big Picture of the Great Depression"

9.4 Franklin D. Roosevelt, "First Inaugural Address" (1933)

9.5 Carolyn Weaver, "Birth of an Entitlement: The Origins of Social Security"

9.6 Huey Long, "Share Our Wealth" (1935)

9.7 Republican Party, "Platform" (1936)

9.1
A Businessman's Reaction to the Crash (1929)

Magnus Alexander

The stock market crash of 1929 brought the prosperity of the 1920s to an end, at least figuratively. The reasons for the crash are complex and have been endlessly argued since the day after the event. This selection presents one businessman's view of the Crash and its potential impact. How would you characterize the attitude of this business leader toward the Crash? Was business responsible for what happened? Who will be affected the most by its consequences?

The recent collapse of stock market prices has no significance as regards the real wealth of the American people as a whole. It has had unfortunate effects in shifting the rights of ownership from some hands to others. But the basic economic concept relating to the welfare of the community is income, not capital. And of itself the stock market deflation has no direct connection with the current income from industrial production. There have been real losses for some individuals. There have been real gains for others. There have been paper losses for still others, and by far the greater part of the calculated reduction in security values have been of this character. Those who owned stocks outright and did not sell them are still entitled to the same income to which they would have been entitled if deflation had not occurred. Their current purchasing power will be in no way affected by the reduction in the capital value of their securities. The individuals who have suffered real losses, on the other hand, are those who had extended their claims to income by acquisition of securities beyond the limits of their own capital. By borrowing, they had purchased capital value with the

Excerpted from "Suggested Telegram to Magnus Alexander" dated October 31, 1929, Series 6, Box 1, Records of The National Industrial Conference Board.

funds of others, and with the shrinkage of these capital values their own margin of ownership has been completely wiped out....Last week's disturbance in the market may well be characterized as a "margin speculator's panic"; a rectification of fictitious values and unrealizable paper profits. In essence, it has no relation to what has happened, or is happening in business. On the very day that stocks declined most, I noticed, the United Steel Corporation declared an extra dividend and the American Can Company increased its dividend rate. According to the newspapers, stocks lost billions in value, yet at the same time the income from two such leading industrial stocks, which is the measure of their present real value to investors, actually increased. It is highly significant, furthermore, that the financial and credit situation in the United States is unusually sound at the present time. Stock speculation during the past few years has been stimulated by the very fact that bank credit has been easy, there being ample money at low rates available. The very fact that the Federal Reserve system at the present time has a higher reserve ratio than at any time since the war indicates the fundamental soundness of the financial situation, as well as emphasizes the fact that the stock market collapse was due to mob-psychology, the same as the previous unprecedented rise in security prices was due to speculative fever which fed on easy money and the prospects of making money easily. The United States has prospered because of its increasing efficiency and productivity. There is therefore no reason whatever for American businessmen to let stock market upsets influence them in their business policies. Adam Smith's famous definition, that the wealth of nations consists not of the unconsumable riches of money but of the consumable goods annually produced by society, still holds true, and the stock market cannot make it any less true. Productivity alone creates purchasing power, a lesson well ingrained in American business philosophy by experience during the past decade. It is now up to American businessmen not to allow a stock quotation flurry to becloud their vision. It is true that stock speculation in earlier years often was able to stimulate or depress business. Business men psychologically then were more easily influenced; the stock market, indeed, was considered a reliable index of future business conditions. Business today has better indices....On the basis of such authentic, reliable and prompt information as is available to modern businessmen through their trade associations, the government and through such organizations as the National Industrial Conference Board and Chambers of Commerce, American industry and trade may well proceed on their course to satisfy the normal wants of the population of the United States and of foreign countries. Paper profits and paper losses in stocks will not change people's total demand for either necessities or luxuries to any considerable extent; and as far as actual stock transactions are concerned, at whatever prices, they can only result in transfers of money from one to another, not in any diminution of the total resources of wealth. Future business prosperity therefore will continue to rest, as it has in the past, on our industrial productivity and well-informed business leadership.

9.2
Lincoln's Birthday Radio Address (1931)

Herbert Hoover

As President during the early stages of the Great Depression, Herbert Hoover tried to calm peoples' fears and lead the nation back to prosperity. In this February 1931 speech, Hoover typifies his conservative, voluntaristic approach to the problem. What solutions does Hoover put forth here? What does he want Americans to do? What do think of his advice? Did it work?

The Federal Government has assumed many new responsibilities since Lincoln's time, and will probably assume more in the future when the states and local communities can not alone cure abuse or bear the entire cost of national programs, but there is an essential principle that should be maintained in these matters. I am convinced that where Federal action is essential then in most cases it should limit its responsibilities to supplement the states and local communities, and that it should not assume the major role or the entire responsibility, in replacement of the states or local government. To do otherwise threatens the whole foundations of local government, which is the very basis of self-government.

The moment responsibilities of any community, particularly in economic and social questions, are shifted from any part of the Nation to Washington, then that community has subjected itself to a remote bureaucracy with its minimum of understanding and of sympathy. It has lost a large part of its voice and its control of its own destiny. Under Federal control the varied conditions of life in our country are forced into standard molds, with all their limitations upon life, either of the individual or the

From Herbert Hoover, "Radio Address on Lincoln's Birthday" (February 12, 1931), in *The State Papers and Other Public Writings of Herbert Hoover*, collected and edited by William Starr Myers (Garden City, N.Y.: Doubleday, 1934), Vol. 1, 503–505.

community. Where people divest themselves of local government responsibilities they at once lay the foundation for the destruction of their liberties.

And buried in this problem lies something even deeper. The whole of our governmental machinery was devised for the purpose that through ordered liberty we give incentive and equality of opportunity to every individual to rise to that highest achievement of which he is capable. At once when government is centralized there arises a limitation upon the liberty of the individual and a restriction of individual opportunity. The true growth of the Nation is the growth of character in its citizens. The spread of government destroys initiative and thus destroys character. Character is made in the community as well as in the individual by assuming responsibilities, not by escape from them. Carried to its logical extreme, all this shouldering of individual and community responsibility upon the Government can lead but to the superstate where every man becomes the servant of the State and real liberty is lost. Such was not the government that Lincoln sought to build.

There is an entirely different avenue by which we may both resist this drift to centralized government and at the same time meet a multitude of problems. That is to strengthen in the Nation a sense and an organization of self-help and cooperation to solve as many problems as possible outside of government. We are today passing through a critical test in such a problem arising from the economic depression.

Due to lack of caution in business and to the impact of forces from an outside world, one-half of which is involved in social and political revolution, the march of our prosperity has been retarded. We are projected into temporary unemployment, losses, and hardships. In a Nation rich in resources, many people were faced with hunger and cold through no fault of their own. Our national resources are not only material supplies and material wealth but a spiritual and moral wealth in kindliness, in compassion, in a sense of obligation of neighbor to neighbor and a realization of responsibility by industry, by business, and the community for its social security and its social welfare.

The evidence of our ability to solve great problems outside of Government action and the degree of moral strength with which we emerge from this period will be determined by whether the individuals and the local communities continue to meet their responsibilities.

Throughout this depression I have insisted upon organization of these forces through industry, through local government and through charity, that they should meet this crisis by their own initiative, by the assumption of their own responsibilities. The Federal Government has sought to do its part by example in the expansion of employment, by affording credit to drought sufferers for rehabilitation, and by cooperation with the community, and thus to avoid the opiates of Government charity and the stifling of our national spirit of mutual self-help.

We can take courage and pride in the effective work of thousands of voluntary organizations for provision of employment, for relief of distress, that have sprung up over the entire Nation. Industry and business have recognized a social obligation to their employees as never before. The State and local governments are being helpful. The people are themselves succeeding in this task. Never before in a great depression has there been so systematic a protection against distress; never before has there been so little social disorder, never before has there been such an outpouring of the spirit of self-sacrifice and of service....

We are going through a period when character and courage are on trial, and where the very faith that is within us is under test. Our people are meeting this test. And they are doing more than the immediate task of the day. They are maintaining the ideals of our American system. By their devotion to these ideals we shall come out of these times stronger in character, in courage, and in faith.

9.3
The Big Picture of the Great Depression

John A. Garraty

In this piece, historian Garraty calls for a re-evaluation of our understanding of the Great Depression. In particular, Garraty believes that the causes of this tragic era and the ways in which world leaders tried to handle its effects have been misunderstood. What does Garraty argue here about the Depression? What lessons might we draw from it if we accept Garraty's arguments?

Back in 1955 John Kenneth Galbraith called the Great Depression of the 1930s "the most momentous economic occurrence in the history of the United States," and thirty-odd years later that judgment, recorded in Galbraith's best seller, *The Great Crash*, still holds. Since then there have been more recessions, some quite severe, but nothing like what happened in the thirties. As dozens of economists and historians have shown, we now know, in theory, how to deal with violent cyclical downturns. We have learned what we should do to manipulate what Lester V. Chandler of Atlanta University has called "the determinants that influence the behavior of employment, output, and prices."

Yet fears of another terrible collapse persist, even among the experts. And the higher the stock market soars, the greater the underlying fear. In *The Great Crash* Galbraith spoke of "fissures" that "might open at …unexpected places," and Chandler warned of some sort of "political deadlock" that might prevent the government from doing the things that would revive a faltering economy.

These fears are not without foundation. The American economy is complex and influenced by forces beyond the control of economists or politicians. More and more, economists are becoming aware of what historians have always known: that they can do a good job of explaining why the economy is the way it is and how it got to be that way, but that know-

---

Reprinted By Permission of *American Heritage Inc.* 1986

ing exactly what to do to make it behave in any particular way in the future is another matter entirely.

The Great Depression of the 1930s was a worldwide phenomenon, great not only in the sense of "severe," but also in the sense of "scope." While there were differences in its impact and in the way it was dealt with from one country to another, the course of events nearly everywhere ran something like this: By 1925 most countries had recovered from the economic disruptions caused by the Great War of 1914-18. There followed a few years of rapid growth, but in 1929 and 1930 the prosperity ended. Then came a precipitous plunge that lasted until early 1933. This dark period was followed by a gradual, if spotty, recovery. The revival, however, was aborted by the steep recession of 1937-38. It took a still more cataclysmic event, the outbreak of World War II, to end the Great Depression. All this is well known.

The effects of the Great Depression on the economy of the United States, and the attitudes of Americans toward both the Depression and the politics of their government, did not differ in fundamental ways from the situation elsewhere. This, too, scarcely needs saying.

However, there has been a tendency among historians of the Depression, except when dealing with specific international events, such as the London Economic Conference, and with foreign relations generally, to concentrate their attentions on developments in a single country or region. The result has been to make the policies of particular nations and particular interest groups seem both more unique and, for good or ill, more effective than they were.

It is true, to begin with, that neither President Calvin Coolidge nor President Herbert Hoover anticipated the Depression. In campaigning for the Presidency in 1928, Hoover stressed the good times, which, he assured the voters, would continue if he was handling the reins of government. After the election, in his last annual message to Congress, Coolidge remarked that "the country can regard the present with satisfaction and anticipate the future with optimism." When the bottom fell out of the American economy some months later, statements such as these came back to haunt Hoover and his party, and many historians have chortled over his discomfiture.

However, the leaders of virtually all the industrial nations were as far off the mark in their prognostications as Hoover and Coolidge were. When the German Social Democrats rode a "wave of prosperity" to power in June 1928, Hermann Müller, the new chancellor, assured the Reichstag that the Fatherland was in a "firm and unshakable" condition.

Great Britain had been plagued by high unemployment and lagging economic growth in the late 1920s, but in July 1929 Prime Minister Ramsay MacDonald scoffed at the possibility of a slump. And as late as December 1929, the French Premier, André Tardieu, announced what he described as a "politics of prosperity." Fewer than a thousand people were out of work in France, and the Treasury was full to overflowing. The government planned to spend five billion francs over the next five years on a "national retooling" of agriculture, industry, commerce, health care, and education. Statesmen of many other nations made similar comments in 1928 and 1929.

Hoover has been subject to much criticism for the way in which he tried to put the blame for the Depression on the shoulders of others. In his memoirs he offered an elaborate explanation, complete with footnote references to the work of many economists and other experts. "The Depression was not started in the United States," he insisted. The "primary cause" was the World War. In four-fifths of what he called the "economically sensitive" nations of the world, including such remote areas as Bolivia, Bulgaria, and Australia, the downturn was noticeable long before 1929, a time when the United States was enjoying a period of great prosperity.

Hoover blamed American's post-1929 troubles on an "orgy of stock speculation" resulting from the cheap-money policies adopted by the "mediocrities" who made up the majority of the Federal Reserve Board in a futile effort to support the value of the British pound and other European currencies. Hoover called Benjamin Strong, the governor of the Federal Reserve Bank of New York, a "mental annex of Europe," because the Fed had kept American interest rates low to discourage foreign investors.

According to Hoover, he had warned of the danger, but neither the Fed nor his predecessor, Calvin Coolidge (whom he detested), had taken his advice. Coolidge's announcement at the end of his term that stocks were "cheap at current prices" was, Hoover believed, particularly unfortunate, since it undermined his efforts to check the speculative mania on Wall Street after his inauguration.

But Hoover could not use this argument to explain the decline that occurred in the United States in 1930, 1931, and 1932, when he was running the country. Instead he blamed the decline on foreign countries. European statesmen "did not have the courage to meet the real issues." Their rivalries and their heavy spending on arms and "frantic public works programs to meet unemployment" led to unbalanced budgets and inflation that "tore their systems asunder." These unsound policies led to the collapse of the

German banking system in 1931, which transformed what would have been no more than a minor economic downturn into the Great Depression. "The hurricane that swept our shores," wrote Hoover, was a European origin.

These squirmings to avoid taking any responsibility for the Depression do Hoover no credit. But he was certainly not alone among statesmen of the time in doing so. Prime Minister MacDonald, a socialist, blamed capitalism for the debacle. "We are not on trial," he said in 1930, "it is the system under which we live. It has broken down, not only on this little island…it has broken down everywhere as it was bound to break down." The Germans argued that the Depression was political in origin. The harsh terms imposed on them by the Versailles Treaty, and especially the reparations payments that, they claimed, sapped the economic vitality of their country, had caused it. One conservative German economist blamed the World War naval blockage for his country's troubles in the 1930s. In the nineteenth century "the English merchant fleet helped build up the world economy," he said. During the war "the British navy helped to destroy it."

When in its early stages the Depression appeared to be sparing France, French leaders took full credit for this happy circumstance. "France is a garden," they explained. But when the slump became serious in 1932, they accused Great Britain of causing it by going off the gold standard and adopting other irresponsible monetary policies, and the United States of "exporting unemployment" by substituting machines for workers. "Mechanization," a French economist explained in 1932, "is an essential element in the worsening of the depression."

Commentators in most countries, including the United States, tended to see the Wall Street crash of October 1929 as the cause of the Depression, placing a rather large burden of explanation on a single, local event. But in a sense the Depression was like syphilis, which before its nature was understood was referred to in England as the French pox, as the Spanish disease in France, the Italian sickness in Spain, and so on.

When the nations began to suffer the effects of the Depression, most of the steps they took in trying to deal with it were either inadequate or counterproductive. Hoover's signing of the Hawley-Smoot protective tariff further shriveled an already shrinking international trade. The measure has been universally deplored by historians, who point with evident relish to the fact that more than a thousand economists had urged the President to veto the bill. The measure was no doubt a mistake because it caused a further shrinking of economic activity, but blaming Hoover for the result ignores the policies of other countries, to say nothing of the uselessness of much of what the leading economists of the day were suggesting about how to end the Depression. Even Great Britain, a nation particularly dependent on international trade, adopted the protective imperial preference system, worked out with the dominions at Ottawa in 1932. Many Latin American countries, desperately short of foreign exchange because of the slumping prices of the raw materials they exported, tried to make do with home manufactures and protected these fledgling industries with tariffs. In Europe, country after country passed laws aimed at reducing their imports of wheat and other foreign food products.

And while the Hawley-Smoot tariff was unfortunate, if Hoover had followed all the advice of the experts who had urged him to veto it, he would surely have been pushing the American economy from the frying pan into the fire, because most of their recommendations are now seen to have been wrongheaded. Opposition to protective tariffs, almost universal among conservative economists since the time of Adam Smith and Ricardo, was no sign of prescience, then as now. In their *Monetary History of the United States,* Milton Friedman and Anna Jacobson Schwartz characterize the financial proposals of the economists of the 1930s as "hardly distinguished by the correctness or profundity of understanding of the economic forces at work." A leading French economic historian, Alfred Sauvy, compares the typical French economist of the period to a "doctor, stuffed with theories, who has never seen a sick person." An Australian historian characterizes the policies of that country as "deeply influenced by shibboleths."

The most nearly universal example of a wrongheaded policy during the Depression was the effort that nations made to balance their annual budgets. Hoover was no exception; Albert Romasco has counted no fewer than twenty-one public statements stressing the need to balance the federal budget that the President made in a four-month period. As late as February 1933, after his defeat in the 1932 election, Hoover sent a desperate handwritten letter to President-elect Roosevelt pleading with him to announce that "there will be no tampering or inflation of the currency[and] that the budget will be unquestionably balanced even if further taxation is necessary."

But Hoover had plenty of company in urging fiscal restraint. Roosevelt was unmoved by Hoover's letter, but his feelings about budget balancing were not very different. In 1928 William Trufant Foster and Waddill Catchings published a book, *The Road to Plenty,* which attracted considerable attention. Roosevelt read it. After coming across the sentence "When business begins to look rotten, more public spending," he wrote in the margin: "Too good to be true—you can't get something for nothing." One of Roosevelt's first actions as President was to call for a tax increase. According to his biographer Frank Freidel, fiscal conservatism was a "first priority" in Roosevelt's early efforts to end the Depression.

Budget balancing was an obsession with a great majority of the political leaders of the thirties, regardless of country, party, or social philosophy. In 1930 Ramsay MacDonald's new socialist government was under pressure to undertake an expensive public works program aimed at reducing Great Britain's chronic unemployment. Instead the government raised taxes by £47 million in an effort to balance the budget. The conservative Heinrich Bruning recalled in his memoirs that when he became chancellor of Germany in 1932, he promised President Hindenburg "that as long as I had his trust, I would at any price make the government finances safe."

France had fewer financial worries in the early stages of the Depression than most nations. Its 1930 budget was designed to show a small surplus. But revenues did not live up to expectations, and a deficit resulted. The same thing happened in 1931 and again in 1932, but French leaders from every point on the political spectrum remained devoted to "sound" government finance. "I love the working class," Premier Pierre Laval told the National Assembly during the debate on the 1932 budget. Hoots from the left benches greeted this remark, but Laval went on: "I have seen the ravages of unemployment....The government will never refuse to go as far as the resources of the country will permit [to help]. But do not ask it to commit acts that risk to compromise the balance of the budget." In 1933, when France began to feel the full effects of the Depression, Premier Joseph Paul-Boncour, who described himself as a socialist though he did not belong to the Socialist party, called for rigid economies and a tax increase. "What good is it to talk, what good to draw up plans," he said, "if one ends with a budget deficit?"

Leaders in countries large and small, in Asia, the Americas, and Europe, echoed these sentiments. A Japanese finance minister warned in 1930 that "increased government spending" would "weaken the financial soundness of the government." Prime Minister William Lyon Mackenzie King of Canada, a man who was so parsimonious that he cut new pencils into three pieces and used them until they were tiny stubs, believed that "governments should live within their means." When King's successor, R. B. Bennett, took office in 1931, he urged spending cuts and higher taxes in order to get rid of a budget deficit of more then eighty million dollars. "When it came to...'unbalancing' the budget," Bennett's biographer explains, "he was as the rock of Gilbraltar."

The Brazilian dictator Getúlio Vargas is reported to have had a "high respect for a balanced budget." When a journalist asked Jaime Carner, one of the succession of like-minded Spanish finance ministers in the early 1930s, to describe his priorities, Carner replied that he had three: " a balanced budget, a balanced budget, and a balanced budget." A recent historian of Czechoslovakia reports that the statesmen of the Depression era in that country displayed an "irrational fear of the inflationary nature of a budget deficit."

These examples could be extended almost without limit. The point is not that Hoover was correct in his views of proper government finance; obviously he was not. But describing his position without considering its context distorts its significance. Furthermore, the intentions of the politicians rarely corresponded to what actually happened. Deficits were the rule through the Depression years because government revenues continually fell below expectations and unavoidable expenditures rose. Even if most budgets had been in balance, the additional sums extracted from the public probably would not have had a decisive effect on any country's economy. Government spending did not have the impact on economic activity that has been the case since World War II. The historian Mark Leff has recently reminded us, for example, that the payroll tax enacted to finance the new American Social Security system in 1935 "yielded as much each month as the notorious income tax provisions of Roosevelt's 1935 Wealth Tax did in a year."

It is equally revealing to look at other aspects of the New Deal from a broad perspective. Franklin Roosevelt's Brain Trust was novel only in that so many of these advisers were academic types. Many earlier Presidents made use of informal groups of advisers—Theodore Roosevelt's Tennis Cabinet and Andrew Jackson's Kitchen Cabinet come to mind. There is no doubt that political leaders in many nations were made acutely aware of their ignorance by the Depression, and in their bafflement they found that turning to experts was both psychologically and politically beneficial. Sometimes the experts' advice actually did some good. Sweden was blessed during the interwar era with a number of articulate, first-rate economists. The Swedish government, a recent scholar writes, was "ready to listen to the advice of [these] economists," with the result that by 1935 Sweden was deliberately practicing deficit spending, and unemployment was down nearly to pre-Depression levels.

Throughout the period British prime ministers made frequent calls on the expertise of economists such as Ralph Hawtrey, A. C. Pigou, and, of course, John Maynard Keynes. In 1930 Ramsay MacDonald, who was particularly fond of using experts to do his thinking for him, appointed a committee of five top-flight economists to investigate the causes of the Depression and "indicate the conditions of recovery." (The group came up with a number of attractive suggestions, but avoided the touchy subject of how to finance them.) The next year MacDonald charged another committee with the task of suggesting "all possible reductions of national Expenditure" in a futile effort to avoid going off the gold standard. Even in France, where political leaders tended to deny that the world depression was affecting their nation's economy and where most economists still adhered to laissez-faire principles, French premiers called from time to time on experts "to search," Sauvy explains, "for the causes of the financial difficulties of the country and propose remedies."

Many specific New Deal policies were new only to America. In 1933 the United States was far behind most industrial nations in social welfare. Unemployment insurance, a major New Deal reform when enacted in 1935, was established in Great Britain in 1911 and in Germany shortly after World War I, well before the Depression struck. The creation of the New Deal Civilian Conservation Corps and the Civil Works Administration, in 1933, and later of the Works Progress Administration and Public Works Administration, only made up for the absence of a national public welfare system before 1936.

The New Deal National Recovery Administration also paralleled earlier developments. The relation of its industrywide codes of "fair" business practices to the American trade-association movement of the 1920s and to such early Depression proposals as the plan advanced by Gerard Swope of General Electric in 1931 are well known. (The Swope Plan provided that in each industry "production and consumption should be coordinated...preferably by the joint participation and joint administration of management and employees" under the general supervision of the Federal Trade Commission, a system quite similar to NRA, as Roosevelt himself admitted.)

That capital and labor should join together to promote efficiency and harmony, and that companies making the same products should consult in order to fix prices and allocate output and thus put a stop to cutthroat competition, all under the watchful eye of the government, were central concepts of Italian fascist corporatism in the 1920s and of the less formal but more effective German system of cartels in that period. The Nazis organized German industry along similar but more thoroughly regimented lines at about the same time as the NRA system was being set up in America. Great Britain also employed this tactic in the 1930s, albeit on a smaller scale. The British government allowed coal companies to limit and allocate production and to fix prices, and it encouraged similar practices by steel and textile manufacturers. The only major industrial power that did not adopt such a policy before the passage of the National Industrial Recovery Act was France. Later, in 1935, the Chamber of Deputies passed a measure that permitted competing companies to enter into "accords" with one another "in time of crisis." The measure would have allowed them to adjust, or put in order, the relations between production and consumption, which is essentially what NRA was supposed to make possible. This *project Marchandeau* died in the French Senate, but some industries were encouraged to cooperate for this end by special decree.

But the area in which American historians of the Depression have been most myopic is New Deal agricultural policy. The extent to which the Agricultural Adjustment Act of 1933 evolved from the McNary-Haugen scheme of the Coolidge era and the Agricultural Marketing Act of the Hoover years has been universally conceded. Beyond these roots, however, historians have not bothered to dig. The stress on the originality of the AAA program has been close to universal. Arthur Schlesinger, Jr., put it clearly and directly when he wrote in his book *Coming of the New Deal* that "probably never in American history has so much social and legal inventiveness gone into a single legislative measure."

Schlesinger and the other historians who expressed this opinion have faithfully reflected statements made by the people most closely associated with the AAA at the time of its passage. Secretary of Agriculture Henry A. Wallace said that the law was "as new in the field of social relations as the first gasoline engine was new in the field of mechanics." President Roosevelt told Congress in submitting the bill that it was a new and untried idea.

In fact, Wallace and Roosevelt were exaggerating the originality of New Deal policy. The AAA did mark a break with the past for the United States. Paying farmers not to grow crops was unprecedented. Yet this tactic merely reflected the constitutional restrictions of the American political system; Congress did not have the power to fix prices or limit production directly. The strategy of subsidizing farmers and compelling them to reduce output in order to bring supplies down to the level of current demand for their products was far from original.

As early as 1906 Brazil had supported the prices paid its coffee growers by buying up surpluses in years of bountiful harvests and holding the coffee off the market. In the 1920s France had tried to help its beet framers and wine makers by requiring that gasoline sold in France contain a percentage of alcohol distilled from French beets and grapes. More important in its effect on the Unites States, Great Britain had attempted in the 1920s to bolster the flagging fortunes of rubber planters in Britain's Asiatic colonies by restricting production and placing quotas on rubber exports. This Stevenson Plan, referred to in the American press as "the British monopoly," aroused the wrath of then Secretary of Commerce Herbert Hoover. It also caused Henry Ford and Harvey Firestone, whose factories consumed huge amounts of imported rubber, to commission their mutual friend Thomas A. Edison to find a latex-producing plan that could be grown commercially in the United States. (Edison tested more than ten thousand specimens and finally settled on goldenrod. Ford then bought a large tract in Georgia to grow and the stuff, although it never became profitable to do so.)

After the Great Depression began, growers of staple crops in every corner of the globe adopted schemes designed to reduce output and raise prices. In 1930 British and Dutch tea growers in the Far East made an agreement to cut back on their production of cheaper varieties of tea. British and Dutch rubber planters declared a "tapping holiday" in that same year, and in 1931 Cuba, Java, and six other countries that exported significant amounts of cane sugar agreed to limit production and accept export quotas. Brazil began burning millions of pounds of coffee in 1931, a tactic that foreshadowed the "emergency" policy of the AAA administrators who ordered the plowing under the cotton and the "murder" (so called by critics) of baby pigs in 1933.

Far from being an innovation, the AAA was actually typical—one of many programs put into effect in countries all over the world in the depths of the Depression to deal with the desperate plight of farmers. The year 1933 saw the triumph nearly everywhere of a simple supply-and-demand kind of thinking that the French called "economic Malthusianism," the belief that the only way to raise prices was to bring output down to the level of current consumption. In February 1933, Indian, Ceylonese, and East Indian tea growers agreed to limit exports and prohibit new plantings for five years. A central committee of planters assigned and administered quotas limiting the exportation of tea. Dutch, British, French, and Siamese rubber growers adopted similar regulations for their product. In April 1933 representatives of nearly all the countries of Europe met in London with representatives of the major wheat-exporting nations, of which the United States, of course, was one of the largest. The gathering produced an International Wheat Agreement designed to cut production in hopes of causing the price of wheat to rise to a point where it would be profitable for farmers, yet still "reasonable" for consumers.

In addition to these international agreements, dozens of countries acted unilaterally in 1933 with the same goals in mind. Argentina adopted exchange controls, put a cap on imports, and regulated domestic production of wheat and cattle. The government purchased most of the 1933 wheat crop at a fixed price, then dumped the wheat abroad for whatever it could get. A Danish law of 1933 provided for government purchase and destruction of large numbers of low-quality cattle, the cost to be recovered through a slaughterhouse tax on all cattle butchered in Denmark. Declining demand caused by British restrictions on importation of Danish bacon led the Danish government to issue a specified number of "pig cards" to producers. Pigs sent to market with such cards brought one price, those without cards a lower one. The Dutch enacted similar restrictions on production of pork, beef, and dairy products.

Switzerland reduced milk production and limited the importation of feed grains in 1933, and Great Britain set up marketing boards that guaranteed dairymen a minimum price for milk. Sweden subsidized home-grown wheat and rye, and paid a bounty to exporters of butter. In 1933 France strengthened the regulations protecting growers of grapes and established a minimum price for domestic wheat. After Hitler came to power, the production, distribution, and sale of all foodstuffs was regulated. Every link from farmer to consumer was controlled.

Looking at the situation more broadly, the growers of staple crops for export were trying to push up prices by reducing supplies, ignoring the fact that higher prices were likely to reduce the demand still further. At the same time, the agricultural policies of the European industrial nations were making a bad situation worse. By reducing imports (and in some cases increasing domestic output) they were injuring the major food-producing countries and simultaneously adding to the costs of their own consumers.

It was, the British historian Sidney Pollard has written, "a world of rising tariffs, international commodity schemes, bilateral trade agreements and managed currencies." The United States was as much a part of Pollard's world as any other country.

One further example of the need to see American Depression policies in their world context is revealing. It involves the recession of 1937-38 and President Roosevelt's supposed responsibility for it. In early 1937 the American economy seemed finally to be emerging from the Depression. Unemployment remained high, but most economic indicators were improving. Industrial production had exceeded 1929 levels. A group of New Dealers who met at the home of the Federal Reserve Board chairman Marriner Eccles in October 1936 were so confident that the Depression was ending that their talk turned to how to avoid future Depressions. The general public was equally optimistic. "When Americans speak of the depression," the French novelist Jules Romains wrote after a visit to this country at that time, "they always use the past tense."

At this point Roosevelt, egged on by his conservative secretary in the treasury, Henry Morgenthau, warned the public in a radio speech that "the dangers of 1929 are again becoming possible." He ordered a steep cut in public works expenditures, and instructed the members of his cabinet to trim a total of $300 million from their departmental budgets. The President promised to balance the federal budget, and in fact brought the 1937 deficit down to a mere $358 million, as compared with a deficit of $3.6 billion in 1936. This reduction in federal spending, combined with the Federal Reserve's decision to push up interest rates and the coincidental reduction of consumer spending occasioned by the first collection of Social Security payroll taxes, brought the economic recovery to a halt and plunged the nation into a steep recession. The leading historian of the subject, K.D. Roose, called the recession a downturn "without parallel in American economic history."

Roosevelt had never been happy with deficits, and he was not much of an economist, but he was far from being alone in thinking that the time had come to apply the brakes to the economy. Economists who were far more knowledgeable than he saw the situation exactly as he did. Prices were still below 1929 levels in most countries, but they were rising rapidly. Using 1929 levels as an index, during 1937 prices jumped from 83 to 96 in Great Britain, from 80 to 93 in Italy, from 87 to 98 in Sweden, and from 80 to 86 in the United States.

These increases caused the grinding deflation of the years since 1929 to be forgotten. Fear of inflation resurfaced. The economist John Maynard Keynes had discounted the risks of inflation throughout the Depression. Inflation was a positive social good, he argued, a painless way to "disinherit" established wealth. But by January 1937 Keynes had become convinced that the British economy was beginning to overheat. He was so concerned that he published a series of articles in the *Times of London* on "How to Avoid a Slump." it might soon be necessary to "retard certain types of investment," Keynes warned. There was even a "risk of what might fairly be called inflation," he added. The next month the British government's Committee on Economic Information issued a report suggesting a tax increase and the postponement of "road improvements, railway electrification slum clearance," and other public works projects "which are not of an urgent character."

During this same period the Federal Reserve Board chairman Marriner Eccles, long a believer in the need to stimulate the economy, warned Roosevelt that "there is grave danger that the recovery movement will get out of hand, excessive rises in prices…will occur, excessive growth of profits and a boom in the stock market will arise, and the cost of living will mount rapidly. If such conditions are permitted to develop, another drastic slump will be inevitable."

It did not take much of this kind of talk to convince President Roosevelt. When Roosevelt's actions triggered the downturn, he reversed himself again, asking Congress for budget-busting increases in federal spending. The pattern elsewhere was similar. In the United States the money was spend on unemployment relief and more public works; in the major European countries the stimulus chiefly resulted from greatly increased expenditures on armaments. In 1939 World War II broke out, and the Great depression came to a final end.

When viewed in isolation, the policies of the United States government during the periods when economic conditions were worsening seem to have at best ineffective, at worst counterproductive. Those put into effect while conditions were getting better appear to have been at least partly responsible for the improvement. This helps to explain why the Hoover administration has looked so bad and the New Dealers, if not always good, at least less bad.

When seen in broader perspective, however, credit and blame are not so easily assigned. The heroes then appear less heroic, the villains less dastardly, the geniuses less brilliant. The Great Depression possessed some of the qualities of a hurricane; the best those in charge of the ship of state could manage was to rid it out without foundering.

Economists and politicians certainly know more about how the world economy functions that their predecessors did half a century ago. But the world economy today is far more complex and subject to many more uncontrollable forces than was then the case. A great depression like the Great Depression is highly unlikely. But a different great depression? Galbraith ended *The Great Crash* with this cynical pronouncement: "now, as throughout history, financial capacity and political perspicacity are inversely correlated." That may be an overstatement. But then again, maybe not.

9.4
First Inaugural Address (1933)

Franklin D. Roosevelt

Arguably the most important president of the twentieth century, Franklin Roosevelt routed Herbert Hoover in the 1932 election, in part by promising a "new deal" for the country. In this famous speech, FDR talks in general terms about what he and America need to do to get the nation back to work and on its feet. How does FDR's address compare to those of Hoover (Document 9.2) and his sixth cousin, Theodore Roosevelt (Document 7.4)? Why do you think FDR's plan was so much more popular than Hoover's?

I am certain that my fellow Americans expect that on my induction into the Presidency I will address them with a candor and a decision which the present situation of our Nation impels. This is preeminently the time to speak the truth, the whole truth, frankly and boldly. Nor need we shrink from honestly facing conditions in our country today. This great Nation will endure as it has endured, will revive and will prosper.

So, first of all, let me assert my firm belief that the only thing we have to fear is fear itself—nameless, unreasoning, unjustified terror which paralyzes needed efforts to convert retreat into advance. In every dark hour of our national life a leadership of frankness and vigor has met with that understanding and support of the people themselves which is essential to victory. I am convinced that you will again give that support to leadership in these critical days.

In such a spirit on my part and on yours we face our common difficulties. They concern, thank God, only material things. Values have shrunken to fantastic levels; taxes have risen; our ability to pay has fallen; government of all kinds is faced by serious curtailment of income; the means of exchange are frozen in the currents of trade; the withered leaves of industrial enterprise lie on every side; farmers find no markets for their produce; the savings of many years in thousands of families are gone.

More important, a host of unemployed citizens face the grim problem of existence, and an equally great number toil with little return. Only a foolish optimist can deny the dark realities of the moment.

Yet our distress comes from no failure of substance. We are stricken by no plague of locusts. Compared with the perils which our forefathers conquered because they believed and were not afraid, we have still much to be thankful for. Nature still offers her bounty and human efforts have multiplied it. Plenty is at our doorstep, but a generous use of it languishes in the very sight of the supply. Primarily this is because the rulers of the exchange of mankind's goods have failed, through their own stubbornness and their own incompetence, have admitted their failure, and abdicated. Practices of the unscrupulous money changers stand indicted in the court of public opinion, rejected by the hearts and minds of men.

True they have tried, but their efforts have been cast in the pattern of an outworn tradition. Faced by failure of credit they have proposed only the lending of more money. Stripped of the lure of profit by which to induce our people to follow their false leadership, they have resorted to exhortations, pleading tearfully for restored confidence. They know only the rules of a generation of self-seekers. They have no vision, and when there is no vision the people perish.

The money changers have fled from their high seats in the temple of our civilization. We may now restore that temple to the ancient truths. The measure of the restoration lies in the extent to which we apply social values more noble than mere monetary profit.

Happiness lies not in the mere possession of money; it lies in the joy of achievement, in the thrill of creative effort. The joy and moral stimulation of work no longer must be forgotten in the mad chase of evanescent profits. These dark days will be worth all they cost us if they teach us that our true destiny is not to be ministered unto but to minister to ourselves and to our fellow men.

Recognition of the falsity of material wealth as the standard of success goes hand in hand with the abandonment of the false belief that public office and high political position are to be valued only by the standards of pride of place and personal profit; and there must be an end to a conduct in banking and in business which too often has given to a sacred trust the likeness of callous and selfish wrongdoing. Small wonder that confidence languishes, for it thrives only on honesty, on honor, on the sacredness of obligations, on faithful protection, on unselfish performance; without them it cannot live.

Restoration calls, however, not for changes in ethics alone. This Nation asks for action, and action now.

Our greatest primary task is to put people to work. This is no unsolvable problem if we face it wisely and courageously. It can be accomplished in part by direct recruiting by the Government itself, treating the task as we would treat the emergency of a war, but at the same time, through this employment, accomplishing greatly needed projects to stimulate and reorganize the use of our natural resources.

Hand in hand with this we must frankly recognize the overbalance of population in our industrial centers and, by engaging on a national scale in a redistribution, endeavor to provide a better use of the land for those best fitted for the land. The task can be helped by definite efforts to raise the values of agricultural products and with this the power to purchase the output of our cities. It can be helped by preventing realistically the tragedy of the growing loss through foreclosure of our small homes and our farms. It can be helped by insistence that the Federal, State, and local governments act forthwith on the demand that their cost be drastically reduced. It can be helped by the unifying of relief activities which today are often scattered, uneconomical, and unequal. It can be helped by national planning for and supervision of all forms of transportation and of communications and other utilities which have a definitely public character. There are many ways in which it can be helped, but it can never be helped merely by talking about it. We must act and act quickly.

Finally, in our progress toward a resumption of work we require two safeguards against a return of the evils of the old order; there must be a strict supervision of all banking and credits and investments; there must be an end to speculation with other people's money, and there must be provision for an adequate but sound currency.

There are the lines of attack. I shall presently urge upon a new Congress in special session detailed measures for their fulfillment, and I shall seek the immediate assistance of the several States....

If I read the temper of our people correctly, we now realize as we have never realized before our interdependence on each other; that we can not merely take but we must give as well; that if we are to go forward, we must move as a trained and loyal army willing to sacrifice for the good of a common discipline, because without such discipline no progress is made, no leadership becomes effective. We are, I know, ready and willing to submit our lives and property to such discipline, because it makes possible a leadership which aims at a larger good. This I propose to offer, pledging that the larger purposes will bind upon us all as a sacred obligation with a unity of duty hitherto evoked only in time of armed strife.

With this pledge taken, I assume unhesitatingly the leadership of this great army of our people dedicated to a disciplined attack upon our common problems.

Action in this image and to this end is feasible under the form of government which we have inherited from our ancestors. Our Constitution is so simple and practical that it is possible always to meet extraordinary needs by changes in emphasis and arrangement without loss of essential form. That is why our constitutional system has proved itself the most superbly enduring political mechanism the modern world has produced. It has met every stress of vast expansion of territory, of foreign wars, of bitter internal strife, of world relations.

It is to be hoped that the normal balance of executive and legislative authority may be wholly adequate to meet the unprecedented task before us. But it may be that an unprecedented demand and need for undelayed action may call for temporary departure from that normal balance of public procedure.

I am prepared under my constitutional duty to recommend the measures that a stricken nation in the midst of a stricken world may require. These measures, or such other measures as the Congress may build out of its experience and wisdom, I shall seek, within my constitutional authority, to bring to speedy adoption.

But in the event that the Congress shall fail to take one of these two courses, and in the event that the national emergency is still critical, I shall not evade the clear course of duty that will then confront me. I shall ask the Congress for the one remaining instrument to meet the crisis—broad Executive power to wage a war against the emergency, as great as the power that would be given to me if we were in fact invaded by a foreign foe. For the trust reposed in me I will return the courage and the devotion that befit the time. I can do no less.

We face the arduous days that lie before us in the warm courage of the national unity; with the clear consciousness of seeking old and precious moral values; with the clean satisfaction that comes from the stem performance of duty by old and young alike. We aim at the assurance of a rounded and permanent national life.

We do not distrust the future of essential democracy. The people of the United States have not failed. In their need they have registered a mandate that they want direct, vigorous action. They have asked for discipline and direction under leadership. They have made me the present instrument of their wishes. In the spirit of the gift I take it.

In this dedication of a Nation we humbly ask the blessing of God. May He protect each and every one of us. May He guide me in the days to come.

9.5
Birth of an Entitlement

Carolyn Weaver

Motivated by the recent movement to "privatize" Social Security, Weaver returns to the origins of the 1935 Social Security Act. She wants to discover what Americans thought about Social Security at its birth (and in the years since) in order to foster a discussion of the more general idea of reforming the system. In short, Weaver wants us to keep the historical perspective in mind as we undertake potential changes to the Social Security system.

When a Social Security advisory council appointed by Health and Human Services Secretary Donna Shalala decides to issue a final report with three reform options, one of which would privatize half the retirement program, and when a Republican presidential candidate not only discusses Social Security privatization but also makes it a key element of his campaign, you know that business is definitely not as usual. In a remarkable turn of events, proposals that once were ignored or denounced as efforts to "smash and destroy" Social Security are being explored as possibly the only real means of saving Social Security. The ongoing support of middle-aged and younger people is clearly threatened by the woefully poor rates of return the program now offers. Numerous proposals circulating on Capitol Hill would move toward a system of true saving, where a portion of a worker's taxes would go directly into a personal retirement account that the worker owns, invests, and earns interest on.

As the idea of privatizing a portion of Social Security gains currency, a debate with the old guard is intensifying over what constitutes "radical" reform. This debate has a certain back-to-the-future quality to it. Far from being universally embraced when first considered, Social Security was bitterly contested in the 1930s and was, at the time, the radical alternative. With real reform now in the wind, it is worth remembering just how close this nation came to maintaining a basically private system of retirement pensions.

FDR's compulsory old-age pension program was nearly stricken from his grander "economic security bill" in the House Ways and Means Committee and again on the House floor, where an amendment to strike the program mustered a third of the votes cast. After this rocky start, the legislation moved to the Senate where an amendment was offered to permit companies to contract out of the public program if they could provide comparable pensions to their employers. Leading to more controversy in the Finance Committee and on the Senate floor than did any other, this amendment was killed in committee by a tie vote, then went on to be approved in the Senate by a wide margin and to stalemate House and Senate conferences.

No doubt the idea that Social Security lacked broad bipartisan support is at odds with many people's understanding of the birth of this mighty program. It is true that the Social Security Act moved through Congress quickly. Introduced on January 17 and signed into law on August 14, 1935, this landmark expansion of the role of the federal government wended its way through Congress and was adopted largely intact in just seven months.

However, what we know as Social Security—the old-age pension program—was just a piece of the Social Security Act that ushered in the modern welfare state. Many now-familiar programs got their start, or at least a federal boost, then too. Federal grants for aid to dependent children (now the AFDC program), aid to the elderly and to the blind (later merged with aid to the disabled into a single program of Supplemental Security Income), and maternal and child health services, to name a few, plus a tax-offset arrangement for unemployment compensation, were all contained in the original Social Security Act.

To appreciate the widespread and bipartisan resistance to Social Security, it is important to recognize the distinction that was made at the time between the problem of *preventing* poverty in old age and the problem of *alleviating* poverty among the elderly poor—a distinction that some find difficult to grasp today. Prevention was seen as a problem of retirement-income planning, of personal saving and continued employment, that could and should be addressed through voluntary employment, that could and should be addressed through voluntary arrangements—by individuals and families working together with employers, trade unions, fraternal organizations, and financial institutions. Alleviation ultimately came to be seen as a problem demanding at least some government intervention at the state or local level.

In the first three decades of this century, many states debated means-tested public assistance for the elderly poor and several states passed laws enabling counties to collect and dispense founds for this purpose. No one, however, introduced legislation to get the federal government involved in poverty relief for the elderly poor—let alone involved in the direct provision of retirement pensions for working Americans.

Advocates of social insurance worked hard to blur the distinction between prevention and alleviation, and between insurance and welfare, in the redsitributive programs they promoted. They met with a decided lack of success. In historian Arthur Schlesinger's words, "While the friends of social security were arguing out the details of the program, other Americans were regarding the whole idea with consternation, if not with horror." Samuel Gompers, leader of the American Federation of Labor for nearly half a century, put his feelings succinctly in 1917. "Compulsory social insurance," he said, "is in its essence undemocratic."

The public was not naive about the political difficulties of controlling public income transfer programs. The federal government had long provided pensions and other special programs for veterans, and the generosity and cost of these programs had been a subject of continuous controversy. In 1920, the federal government set up a retirement program for its own employees, spending on which quickly outstripped original projections. And, of course, two or three decades' worth of experience with state and local pension funds for teachers, firemen, and other public employee groups revealed the inevitable pressures to increase benefits, defer tax costs, and shift burdens to future generations. Overexpansion, severe underfunding, and even cutbacks in benefits were not unheard of. In some ways, the political risks attached to long=term benefit promises by government were better understood in the 1920s than they have been since—or at least until very recently.

With the onset of the Great Depression in 1929 and the election of Franklin Roosevelt in 1932, the political landscape began to shift. Old-age assistance programs cropped up in many states, but were strained severely by burgeoning numbers of poor people and shrinking local tax bases. Pressures mounted—especially in the larger, more industrialized states—for federal assistance and a redistribution of tax costs. In 1934, a bill to provide federal matching funds to states operating old-age assistance programs received unanimous approval in both the House Labor Committee and the Senate Finance Committee, revealing broad, bipartisan support for public assistance for the elderly poor.

In a masterful political ploy, however, FDR refused to support the bill and it died at the end of the session. FDR's strategy, clear to all observers at the time, was to take the substantial momentum behind federal assistance for the poor—especially the elderly poor—and leverage it into support for his Social Security Act, a comprehensive legislative program whose heart was the compulsory, government administered pension program.

Across party lines, members of Congress recognized and complained that they were being put in the position of voting for everything or being labeled as opposed to "social security." As Abraham Epstein, an early proponent of social insurance, described the dilemma for members of Congress. "Their choice was 'all-or-none,' [so] they voted for all and left it to the Supreme Court to separate the good from the bad." (Interestingly, the terms *pension*, *annuity*, and *insurance* appeared nowhere in the original Social Security Act because of the concern that a compulsory pension program would be found unconstitutional.)

FDR was well aware of the battle to be waged over compulsory old-age pensions. When his Committee on Economic Security submitted its comprehensive legislative package to Congress in 1935, the Great Depression had been raging for six years. The Depression wreaked havoc on everyone—nearly 20 million Americans were on direct relief from the government—but it hit the aged especially hard. Yet not a single bill had been introduced into either chamber of Congress to establish a compulsory old-age pension program. FDR's social-insurance proposal was the first of its kind, even though social insurance had emerged in Europe nearly a half-century earlier, had spread widely among industrial nations, and had been a topic of debate in the United States for more than two decades.

The battle for Social Security began in earnest in the Senate when Sen. Bennett Clark (D-Mo.) Offered an amendment to allow companies with private pensions to opt out of the public program. Under the amendment, any company could contract out of the public program if it had a pension plan that offered benefits at least a generous as the federal program, provided that the plan was available to all employees, that premiums were deposited with an insurance company or approved trustee, that employee contributions plus interest were refunded to government in the event an employee's job was terminated, and that the company was willing to subject its books to federal scrutiny. Employees of companies that contracted out would have their choice of the public or private plan. (Those familiar with modern social security systems will recognize the concept of company-wide contracting out from systems in the United Kingdom and in Japan.)

While the Clark amendment conceded a great deal to Social Security proponents—it accepted, for instance, the premise of compulsory participation and left companies exposed to substantial federal regulation—it nevertheless would have given workers some degree of choice and given employers the right to compete with the government in providing retirement pensions. Individual choice and competition in supply would help ensure maximum value for workers' tax "contributions," protect workers' non-contractual rights to future benefits, and provide a much-needed check on the use of Social Security for the purposes of income redistribution.

According to University of Chicago economist Paul Douglas, a leading figure in the social-insurance movement and later a U.S. senator, the fight over the Clark amendment was "the most vigorous" of the debates surrounding the economic security bill. And little wonder: In less than 10 sentences, the amendment cut through the "insurance" rhetoric and exposed the redistributive underpinnings of Social Security.

Clark and his supporters argued that the amendment would preserve competition in the supply of pensions and allow freedom of choice for workers, while ensuring the nation's elderly a level of protection at least as generous as the federal program. Why stifle the development of private pensions, they reasoned, that potentially could provide higher benefits for retirees while building good will with workers? Company pension plans were spreading rapidly among large companies in the 1920s, having first emerged in the 1880s, and coverage was destined to expand as the tax and business environment improved.

It was in 1926, for example, that the basic features of the tax code pertaining to pensions were established, effectively eliminating the double taxation that penalized ordinary savings. (The favorable tax treatment of employer-sponsored pensions did not extend to individual retirement savings until much later—individual retirement accounts and Keogh plans are creature s of the 1960s and 1970s.)

But critics recognized that the Clark amendment, if passed, would put the federal government in the position regulating and competing with private pensions plans rather than monopolizing its own. That competition would have profound implications for the ability to use Social Security for purposes of income redistribution. As Sen. Robert LaFollette (Prog-Wisc.) put it, "If we shall adopt the amendment, the government...would be inviting and encouraging competition with its own plan which ultimately would undermine and destroy it."

The critics' key argument was that contracting out would leave the public program at a great disadvantage. The feds' benefit formula, weighted in favor of this near retirement (and with lower earnings), would attract people who were relatively more costly to "insure," thus making the government program more expensive, if not prohibitively so. Critics reasoned that firms with relatively young workers would establish or maintain pension plans, choosing to contract out of the public plan (at a savings). Firms with older workers would discontinue or fail to establish plans, allowing their workers to gain retirement protection through the government (also at a savings). Said Sen. Robert Wagner (D-N.Y.), one of the bill's sponsors, "I am firmly convinced that if this amendment were adopted we should find the government holding the bag for older men...while industries would take care of only the younger men who earned every bit of annuity they received."

Undoubtedly the critics were right. In a competitive setting and in the absence of coercion, workers would be compensated whether in the form of wages, pensions, or some other form of benefit or payment—in relation to the value of their output. There would be little room for anything unearned. But, as proponents of the Clark amendment reasoned, if the purpose of the new program was to provide pensions based on earnings and contributions, not to redistribute income, the private sector was perfectly capable of performing this function. Unearned benefits, not competition, were the source of the problem.

FDR and his allies went to some lengths to kill the Clark amendment, including threatening to veto the entire bill—and thus to block all federal assistance for the poor—if the amendment were passed. Such efforts didn't work, at least initially: The Clark amendment was passed by the Senate (where Democrats held a 44-vote margin) by a vote of 51 to 35. Paul Douglas later acknowledged that, "In view of all the safeguards, it seemed to the majority of the Senate and to a goodly section of the public that there was really no legitimate objection against granting such an exemption." The Senate then approved the economic security bill as amended by a vote of 77-6. The House had already approved the legislation—without the Clark amendment—by a vote of 372-33.

When the House and Senate bills reached conference early in July 1935, negotiators spent a couple of weeks resolving all matters of disagreement in the various welfare programs, the unemployment compensation program, and the compulsory old-age pension program, with the exception of one—the Clark amendment. The House strongly opposed the amendment on the grounds that it would ruin the federal program and could, by resulting in different tax treatment of employers who had and had not contracted out, render the federal program unconstitutional. The Senate refused to budge. On July 16, conferees returned their reports to their respective houses, seeking approval on all issues except the Clark Amendment and seeking further instructions. Both houses responded with instructions to adhere to their positions.

Negotiations dragged on for several more weeks until the conferees decided that a further delay of the entire economic security bill—over a single amendment to a single program—could not be justified. They dropped the Clark amendment with the understanding that a special joint legislative committee would be formed to prepare an amendment, for consideration during the next session of Congress, that embodied the essence of the Clark amendment without rasing the constitutional complications.

This, of course, was a major victory for FDR and his allied. The House and Senate accepted the conference report on August 8 and 9, respectively, and the president signed the Social Security Act into law on August 14. The Clark amendment was never reconsidered.

Just five years later, Social Security's income-transfer machinery began churning out checks to elderly people who had paid taxes for at most three years and to people who had paid no taxes at all (elderly spouses and widows, young widows with children, and children of retired or deceased workers). Financed on a quasi-pay-as-you-go basis, the program grew in size and scope in the decades that followed, delivering lifetime annuities to a broader and broader segment of the population at a fraction of the true cost—and piling up larger and larger liabilities to be met by younger generations. Worries about the political risks attached to the government's long-term benefit promises seemed to evaporate.

It was not until the 1970s that reality began to pinch. This is when Social Security first began running gaping long-term deficits and when, as a "mature" pay-as-you-go system, its ability to produce large windfall gains to retirees was fast disappearing. Nothing's been quite the same since.

Today, middle-aged and younger workers, who face the prospect of potentially large wealth losses under the system, naturally seek the right to save privately for retirement, both to reap the gains of investing in higher yielding real capital and to secure their rights to future income. Neither steeped in the traditions of New Deal programs nor beneficiaries of the windfalls those programs delivered in decades past, these workers question the value of Social Security as a retirement savings vehicle in the next century and seek new solutions to the age-old problem of retirement income security. In this case, the best new solutions lie in some old ideas.

When Congress takes up the issue of Social Security reform, it can aim much higher than proponents of the Clark amendment were able to in the 1930s. With modern financial markets, a mature private pension system, and extensive experience with IRAs, 401(k) plans, and other self-directed investment plans, there is no reason to be limited by the idea of company-wide contracting out. Giving individual workers the right to fund and control the investment of their own retirement accounts is now a viable alternative that demands consideration—whether on a limited basis, as envisioned in the legislation introduced by Senators Kerrey (D-Neb.) and Simpson (R-Wyo.), or on a large-scale basis, as under the system adopted in Chile over a decade.

9.6
Share Our Wealth (1935)

Huey Long

*One of the most popular critics of FDR and his New Deal was
Louisiana politician Huey Long. More homespun and colloquial than
the patrician Roosevelt, Long's "Share Our Wealth" was a much more
radical solution to the problems of the Depression. Long was elected
to the Senate in 1932, swept in on FDR's coattails, but he shortly
thereafter began to oppose FDR's policies. Why might FDR and other
Democrats have looked at the "Share Our Wealth" as a threat to the
popularity of the New Deal?*

Here is the whole sum and substance of the Share Our Wealth movement:

1. Every family to be furnished by the government a homestead
    allowance, free of debt, of not less than one-third the average family
    wealth of the country, which means, at the lowest, that every family
    shall have the reasonable comforts of life up to a value of from $5,000
    to $6,000: No person to have a fortune of more than 100 to 300 times
    the average family fortune, which means that the limit to fortune is
    between $1,500,000 and $5,000,000, with annual capital levy taxes
    imposed on all above $1,000,000.

2. The yearly income of every family shall be not less than one-third of
    the average family income, which means that, according to the
    estimates of the statisticians of the U. S. Government and Wall Street,
    no family's annual income would be less than from $2,000 to $2,500:
    No yearly income shall be allowed to any person larger than from
    100 to 300 times the size of the average family income, which means
    that no person would be allowed to earn in any year more than
    $600,000 to $1,800,000, all to be subject to present income tax laws.

From Congressional Record, 73rd Congress, 2nd. Sess. (1934).

443

3. To limit or regulate the hours of work to such an extent as to prevent over-production; the most modern and efficient machinery would be encouraged so that as much would be produced as possible so as to satisfy all demands of the people, but also to allow the maximum time to the workers for recreation, convenience, education, and luxuries of life.

4. An old age pension to the persons over 60.

5. To balance agricultural production with what can be consumed according to the laws of God, which includes the preserving and storing of surplus commodities to be paid for and held by the Government for emergencies when such are needed. Please bear in mind, however, that when the people of America have had money to buy things they needed, we have never had a surplus of any commodity. This plan of God does not call for destroying any of the things raised to eat or wear, nor does it countenance whole destruction of hogs, cattle or milk.

6. To pay the veterans of our wars what we owe them and to care for their disabled.

7. Education and training for all children to be equal in opportunity in all schools, colleges, universities and other institutions for training in the professions and vocations of life; to be regulated on the capacity of children to learn, and not on the ability of parents to pay the costs. Training for life's work to be as much universal and thorough for all walks in life as has been the training in the arts of killing.

8. The raising of revenues and taxes for the support of this program to come from the reduction of swollen fortunes from the top, as well as for the support of public works to give employment whenever there may be any slackening necessary in private enterprise.

9.7
Platform (1936)

Republican Party

A more traditional kind of opposition to the New Deal came from the Republican Party. Having shed themselves of the unpopular Hoover, the Republicans in 1936 nominated Alf Landon and approved the following selection as their party platform. What attitudes about FDR and the New Deal does this document evidence? Have the Republicans completely abandoned the ideas of Hoover as expressed in Document 9.2? Does the platform give you any understanding as to the reasons why Landon (and Republican Congressional candidates) went down to a crushing defeat in 1936?

America is in peril. The welfare of American men and women and the future of our youth are at stake. We dedicate ourselves to the preservation of their political liberty, their individual opportunity and their character as free citizens, which today for the first time are threatened by Government itself.

For three long years the New Deal Administration has dishonored American traditions and flagrantly betrayed the pledges upon which the Democratic Party sought and received public support.

The powers of Congress have been usurped by the President.
The integrity and authority of the Supreme Court have been flouted.
The rights and liberties of American citizens have been violated.
Regulated monopoly has displaced free enterprise.
The New Deal Administration constantly seeks to usurp the rights reserved to the States and to the people.

From Proceedings, 21st Republican National Convention.

It has insisted on the passage of laws contrary to the Constitution.

It has intimidated witnesses and interfered with the right of petition.

It has dishonored our country by repudiating its most sacred obligations.

It has been guilty of frightful waste and extravagance, using public funds for partisan political purposes.

It has promoted investigations to harass and intimidate American citizens, at the same time denying investigations into its own improper expenditures.

It has created a vast multitude of new offices, filled them with its favorites, set up a centralized bureaucracy, and sent out warms of inspectors to harass our people.

It had bred fear and hesitation in commerce and industry, thus discouraging new enterprises, preventing employment and prolonging the depression.

It secretly has made tariff agreements with our foreign competitors, flooding our markets with foreign commodities.

It has coerced and intimidated voters by withholding relief from those opposing its tyrannical policies.

It has destroyed the morale of many of our people and made them dependent upon Government.

Appeals to passion and class prejudice have replaced reason and tolerance.

To a free people these actions are insufferable. This campaign cannot be waged on the traditional differences between the Republican and Democratic parties. The responsibility of this election transcends all previous political divisions. We invite all Americans, irrespective of party, to join us in defense of American institutions.

Constitutional Government and Free Enterprise

We Pledge Ourselves:

1. To maintain the American system of constitutional and local self government, and to resist all attempts to impair the authority of the Supreme Court of the United States, the final protector of the rights of our citizens against the arbitrary encroachments of the legislative

and executive branches of Government. There can be no individual liberty without an independent judiciary.

2. To preserve the American system of free enterprise, private competition, and equality of opportunity, and to seek its constant betterment, in the interests of all.

Reemployment

The only permanent solution of the unemployment problem is the absorption of the unemployed by industry and agriculture. To that end, we advocate:

Removal of restrictions on production. Abandonment of all New Deal policies that raise production costs, increase the cost of living, and thereby restrict buying, reduce volume and prevent reemployment.

Encouragement instead of hindrance to legitimate business.

Withdrawal of Government from competition with private payrolls.

Elimination of unnecessary and hampering regulations.

Adoption of such policies as will furnish a chance for individual enterprise, industrial expansion, and the restoration of jobs.

Relief

The necessities of life must be provided for the needy, and hope must be restored pending recovery. The administration of relief is a major failure of the New Deal. It has been faithless to those who most deserve our sympathy. To end confusion, partisanship, waste and incompetence,

We Pledge:

1. The return of responsibility for relief administration to non-political local agencies familiar with community problems.
2. Federal grants-in-aid to the States and Territories while the need exists, upon compliance with these conditions: (a) a fair proportion of the total relief burden to be provided from the revenues of States and local governments; (b) all engaged in relief administration to be selected on the basis of merit and fitness; (c) adequate provision to be made for the encouragement of those persons who are trying to become self-supporting.
3. Undertaking of Federal public works only on their merits and separate from the administration of relief.
4. A prompt determination of the facts concerning relief and unemployment.

Security

Real security will be possible only when our productive capacity is sufficient to furnish a decent standard of living for all American families and to provide a surplus for future needs and contingencies. For the attainment of that ultimate objective, we look to the energy, self-reliance and character of our people, and to our system of free enterprise.

Society has an obligation to promote the security of the people, by affording some measure of protection against involuntary unemployment and dependency in old age. The New Deal policies, while purporting to provide social security, have, in fact, endangered it.

We propose a system of old age security....

We propose to encourage adoption by the States and Territories of honest and practical measures for meeting the problems of unemployment insurance.

The unemployment insurance and old age annuity sections of the present Social Security Act are unworkable and deny benefits to about two-thirds of our adult population, including professional men and women and all those engaged in agriculture and domestic service, and the self employed, while imposing heavy tax burdens upon all. The so-called reserve fund estimated at forty-seven billion dollars for old age insurance is no reserve at all, because the fund will contain nothing but the Government's promise to pay. while the taxes collected in the guise of premiums will be wasted by the Government in reckless and extravagant political schemes.

Labor

The welfare of labor rests upon increased production end the prevention of exploitation. We pledge ourselves to:

Protect the right of labor to organize and to bargain collectively through representatives of its own choosing without interference from any source.

Prevent governmental job holders from exercising autocratic powers over labor.

Support the adoption of State laws and interstate compacts to abolish sweatshops and child labor, and to protect women and children with respect to maximum hours, minimum wages and working conditions. We believe that this can be done within the Constitution as it now stands.

Agriculture

The farm problem is an economic and social, not a partisan problem, and we propose to treat it accordingly....

Our paramount object is to protect and foster the family type of farm, traditional in American life, and to promote policies which will bring about an adjustment of agriculture to meet the needs of domestic and foreign markets. As an emergency measure, during the agricultural depression, Federal benefit payments or grants-in-aid when administered within the means of the Federal Government are consistent with a balanced budget.

We Propose

1. To facilitate economical production and increased consumption on a basis of abundance instead of scarcity.
2. A national land-use program, including the acquisition of abandoned and non-productive farm lands by voluntary sale or lease, subject to approval of the legislative and executive branches of the States concerned, and the devotion of such land to appropriate public use, such as watershed protection and flood prevention, reforestation, recreation, and conservation of wild life.
3. That an agricultural policy be pursued for the protection and restoration of the land resources, designed to bring about such a balance between soil-building and soil-depleting crops as will permanently insure productivity, with reasonable benefits to cooperating farmers on family type farms, but so regulated as to eliminate the New Deal's destructive policy towards the dairy and live-stock industries.
4. To extend experimental aid to farmers developing new crops suited to our soil and climate....

Regulation of Business

We recognize the existence of a field within which governmental regulation is desirable and salutary. The authority to regulate should be vested in an independent tribunal acting under clear and specific laws establishing definite standards. Their determinations on law and facts should be subject to review by the Courts. We favor Federal regulation, within the Constitution, of the marketing of securities to protect investors. We favor also Federal regulation of the interstate activities of public utilities....

Government Finance

The New Deal Administration has been characterized by shameful waste and general financial irresponsibility. It has piled deficit upon deficit. It threatens national bankruptcy and the destruction through inflation of insurance policies and savings bank deposits.

We Pledge Ourselves to:

Stop the folly of uncontrolled spending.

Balance the budget—not by increasing taxes but by cutting expenditures, drastically and immediately.

Revise the Federal tax system and coordinate it with State and local tax systems.

Use the taxing power for raising revenue and not for punitive or political purposes.

Money and Banking

We advocate a sound currency to be preserved at all hazards.

The first requisite to a sound and stable currency is a balanced budget.

We oppose further devaluation of the dollar.

We will restore to the Congress the authority lodged with it by the Constitution to coin money and regulate the value thereof by repealing all the laws delegating this authority to the Executive.

We will cooperate with other countries toward stabilization of currencies as soon as we can do so with due regard for our national interests and as soon as other nations have sufficient stability to justify such action.

Conclusion

We assume the obligations and duties imposed upon Government by modern conditions. We affirm our unalterable conviction that, in the future as in the past, the fate of the nation will depend, not so much on the wisdom and power of Government, as on the character and virtue, self-reliance, industry and thrift of the people and on their willingness to meet the responsibilities essential to the preservation of a free society.

Finally, as our party affirmed in its first Platform in 1856: "Believing that the spirit of our institutions as well as the Constitution of our country guarantees liberty of conscience and equality of rights among our citizens, we oppose all legislation tending to impair them," and "we invite the affiliation and cooperation of the men of all parties, however differing from us in other respects, in support of the principles herein declared."

The acceptance of the nomination tendered by this Convention carries with it, as a matter of private honor and public faith, an undertaking by each candidate to be true to the principles and program herein set forth.